Phonetics

Blackwell Textbooks in Linguistics

The books included in this series provide comprehensive accounts of some of the most central and most rapidly developing areas of research in linguistics. Intended primarily for introductory and post-introductory students, they include exercises, discussion points and suggestions for further reading.

1. Liliane Haegeman, *Introduction to Government and Binding Theory* (Second Edition)
2. Andrew Spencer, *Morphological Theory*
3. Helen Goodluck, *Language Acquisition*
4. Ronald Wardhaugh, *An Introduction to Sociolinguistics* (Fifth Edition)
5. Martin Atkinson, *Children's Syntax*
6. Diane Blakemore, *Understanding Utterances*
7. Michael Kenstowicz, *Phonology in Generative Grammar*
8. Deborah Schiffrin, *Approaches to Discourse*
9. John Clark, Colin Yallop, and Janet Fletcher, *An Introduction to Phonetics and Phonology* (Third Edition)
10. Natsuko Tsujimura, *An Introduction to Japanese Linguistics* (Second Edition)
11. Robert D. Borsley, *Modern Phrase Structure Grammar*
12. Nigel Fabb, *Linguistics and Literature*
13. Irene Heim and Angelika Kratzer, *Semantics in Generative Grammar*
14. Liliane Haegeman and Jacqueline Guéron, *English Grammar: A Generative Perspective*
15. Stephen Crain and Diane Lillo-Martin, *An Introduction to Linguistic Theory and Language Acquisition*
16. Joan Bresnan, *Lexical-Functional Syntax*
17. Barbara A. Fennell, *A History of English: A Sociolinguistic Approach*
18. Henry Rogers, *Writing Systems: A Linguistic Approach*
19. Benjamin W. Fortson IV, *Indo-European Language and Culture: An Introduction*
20. Liliane Haegeman, *Thinking Syntactically: A Guide to Argumentation and Analysis*
21. Mark Hale, *Historical Linguistics: Theory and Method*
22. Henning Reetz and Allard Jongman, *Phonetics: Transcription, Production, Acoustics, and Perception*

Phonetics

Transcription, Production, Acoustics, and Perception

Henning Reetz and Allard Jongman

WILEY-BLACKWELL

A John Wiley & Sons, Ltd., Publication

Blackwell Publishing was acquired by John Wiley & Sons in February 2007. Blackwell's publishing program has been merged with Wiley's global Scientific, Technical, and Medical business to form Wiley-Blackwell.

Registered Office
John Wiley & Sons Ltd, The Atrium, Southern Gate, Chichester, West Sussex, PO19 8SQ, United Kingdom

Editorial Offices
350 Main Street, Malden, MA 02148-5020, USA
9600 Garsington Road, Oxford, OX4 2DQ, UK
The Atrium, Southern Gate, Chichester, West Sussex, PO19 8SQ, UK

For details of our global editorial offices, for customer services, and for information about how to apply for permission to reuse the copyright material in this book please see our website at www.wiley.com/wiley-blackwell.

Library of Congress Cataloging-in-Publication Data

Reetz, Henning.
  Phonetics : transcription, production, acoustics and perception / Henning Reetz and Allard Jongman.
     p. cm. — (Blackwell textbooks in linguistics ; 22)
  Includes bibliographical references and index.
  ISBN 978-0-631-23225-4 (hardcover : alk. paper) — ISBN 978-0-631-23226-1 (pbk. : alk. paper) 1. Phonetics. 2. Speech. I. Jongman, Allard. II. Title.

  P221.R37 2009
  414′.8—dc22

                                                                      2007052357

A catalogue record for this book is available from the British Library.

Set in 10/13 point Sabon by Graphicraft Limited, Hong Kong
Printed in Singapore by C.O.S. Printers Pte Ltd

6   2013

Contents

Preface

Phonetics is traditionally subdivided into three areas: articulatory phonetics concerns the way in which speech is produced and requires an understanding of the physiology of the speaking apparatus; acoustic phonetics investigates the acoustic characteristics of speech such as frequency, intensity, and duration, and requires knowledge of sound waves; auditory phonetics addresses the perception of speech and requires awareness of the function of the auditory system and memory. Phonetics thus spans several related disciplines, including linguistics, biology, physics, and psychology. In addition, students of phonetics should be familiar with phonetic transcription, the use of a set of symbols to "write" speech sounds.

Some courses in phonetics cover primarily articulatory phonetics and phonetic transcription while others focus on acoustic or auditory phonetics. However, in our teaching experience, we have found it more rewarding to combine these subjects in a single course. For example, certain speech patterns are better explained from an articulatory point of view while others may be more readily motivated in terms of auditory factors. For these reasons, we decided to write this textbook.

This book covers in detail all four areas that comprise phonetics: articulatory, acoustic, and auditory phonetics as well as phonetic transcription. It is aimed at students of speech from a variety of disciplines (including linguistics, speech pathology, audiology, psychology, and electrical engineering). While it is meant as an introductory course, many areas of phonetics are discussed in more detail than is typically the case for an introductory text. Depending on their purpose, readers (and instructors) will probably differ in terms of the amount of detail they require. Due to the book's step-wise approach, later chapters are accessible even if sections (for example, those containing too much technical detail) of preceding chapters are skipped. While some technical detail is, of course, inevitable (for example, to understand a spectrogram), little knowledge of physics or mathematics beyond the high school level is required. Technical concepts are introduced with many examples. In addition, more advanced technical information can be found in Appendices A amd B in order to maintain a readable text. This book thus employs a modular format to provide comprehensive coverage of all areas of phonetics with sufficient detail to challenge to a deeper understanding of this complex interdisciplinary subject.

Phonetics as a science of speech should not be geared toward any particular language. Nonetheless, many examples in this textbook are from English, simply because this book is written in English. We do, however, include examples from a variety of languages to illustrate facts not found in English, but in-depth knowledge of those languages by the reader is not required.

This book reflects the ideas and research of many speech scientists, and we feel fortunate to be part of this community. For discussions about speech over the years, we are first and foremost indebted to Aditi Lahiri and Joan Sereno without whose continued support and guidance this book would never have been finished. It is to them that we dedicate this book. In addition, we thank our teachers and mentors who initially got us excited about phonetics: Sheila Blumstein, Philip Lieberman, and James D. Miller. And our students who kept this excitement alive: Mohammad Al-Masri, Ann Bradlow, Tobey Doeleman, Kazumi Maniwa, Corinne Moore, Alice Turk, Travis Wade, Yue Wang, Ratree Wayland, as well as the many students in our introductory and advanced classes who – through their questions – made us realize which topics needed more clarification. We are also grateful to Ocke-Schwen Bohn, Vincent Evers, Carlos Gussenhoven, Wendy Herd, Kazumi Maniwa, Travis Wade, Ratree Wayland, and Jie Zhang, who provided valuable comments on previous versions of the text. A very special thank you goes to Regine Eckardt, who provided the artistic drawings. Finally, we thank Wim van Dommelen, Fiona McLaughlin, Simone Mikuteit, Joan Sereno, Craig Turnbull-Sailor, Yue Wang, and Ratree Wayland for providing us with their recordings. Needless to say, none of these individuals is responsible for any inaccuracies of this book.

We especially thank Aditi Lahiri for her extensive financing at many stages of the book through her Leibniz Prize. We also thank the Universities of Konstanz and Kansas for travel support and sabbatical leave to work on this book.

Henning Reetz
Allard Jongman

1 About this Book

Phonetics is the study of speech. It is a broad and interdisciplinary science whose investigations cover four main areas:

- how speech can be written down (called **phonetic transcription**);
- how it is produced (**speech production** or **articulatory phonetics**);
- what its acoustic characteristics are (**acoustic phonetics**);
- how it is perceived by listeners (**speech perception** or **auditory phonetics**).

This book provides a coherent description of phonetics in these four areas. Each of these areas of phonetics is related to other scientific disciplines and has its own methodology. For example, the transcription of speech sounds is based on (supervised) introspection, careful listening, and speaking. The study of speech production and acoustics is related to physiology, anatomy, and physics. Finally, the study of speech perception is more oriented toward psychology. This book tries to familiarize the reader with important concepts of these other, sometimes rather "technical," areas by means of everyday examples. This approach is based on the conviction that *understanding* is an important key to *knowledge*.

Given this range, this textbook is not only intended for students of phonetics or linguistics, but also for students of related disciplines such as psychology, computer science, medicine, speech pathology, and audiology – indeed, for anyone interested to learn more about how we speak and hear. Phonetics as the science of speech is not geared toward any particular language. Nonetheless, many examples are taken from English, simply because this book is written in English. We do, however, include many examples from other languages to illustrate facts not found in English, but in-depth knowledge of those languages by the reader is not required.

1.1 Phonetics in a Nutshell

This section introduces some basic concepts of phonetics, which are explained in detail throughout the book. They are represented in Figure 1.1 and include, from

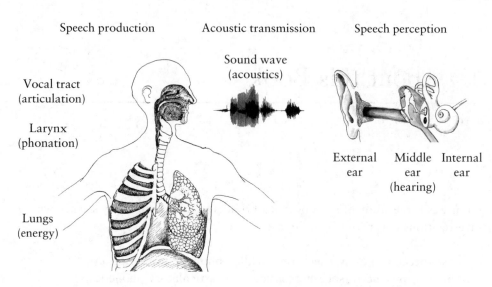

Figure 1.1 The main elements of speech production, acoustic transmission, and speech perception.

left to right: the anatomical structures that enable us to speak, the acoustic signal that these structures produce, and the anatomical structures that enable us to hear.

The anatomical organs which play a role in speech production can be organized into three main areas (see left part of Figure 1.1): the **lungs**, the **larynx**, and the **vocal tract**, which itself consists of mouth, nose, and pharynx.

The lungs, which are used for breathing, are the main source of energy to produce speech sounds. Air that flows from the lungs outward has to pass through the larynx in the neck, where the vocal folds are located. The vocal folds can vibrate in the airstream and this gives the speech its pitch: the vocal folds in the larynx vibrate slower or faster when we produce a melody while we are speaking. This important process is called **phonation**, and speech sounds that are produced with vibrating vocal folds are called **voiced** sounds. The phrase "I lost my voice" actually refers to this process, since somebody who lost his voice is not completely silent but is rather whispering because his vocal folds do not vibrate. The area between the vocal folds is the source of many speech sounds; consequently, it has its own name, the **glottis**. Finally, the vocal tract (mouth, nose, and pharynx) are the central structures for producing speech sounds, a process which is called **articulation**. The structures involved in this process are called the **articulators**. The tongue is the most important organ here, and as the terms *mother tongue* or *language* (from the Latin word *lingua* 'tongue') indicate, this was well known by our ancestors.

Since the larynx has the role of a separator in this system, the part of the speech apparatus above the larynx is referred to as the **supralaryngeal system** and the part below it as the **subglottal system**.

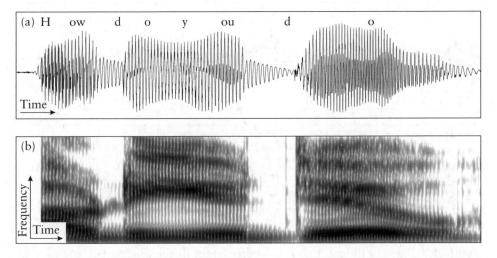

Figure 1.2 (a) Oscillogram and (b) spectrogram of the phrase *How do you do?*

Speech sounds formed by the human **vocal apparatus** travel through the air as **sound waves,** which are essentially small air pressure fluctuations. In an **oscillogram,** these small fluctuations can be graphically represented with time on the horizontal *x*-axis and pressure at each instant in time on the vertical *y*-axis (see Figure 1.2a for an oscillogram of the sentence *How do you do?*). A surprising experience for many looking for the first time at a graphic representation of a speech signal is that there are no pauses between the words (like there are nice spaces between printed words) and that the sounds are not as nicely separated as letters are. In fact, speech sounds merge into each other and speakers do not stop between words. It actually sounds very strange if a speaker utters words with pauses between them (*How – do – you – do*) and in normal speech the phrase sounds more like *howdjoudou* with the *dj* like the beginning of the word *jungle*. This continuation of sounds and lack of breaks between words is one of the problems an adult learner of a foreign language faces: the native speakers seem to speak too fast and mumble all the words together – but this is what any speaker of any language does: the articulators move continuously from one sound to the next, and one word joins the next. The graphic display of this stream of sounds is therefore very helpful in the analysis of what actually has been produced.

If a sound is loud, its air pressure variations are large and its **amplitude** (i.e. the vertical displacement) in the oscillogram is high, just like an ocean wave can be high. If a sound wave repeats itself at regular intervals, that is, if it is **periodic,** then the signal in the oscillogram shows regular oscillations. If the sound is irregular, then the display of the signal on the oscillogram is irregular. And when there is no sound at all, there is just a flat line on the oscillogram. The oscillogram therefore is an exact reproduction of the sound wave.

Analyzing the signal and representing it in a **spectrogram** is often a useful method to gain further insight into the acoustic information transmitted by a speech signal

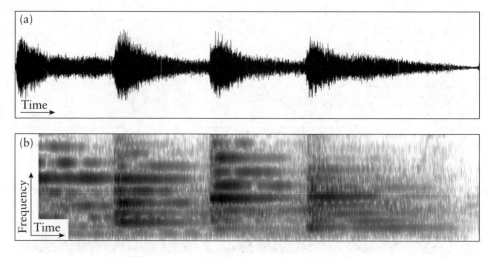

Figure 1.3   (a) Oscillogram and (b) spectrogram of the first part of the tune of "Big Ben."

(see Figure 1.2b for a spectrogram of the same utterance of Figure 1.2a). On a spectrogram, time is also displayed on the horizontal axis as in the oscillogram, but the vertical axis shows the energy in different pitch regions (or, more precisely, frequency bands). Frequency increases along the vertical axis, with higher frequencies displayed toward the top of the axis. In addition, intensity is represented by the darkness of the display, with areas of greater intensity showing up as darker parts of the spectrogram.

As a further example, Figure 1.3 represents the first half of the tune played by London's "Big Ben" bell. The oscillogram (Figure 1.3a) shows that there are four acoustic events, but without further analysis it is not possible to differentiate the musical notes played by the bells. From the spectrogram, an experienced person could infer that the tones were produced by bells, and not, for example, by a trumpet, and determine the frequencies of the bells (what we perceive as their pitch). Comparing Figures 1.2 and 1.3, it is obvious that speech sounds are far more complex than the rather simple signals of bells.

The speech sounds eventually reach the **ear** of a listener (see right-hand side of Figure 1.1). The ear is not only the external structure on the side of the head, which is visible as the ear auricle, but includes the central hearing organ, which sits deep inside the head in the internal ear. The transmission of sound energy from the external ear to the internal ear is performed by a mechanical system in the middle ear that translates the airborne sound waves to pressure waves inside the fluid-filled cavities of the internal ear. Our brain, finally, makes sense of the signals generated by the sensory nerves of the internal ear and transforms them into the perception of speech. Although we cannot directly observe what is going on in this process, we can develop theories about the perception of speech and test these with clever experiments. This situation is somewhat similar to an astronomer who can make theories about a distant planet without actually visiting it. Unfortunately, our perception cannot be measured as easily as the physical properties of a signal, which we examine with an oscillogram or a spectrogram. For example, while it is easy to measure the amplitude of a signal, that is, how "high" sound waves are, this amplitude does not directly relate to the sensation of how "loud" a signal is perceived. This effect is well known by listening to music in a car on the highway and then stopping for a break: the music sounds extremely loud when the car is re-started after a few minutes. The physical amplitude of the signal is the same on the freeway and in the parked car, but the perception changes depending on the background noise and how long a person has been exposed to it.

All activities – producing, transmitting, and perceiving speech – are related to a sound wave and "run in real time": if a DVD is paused, the picture can be frozen but the sound disappears. How, then, can speech sounds be described and captured on paper in order to talk about them? The oscillogram and spectrogram are ways to put signals on paper but they are not easy to understand and it is very complicated to infer from these pictures what a person has said. Normally, we write down the words that we hear, but we do this by knowing the spelling of a language, which might not be related to the way the words are pronounced. For example, the English words *cough*, *though*, *through*, and *thorough* all share the same letters – *ough* – but these letters are pronounced very differently. Thus, the orthography is often not a good way to represent the pronunciation of words. Therefore, speech sounds are "written" with the special symbols of the **International Phonetic Alphabet (IPA)**. Some of these symbols look very much like the letters we use in writing, but these phonetic IPA symbols reflect *sounds* and not *letters*. To make this distinction obvious, IPA symbols are enclosed in square brackets. In this book, we use double quotation marks for letters. For example, the English word *ski* is written in IPA as [ski]. In our example, the words *cough*, *though*, *through*, and *thorough* are represented in IPA as [kɔf, ðou, θɹu, 'θʌɹə]. This writing with phonetic symbols is called phonetic transcription. And although this transcription may look foreign, it is obvious that the underlined sound sequences are different for these words and reflect the way the words are pronounced in this particular dialect of English. It is very important to keep this distinction in mind between the IPA symbols used for *sounds* and the *letters* that many languages use for writing.

Recall that Figure 1.2a shows a speech waveform (oscillogram) of the phrase *How do you do?*, which is a true representation of the air pressure fluctuations that make up this speech signal. When looking at such a waveform, it becomes clear that speech is not a sequence of isolated sound segments. Unlike printed characters that are a sequence of isolated letters grouped into words, nicely separated by spaces, a speech signal is a continuous, ever-changing stream of information. The transcription into sound segments is a rather artificial process that reflects our impression that speech is made up of a sequence of sounds. But even a single sound, like the consonant *p* in the word *supper*, is a complex event, that in a fraction of a second requires a precise coordination of the different muscle groups of the lips, tongue, and larynx. The outcome is a complex acoustic structure with different components, which are nevertheless perceived as one **sound segment**. On the other hand, even the removal of this sound segment from a speech stream leaves traces of its articulatory maneuvers in the adjacent speech segments, and the speech sound can often still be perceived after it has been removed from the signal. In this book, we explain how such a sound is produced, analyzed, perceived, and transcribed.

Additionally, there are other characteristics related to speech that affect more than one segment. Because these characteristics extend beyond a single segment, they are called **suprasegmentals**. An important notion here is the **syllable**, which groups several sounds together. When we speak, we usually produce individual syllables of a word with more or less stress. For example, we say *contráry* as an adjective in the nursery rhyme *Mary, Mary, quite contráry*, stressing the second syllable, but when we say it as a noun, we stress the first syllable, in a phrase like *On the cóntrary, I said the opposite.* The stress on a word can even change its meaning; for example, *desért* means *to abandon* whereas *désert* means *wasteland*, and it is obvious that the stress is important to understand the utterance, although it is not reflected in the orthography of the written text (but you will note a change in quality in the related vowels due to the difference in stress). Another suprasegmental phenomenon is the **intonation** or melody we give a sentence when we speak. For example, in making the statement *It is 10 o'clock.* the pitch of the voice goes down at the end whereas in the question *It is 10 o'clock?*, expressing surprise, the pitch goes up. In both cases, the segmental material (i.e. the speech sounds) is the same and only the intonation differs. There are languages that change the intonation of individual syllables to alter the meaning of a word. The stand-ard example here is Mandarin Chinese, where the word *ma* means 'mother', 'hemp', 'horse', or 'scold', depending on whether the pitch stays flat, rises slightly, falls and rises, or falls sharply, respectively, on *ma*. This usage of pitch, known as tone, might sound strange to someone whose language does not have this feature, but many speakers of the world actually use pitch in this way.

1.2   The Structure of this Book

This book covers the four areas of phonetics: speech transcription, production, acoustics, and perception. We do not want to separate these fields and there is a certain overlap. This illustrates how we think about speech in phonetics: to understand speech one has to know how to write down a sound, how it is produced, what its acoustic correlates are, and how listeners perceive a speech sound. But to be able to do these four things in parallel, each area must be known beforehand – for that reason, this textbook presents these four areas as some-what separate. Whenever we have to use certain terms before they are explained in more detail later in the book, we try to give a short description when they are first introduced. Additionally, certain technical details require a longer motivation and explanation. We have put some of this background information into separate appendices to maintain a readable main text, even when the information in the appendices is crucial for a deeper understanding.

In Chapter 2 we describe the structures of the vocal apparatus that are easy to observe: the phonation at the larynx and the articulation in the vocal tract. In Chapter 3 we introduce the principles of how the sounds of the English language that are produced by these structures are transcribed with the IPA. Chapter 4 goes systematically through the transcription of many consonants of the world's languages. Chapter 5 presents a detailed discussion of the anatomy and physiology of the respiratory system and the larynx. Alternative ways of producing sounds by means of different airstream mechanisms are explained in Chapter 6. Chapters 7 and 8 provide basic knowledge about sound in physical terms, ways to analyze and measure sound, and survey the methods that are available on computers to analyze speech sounds. Chapter 9 introduces the acoustic theory of speech production based on the concepts introduced in Chapters 7 and 8. These three chapters are rather "technical" but we try to convey the principles in a way that can be followed by a reader without an extensive mathematical background. The concepts and methods introduced in Chapters 7 to 9 are then applied to speech sounds in Chapter 10. Interestingly, consonants are easy to describe in articulatory terms whereas vowels are easier to describe in acoustic terms. That is why we provide a somewhat hybrid articulatory and acoustic description of the sounds. A similar principle applies to the last three chapters of this book: speech is not a sequence of isolated sound segments but rather a continuous flow of larger sound structures that are eventually perceived by listeners. Since these larger sound structures, which are essential to speech, require an understanding of the individual elements (the sound segments), they are covered relatively late in the book, in Chapter 11. Ultimately, speech exists only because it is perceived. Even though a child typically perceives speech before it is able to produce it, hearing and perception come last in the book because an overview of these two areas requires a basic understanding of the acoustics of speech. Chapter 12 lays out the structures of our hearing organs and Chapter 13 reports on findings about the perception of speech. The appendices explain some more technical terms in more detail for the interested reader. In sum, the 13 chapters discuss how to transcribe speech, how it is produced, what its acoustic characteristics are, and how it is perceived.

1.3 Terminology

Whenever a term is introduced, it is printed in **bold** in the text and its transcription is given in the index if it is an usual word. Technical measures are based on metric units, which are used in this book. Everyday examples use parallel metric units (with meters and kilograms) and the Imperial system (with inches and pounds) so that they are familiar to readers of varying backgrounds.

1.4 Demonstrations and Exercises

We have included exercises at the end of each chapter. These exercises are meant to check and enhance understanding of the key concepts introduced in the chapters. Many more exercises, particularly those that involve the use of sound and graphic representations such as oscillogram and spectrogram and some acoustic and visual demonstrations related to this book are presented on an accompanying website (http://www.blackwellpublishing.com/phonetics). The website refers back to this book. This allows us to continually make updates, additions, and changes to the website.

Exercises

1 List and briefly define the four areas of phonetics.
2 What are the three main areas involved in speech production? Briefly describe their role in speech production.
3 How does an oscillogram reproduce a sound wave? How does it differ from a spectrogram?
4 Justify the use of IPA symbols instead of orthographic representations to represent the pronunciation of words.
5 Define and provide one example of a suprasegmental.

2 Articulatory Phonetics

An important component of phonetics is the description of sounds. One mode of description is articulatory; that is, it involves an articulatory description of how speech sounds are produced. First of all, the production of any kind of sound requires a source of energy. For speech this energy source is the flow of air. For most sounds of the world's languages, this airflow is generated by the lungs, which are described in detail in Section 5.1. Air flows from the lungs through the trachea (windpipe) and then through the larynx (voice box), where the vocal folds are located. The larynx and its role in the complex process of voice formation are discussed in detail in Section 5.2. Finally, the physiological details of the upper part of the speaking apparatus, namely the pharynx (throat), oral tract (mouth), and nasal tract (nose) are presented in Section 5.3. In this chapter, aspects of the speaking apparatus that are easy to observe will be introduced, including phonation at the larynx and articulation in the vocal tract. This description will help to explain terms used for phonetic transcription (Chapter 3).

2.1 Phonation at the Larynx

The larynx (voice box) is located at the bottom of the pharynx (throat) on top of the trachea (windpipe) and consists of cartilage, muscle, ligament, and tissue. For some speakers, the larynx is visible as the Adam's apple, moving up and down during swallowing and speaking. It is not this movement that is central for speech production but the operation of two small muscular folds inside the larynx. These are known as the vocal folds (or vocal cords) and airflow generated by the lungs must pass through them. The vocal folds can be either apart, close together, or tightly closed. When they are apart (as in normal breathing), air travels through without much obstruction. When they are tightly closed, no air passes through, which prevents, for example, food from entering the trachea. When they are close together, the airstream from the lungs will make them vibrate. This vibration is known as **voicing** or phonation. It is important to note that **voiced sounds** such as vowels and many consonants are produced with vocal fold vibration (vocal folds close together) while **voiceless sounds** are produced without vocal

fold vibration (vocal folds apart). The presence and absence of vocal fold vibration can be determined by placing your finger loosely on your Adam's apple and
prolonging the sound at the beginning of a word like *zip* ("zzzzzzzz"). This is a
voiced consonant produced with vocal fold vibration and you should be able to
feel this vibration with your finger. The beginning of a word like *sip* ("ssssssss")
has a voiceless consonant that is produced without vocal fold vibration. You should
not feel any vibration. Another way to test this difference is to place your hands
over your ears and then produce the sounds. For the voiced sound ("zzz") there
should be a humming in your head which is not there when the voiceless sound
("sss") is produced. This hum is caused by the vibration of the vocal folds.

The space between the vocal folds is known as the glottis. Adjustments of the
vocal folds and hence the glottis can result in whisper, breathy voice, or other
modifications of the voice quality (see Section 6.2).

2.2   Basic Articulatory Terms

Figure 2.1 shows a side view (also known as a midsagittal view) of the part of
the speech production apparatus from the larynx up. The air passages above the

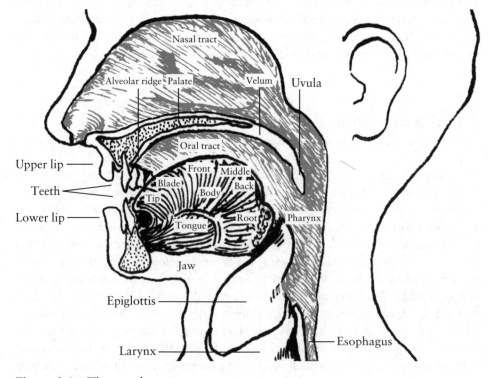

Figure 2.1   The vocal tract.

larynx are collectively known as the vocal tract and the organs above the larynx are sometimes collectively referred to as supralaryngeal organs. These air passages include the pharynx (throat), the oral tract (mouth), and the nasal tract (nose).

The parts of the vocal tract that can be used to form sounds are called articulators. The basic principle in describing and producing sounds is that an articulator comes near or touches another articulator. Often, the articulators that form the lower surface of the oral tract move toward those that form the upper part. We will now describe the principal articulators or supralaryngeal organs, moving from the front of the vocal tract toward the back, that is, from lips to larynx:

1 **Lips**. Both the upper and lower lip can be used to produce speech sounds. Sounds involving the lips are known as **labial sounds**.
2 **Teeth** (primarily the upper incisors). Sounds involving the teeth are known as **dental sounds**.
3 **Alveolar ridge**. This is a slight protrusion directly behind the upper front teeth. Its prominence varies among individuals. The alveolar ridge is sometimes known as the gum ridge. Sounds produced here are known as **alveolar sounds**.
4 **Palate**. This is the hard and bony part that forms the front part of the roof of the mouth. It is sometimes referred to as the **hard palate**. Sounds produced here are known as **palatal sounds**.
5 **Velum**. This is the soft muscular rear part of the roof of the mouth, also known as the **soft palate**. Sounds produced here are known as **velar sounds**. The velum also serves another purpose in the production of speech sounds. It can be raised to close off the nasal cavity from the rest of the vocal tract, for example during oral breathing. In this case, air can only escape through the mouth. This closing of the nasal cavity is known as the velic or **velopharyngeal closure**. Sounds produced with a raised velum are called **oral sounds**. When the velum is lowered, the passage between the nasal and oral cavities is open, as in nasal breathing. Air can now go out through the nose and the mouth, producing in this way **nasal** or **nasalized sounds** (see Section 3.4.2.2 for a discussion of the difference between nasal and nasalized sounds). If, in addition to lowering the velum, the airstream is blocked from flowing out of the oral cavity, the air can only escape through the nasal cavity. In this case a **nasal stop** is produced.
6 **Uvula**. This is a small wedge-shaped object hanging down from the end of the velum. It can be seen when looking in the mirror with the mouth wide open and keeping the tongue low and flat or holding it down with a tongue depressor, as when saying "aaa" at the doctor's office. Sounds produced here are known as **uvular sounds**.
7 **Pharynx**. This is the cavity between the uvula and the larynx, in everyday language referred to as the throat. The back wall of the pharynx can be considered an articulator on the upper surface of the vocal tract. Sounds produced here are known as **pharyngeal sounds**.

After reviewing these parts of the upper surface of the vocal tract and before going over the lower surface of the vocal tract, we should discuss what in common terms is known as the "voice box."

8   **Larynx**. Usually this is the source of all voiced sounds. But the vocal folds in the larynx can also be the narrowest constriction in the production of a speech sound and hence the larynx can also serve as an articulator. Sounds produced in this way are called **glottal sounds**.

  The articulators forming the lower surface of the vocal tract include:

1   Lower lip, which can actively approximate or touch the upper lip or the upper teeth, resulting in bilabial or labiodental sounds, respectively.
2   Lower teeth, which take part in the production of certain dental sounds.
3   Most important, however, is the tongue, the muscle that is attached to the lower jaw (mandible). The tongue can be divided into the following six regions, going from front to back:
    (a) **Tongue tip**. This is the frontmost part of the tongue. Sounds produced with the tongue tip (apex of the tongue) are known as **apical** sounds.
    (b) **Tongue blade**. This is a short section following the tip. It is below the alveolar ridge when the vocal tract is in its neutral or rest position. Sounds produced with the tongue blade (lamen) are known as **laminal** sounds.
    (c) Front of the **tongue body**. This is the *front part* of the *tongue body* so it is actually more the *middle* portion of the *tongue*. It is that part of the tongue that is below the palate when the tongue is in its rest position.
    (d) Center of the tongue body. This middle part of the tongue body is roughly beneath the palate and the velum at rest position.
    (e) Back of the tongue body. This rear portion of the tongue body is the part beneath the velum. It is also known as the **tongue dorsum**.
    (f) **Tongue root**. This is the part of the tongue opposite the back wall of the pharynx. Sounds produced with the root (radix) are referred to as **radical sounds**.
4   **Epiglottis**. It is a cartilaginous structure moving downward and backward with the tongue. As the tongue moves backward during swallowing, the epiglottis folds down and covers the glottis, thus channeling food and fluids to the esophagus. There is some debate about the status of the epiglottis as an articulator. While some view the epiglottis as a passive articulator that merely moves in tandem with the tongue, others indicate that it is an active articulator as, for example, in the production of certain consonants in Hebrew.

This, then, provides a basic overview of the organs and structures in the vocal tract. As we said before, the basic principle in speech production is that one articulator approaches or touches another articulator. Those articulators that move are called the **active articulators** (lips, tongue tip, tongue blade, front, middle, and back of the tongue body, tongue root, epiglottis, velum, and larynx) and those that are stationary are called the **passive articulators** (lips, teeth, alveolar ridge, palate, velum, uvula, and pharynx wall).

Notice that two of the articulators can be either active or passive. The lips are considered both active and passive articulators. The lower lip is typically the active articulator while the upper lip is usually a passive articulator. That is, the lower lip usually moves up and makes contact with the upper lip. The velum can also be either active or passive. The velum is active in the distinction between oral and nasal sounds. When the velum moves up and makes contact with the pharynx wall, air cannot pass through the nasal cavity and hence the resulting sound will be oral. When the velum moves down, the passage to the nasal cavity is opened up and the resulting sound is nasal or nasalized. The velum can also be a passive articulator, in which case some part of the tongue (the active articulator) approaches or makes contact with the velum, resulting in a velar sound. While the uvula does vibrate (or trill), its motion does not result from muscular effort. Instead, the uvula is set into vibration by the airflow from the lungs, much like a leaf on a tree can be set into motion by the wind. The uvula is therefore considered a passive articulator. With the exception of the lips, velum, and uvula, all passive articulators are immobile rigid structures.

2.3   The Articulation of Consonants

The preceding review of the individual articulators and structures of the vocal tract now allows for the description of specific speech sounds. A very basic distinction between two major classes of speech sounds is that between **consonants** and **vowels**. (Linguists often abbreviate consonants as C and vowels as V, such that the structure of the word *milk* can be represented as CVCC.) Sounds are classified as consonants or vowels mainly on the basis of how they are articulated or produced. For the articulation of vowels, the oral cavity is relatively open – in other words, the airflow is quite unobstructed. In addition, the vocal folds are usually vibrating. For consonants, on the other hand, the airstream is affected in a number of ways; it can either be:

1   blocked, resulting in an (oral) stop consonant;
2   impeded, resulting in either a fricative with a major constriction or an approximant with a minor constriction;
3   diverted through the nasal cavity, resulting in a nasal consonant.

In addition, the vocal folds may or may not be vibrating, resulting in voiced or voiceless (= unvoiced) sounds.

From now on, speech sounds will be classified as either consonants or vowels. We will start with the consonants. In order to produce a consonant, the airstream through the vocal tract must be obstructed in some way. Consonants can therefore be classified according to the location and extent of this obstruction, or, in linguistic terms, the **place and manner of articulation**. We start by describing the consonants of English in terms of their place and manner of articulation. In Chapter 4 we expand this description to sounds found in other languages of the world.

2.3.1   Place of articulation

Going from front to back in the vocal tract, the following places of articulation can be distinguished in English:

1   **Bilabial**. Bilabials are produced with both lips. Examples in English are the initial sounds in the words *peak*, *beak*, and *meek*.
2   **Labiodental**. The lower lip makes contact with the upper front teeth. Examples are the initial sounds in the words *fine* and *vine*.
3   **Dental**. Dental consonants involve the tip or blade of the tongue and the upper front teeth. Examples are the initial sounds in *thigh* and *thy*.
4   **Alveolar**. These sounds involve the tip or blade of the tongue and alveolar ridge as in *tip*, *dip*, *sip*, *zip*, *lip*, *rip*, and *nip*. (For a discussion of the retroflex variant of "r," see Section 3.1.5.)
5   **Postalveolar**. These sounds involve the tongue tip or blade and the back of the alveolar ridge. The tongue is raised towards the alveolar ridge and the front of the hard palate. Examples are the initial sounds in *sheep*, *genre*, *cheap*, and *jeep*.
6   **Palatal**. Palatal consonants involve the front of the tongue and the hard palate, as in the initial sound in *yes*.
7   **Velar**. These consonants involve the back of the tongue and the velum. Examples are the initial sounds in *coal* and *goal*, and the final sound in *sing*.
8   **Glottal**. English has one sound that is produced at the glottis, the initial sound in words such as *heat*. This sound is created when air is blown through widely separated vocal folds.

As can be seen by the examples given above, there are often several different sounds at each place of articulation, which differ in their voicing and manner of articulation.

2.3.2   Manner of articulation

Another dimension along which consonants are classified refers to the degree of obstruction, which relates directly to the way they are produced. This dimension is called manner of articulation. Recall that for consonants, the airstream can be completely blocked, it can be impeded, or it can be diverted through the nasal tract. Consequently, the following manners of articulation for consonants are distinguished:

1 **Plosive** or **stop**. In the production of plosives, the articulators come together to form a constriction and completely block or stop the oral flow of air for a brief moment. For (oral) stops, the velum is raised, blocking the nasal cavity, so that no air can escape through either the mouth or the nose. As air continues to travel up from the lungs into the oral cavity, pressure in the mouth will build up behind the constriction. When the articulators then come apart, for the production of the next speech sound, the air pressure will be released in a small burst of sound (see the vertical "spike" at point A on the spectrogram in Figure 2.2b). This burst of sound can be considered a small explosion and that is why stop consonants are also known as plosives. Because stop consonants involve a temporary blockage of the airstream, they cannot be perceived in isolation. In order to hear the release, a vowel context is typically required. Examples of voiced plosives are the initial sounds in the words _buy_, _die_, _guy_. Examples of voiceless plosives are the initial sounds in _pea_, _tea_, _key_. English has plosives at three places of articulation: bilabial (_pie_, _buy_), produced by closing the lips, alveolar (_to_, _do_), produced by placing the tongue tip or blade against the alveolar ridge, and velar (_cot_, _got_), produced by placing the back of the tongue against the velum.
2 **Nasal**. In the production of a nasal (or nasal stop), air is diverted through the nasal cavity. For nasals, similar to plosives, a complete constriction is again present in the oral cavity so that no air can escape through the mouth. But since the velum is lowered for nasals, air can escape through the nose. The result is a nasal stop. English nasals are voiced and occur at the same three places of articulation as plosives: bilabial (_me_), alveolar (_no_), and velar (the final sound in _long_). That is, the articulation in the oral cavity is identical to that for a plosive at the same place of articulation. The only difference is that nasals are produced with a lowered velum.
3 **Fricative**. In the production of a fricative, one articulator comes very close to another, creating a narrow passage. The air coming from the lungs is forced, under considerable pressure, through this narrow constriction. This creates noisy turbulence of air, which produces a sound with a hissing quality (see, for example, the dark high-frequency region at point D in Figure 2.2b). Since there is no complete blockage of the airstream in the production of these sounds, fricatives can be sustained in isolation. English has fricatives at five places of articulation: labiodental (_fine_, _vine_), produced by raising the lower lip toward the upper front teeth; dental (_thigh_, _thy_), produced by creating a narrow channel between the tip or blade of the tongue and the upper front teeth; alveolar (_sip_, _zip_), produced by raising the tongue tip or blade toward the alveolar ridge; postalveolar (as in the medial sounds in _pressure_ and _measure_),

produced by raising the tip or blade of the tongue towards that part of the roof of the mouth behind the alveolar ridge and extending into the palatal region; and glottal (*high*), produced by air passing through an open glottis.

4 **Affricate**. Production of an affricate involves a combination of two manners of articulation, stop and fricative, in this sequence. Since the stop and fricative are produced at nearly the same place of articulation (are **homorganic**), they act as a single unit, resulting from one articulatory movement. In English, affricates are combinations of postalveolar plosives and postalveolar fricatives, as the first sound in *chin* and *gin*. First, the tip or blade of the tongue is raised to make contact immediately behind the alveolar ridge. Next, the contact between tongue tip and roof of the mouth is slackened to form a fricative at the same place of articulation.

5 **Approximant**. In the production of an approximant, one articulator approaches the other but not sufficiently to create friction. The extent of the constriction is somewhat greater than for a vowel but much smaller than for a fricative. Approximants have some characteristics of both vowels and consonants, which is why they are sometimes called **semi-vowels**. Like vowels, they are produced without a severe constriction but like consonants, airflow is partially obstructed. Approximants are also like consonants in terms of their behavior in the world's languages. For example, approximants do not occur alone, similar to consonants, whereas isolated vowels can constitute words, as, for example, in English *I* or *awe*. A distinction is made between **central approximants** and **lateral approximants**. Central approximants are characterized by a "central" airflow in the middle (midsagittal) section of the oral cavity. English has central approximants at three places of articulation: labial-velar (*way*), produced simultaneously with the back of the tongue raised toward the velum and with pursed or rounded lips; alveolar (*rye*), produced with the tongue tip raised toward the alveolar ridge; and palatal (*you*), produced with the front of the tongue raised toward the palate. In a lateral approximant, the central pathway is blocked and the air flows sideways (laterally) around the blockage. English has one lateral approximant, with an alveolar place of articulation, as in the word *lie*. In the production of a lateral alveolar approximant, the tip of the tongue makes full contact with the alveolar ridge. However, the airflow is not interrupted because air passes around the sides of the tongue.

To summarize, consonants can be described in terms of voicing, and place and manner of articulation. Voicing indicates whether a sound is voiced or voiceless. Places of articulation for English sounds are bilabial, labiodental, dental, alveolar, postalveolar, palatal, velar, and glottal. Manners of articulation are plosive, nasal, fricative, affricate, and approximant. In addition, two more dimensions can be used to fully specify consonants: oral/nasal to indicate whether a sound is oral or nasal, and central/lateral, to indicate whether air flows out through the center of the mouth or along the sides of the mouth.

As an example, the initial consonant in the word *zest* can be described as a "voiced alveolar central oral fricative." In English, the vast majority of speech sounds involves a central articulation (only "l" is a lateral). In addition, most sounds are oral, produced with a velic closure (only "m," "n," and "ng" are nasal). Central and oral are therefore typically considered default values for these categories and can be left out of the specification. As a result, the description of "z" can be simplified to "voiced alveolar fricative."

It is important to note that the articulatory description of consonants typically only involves mention of the passive articulator while it is assumed that the active articulator is the tongue. The tongue will touch or approximate a passive articulator. For example, if the tongue is raised to touch the alveolar ridge, we speak of an alveolar plosive. Likewise, if the tongue is raised to form a narrow channel at the alveolar ridge, we speak of an alveolar fricative. Even though the tongue does all the moving, it is not mentioned in the articulatory description. One advantage is the avoidance of cumbersome terms such as lingua-alveolar. However, both articulators are mentioned if:

1   neither articulator is the tongue, such as in bilabial or labiodental sounds;
2   a more precise description is needed. For example, either the tip or the blade of the tongue may touch the alveolar ridge. Either sound is simply described as an *alveolar*. But if it is important to specify this difference, one could distinguish an apico-alveolar from a lamino-alveolar sound.

2.3.3   Other classification schemes

In closing this section on consonants, it is useful to mention a few more terms that are sometimes used to classify consonants. Plosives, affricates, and fricatives are sometimes grouped together because they all involve a severe obstruction of the airflow and they are collectively referred to as **obstruents**. The class of approximants can be divided into **glides** and **liquids**. These terms express that glides are "gliding" from one position to the other and that liquids lack any "harshness." In English, the labial-velar (*way*) and palatal (*you*) approximants are glides while the central alveolar (*rye*) and lateral alveolar (*lie*) approximants are liquids. Finally, nasals and approximants are sometimes collectively referred to as **sonorant** consonants. Since the class of sonorant segments includes those sounds that are produced without a complete interruption of the vocal tract and without turbulence, vowels classify as sonorants as well. Sonorants are distinct from obstruents in that they lack an increase in air pressure behind the constriction.

Places of articulation are also sometimes subdivided into broader classes, namely the labial sounds, which are produced involving the lips, **coronal sounds**, which are produced with the tongue tip, blade, or front of the tongue body, **dorsal sounds**, which are produced with the tongue dorsum, and **guttural sounds**, which are produced in the pharynx and by the larynx. This subdivision is less precise, but reflects the observation that many languages of the world have only one sound contrast in each of these four areas and that these four areas are controlled by three rather independent groups of muscles.

The types of sounds discussed so far can be easily identified in an oscillogram and spectrogram of the word *conceptualizing* (Figure 2.2). Stop consonants (points A and F in Figure 2.2) are identifiable by their zero amplitude on the oscillogram and by white gaps on the spectrogram. These areas correspond to the period during which the airflow from the lungs is blocked because of a constriction somewhere in the vocal tract. A voiceless fricative (point D) is produced with a severe constriction in the vocal tract, which results in a very irregular pattern, as shown by the random variations in air pressure on the oscillogram and by a concentration of energy in the higher frequencies (toward the top of the vertical axis) on the spectrogram. In comparison, a voiced fricative (point K) has a lower amplitude, as shown by the much smaller variations in pressure on the oscillogram and weaker (less dark) striations on the spectrogram. Voicing is most clearly seen on the spectrogram in the form of dark regular striations of a very low frequency (at the very bottom of the vertical axis). The acoustics of approximants may be appreciated in comparison to those of vowels. Vowels are produced with relatively little obstruction; as a result, they are characterized by relatively large amplitudes on the oscillogram. On the spectrogram, vowels stand out by having dark bands at multiple frequencies (points B, E, H, J, and L). Since the production of approximants requires a constriction that is somewhat greater than that for a vowel, approximants show a vowel-like pattern but with a lower amplitude, as shown in I on both the oscillogram and spectrogram. Finally, spectrograms for nasals typically show dark regular striations of a very low frequency that represent voicing; additional bands of energy at higher frequencies may be weak (as in C) or absent (as in M).

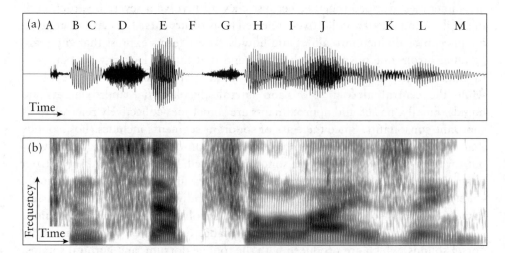

Figure 2.2   (a) Oscillogram and (b) spectrogram of the word *conceptualizing*.

Affricates display aspects of both stops and fricatives, as shown in point G. The stop portion of the voiceless affricate shows up as an area of low amplitude on the oscillogram and corresponding white gap in the spectrogram. The release, in turn, is immediately followed by a fricative, with random variation in air pressure in the oscillogram and a concentration of high-frequency energy in the spectrogram.

2.4   The Articulation of Vowels

In the production of vowels, the articulators do not come as closely together as for consonant production. The airstream is therefore relatively unobstructed. In addition, the vocal folds almost always vibrate and serve as a sound source. Different vowels are produced by changing the size and shape of the vocal tract, and the shape of the tongue is the primary factor in determining the shape of the vocal tract, which affects the sound produced at the glottis. However, rather than specifying the entire shape of the tongue, articulatory descriptions of vowel sounds focus only on the position of the highest point of the tongue. In addition, the position of the lips can also affect the quality of a vowel. In general, there are three major articulatory dimensions used in classifying the vowels:

1   **Frontness**. Most vowels are produced with a certain arching of the tongue. This arching may be toward the front, center, or back of the oral cavity. This horizontal dimension is referred to as the frontness (or backness) of the vowel.
2   **Height**. By moving the tongue body up and down within the lower jaw, the oral cavity can be made narrower or wider. This vertical dimension is called the height of the vowel. While the lower jaw and tongue often move in tandem, the tongue can move independently of the jaw.
3   **Lip rounding**. Vowels may be produced with the lips rounded or in a neutral (unrounded or spread) position.

For English, two groups of vowels are distinguished, namely front vowels and back vowels. And for each of these groups, a vowel can be either high, mid, or low. In English, unlike many other languages, there are no words that differ only in the rounding of vowels. This is different, for example, in German, which has many word-pairs differing only in vowel rounding like *lesen* 'to read' with a mid front unrounded vowel and *lösen* 'to loosen' with a mid front rounded vowel (see Section 10.1).

To illustrate the parameters of frontness, height, and rounding as descriptors of vowel quality, we start with the vowel in the word *beat*. The tongue body is raised upward and is relatively far forward. Notice that the tip of the tongue touches lightly behind the lower front teeth. The middle to front portion of the tongue is raised. This is also the case for the vowels in the words *bit*, *bet*, *bait*, and *bat*. Since for these five vowels the highest point of the tongue is in the front of the mouth, these vowels are all known as front vowels.

The five front vowels of English differ along the height parameter. For the vowel in *beat*, the tongue is raised close toward the palate. For the vowel in *bit*, the highest point of the tongue is a little lower, and it is progressively lower for the vowels in *bait*, *bet*, and *bat*, respectively. In fact, in *bat* the tongue is quite flat in the mouth. Vowel height is thus a vertical dimension. In the description of vowel height, the terms **high**, **mid**, and **low** are typically used. For example, the vowels in *beat* and *bit* are high, those in *bet* and *bait* are mid, and that in *bat* is a low vowel. The distinction between *beat* and *bit* and *bait* and *bet*, respectively, is typically captured by means of the distinction between tense and lax segments, discussion of which will be postponed until Section 3.2. In some descriptions, high and low are referred to as **close** and **open**, respectively, because the oral pathway is relatively closed for the high vowels and relatively open for the low vowels. All front vowels of English are unrounded.

Combining the dimensions of frontness, height, and rounding, the vowel in *beat* can be described as a high (or close) front unrounded vowel, and that in *bat* as a low (or open) front unrounded vowel. The remaining vowels in *bit*, *bait*, and *bet* can be described as high front unrounded (and lax), mid front unrounded (and tense), and mid front unrounded (and lax), respectively.

For the back vowels, the same approach can be used. Starting with the vowel in the word *boot*, the highest point of the tongue is raised close to the velum in the back of the oral cavity. Since for these vowels the highest point of the tongue is toward the back of the vocal tract (for more on this, see Section 3.2), these vowels are known as back vowels. For the vowel in *boot*, then, the tongue is close to the back surface of the vocal tract. This is also the case for the vowels in *cook*, *coat*, *caught*, and *cot*. (It should be mentioned that for many speakers of American English, the words *caught* and *cot* have the same vowel. A speaker of this variety of English produces both words with the vowel as in *father* and has four back vowels instead of five.)

This illustration of a difference between varieties of English makes it clear that it is important to specify the variety of English that we are describing. In this and other chapters, we are concerned with a variety of English spoken in North America known as General American (GA). GA is often heard in national broadcasts and is relatively free of regional markers. GA excludes varieties of American English spoken in the south and eastern seaboard, particularly New England and New York City. For speakers of GA, the words *cot*, *palm*, and *father* all contain the same (low back) vowel. Even within GA, there are regional differences. Most notably, for speakers in the Midwest and West of the US, as well as Canada, the vowels in *cot* and *caught* are the same (low back) vowel. Unless stated otherwise, it is this variety of GA that we have in mind when we speak of English and that we use in our descriptions and transcriptions.

Most of the variation in accents occurs among the vowels. In the United Kingdom, the language traditionally used by national broadcasts is Received Pronunciation (RP, also referred to as Standard Southern British English). RP has more vowels than GA. For example, the words *pot*, *palm*, and *father* contain three distinct vowels. In addition, RP is a non-rhotic accent in which the non-prevocalic "r" is not pronounced.

Returning to the back vowels, they can once again be distinguished in terms of height (or openness), with the vowels in *boot* and *cook* being high (close) and that in *cot* being low (open). The vowels in *coat* and *caught* can be described as mid back. The vowel in *coat* is tense while that in *caught* is lax.

For English, there are only three vowels left. They are all articulated at the midpoint along the horizontal front–back dimension, and are known as **central** vowels. One very common vowel is the unstressed vowel as at the beginning of *about*. This vowel is articulated at the approximate midpoint of both height and frontness and is therefore described as a mid central vowel. This unstressed vowel in *about* is called **schwa**. Its articulatory point is in an intermediate "neutral" position, neither high nor low, nor front nor back. Another central vowel is that in words such as *fur*. Rather than describing this as a sequence of schwa and "r," the production of this vowel involves a nearly complete temporal overlap of the vocalic and consonantal articulations for –*ur*. It is therefore considered a single phonetic segment, described as a mid central r-colored vowel. Finally, the vowel in words such as *cut* is described as a low central vowel. It is similar to schwa but stressed and slightly lower.

We have left out a few sounds that are typically referred to as vowels. Specifically, the vowel sounds in the words *buy*, *cow*, and *boy*, have not yet been discussed. This is because these sounds constitute a special kind of vowel that is known as a **diphthong**. A diphthong is a vowel whose quality changes substantially during its articulation. A diphthong can be described as a movement from one vowel to another vowel where the first part of the diphthong is usually more dominant. Vowels that do not involve significant articulatory movement are sometimes called **monophthongs**, or pure vowels, in order to distinguish them from the diphthongs.

The English diphthongs can be described as follows. For the diphthong in *buy*, the articulators start with a low central unrounded vowel and move to a high front unrounded vowel. In *cow*, the articulators start with the same low central unrounded vowel and move to a high back rounded vowel. Finally, the diphthong in *boy* starts out as a low back rounded vowel and ends up as a high front unrounded vowel. An easy way to determine that a diphthong consists of two parts is by prolonging or sustaining it. Either the first or the second part is prolonged but the vowel sound cannot be prolonged in its entirety. While we have described diphthongs as combinations of two vowels, some diphthongs do not begin with any of the monophthongal vowels found in English. The diphthongs in *buy* and *cow* both start with a low central unrounded vowel.

The diphthongs in *buy*, *cow*, and *boy* are sometimes referred to as "true" diphthongs to distinguish them from the vowels in *bait* and *boat*. The vowel sounds in these two words involve considerable articulatory movement but not as substantial as that in the three "true" diphthongs. In English, the vowels in *bait* and *boat* are said to be **diphthongized**. That is, the articulatory movement results in a substantial change in the quality of these vowels, known as an **offglide**, toward the end of their articulation. The vowels in *bait* and *boat* can be described as mid front unrounded and mid back rounded diphthongized vowels, respectively.

In summary, vowels are described in terms of three dimensions (height, frontness, and rounding) and diphthongs are considered a special class of vowels that combine two vowel articulations. Additional dimensions relating to voice quality will be discussed in Section 6.2. Having introduced an articulatory description of consonants and vowels, the next chapter will discuss a way of representing the sounds of any spoken utterance by means of a set of symbols, a process known as phonetic transcription.

Exercises

1 Describe the process of voicing or phonation.
2 With which articulator are apical, laminal, and dorsal sounds produced? What is the difference between them?
3 What is the difference between passive and active articulators? Using an example, explain how an articulator can be both an active and a passive articulator.
4 What is the place and manner of articulation of the underlined segments in each of the following words: *junk*, *did*, *shy*, *my*, *yes*.
5 Name and define the articulatory dimensions introduced in this chapter to classify vowels.
6 Using the above dimensions, classify the vowels in the following words: *sat*, *look*, *weep*, *cup*, *odd*.

3   Phonetic Transcription

While a detailed articulatory description of sounds can provide a reasonably good idea of what a spoken utterance sounds like, it is quite cumbersome to label each sound in terms of its articulation. For example, the word "speech" would consist of a voiceless alveolar fricative, followed by a voiceless bilabial plosive, which is in turn followed by a high front unrounded vowel, followed by a voiceless postalveolar affricate. In order to provide a more efficient means of describing speech, phoneticians have devised a set of symbols, known as the International Phonetic Alphabet (IPA). IPA symbols are by convention enclosed in square brackets ([ ]). Founded in 1886, the International Phonetic Association, which is also abbreviated IPA, continues to modify the alphabet in order to accommodate newly documented sounds. Ideally, anyone properly trained in the use of this alphabet should be able to use it to **transcribe** the sounds of any language. Proper training should help in listening as objectively as possible in order to minimize any influence of the native language or dialect. The final transcription should enable anyone with proper training to reconstruct the sounds of the original message. The extent to which the original sounds can be reconstructed is of course a function of the level of detail and precision of the transcription.

The truest representation of the sounds of a spoken utterance is a recording. But sounds cannot be printed on paper, and even a graphic representation such as an oscillogram or spectrogram may be impossible to "read." The most detailed way of representing speech sounds with printed symbols is a close or **narrow transcription**. Such a transcription tries to represent as much detail as possible and encodes dialectal details and peculiarities of a speaker. Such a detailed transcription would not be very helpful for a language learner looking up the pronunciation of a word in a dictionary, because there can be many possible narrow transcriptions for one word in a given language. For such a purpose, an idealized or **broad transcription** is much more appropriate. Such a transcription shows much less detail but represents the essential sounds that have to be used to pronounce a word correctly without including details that might be language-specific or speaker-specific. For example, a "p" at the beginning of a word in English is pronounced with **aspiration**; that is, it is produced with a certain amount of audible airflow after the release of the plosive. A dictionary would transcribe only a [p]. In French, such a release has to be produced without this flow of air (i.e. without aspiration), but the dictionary would also transcribe a [p]. Both transcriptions still refer to a voiceless bilabial plosive, but its language-dependent realization with or without aspiration need not be noted in the broad transcription (but a good dictionary should explain the proper production of the sounds in the language in its introduction). The speech sounds that are represented in a narrow or broad transcription are called **phones** and are also sometimes called sound segments.

Actually, there are many possible intermediate levels of transcription between a broad and a narrow transcription. The amount of detail depends on the application and on the experience and training of the transcriber. Imagine that the assignment is to transcribe an unknown language. It is not known which phonetic properties will turn out to be important, and, consequently, you will have to initially include as much phonetic detail as possible. Such a transcription will be very narrow and lack word boundaries because no words of the language are known yet. This level of transcription is known as an **impressionistic** or **general phonetic** transcription. Impressionistic and narrow transcriptions always require a (live or recorded) speech signal. In contrast, a broad transcription can be generated without access to the signal.

The existence of different transcriptions might confuse a novice in the field, but in real life we often use different levels of detail for various purposes. For example, a car driver requires a different map for the same stretch of land than a hiker, who needs a map that indicates slopes which might be irrelevant for a car driver, who, in turn, would be very upset if steps were not marked. A map that has all details for all applications would become unreadable. An ideal map often fits a specific purpose. The same is true for a transcription: depending on how much detail has to be covered and how much is known about how to produce the sounds of a language, the transcription will carry more or less detail.[1]

The reduction from the actually produced details covered by a narrow transcription to a more generalized pronunciation in a broad transcription can be carried even further to a more abstract **phonemic** representation that captures the speaker's mental representation of the sounds. A phonemic transcription focuses on the **phonemes** of a language and does not, therefore, contain phonetic detail. To be able to differentiate the physically realized *phones* from the *phonemes*, which exist as a mental representation in the mind of a speaker, the latter are enclosed in two slashes in the transcription. To illustrate this difference, take a word like *handbag*, which may be pronounced as *ha*[mb]*ag*. This broad transcription indicates that the "d" was deleted and the "n" adopted the place of articulation of the following bilabial "b." In contrast, the phonemic transcription of this word would be *ha*/ndb/*ag*, which is a representation of the way in which the word may be stored in the speaker's mental lexicon. The science that is concerned with this more abstract representation of sounds and their interaction is **phonology**. The difference between a more abstract representation and the physical reality is known to users of a Roman writing system: they have a concept of the letter "A," which is rather abstract, since the letter can be written as "A," "a," "ɑ," "a," "*a*," etc., which are different physical realizations.

We will concentrate here on broad transcription and add further details that are needed for a narrow transcription, since mastering narrow transcription requires extensive training. But it must be kept in mind that transcriptions are always language-dependent, and, as we will show in Section 13.4, it is very hard not to be influenced in perception by one's mother tongue. It is also common for a sound in one language to be realized in rather different ways without conscious awareness by a native speaker. In another language, the same differences might be related to two different phonemes and a speaker of that language can differentiate them with ease. Take for example the distinction between the two sounds "l" and "r" in English. These sounds are often perceived as the same by Japanese speakers. On the other hand, an English speaker will often not hear the difference between *ma* with a rising tone (meaning 'hemp') and *ma* with a falling-rising tone (meaning 'horse'), and will find it difficult to learn this difference (without proper training), whereas a three-year old Mandarin child has no problems perceiving them as distinct.

The general principle in phonetic transcription is that, for a given language, each **distinctive sound** is represented by a unique symbol. But how does one decide what the distinctive sounds of a language are? A native speaker of a language may never have considered how many distinctive speech sounds his or her native language has. How would one document a language encountered for the first time? One usually begins with a **minimal pair** test. Using English as our example, we start with a known word, like *tip*. Systematically, only one sound in a given position is changed and it is checked (by yourself, or with the help of a native informant) whether or not this results in a different word. For example, replacing the initial "t" by "d" would result in a different word, namely *dip*. If a different word is the result, it can be concluded that, in English, "t" and "d" must be distinct sounds. If they were not distinct, there would be no way to distinguish the two words *tip* and *dip*. These distinct phonemes are the smallest segments of sound that serve to distinguish meaning. In other words, if substituting [t] by [d] does not result in a different word, [t] and [d] would not be distinct phonemes. All different positions in a word can be used in a minimal pair test. The sound in medial position ("i") can be changed from "i" in *tip* to "o" in *top*, leading to a different word. Likewise, changing the final "p" to "n" gives the word *tin*. Sometimes, phonemes do not appear in all positions of a word. For example, the voiced velar nasal in *long* does not occur in initial position in English and the glottal fricative in *hat* never occurs in final position. Although using the minimal pair test is not always successful in finding contrasting words since not all segments of a word can be changed to create different words, this test is often sufficient to identify the phonemes of a language.

Consider again the pronunciation of the initial sound in *tip*. At the level of a narrow transcription, there is variation in how this sound is pronounced. For example, it can be pronounced by placing the blade of the tongue against the alveolar ridge (voiceless lamino-alveolar plosive), by placing the tongue tip against the alveolar ridge (voiceless apico-alveolar plosive), or by placing the tip or the tongue blade right behind the teeth (voiceless dental plosive). Although this may result in slightly different-sounding "t"s, these differences do not distinguish two words in the English language. That is, *tip* produced with a lamino-alveolar plosive, *tip* with an apico-alveolar, or *tip* with a dental plosive do not make distinct words in English. The different versions of "t" are said to be **allophones** of the phoneme /t/. Allophones are different realizations of the same phoneme that are not associated with a difference in meaning. Allophones can result from differences in the position in which the phoneme occurs. For example, English light and dark "l" are allophones that typically occur in word-initial and word-final position, respectively (see Section 3.1.5). The **context** in which a phoneme occurs, that is, the sounds that immediately precede or follow it, can also result in different allophones (see, for example, our discussion of anticipatory coarticulation in Section 3.4.1.2). For a language in which these differences are allophonic, they do not have to be captured in a transcription that focuses on linguistically relevant aspects. However, if a language phonemically contrasts lamino- and apico-alveolar plosives, for example, it is crucial to convey this distinction in the transcription.

In a phonemic transcription, phonemic contrasts are highlighted, focusing on those segments that serve to distinguish meaning. Phonemes are placed between two slashes. Hence, the phonemic transcription for *tip* is /tɪp/ (the missing dot on the "i" is important, as will be explained shortly). In a broad transcription, the symbols for the sound segments are enclosed in square brackets to indicate that these are phones that are actually produced. Hence, the broad transcription for *tip* is [tɪp]. For this example, it seems as if only the brackets have changed, and in fact the /tɪp/ that is stored in the memory of the speaker is realized as [tɪp]. But a word like *handbag* /hændbæg/ will be realized as [hæmbæg] as discussed before. The use of the same symbols in a phonemic and a broad transcription might confuse a novice user of these systems but it saves us from having to learn two different alphabets. Note, though, that in a broad transcription, each symbol represents a rather broad range of possible pronunciations. For example, the symbol [t] would represent a variety of articulations, including the lamino-alveolar, apico-alveolar, and dental ones discussed above. In a narrow transcription of a Frenchman speaking English the transcription of *tip* could be [t̪ip] or an Englishman could say [tʰɪpˑ] – the square brackets indicate that it is an actual pronunciation and the great amount of detail indicates that this is a rather narrow transcription.

The next two sections provide an overview of the transcription of the consonants and vowels of English.

3.1   Consonants

Table 3.1 provides the IPA symbols for the English consonants while Table 3.2 gives an illustration of words containing those consonants. We will now go through these symbols in more detail.

Table 3.1 shows that quite a few symbols correspond to letters found in the English alphabet. However, that does not necessarily mean that the sound

Table 3.1 IPA symbols for the consonants of English. Place of articulation is represented from left to right while manner of articulation is represented from top to bottom. Symbols on the left-hand side of a cell represent voiceless consonants while those on the right-hand side represent voiced consonants

	Bilabial	Labiodental	Dental	Alveolar	Postalveolar	Palatal	Velar	Glottal
Plosive	p b			t d			k ɡ	
Nasal	m			n			ŋ	
Fricative		f v	θ ð	s z	ʃ ʒ			h
Affricate					t͡ʃ d͡ʒ			
Approximant				ɹ		j	w	
Lateral approximant				l				

Table 3.2 English words illustrating the IPA symbols introduced in Table 3.1. A given IPA symbol from Table 3.1 represents the sound associated with the underlined characters in the corresponding cell in this table. For example, the initial sound in *this* is the symbol [ð]

	Bilabial	Labiodental	Dental	Alveolar	Postalveolar	Palatal	Velar	Glottal
Plosive	pat bat			tip dip			came game	
Nasal	mat			not			long	
Fricative		fine vine	thistle this	sue zoo	shoe measure			ham
Affricate					cheap jeep			
Approximant				read		you	will	
Lateral approximant				lead				

segments represented by these symbols correspond to the way the letters are pronounced. For example, while the symbol [m] does correspond with the way in which the letter "m" is pronounced (as in *mill*), the symbol [j] corresponds to the way the letter "y" is pronounced (as in *yoke*) rather than the letter "j" (as in *joke*). In addition to symbols that correspond to letters, a number of IPA symbols are not part of the Roman alphabet that is used for writing English (e.g. [ʃ, ŋ]).

Table 3.1 is organized by phonetic principles: the manner of articulation (see Section 2.3.2) is listed in rows going from the most obstructed (plosives and nasals) to the least obstructed (approximants) consonants, and the place of articulation (see Section 2.3.1) appears in different columns ranging from the lips at the left to the glottis at the right. In each cell (place and manner of articulation), the voiceless sounds (see Section 2.1) are written on the left and the voiced on the right. We will now introduce the individual sounds of English and discuss some of them in more detail later. In Chapters 4 and 6, we will add more sounds and details that will cover many of the world's languages.

3.1.1   Plosives

The symbols for the plosives (or oral stops) [p, b, t, d, k, g] are familiar to anyone who uses the English orthography. Importantly, however, as pointed out earlier, these symbols represent unique *sounds* that are articulatorily defined in terms of place and manner of articulation and voicing and are not *letters* that are defined by convention. It is easy to find minimal pairs for the voiceless–voiced contrast for all plosives (e.g. initial: *pie–buy*, *tie–dye*, *coast–ghost*; final: *rope–robe*, *sight–side*, *back–bag*) and for the place oppositions (e.g. *by–die–guy*, *pair–* (to) *tear–care*, *bib–bid–big*, *ape–eight–ache*).

3.1.2   Nasals

The symbols for the nasals are [m, n, ŋ]. The bilabial nasal [m] and alveolar nasal [n] are familiar to a speaker (or writer) of English – and, again, the IPA symbols are similar to the orthographic letters, which are often pronounced as these sounds. That these are sounds and not letters becomes more obvious for the velar nasal, which is represented by the symbol [ŋ]. This IPA symbol is not part of the English orthography. Note that the IPA symbol has a small hook on the right leg of the "n," which is turned backward (the orientation and direction of this hook are important because there are other IPA symbols that differ in this respect). Minimal pairs for the labial and alveolar nasals are easy to find (*might–night*, *tumor–tuner*, *beam–bean*). Minimal pairs (triplets) for all three places of articulation are more difficult to find since velar nasals do not occur in word-initial position in English. However, a number of examples can be found in medial and final positions (e.g. *simmer–sinner–singer* and *sum–son–sung*).

In case you are not convinced that the last sound in *king* ([ŋ]) is different from that in *kin* ([n]), stick a finger in your mouth while producing the last sound of the two words. The tongue is in the front of the mouth for the word *kin* and the finger hits the tongue much farther back for the word *king*. *Kin* ends with the alveolar nasal [n] whereas *king* ends with the velar [ŋ]. Remember that nasal and oral stops are both produced at the same place of articulation and that the tongue might have exactly the same shape. But for the nasal stops the velum is lowered, and for the oral stops the vocal folds do not vibrate if they are voiceless.

3.1.3   Fricatives

For the fricatives, we see a bit more variation in the places of articulation and we encounter a few new symbols. The voiceless labiodental fricative [f] is common in many English words. The voiced variant of this sound [v] is again produced with the same position of the articulators but the vocal folds vibrate, as can be easily felt (see Section 2.1). Minimal pairs in initial, medial, and final positions are *fan–van*, *surface–service*, *leaf–leave*.

There are also two dental fricatives in English, voiceless [θ] and voiced [ð]. There are few minimal pairs in English that differ only in terms of the voicing of the dental fricative (e.g. *thigh–thy*, *teeth–teethe*). But there are many contrasts for the voiceless and voiced dental fricatives with other sounds in initial, medial, and final position (e.g. *thigh–tie*, *both–boat*, *though–dough*, *worthy–wordy*, *breathe–breed*, etc.)

There are many minimal pairs for the voiceless alveolar fricative [s] and its voiced counterpart [z] (*seal–zeal*, *lacy–lazy*, *ice–eyes*). As mentioned before, speakers might differ in terms of whether they produce these sounds as apical or laminal. Nevertheless, the acoustic result is nearly identical and in any broad and most narrow transcriptions this individual difference is not transcribed.

The postalveolar fricatives are voiceless [ʃ] and voiced [ʒ]. Other than *Confucian–confusion* there are no minimal pairs for [ʃ] and [ʒ]. While [ʃ] is quite common (e.g. *sure*, *machine*, *rush*), [ʒ] occurs word-initially and finally only in borrowings (e.g. *genre*, *massage*). Word-medial [ʒ] may be found in words such as *usual*. Common non-IPA symbols for [ʃ] and [ʒ] are [š] and [ž], respectively.

There are both velar plosives and nasals but there are no velar fricatives in English, neither voiced nor voiceless. This is a sort of "gap" in the language. English once had these sounds but "lost" them. This can be seen in the spelling of words like *laugh*. These days, this word is produced with a labiodental fricative but the spelling still uses a velar consonant "g" followed by the "h," which reflects that this word was once produced with a velar fricative.

There is an additional voiceless fricative, namely the glottal fricative [h]. The place of articulation of this sound is taken as the glottis and the rest of the vocal tract is rather free to take any position. Usually, this will be the position of the following vowel and some linguists consider [h] as a voiceless variant of the accompanying vowel.

3.1.4 Affricates

For the affricates, there are voiceless and voiced postalveolar sounds ([t͡ʃ] and [d͡ʒ], respectively). The IPA does not have separate symbols for affricates but combines the plosive and fricative with a tie bar [͡]. The reason for this lack of symbols is that (1) affricates can be easily represented by this procedure and it reduces the number of symbols that have to be remembered, and (2) there is a debate whether affricates are really only a single sound segment or not. It is sometimes more a matter of whether the sounds are felt to be one segment or whether the plosive and affricate are two sounds that appear together as a coincidence. For example, the initial sounds in the English words *cheap* (with an initial [t͡ʃ]) and *jeep* (with an initial [d͡ʒ]) are considered affricates because English generally does not allow clusters of a plosive followed by a fricative at the beginning of a word. On the other hand, the words *pants* and *hands* end in the plural marker "-s" and [ts] and [dz] at their ends are considered as a sequence of a plosive and a fricative, because the fricative is not really part of the word but the result of the attachment of the plural "-s" to the final plosives of the words. The case is different in, for example, German, where the sound [t͡s] patterns like a single sound (similar to [t͡ʃ] in English). As a result, German [t͡s] occurs at the beginning, middle, and end of words such as *Ziel* [t͡siːl] 'target,' *Konzept* [kɔnˈt͡sɛpt] 'concept,' *Schutz* [ʃʊt͡s] 'protection'). Because the definition of an affricate is partly dependent on this structural behavior of a language, some phoneticians always treat affricates as a sequence of two sound segments and not as one phone or phoneme. When it is treated as one unit, keep in mind that it must always be a homorganic articulation (see Section 2.3.2; i.e. [ks] is not an affricate because the places of articulation for plosive and fricative are different) and it must be the sequence plosive–fricative and not the other way round (i.e. [st] is not an affricate). Common non-IPA symbols for [t͡ʃ] and [d͡ʒ] are [č] and [ǰ], respectively.

3.1.5 *Approximants*

All the sounds we have discussed so far are characterized by a total obstruction of the oral pathway (plosives, nasals, and affricates) or a rather severe constriction (fricatives). For the approximants, which are all voiced in English, as they are for most languages of the world, the pathway is more open. The pathway can be blocked in the midsagittal part, as for the lateral approximant [l], which is known from words as *leek* or *little*, but in that case at least one side of the tongue is lowered, allowing a reasonably unrestricted airflow.

Listening carefully or watching yourself when producing words with an [l], you may notice that the quality of the [l] in *like* differs from that in *ball*. When you inhale while producing them, you will also realize that slightly different parts of your mouth are getting cold and – in case the airstream produces a sound while inhaling – that they sound differently. In English, the /l/ produced at the end of a word (e.g. *ball* or *felt*), is produced with the back of the tongue raised toward the velum. When /l/ is produced with such a secondary constriction near the velum it has a certain "dark" auditory quality, which is why it is known as a **dark l**. Many dialects of American English do not distinguish word-final "dark l" from word-initial "light l" and have only dark l, represented as [ɫ] (see the discussion of velarization in Section 3.4.1.6).

Another common approximant of English is the "r" sound. There are actually several variants of this sound, including the alveolar [ɹ] and the **retroflex** variant [ɻ]. The alveolar variant is often produced as a "bunched r," with the tip of the tongue drawn back into the tongue body and the major constriction near the alveolar or postalveolar region. For the retroflex variant, the tip of the tongue or underside of the tongue tip or blade faces the postalveolar region of the roof of the mouth (see Laver 1994, pp. 299–302, for a detailed review). English has no minimal pairs that differ in terms of these two sounds and they can therefore be viewed as two allophones of the same underlying phoneme. Many authors use the symbol /r/ for this phoneme, which actually represents an alveolar trill in the

IPA transcription (see Section 4.2). Despite the fact that this symbol represents a different manner of articulation, it is sometimes even used in broad transcriptions to indicate that an "r" sound is made. But the user must be aware that this is only a sluggish convenience or done to ease typography, and that the symbol is defined in the IPA with a specific manner of articulation.

The English language has only one palatal sound, namely the approximant [j]. This sound appears at the beginning of words like *you* and in the middle of words like *bayou*. Additionally, [j] occurs in words like *few*, *beauty*, *pure*, *cute* between certain consonants and the vowel you find in *boot*. Many speakers of British English also have it as a gliding sound between an alveolar plosive and a vowel in words like *due*. A speaker of this dialect will produce two different pronunciations for the words *do* and *due*, whereas a speaker of GA will pronounce both words in the same way.

The symbol [w] as in the word *way* had been described in Section 2.3.2 as a labial-velar approximant, yet it is listed here as a velar. A labial-velar involves a **double articulation** whose description indicates that the labial articulation (lip rounding) and the velar constriction (raising of the back of the tongue towards the velum) are of equal importance. It is not possible to capture this double articulation in an IPA table such as Table 3.1. The decision, then, to list [w] as either velar, as we do, or labial, is arbitrary. An unsatisfactory solution would be to list [w] both at the labial and velar places of articulation. This may lead to confusion, suggesting that there are two different sounds represented by the same symbol, which would violate one of the basic principles of the IPA. Another option is to simply list this sound separately from the table, which is also often done.

3.2 Vowels

Figure 3.1 provides the IPA symbols for the English vowels and Figure 3.2 provides an illustration of words containing those vowels.

As introduced in Section 2.4, vowels are categorized by their height (high, mid, low), frontness (front, central, back), and rounding (rounded, unrounded, spread). In addition, vowels can be characterized as tense or lax. In Figure 3.1, the vowels are written in a chart that roughly represents the height and frontness of idealized tongue positions. This representation is known as a **vowel quadrilateral**. There is some debate about whether a vowel quadrilateral is in fact an articulatory representation, or should be considered an acoustic representation of vowels; we will take up this issue in Section 10.1.

In contrast to consonants, whose place and manner of articulation can be reasonably determined by self-observation, it is more difficult to determine the tongue positions for vowels, and they can vary considerably across speakers. Furthermore, there is a substantial divergence in the exact quality of vowels produced in different varieties of English. For example, an Australian English speaker

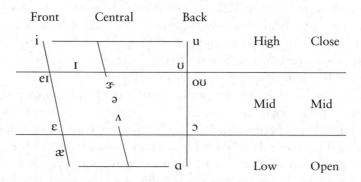

Figure 3.1 Vowel quadrilateral with IPA symbols for the monopthongal and diphthongized vowels of American English.

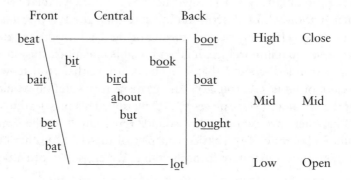

Figure 3.2 Words exemplifying the monophthongal and diphthongized vowels of American English. A given IPA symbol from Figure 3.1 represents the sound associated with the underlined characters in the corresponding cell in this figure. For example, the symbol [æ] represents the vowel sound in *bat*.

saying *today* might sound like an American English speaker saying *to die*. We will concentrate here on General American English but the reader should keep in mind that his or her vowel quality might differ for the given examples and that the tongue and lips may be in slightly different positions. In Section 10.1, we will provide a more objective acoustic representation of vowels, which can be related to the articulatory description given here.

The high front unrounded vowel [i] as in the word *feet* is realized in English with a fronted tongue body raised toward the palate. The vowel in *fit* has a different quality: the vowel is realized a bit lower and further back, which is indicated by the position of [ɪ] in the vowel quadrilateral. This vowel is also shorter. The duration of the vowels in the words *feet* and *fit* differs; that is, the **quantity** of the vowels is different. This quantity difference goes along with a **quality** difference in English: the vowel in *feet* is not only longer than in *fit*, it also sounds a bit different. This can be tested by saying the word *feet* but making the vowel very short (or using a computer program to shorten the vowel). The word will not sound like *fit* but like a fast version of *feet*. And, if the vowel in *fit* is pro-longed (by making it longer without changing the tongue position) it will *not* lead to an "i"-like sound as in *feet*. This illustrates that the two vowels differ primarily in terms of their acoustic quality (i.e. position in the vowel quadrilateral), and only secondarily in terms of quantity (length). And that is why we prefer to distin-guish these English vowels on the basis of their quality, as shown in Figure 3.1.

In addition to descriptions such as "long" and "short," English vowels can also be classified as **tense** and **lax**. These terms originally referred to an increased and decreased muscular tension, respectively, of the vocal tract relative to that for the neutral schwa. However, the difference between these two groups of vowels is not always a matter of muscular tension. We will therefore use the terms "tense" and "lax" as labels to distinguish two groups of vowels that differ in certain articu-latory and acoustic aspects. Essentially, it is a quality and length difference: lax vowels occupy a less extreme position in the vowel quadrilateral and are shorter relative to their tense counterparts. A practical way of determining whether a vowel is tense or lax is to check whether or not it can occur *only* in closed syllables. An **open syllable** is a syllable that ends in a vowel (e.g. *sea*); conversely, a **closed syllable** ends in a consonant (e.g. *seat*). Tense vowels can occur in both open and closed stressed syllables, while lax vowels can only occur in closed syllables. In sum, the vowel [i] is classified as a high front unrounded tense vowel while the vowel [ɪ] is classified as high front unrounded lax.

Since we consider the difference between [i] and [ɪ] to be primarily in terms of quality, the difference in duration need not be indicated in a broad transcription. However, in a more narrow transcription, this duration difference can be noted. The length of a sound (vowel or consonant) is indicated in the IPA transcription by a **length mark** (two small triangles like a colon) after the sound. The narrow transcription of the word *feet* with the indication of vowel length is [fiːt]. The vowel [ɪ] is always short in English and the transcription of *fit* is [fɪt].

For the back vowels, similar patterns can be observed. The high back rounded vowel in *suit* is produced with a retracted tongue body raised toward the velum. In addition, speakers purse (or round) their lips when making this sound. This vowel [u] is tense. Just as *feet* and *fit* form a minimal high front pair in terms of vowel quality, so are *suit* and *soot* a complementary pair for the high back vowels. The vowel in *suit* is tense and realized a bit higher than the vowel in *soot*, which is lax, and it is a bit more retracted. Again, this difference in position is indicated by the position in the vowel quadrilateral, where the symbol for the vowel in *soot* is the so-called "upsilon" [ʊ], which is a high back rounded lax vowel. Because both lax variants ([ɪ] and [ʊ]) of the high vowels ([i] and [u]) are closer to the center of the system, they are said to be **centralized**.

If we lower the tongue more than in the word *fit*, we get the word *fate*. This is a mid front unrounded tense vowel. When it is produced without articulatory movement, this mid front vowel is transcribed as [e]. However, most varieties of American English have a diphthongized (see Section 2.4) version of the vowel [e]. That is, this vowel is usually pronounced with a slight movement of the tongue (offglide) at the end towards an [ɪ], and is therefore more accurately transcribed using the symbol [eɪ]. Lowering the tongue a bit more results in the production of the vowel in words such as *fed*. This vowel is lax and the symbol for this mid front unrounded lax vowel is the "epsilon" [ɛ]. The word *fed* is transcribed as [fɛd].

When the tongue is moved further down, as in the word *f<u>a</u>t*, a low front vowel is formed. Although this vowel is long, it is labeled lax since it does not occur in open syllables. The low front unrounded lax vowel of this word is transcribed as [æ], the so-called "ash" symbol. The transcription of *fat* is [fæt].

For the back vowels, we find a pattern similar to that for the front vowels. We already mentioned that the relation between the high back vowels [u] and [ʊ] is similar to that for the high front vowels [i] and [ɪ]. Lowering the tongue from the high back rounded lax vowel [ʊ] as in *pull* will lead to the slightly lower vowel [o] as in *pole*. This is a mid back rounded tense vowel. Just as with the vowel [e], [o] is typically diphthongized in American English, involving a slight offglide of the tongue at the end of the vowel towards [ʊ], and is therefore transcribed as [oʊ]. Lowering the tongue again, we produce the mid back rounded lax vowel [ɔ] as in *c<u>au</u>lk*. Finally, if the tongue is lowered again, the low back unrounded tense vowel [ɑ] as in *c<u>o</u>t* is produced. While the vowels [ɔ] and [ɑ] are distinct in British English and East Coast varieties of American English, we mentioned in Section 2.4 that many varieties of American English do not distinguish these two sounds, merging both into the low back unrounded tense [ɑ]. Thus, these speakers treat *cot* and *caught* as **homophones**; that is, as two words that sound the same ([kɑt]) but are spelled differently.

In Figure 3.1, there are three central (in terms of frontness) unrounded vowels. The vowel in the word *bird* is a mid central unrounded **rhotacized** or "r-colored" tense vowel ([ɝ]). The rhotacized vowel occurs in American English in stressed position in words such as *b<u>ir</u>d* [bɝd]. Rhotacization is indicated by the little hook [˞] that can be added to the IPA symbol of any vowel. For example, *bar* can be transcribed as ['bɑ˞]. In many varieties of British English, "r" is not pronounced, and *bird* would be transcribed as [bɜd]. However, the non-rhotacized vowel [ɜ] does not occur in American English. The mid central unrounded lax vowel schwa [ə], also known as the "neutral" vowel because of its position in the middle of the vowel quadrilateral, occurs only in unstressed position, as in *<u>a</u>loof* [əluf]. Finally, there is another mid central unrounded lax vowel as in *c<u>u</u>t* [kʌt]. This vowel is very similar in quality to schwa and many speakers of American English do not differentiate the two. However, some speakers produce [ʌ] in stressed positions and [ə] in unstressed positions.

There are three "true" diphthongs in English, [ɔɪ], [aɪ], and [aʊ]. The movement of the tongue during their production is much more substantial than that for diphthongized [eɪ] and [oʊ]. The diphthong in *b<u>oy</u>* starts as a mid back vowel ([ɔ]) and ends as a high front vowel ([ɪ]). The IPA symbol [ɔɪ] represents this change. The diphthong in the word *b<u>uy</u>* starts with a low central vowel that does not occur in isolation in GA, the low central vowel [a], which is more fronted than low

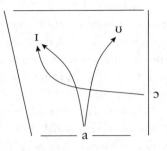

Figure 3.3 Vowel quadrilateral for the diphthongs of American English. The starting and ending point of the articulation of each diphthong is indicated by the base and tip, respectively, of its arrow.

back [ɑ]. The diphthong ends as a high front vowel ([ɪ]). It is represented by the IPA symbol [aɪ]. Finally, the diphthong in the word *how* starts with the same low central vowel ([a]) and ends as a high back vowel ([ʊ]), and is represented by the IPA symbol [aʊ]. Note that the true diphthongs are not included in Figure 3.1. Since the articulation changes during their production, diphthongs cannot be properly characterized as belonging to any one single cell. An attempt at capturing the dynamic character of diphthongs is shown in Figure 3.3, using a vowel quadrilateral in which arrows indicate the starting and end points of each diphthong.

In sum, the vowels of American English include the front vowels [i, ɪ, eɪ, ɛ, æ], the back vowels [u, ʊ, oʊ, ɔ, ɑ], the central vowels [ɝ, ə, ʌ], and the diphthongs [ɔɪ, aɪ, aʊ]. Some of these vowels can be grouped into tense–lax pairs by pairing a tense vowel with the lax vowel that is most similar in quality. English has three such pairs: [i, ɪ], [eɪ, ɛ], and [u, ʊ]. For each of these pairs, the lax member is shorter, lower in tongue height, and more centralized than its tense counterpart. The tense vowels of English are [i, eɪ, ɑ, ɔ, oʊ, u, ɝ, aɪ, aʊ, ɔɪ] and the lax vowels are [ɪ, ɛ, æ, ə, ʌ, ʊ]. In contrast to the consonants, the orthographic symbols for vowels rarely correspond to the phones that are produced (e.g. m*ea*t, m*ee*t, P*e*te: [i], t*o*, tw*o*, t*oo*, sh*oe*, thr*ough*, fl*ew*, h*ue*, H*ugh*: [u]).

3.3 Diacritics and Other Symbols

As mentioned earlier, in a broad transcription each sound is typically represented by a unique symbol. The level of accuracy of a transcription can be conceived of as a continuum. At one end is the broad transcription as we introduced it for English. At the other end of the continuum is the narrow transcription. As we said, a narrow transcription conveys, as accurately as possible, how one speaker pronounces an utterance on one given occasion. A narrow transcription therefore tries to capture as much detail as possible. While a broad transcription usually contains only symbols, a narrow transcription also includes **diacritics** as a way to provide additional detail. Diacritics are additional marks that can be attached to both consonant and vowel symbols to refine their description. Returning to an earlier example, while the initial consonant in *tip* is transcribed as [t] in a broad transcription, a narrow transcription would differentiate the different allophonic pronunciations (e.g. produced with either the tip or the blade of the tongue at either the alveolar ridge or the teeth) with the help of diacritics. The alveolar consonant pronounced with the tip of the tongue (apical) is transcribed as [t̺] while that produced with the blade of the tongue (laminal) is transcribed as [t̻]. The dental consonant would be transcribed as [t̪] which could be combined with other diacritics to indicate its apical or laminal production, as in [t̪̺] and [t̪̻], respectively. A narrow transcription is particularly useful for capturing idiosyncratic aspects of pronunciation that can be due to dialectal differences, stages in speech development, speech disorders, or even foreign accent.

It is also possible to have more than one broad transcription of an utterance. It is sometimes the case that a word has a number of different pronunciations depending on the context in which it occurs. For example, the vowel in the word *get* has a number of allophones, according to phonetic environment, which mostly fall between [ɪ] and [ɛ]; for example, *You must g[ɛ]t a coffee* versus *G[ɪ]t me a coffee*. Depending on context, either symbol can be used to represent the vowel phoneme. Different transcriptions may also result from alternative ways of representing a particular contrast. We have transcribed the vowels in the words *beat* and *bit* as [i] and [ɪ], respectively. This transcription represents our opinion that the primary difference between these two vowels is in terms of quality. However, to express that duration is also an important correlate of the distinction, the two vowels could be transcribed as [iː] and [ɪ], respectively. The length mark [ː] indicates that [i] is relatively long. Finally, if it should be conveyed that duration is the primary difference between the two vowels, the vowels could be represented by [iː] and [i]. All of these transcriptions conform to the principles of the IPA, as long as the particular transcription adopted is used consistently for all comparable vowel contrasts in the language.

We have only discussed symbols that represent individual speech sounds of English. There are also symbols that represent properties of speech that extend over more than one sound, such as stress. **Primary** or **main stress** is indicated by the symbol ['] before the syllable that carries stress, as in *speaking* ['spikɪŋ] or *request* [ɹɪ'kwɛst], and a weaker **secondary stress** is indicated by a [ˌ] as in [ˌmækə'ɹouni]. Determining where primary or secondary stress is located in a word is sometimes difficult even for native speakers. On the other hand, stressing the wrong syllable sounds "strange," as when, for example, pronouncing *telephone* ['tɛlə,foun] (with primary stress on the first syllable) as [ˌtɛlə'foun] (with primary stress on the last syllable). This indicates that speakers know which syllable to stress but are not always overtly aware of it.

3.4 Transcription of General American English

Up to now, we have attempted to present the guiding principles for a broad transcription. As mentioned earlier, speakers of English produce allophones of phonemes depending on the context in which the phonemes occur or on other factors such as stress. For example, the usage of the two phones "dark l" and "light l" depends on the position of the phoneme /l/ in a word (see Section 3.1.5). We will now make some of these rules more explicit and introduce allophonic variants and their symbols in the rest of this section. We should emphasize, though, that we do not provide a complete and detailed description of English and all its variants. This section should serve more to increase awareness of some regular processes of English and how they are transcribed. For in-depth treatment of English (or any other language), textbooks for language training are recommended.

In this section, we will concentrate on the transcription of GA English to illustrate some of the principles introduced above. Our aim is to provide the descriptions for an allophonic transcription of American English, including an explicit account of the rules and conventions that are often used. Adoption of an explicit set of conventions relieves the transcriber from having to incorporate details that are expressed by these predictable conventions. While these details must be included in a narrow transcription, knowledge of the conventions that guide allophonic variation will facilitate this process. We will again consider consonants and vowels separately.

3.4.1 *Consonants*

We will begin our discussion of consonants with the closely related issues of aspiration, voicing, and devoicing.

3.4.1.1 ASPIRATION, VOICING, AND DEVOICING

Voiceless plosives are often produced with an audible air flow after the release of their constriction. Plosives produced in this way are called **aspirated** plosives. Aspiration involves a period of voicelessness after the release of the constriction. In the production of an aspirated plosive, the vocal folds are still separated when the consonantal constriction is released. As a result, there is a brief interval during which air rushes through the open glottis. The sound generated during this interval is known as aspiration (see Section 6.3 for a more detailed account of aspiration). The presence or absence of aspiration can be checked by holding your hand in front of your mouth during the production of these words. A small puff of air should be felt for the aspirated [pʰ], but not the unaspirated [p]. In isolation, the aspiration is similar to a short [h], which is why, in a narrow transcription, aspiration is indicated by the diacritic [ʰ] following the plosive as in *top* [tʰɑp]. In English, aspiration is allophonic, occurring only in specific environments.

Voiceless plosives are aspirated in GA if:

1   they are in absolute word-initial position; that is, they are the very first sound in a word, as in *top* [tʰɑp] or *today* [tʰə'deɪ].
2   they precede a stressed vowel. Compare aspirated /p/ in *appeal* [ə'pʰil] to un-aspirated /p/ in *apple* ['æpəɫ]. The "p" in *appeal* precedes a stressed vowel and is therefore aspirated.

In most other positions, voiceless plosives are not aspirated. For example, voiceless plosives are not aspirated if they are preceded by /s/, as in *stop* [stɑp]. There are languages, however, that have aspirated and non-aspirated plosives in their phonemic inventory. In these languages, aspiration has to be indicated in both the broad and narrow transcription. For example, in Thai, the word [tam] means *to pound*, and [tʰam] *to do*.

Aspiration can also affect the voicing of following approximants. In these cases, the vocal folds start vibrating later and the approximants become partially voiceless (or **devoiced**) after aspirated plosives. This is represented by the diacritic [̥] as in *please* [pl̥iːz] or *quick* [kw̥ɪk]. In these cases, the aspiration does not need to be indicated separately. The difference between the voiceless [l̥] in *please* and the voiced [l] in *lease* can be checked by feeling the vibrating vocal folds. By placing a finger on the larynx, the vocal fold vibration during /l/ can be felt in *lease* but not in *please*.

Final voiced consonants, both plosives and fricatives, may become partially or fully devoiced at the end of a word or phrase. Full devoicing can be easily indicated in a broad or narrow transcription by the use of the symbol for the corresponding voiceless sound. This works for plosives and fricatives, where a devoiced /z/, for example, can be represented by [s]. However, for approximants, because they lack voiceless counterparts, such a simple solution is not available. In these cases, devoicing (full or partial) is indicated in a narrow transcription by the diacritic [̥]. Note that this may create ambiguity: while [z̥] is partially devoiced (if it were fully devoiced, [s] would have been used), [m̥] may be either partially or fully devoiced.

While /h/ is typically voiceless, it can be voiced when it does not occur at the beginning of a word. Voiced /h/ is transcribed as [ɦ]. The narrow transcription of a word pair such as *head–ahead* is [hɛd–ə'ɦɛd].

3.4.1.2   COARTICULATION

Coarticulation refers to the phenomenon that speech sounds are usually produced with some articulatory overlap. That is, in the production of a sequence of sounds, the articulatory maneuvers for one sound typically overlap a preceding or following sound. Two types of coarticulation are distinguished, anticipatory and perseverative coarticulation. **Anticipatory coarticulation** occurs when the articulation of a particular sound is affected by that of a later-occurring sound. Anticipatory coarticulation is also known as **"right-to-left" coarticulation**, because the influence spreads from a later-occurring (right) segment to an earlier one (on the left), in right-to-left fashion, or as **regressive coarticulation** because a sound influences in a "backwards" manner the previous sound. An example can be found in the behavior of velar plosives ([k, g]). Velar plosives become fronted when preceding front vowels, as in *keel*. In other words, in anticipation of the upcoming front vowel [i], which requires a fronted tongue body, the tongue in [k] contacts the velum at a substantially more forward location. In a narrow transcription, this is indicated by the diacritic [₊] as in [sk̟iː].

Another example of coarticulation can be found in the behavior of alveolar consonants. All alveolar consonants, except for fricatives, coarticulate with following dentals. For example, the alveolar plosive [t] is produced as a dental when preceding a dental as in the word *width*. The narrow transcription would be [wɪt̪θ], where the diacritic [̪] indicates a dental place of articulation. This again is an instance of anticipatory coarticulation in that the alveolar is produced as a dental in anticipation of the following dental sound. Vowels can also show effects of anticipatory coarticulation, as discussed in Section 3.4.2.2 on vowel nasalization, such that a vowel preceding a nasal consonant becomes nasalized because the velar port starts opening during the vowel in anticipation of the upcoming nasal.

Perseverative coarticulation occurs when the prolonged effect of a sound affects a later-occurring sound. This type of coarticulation is typically ascribed to inertia of the articulators. Perseverative coarticulation is also known as **carry-over** or **"left-to-right" coarticulation**, spreading from earlier sounds to later-produced sounds. This coarticulation is also known as **progressive coarticulation** because a sound influences an "upcoming" sound. The devoicing of approximants following voiceless aspirated plosives described in the preceding section can be viewed as an instance of perseverative coarticulation, with the voicelessness of the initial plosive carrying over to the following approximant, as in *please* [pl̥iːz].

3.4.1.3 CONSONANTAL RELEASE

There is considerable variability in the way speakers pronounce (or do not pronounce) plosives at the end of a word or phrase. In Section 2.3, we described plosives as being characterized by a brief burst following the release of the constriction. Our discussion primarily concerned syllable- or word-initial plosives. Final plosives, on the other hand, may be released abruptly (just like initial plosives), or may be released gradually, in which case the release may be inaudible, or not at all. For example, final voiced plosives can be realized as voiced, as (partially) devoiced, or without an audible release (i.e. the closure is made but the word "ends" without opening the vocal tract again), as in *rib* [ɹɪb], [ɹɪb̥], or [ɹɪb̚]. In the latter case, the diacritic [̚] indicates the absence of an audible release.

Final voiceless plosives can be realized as voiceless, aspirated, or without release, as in *up* [ʌp], [ʌpʰ], or [ʌp̚]. Voiced and voiceless plosives are often unreleased when they occur at the end of a word and are preceded by an approximant, as in *bulb* [bʌɫb̚] or *harp* [hɑɹp̚].

When considering word-final **consonant clusters** – that is, a sequence of consonants at the end of a word – a final plosive in a cluster tends to be released when it is similar in place of articulation to the preceding consonant, as in *bump* [bãmp] or [bãmpʰ] (the diacritic [˜] indicates nasalization; see Section 3.4.2.2). If the final plosive were not released, it would be difficult to distinguish [bãmp̚] from [bãm]. Likewise, for manner of articulation, if the final two consonants are both plosives, the second one tends to be released, as in *picked* [pʰɪkt], in order to distinguish it from *pick* [pʰɪk]. However, in such word-final plosive consonant sequences, the first of the two word-final plosive consonants is usually unreleased. For example, in *apt*, the bilabial plosive is not released or if it is, it is often inaudible: when the bilabial closure for the [p] has been made, the tongue is free to move toward the constriction for the following [t]. When the lips separate to release the [p], the closure of the [t] blocks airflow and the articulation of the [t] masks the release of the [p]. This results in an inaudible release for the bilabial plosive: [æp̚t]. Acoustically, the transition of the vowel [æ] to the upcoming [p] does contain some information indicating that it was followed by a bilabial closure but the release is produced as a [t]. For this reason, [æp̚t] sounds quite different from a word like *at*, which is produced as [æt] or [æt̚], without any bilabial influence.

3.4.1.4   FLAPS AND TAPS

Another change often observed in alveolar plosives is flapping. The pervasive use of **flaps** (or **taps**) in GA distinguishes it from British English. The flap consists of a single flick of the tongue tip against the alveolar ridge. It is therefore a very brief sound, and it is voiced. Figure 3.4 shows realizations of the phoneme /t/ in three different ways. Figure 3.4a shows the /t/ in *attack* as an aspirated voiceless plosive [tʰ]: a long silent closure duration (approximately 90 ms) is followed by a release burst and a long (approximately 60 ms) period of aspiration. In Figure 3.4b, the phoneme is realized as a voiced plosive ([d]): a voiced closure portion (approximately 50 ms) is followed by a (weak) release burst and no aspiration. Figure 3.4c shows the realization of the same phoneme as a flap ([ɾ]): the oscillogram shows a short voiced closure duration (approximately 35 ms) without a discernable burst and without aspiration. Alveolar plosives are usually realized as flaps when they follow a vowel or central approximant and precede an unstressed vowel. The flap is transcribed as [ɾ]. For example, in GA the words *latter* and *ladder* are both pronounced as ['læɾɚ]. It is important to know that flaps do not occur when the alveolar precedes a stressed syllable: compare *phonetician* [ˌfoʊnəˈtʰɪʃ ə̃n] without a flap and *phonetics* [fənˈɛɾɪks] with a flap.

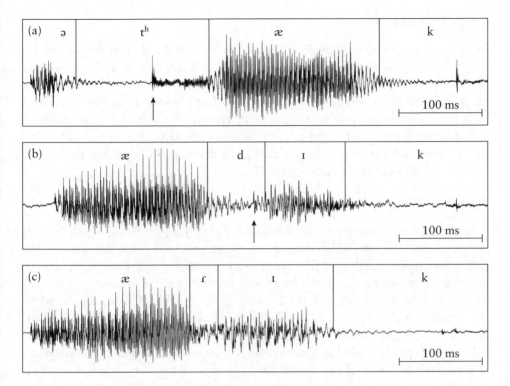

Figure 3.4 Oscillograms of the words (a) *attack* with an aspirated voiceless plosive [ə'tʰæk], (b) *attic* with a (fully) voiced plosive ['ædɪk], and (c) with a flap ['æɾɪk]. Segments are indicated by vertical markers and the arrows in (a) and (b) point to the release of the medial plosives.

3.4.1.5 GLOTTAL PLOSIVES

We saw in Section 3.4.1.4 that alveolar plosives are pronounced as flaps in certain circumstances. In addition, voiceless alveolar /t/ is often pronounced as a glottal plosive (often referred to as a "glottal stop"), both in GA and British English. The glottal plosive [ʔ], an allophone of /t/ in English, is produced by tightly closing the vocal folds for a brief period. In certain varieties of British English, it can replace /t/ in words such as *butter* ['bʌʔə]. The glottal plosive is also often used to separate two words when the first ends with a vowel and the next begins with a vowel: *the only* [ðə'ʔõũnli], *she eats* [ʃi'ʔits]. In addition, many speakers insert a glottal plosive before word-final voiceless plosives as in *cup* [kʰʌʔp] or *pack* [pʰæʔk]; that is, they close their vocal folds at the end of the vowel rather than keeping them open while producing the plosive. Finally, [ʔ] may occur in words such as *mountain* ['mãũʔn̩], *sentence* ['sɛ̃ʔn̩s], *button* ['bʌʔn̩] (see Section 3.4.1.7 for [n̩] and other syllabic consonants), or *camps* [kæ̃ʔps].

3.4.1.6   VELARIZATION

In Section 3.1.5, we already briefly discussed the fact that the alveolar lateral approximant /l/ has two allophones, light l and dark l. Light (or clear) l is produced with the tip of the tongue against the alveolar ridge and a relatively low tongue body. In general, /l/ is light when preceding a front vowel, as in *leaf* [lif]. For a dark l, the tongue tip rests near the lower incisors and the back of the tongue is raised towards the velum, which is why this allophone is also known as "velarized l." Generally, postvocalic /l/ is dark. The diacritic [~], placed in the middle of the symbol, indicates velarization: [ɫ].

3.4.1.7   SYLLABIC CONSONANTS

When schwa is followed by a word-final nasal ([m, n, ŋ]) or liquid ([l, ɹ]) [ə] may be deleted and the following consonant acts as a sort of syllable (as in *able* – the [bl] is the second syllable of the word). Such word-final consonants are known as **syllabic consonants**, indicated by a small vertical line [ˌ] *below* the consonant. They may take up the full durational value of the syllable. This is clearest when the consonants share place of articulation. For example, in *sudden* ['sʌdn̩], a closure is made for the alveolar plosive with the tongue tip, after which the velum is lowered to produce the [n]. Since the final two consonants share the same place of articulation, the tip of the tongue need not move when the [d] is released as a nasal [n]. This is known as **nasal plosion**. Likewise, for a **lateral plosion**, a closure is made for the alveolar plosive, after which the sides of the tongue are lowered for the alveolar lateral, as in *channel* ['t͡ʃænɫ]. Since the constriction is maintained throughout both consonants, there is no intervening vowel and the consonant acts like a syllable. However, the deletion of a schwa may also occur when both consonants do *not* share place, as in, for example, *motion* ['mouʃn̩] and *uncle* ['ʌŋkɫ].

3.4.1.8   INTRUSION

In Section 3.4.1.3 we described cases of releases where phones become partly inaudible. The opposite are **intrusions**, where phones are inserted. These insertions can serve to break up consonant clusters in some languages (e.g. in Dutch, words like *melk* [mɛlk] 'milk' are often pronounced as ['mɛlək]), or result from coarticulation. In English, this happens when a nasal consonant precedes a voiceless fricative, as in the word *something*. In these cases, a voiceless plosive with the same place as the nasal may intrude between the nasal and the voiceless fricative. Namely, to produce the nasal, the oral pathway has to be closed completely (similar to an oral stop) and the velum is lowered. Next, in the production of the following fricative, the velum is raised and the plosive closure is released at the same time to allow turbulent airflow for the fricative. If the velum is closed first and the oral closure is released slightly later, the articulation is the same as an oral stop: an oral closure with raised velum and a release. As a result, an oral stop

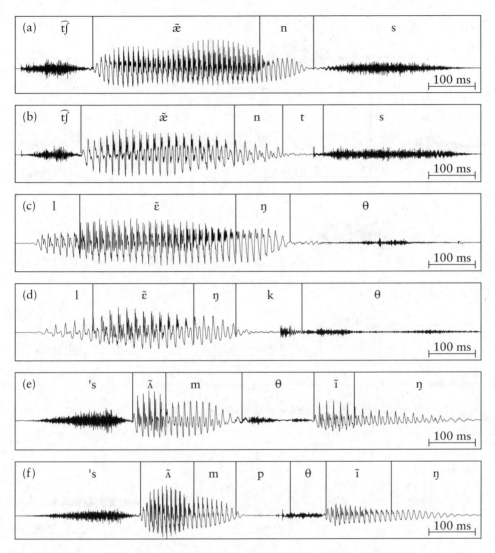

Figure 3.5 Oscillograms of the words *chance*, *length*, and *something* (a, c, e) without and (b, d, f) with intruding plosives.

has been inserted. For example, *chance* [t͡ʃæns] can become [t͡ʃænts], *length* [lɛ̃ŋθ] can become [lɛ̃ŋkθ], or *something* ['sʌ̃mθɪ̃ŋ] can become ['sʌ̃mpθɪ̃ŋ]. Figure 3.5 shows oscillograms of words without and with intrusive plosives. In the latter case, the intrusive voiceless plosives [t, k, p] show a clear voiceless closure portion followed by a distinct release burst.

3.4.1.9 DURATION

When identical consonants join at the end of one word and the beginning of the next, they are usually produced as one sound with a slightly longer duration: compare

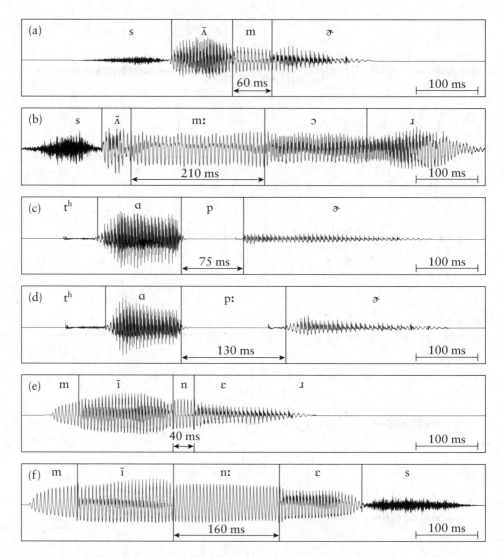

Figure 3.6 Oscillograms of the words (a) *summer*, (b) *some more*, (c) *top air*, (d) *top pair*, (e) *meaner*, and (f) *meanness*. (The duration of the nasals in (a), (b), (e), and (f) were determined with the help of spectrograms not displayed here.)

summer ['sʌ̃mɚ] and *some more* [sʌ̃'mːɔɹ], or *top air* [tʰɑp'ɚ] and *top pair* [tʰɑ'pːɚ]. For an example that does not require two words, compare *meanest* ['mĩnəst] and *meanness* ['mĩnːəs]. Figure 3.6 shows oscillograms of these three word pairs. Note that in Figure 3.6b, 3.6d, and 3.6f, the consonant is substantially longer than in Figure 3.6a, 3.6c, and 3.6e. This is indicated in the transcription by the length mark [ː], which was introduced in our discussion of vowel length in Section 3.2.

3.4.2 Vowels

There is a large variety of vowel qualities in the different English dialects, as we already mentioned in Section 3.2. A discussion of all effects is a research topic of its own (see, for example, Hughes and Trudgill 1996; Wolfram and Schilling-Estes 1998). In section 9.5.1, we give articulatory and acoustic descriptions of vowel quality, and we extend these to non-English vowels in Section 10.1. Here, we will limit our discussion of the transcription of vowels to issues concerning their duration and the way vowel quality is affected by following consonants, two critical issues in vowel transcription.

3.4.2.1 DURATION

Vowels can be long or short, as was discussed in Section 3.2. Recall we use the length mark [ː] to indicate length in both vowels and consonants. In addition, the same vowel can be lengthened or shortened depending on whether it occurs in a stressed or unstressed syllable. Compare the length of the vowel [aɪ] in the words *insight* ['ɪn,saɪt] without primary stress and *incite* [,ɪn'saɪt] with primary stress (see Figure 3.7). The vowel is noticeably longer in the latter word. This lengthening can be indicated by the length mark [ː], or, if the lengthened vowel is not as long as a "true" long vowel, by a half-length mark [ˑ]. As we discussed in Section 3.2, a quantity difference (length) often goes along with a quality difference (type of vowel). Consequently, when vowels in stressed syllables are longer than in unstressed syllables, the shorter vowels can also differ in quality.

We already introduced the distinction between open and closed syllables in our discussion of tense and lax vowels in Section 3.2. It turns out that vowels are substantially longer in open syllables than in closed syllables, an effect that is called

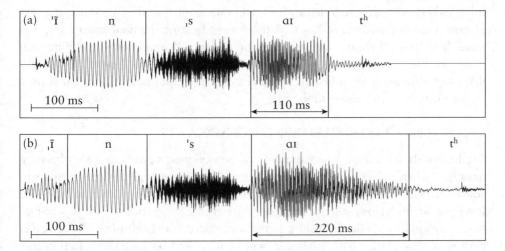

Figure 3.7   Oscillograms of the words (a) *insight* and (b) *incite*.

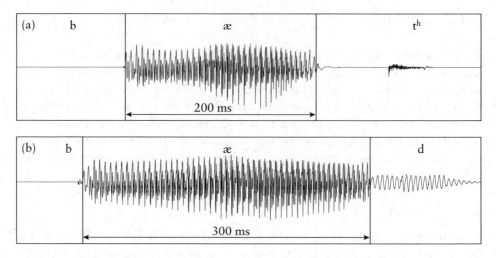

Figure 3.8 Oscillograms of the words (a) *bat* and (b) *bad*.

open syllable lengthening. For example, the vowel in *bee* is longer than in *beat*. It is almost as if the vowel in *beat* is shortened or clipped by the following consonant. The length mark [ː] can again be used to indicate this extra length on the vowel.

Vowels are also longer when preceding a voiced consonant relative to a voiceless consonant. Compare the vowels in *bat* and *bad* (see Figure 3.8). The lengthening of the vowel preceding voiced consonants appears to occur in the vast majority of languages for which it has been investigated. However, the difference in duration between vowels preceding voiceless and voiced consonants seems to be much larger in English than in most other languages. In fact, the voicing of the consonants is often inferred from the length of the preceding vowel, especially for speakers who do not release the final consonant (i.e. they produce the last plosive with an inaudible release). Without even hearing the final consonant, it is possible to hear differences between *bat* and *bad*, based simply on vowel duration.

As we mentioned before, in a narrow transcription, all length differences discussed above can be indicated by means of the length mark [ː], or, if it is only a "half-length," with the symbol [ˑ].

3.4.2.2 EFFECTS OF FOLLOWING CONSONANTS

While vowels are longer preceding voiced consonants, vowels can also become nasalized when preceding a nasal consonant, another instance of the anticipatory coarticulation that was discussed in Section 3.4.1.2. In a word such as *ban*, the lowering of the velum starts during the vowel in anticipation of the upcoming nasal consonant. While the velum is initially raised, the beginning of the vowel may be oral. Its latter part, however, will be nasalized because the velum begins to lower for the upcoming nasal consonant while the oral cavity is still open.

In a narrow transcription, this is indicated by means of the diacritic [˜] over the vowel; compare the nasalized vowel in *ban* [bæ̃n] and the oral vowel in *bad* [bæd]. There are languages that have "true" nasal vowels; that is, there are minimal pairs in the language that differ only in the state of the nasality of the vowel. For example, in Bengali [tɑt] means 'warmth' and [tɑ̃t] means 'loom.' In this case, the term **nasal vowel** rather than **nasalized vowel** is used to indicate that the nasal vowel is phonemic.

Vowel quality is substantially affected when vowels are followed by /ɹ/ and /l/, resulting in allophones that are produced with a more retracted tongue body. Before syllable-final /ɹ/, the number of distinct vowel qualities is substantially reduced because the contrasts between [i] and [ɪ], [u] and [ʊ], and [eɪ] and [ɛ] are neutralized. The word *bear* could therefore be transcribed as either [bɛɹ] or [beɪɹ]. The influence of /ɹ/ on the quality of the preceding vowel is known as **r-coloring** or **rhotacization**. The diphthongs [eɪ] and [oʊ] may lose their offglide when preceding /l/ and become monophthongs, as in *bail* [beł] and *bowl* [boł].

This completes our brief overview of the transcription of American English. The rules outlined above should help in specifying the phonetic realization of the speech sounds produced by most speakers of GA. This set of rules is by no means exhaustive. It is meant, however, to increase awareness of a number of phenomena that play a role in GA and in some other varieties of spoken English. Understanding rules of transcription increases awareness of some of the ways in which sounds are pronounced. It should also be clear that there are often a variety of ways to transcribe pronunciations. Consistency is therefore an important part of a transcription. Once a particular approach to transcribing a specific sound has been adopted, it should always be used when transcribing that same sound, because a different transcription implies a different pronunciation.

Exercises

1 What are the differences between a narrow and a broad transcription? Between a broad and a phonemic transcription? Describe separate contexts in which each would prove useful.
2 Explain the difference between phones, phonemes, and allophones.
3 In what three ways do tense and lax vowels differ in GA English?
4 How is aspiration produced? Why is aspirtion allophonic in English? Use examples other than those in the textbook to support your answer.
5 What are the differences between and some examples of anticipatory and perseverative coarticulation?
6 Write the GA English words that correspond to the following transcriptions: [əˈnʌf], [ˈd͡ʒʌŋgl̩], [ˈkwaɪət], [ˈlɪsn̩], [ˈkɹit͡ʃɚ], [ˈd͡ʒʌstəˌfaɪ], [əˈbaʊt], [ˈfit͡ʃɚz], [ˈfeɪljɚ], [ˈfoʊɾoʊ].

7 Provide a broad transcription of the following words: *judge, literature, language, phonation, whistle, youth, television, peaceful, fountain, rather.*

Note

1 For a more detailed discussion of different types of transcription, see Laver (1994, ch. 18) and the *Handbook of the International Phonetic Association* (1999, pp. 28–30).

4 Place and Manner of Articulation of Consonants and Vowels

In Chapter 3, we described the English consonants in terms of voicing, place of articulation, and manner of articulation. We also described the English vowels in terms of frontness, height, and lip rounding. This use of different dimensions in the description of consonants and vowels suggests that the articulation of these two classes of sounds has little in common. However, the articulatory description of both consonants and vowels is largely based on location of constriction ("place of articulation" in consonants, "frontness" in vowels) and degree of constriction ("manner of articulation" in consonants, "height" in vowels). It is therefore reasonable to use the terms place and manner of articulation in the description of both consonants and vowels.

The speech sounds of English form a subset of all the speech sounds that have been documented across the languages of the world. Currently, it is estimated that there are approximately 6,000–7,000 languages in the world. However, many of these languages are spoken by only a few native speakers and are in danger of disappearing. Nevertheless, all languages are equally valuable. The fact that only a few people speak a particular language does not mean that this language is "strange" or "unnatural" – it is simply a consequence of historical (political or economic) developments. It has recently been estimated that more than half of all languages that are currently spoken will be extinct a hundred years from now. Fortunately, the languages that have been documented so far provide us with a rich inventory of speech sounds used throughout the world. The IPA chart on the last page of this book shows the inventory of IPA symbols that are available to transcribe many sounds of the world's languages. It is clear that there are a large number of non-English sounds in other languages that we have not covered in the previous chapter on English consonants and vowels. It must be noted that the IPA was originally devised by Western European scientists and that the selection of sounds that are represented with single symbols still reflects those original languages, which also accounts for the left-to-right writing of the symbols to indicate a sequence of sounds. The current IPA is therefore a rather arbitrary mixture of symbols corresponding to letters of the Roman and Greek alphabets, modifications (e.g. inversion) of these letters, as well as borrowings from other writing and symbol systems. This choice of symbols has the disadvantage that the organizing principles of place and manner of articulation are not inherently represented. For example, it is not the case that all symbols representing fricatives share a particular graphic characteristic that distinguishes them as a class from all other symbols. Likewise, the symbols for all bilabials do not have anything in common. Nevertheless, the current set of IPA symbols can be used to represent most sounds of the world's languages.

In this chapter, we will briefly survey the great variety in consonants and vowels that exists across the languages of the world and introduce IPA symbols for their transcription. In the collection of examples, we have found two sources very valuable, Laver (1994) and Ladefoged and Maddieson (1996). For audio examples of many of these sounds, please visit the website accompanying this book and the links given there. In addition, the so-called "sowl" (sounds of the world's languages) website (http://hctv.humnet.ucla.edu/departments/linguistics/VowelsandConsonants) is a very useful source.

4.1 Consonants

Table 4.1 shows the IPA symbols that are available to transcribe many of the world's consonants. While most languages use the same places of articulation as English, so that adding symbols to the existing cells of the table does not cause too many problems, many languages use additional manners of articulation. For example, while English has only dental fricatives and no dental plosives, other languages such as French do have dental plosives. Some of these sounds may occur as allophones in English, but they can be phonemes in other languages. Languages that contrast dental and alveolar plosives are also found.

The consonant chart in Table 4.1 has three types of cells: cells with phonetic symbols, cells without symbols, and cells that have been shaded. The cells without symbols represent speech sounds that are possible but that have not yet been attested in the world's languages. For example, the empty cell at the intersection of the column labeled "labiodental" place of articulation and the row labeled "trill" manner of articulation indicates that no language has (yet) been documented that has a labiodental trill. However, since there are no known anatomical or aerodynamic reasons why such a sound could not be produced, chances are that as new languages are documented, this sound will be found to exist (at which point a new IPA symbol must be added). In contrast, shaded cells represent articulations that are deemed impossible. It is a good exercise to come up with a reason for why each shaded cell is impossible. For example, why can no language have a pharyngeal nasal, according to this chart?

We will now discuss those consonants that we did not encounter in English, and we will do so by going from left to right, or, in other words, from lips to glottis in terms of place of articulation. For the moment, we restrict our survey to those manners of articulation that we already discussed for English, namely,

Table 4.1 IPA symbols for pulmonic consonants based on IPA 1993, revised 2005. We include "epiglottal" as a column for place of articulation, "affricate" as a row for manner of articulation, and list the labial-velar approximant under the velar place

	Bilabial	Labiodental	Dental	Alveolar	Postalveolar	Retroflex	Palatal	Velar	Uvular	Pharyngeal	Epiglottal	Glottal
Plosive	p b			t d		ʈ ɖ	c ɟ	k ɡ	q ɢ		ʡ	ʔ
Nasal	m	ɱ		n		ɳ	ɲ	ŋ	ɴ			
Trill	ʙ			r					ʀ			
Tap/flap		ⱱ		ɾ		ɽ						
Fricative	ɸ β	f v	θ ð	s z	ʃ ʒ	ʂ ʐ	ç ʝ	x ɣ	χ ʁ	ħ ʕ	ʜ ʢ	h ɦ
Lateral fricative				ɬ ɮ								
Affricate		p͡f		t͡s d͡z	t͡ʃ d͡ʒ			k͡x				
Approximant		ʋ		ɹ		ɻ	j	ɰ w ɥ				
Lateral approximant				l		ɭ	ʎ	ʟ				

plosives, nasals, fricatives, affricates, and approximants. We return to the additional manners of articulation (trill, tap/flap, lateral fricative) at the end of this chapter. As in the preceding chapters, all sounds discussed here are produced with an outward flow of air generated by the lungs, that is, a pulmonic airstream. Sounds produced with a different source or direction of airflow are surveyed in Section 6.1.

4.1.1 Labials

The first column in Table 4.1 represents *bilabials*. English has bilabial plosives [p, b] and the nasal [m] but no bilabial fricatives. Bilabial fricatives are actually common across the world's languages. Many Bantu languages have bilabial fricatives. For example, Northern Sotho, a Niger-Congo language spoken in South Africa, distinguishes the voiceless bilabial fricative [ɸ] as in ['ɸeta] 'to pass' from the voiced bilabial fricative [β] as in ['βeta] 'to choke.'

Spanish has the voiced [β] as an allophone of the phoneme /b/ in intervocalic position. For example, the phrase *Barcelona and Valencia* is pronounced as *[b]arcelona y [β]alencia* and the phrase *Valencia and Barcelona* as *[b]alencia y [β]arcelona* (the *y* 'and' is pronounced as [i]). As can be seen, the initial sound of the two cities is pronounced as [b] when it appears at the beginning of the phrase but as a bilabial voiced fricative [β] after a voiced sound. That is, a Spanish speaker realizes a [b] or [β] depending on the context, that is, the phonemes surrounding it.

Moving slightly back brings us to the labiodental place of articulation. Labiodental plosives have not been attested, perhaps because it is difficult to create a firm complete constriction by touching the upper teeth with the lower lip. Labiodental nasals appear to be very rare. Teke-Kukuya, a Niger-Congo language spoken in the Congo (former Brazzaville), seems to be the only documented language with a phonemic labiodental nasal [ɱ], as in [ɱîî] 'eyes' versus [mîî] 'urine' ([́] and [`] indicate high and low tones, respectively; see Section 11.4.1). The labiodental nasal occurs in English as an allophone of bilabial [m] or alveolar [n] preceding [f, v] as in *symphony* ['sɪɱfəni] or *envelope* ['ɛɱvəloʊp]. In fact, most labiodental nasals seem to be the result of coarticulation with a following labiodental fricative.

English has labiodental fricatives [f, v]. While many languages have either bilabial or labiodental fricatives, only a few languages contrast the two. An example is Ewe, a Niger-Congo language spoken in Ghana, that contrasts bilabial ([ɸ, β]) and labiodental ([f, v]) fricatives, as shown in Table 4.2.

A rare sound in the world's languages is the voiceless labiodental affricate [p͡f], where a bilabial plosive is released into a labiodental fricative. This sound has only been attested in German and in Beembe, a Niger-Congo language spoken in Congo. The affricate is rather similar to the labiodental fricative [f], but German has minimal pairs like *fad* [faːt] 'without taste' and *Pfad* [p͡faːt] 'path.' The voiced labiodental approximant [ʋ] occurs in Dutch, where, for some speakers, it

Table 4.2 Examples of bilabial and labiodental fricatives from Ewe

Bilabial	Gloss	Labiodental	Gloss
[ɸu]	'bone'	[fu]	'feather'
[βu]	'boat'	[vu]	'to tear'

contrasts with the labiodental fricative [v] as in *wol* [ʋɔl] 'wool' and *vol* [vɔl] 'full.' Most commonly, languages have bilabial plosives, bilabial nasals, and labiodental fricatives.

4.1.2 Coronals

The next column in Table 4.1 is labeled *Dental/Alveolar/Postalveolar*. These three labels together form one column because contrasts between them, especially between dentals and alveolars, are rare. For example, most languages have either dental or alveolar or postalveolar plosives but not all three. When there is no contrast, the exact place of articulation (dental, alveolar, postalveolar), as well as the tongue position (apical or laminal), may vary considerably. Postalveolar is a broad term to represent any primary articulation that falls in the region between the alveolar ridge and the palate. Cross-linguistically, dental plosives are more common than alveolar plosives. While English and German have alveolar plosives, nearly all other Indo-European languages have dental plosives. Nevertheless, the dental diacritic [̪] is usually not used to transcribe the dental plosives of these languages and the alveolar symbols are simply used with the convention that these sounds are produced as dentals. For example the dental plosive in French *tous* 'all' is transcribed as [tu] without the dental diacritic.

English has the dental fricatives [θ, ð], and dental plosives occur in English as allophones when preceding dental fricatives, as in *eighth* [eɪt̪θ]. Alveolar plosives [t, d], alveolar nasals [n], and alveolar fricatives [s, z] are very common in English. The voiceless alveolar affricate [t͡s] can be found in German (*Zahl* [t͡saːl] 'number'). Bulgarian has both the voiceless and voiced affricates as in [t͡sar] 'czar' and [d͡zar] 'tar.' The alveolar approximant [ɹ] is found in English, as is the alveolar lateral approximant [l]. The English postalveolar fricatives [ʃ, ʒ] and affricates [t͡ʃ, d͡ʒ] were introduced in Sections 3.1.3 and 3.1.4.

Moving further back in the vocal tract, the next place of articulation is retroflex. In a retroflex articulation, the tip of the tongue curls ("flex") back ("retro") to the anterior (front) portion of the palate. *Retroflex* consonants can be found in many languages spoken in South Asia. For example, Bengali, an Indo-European language spoken in Bangladesh and India, contrasts the words [t̪an] 'tune,' [ʈan] 'pull,' [d̪an] 'right,' and [ɖan] 'charity.' The IPA symbols for retroflex consonants are very similar to those for their non-retroflex counterparts, except that they extend

Table 4.3 Phonemic contrasts at three places of articulation for both plosives and nasals in Malayalam

Dental	Gloss	Alveolar	Gloss	Retroflex	Gloss
[kuṯːi]	'stabbed'	[kutːi]	'peg'	[kuʈːi]	'child'
[paṉːi]	'pig'	[kanːi]	'virgin'	[kaɳːi]	'link in chain'

further down and have a small hook pointing rightward, as in alveolar [t] and retroflex [ʈ]. (In previous versions of the IPA, retroflexion was indicated by means of a small dot [.] below the symbol, as in [ṭ]. The current IPA uses this diacritic for "whisper"; see Section 6.2.)

Malayalam is a language that has the retroflex nasal [ɳ] as in ['paɳam] 'money.' In fact, Malayalam contrasts both plosives and nasals at each of the three places of articulation discussed above, dental, alveolar, and retroflex, as shown in Table 4.3.

These sounds appear to be very similar or even identical to a speaker of a language that does not have such a contrast, because they are perceived as variants of the same phoneme in the language (see Section 13.4). Of course, a person who grew up speaking a language with these contrasts will find that these sounds are clearly different and that this is a very natural distinction.

Retroflex fricatives [ʂ, ʐ] can be found in Polish, as in [kaʂa] 'buckwheat' and [kazʐa] 'gauze.' Mandarin Chinese has voiceless [ʂ] as in [ʂāŋhaj] 'Shanghai.'

We mentioned in Section 3.1.5 that in English the "r" – sound is often pronounced as a retroflex consonant. The IPA symbol for "retroflex r" is [ɻ]. For these sounds, the tip of the tongue is curled up and back behind the alveolar ridge, without contacting it. In English, retroflex plosives may also occur, allophonically, when preceding retroflex [ɻ]. For example, prepare to say the words *tea* [ti] and *tree* [tɻi]. Instead of producing the words, hold the articulation at the initial [t]. When comparing the positions of the tongue for the [t]s, a difference between the two words can be noticed. Specifically, [t] in *tree* is often produced as a retroflex [ʈ] in anticipation of the following [ɻ]. If that is the case in your speech, you should notice that the tip of your tongue is somewhat curled back. This articulation is very similar to that of retroflex [ʈ] in a language like Bengali.

The retroflex lateral [ɭ] can be found in Dravidian languages. For example, Tamil, spoken in South India, has both alveolar and retroflex laterals, as in [baːlaː] 'a proper name' and [meːɭaː] 'festival.'

Palatal consonants are not very common except for the palatal approximant [j]. Palatal plosives can be found in languages such as Czech, which contrasts voiceless and voiced palatal plosives [c] and [ɟ] as in *tělo* ['cɛlo] 'body' and *dělo* ['ɟɛlo] 'gun,' respectively. Palatal nasals are found in languages such as Spanish and French; for example, Spanish *año* ['aɲo] 'year,' or French *agneau* [a'ɲo] 'lamb.' Palatal fricatives, voiceless [ç] and voiced [ʝ], are also rare. German is a language that has the voiceless palatal fricative in its inventory in words like *ich* [ɪç], 'I.' The voiced palatal fricative [ʝ] appears in Greek, as in [ˈʝɛɾi] 'old men' versus [ˈçɛɾi] 'hand.' Palatal fricatives do occur frequently as allophones of palatal approximants in a variety of languages, including English. There are varieties of English where the words *you* and *Hugh* do not start with the same sound. In that case, the speaker may differentiate *you* [ju] with a voiced palatal approximant, from *Hugh* [çu] by starting the latter with a voiceless palatal fricative. The palatal lateral approximant [ʎ] occurs in Italian, as in *figlio* [ˈfiʎo], 'son.'

4.1.3 Dorsals

Velars can be produced by approaching or contacting any part of the soft palate. This allows for a considerable range, as evidenced by the fact that, due to coarticulation, the place of articulation for the voiceless velar plosive [k] in a word such as English *key* [ki] can be as much as 1 centimeter more anterior than that in *coup* [ku]. In addition to [k], English has the voiced velar plosive [g].

While the velar nasal [ŋ] is more common in syllable-final position than in syllable-initial position, velar nasals occur in both positions in languages such as Cambodian, Laotian, Thai, and Vietnamese, as in Thai [ŋāːn] 'work' ([ˉ] indicates a mid tone; see Section 11.4.1). Farsi (Persian) is an example of a language with the voiceless velar fricative [x] and the voiced velar fricative [ɣ] as in [xæm] 'bend' and [ɣæm] 'sorrow,' respectively. In languages with both palatal and velar fricatives, such as German and Greek, the place of articulation is usually conditioned by the vowel. For example, German exhibits an alternation between voiceless velar fricative [x] and palatal fricative [ç], which is conditioned by the backness or frontness of the preceding vowel, as shown in Table 4.4.

The rare velar affricate [k͡x] is a phoneme in Swiss German, where it occurs in words like [tːaŋk͡x] 'tank.'

English has the labial-velar approximant [w], which we placed in the velar column for convenience (see Section 3.1.5). The velar approximant [ɰ] seems to be quite rare and descriptions of languages claimed to have it as a phoneme are usually not detailed enough to decide whether it is the velar approximant [ɰ] or the labial-velar approximant [w].

Table 4.4 Vowel-conditioned alternation between palatal [ç] and velar [x] voiceless fricatives in German

Front vowels		Gloss	Back vowels		Gloss
siechen	[ˈziçən]	'to decay'	*suchen*	[ˈzuxən]	'to search'
rächen	[ˈʁɛçən]	'to avenge'	*Rochen*	[ˈʁɔxən]	'ray'

The voiced velar lateral [ʟ] occurs in Mid-Waghi, a Papuan language spoken in Papua New Guinea, as in [aʟaʟe] 'dizzy.'

Uvular plosives involve a constriction slightly further back than the velum, by raising the back of the tongue against the uvula. Arabic has a voiceless uvular plosive [q] as in [qalb] 'hear.' The voiced uvular plosive [ɢ] occurs in Dargi (Mehegi dialect), a Caucasian language spoken in Russia, as in [ɢaraʔul] 'watch (absolutive).' The voiced uvular plosive [ɢ] is rare, possibly because it is very difficult to maintain voicing with a constriction that close to the larynx. Since the air pressure above the larynx will soon equal that below the glottis, air will stop flowing from the lungs and vocal fold vibration will cease.

The uvular nasal [ɴ] is found in Inuit, an Eskimo-Aleut language spoken in Greenland and Canada, as in [eɴina] 'melody.' It may be difficult to find a language with true voiceless and voiced uvular fricatives since the uvula often vibrates during their production, thus creating uvular trills, rather than uvular fricatives. Voiced uvular fricatives can be found in French, as in *roux* [ʁu] 'reddish,' and the voiceless uvular fricative occurs as an allophone of [ʁ], as in *lettre* [lɛtχ] 'letter.'

4.1.4 Gutturals

The class of gutturals includes pharyngeals, epiglottals, and glottals. Pharyngeals are produced in the middle part of the pharynx, epiglottals are produced toward the lower part of the pharynx, while glottals are produced at the level of the glottis. *Pharyngeals* – that is, sounds produced by pulling the tongue root back toward the pharynx – are said to occur in many Semitic languages. For example, the Oriental dialect of Modern Hebrew has both the voiceless pharyngeal fricative [ħ] as in [ħaːli] 'my condition' and the voiced pharyngeal fricative [ʕ] as in [ʕor] 'skin.' However, there is some debate as to whether the pharyngeals found in languages such as Arabic and Hebrew are truly pharyngeal or whether they are actually epiglottal. For *epiglottals*, the epiglottis is the active articulator and forms a constriction near the back wall of the pharynx.

A rare example of a language that has both pharyngeal and epiglottal sounds is the Burkikhan dialect of Agul, spoken in the Caucasus. This language has a voiceless epiglottal plosive [ʡ], as in [jaʡar] 'centers.' It also contrasts the voiceless pharyngeal fricative [ħ], the voiced pharyngeal fricative [ʕ], and the voiceless epiglottal fricative [ʜ], as in [muˈħar] 'barns,' [muˈʕar] 'bridges,' and [mɛˈʜɛr] 'wheys.' The voiced epiglottal fricative [ʢ] is found in Dargi, as in [ʢuʃːaː] 'you.' For *glottals*, a constriction is formed at the level of the vocal folds. The glottal plosive was introduced as an allophone of /t/ in English in Section 3.4.1.5. The glottal plosive occurs phonemically in Hawaiian, as in [ʔaʔa] 'dare.' The voiceless and voiced glottal fricatives [h, ɦ] have also been introduced in our discussion of English sounds.

4.2   Additional Manners of Articulation

We now return to those manners of articulation listed in Table 4.1 that do not occur phonemically in English, namely trill, tap/flap, and lateral fricative.

When producing a **trill**, one articulator is held in close proximity to another so that the flow of air between them sets one of them in vibration. This vibration is caused aerodynamically, without muscle contraction, in that an articulator is made to vibrate rapidly by blowing air over it. As shown in Table 4.1, this aerodynamic vibration can occur at a number of different places of articulation: the lips, tongue tip, and uvula can be trilled; trills can be voiced or voiceless. A voiced bilabial trill [ʙ] may seem exotic but is quite easy to produce. The lips need only to be placed loosely together and are set in vibration by blowing air through them. The voiced alveolar trill [r] is made by placing the tip or blade of the tongue just below the alveolar ridge. This sound may be difficult to produce if it has not been learned during childhood, since the tongue tip must be tensed to reach the alveolar ridge but must also be relaxed enough to 'flutter' in the air. Spanish has alveolar trills, as in *perro* ['pero], 'dog.' The uvular trill [ʀ], which is produced by trilling the uvula as if someone is gargling, can be found in the initial sound of *rok* [ʀɔk], 'skirt' in certain varieties of Dutch.

A *tap* or *flap* is caused by a single contraction of the muscles so that one articulator briefly touches the other, resulting in a closure that is much shorter than for a plosive. The IPA recently added a new symbol for the labiodental flap that occurs in many languages spoken in central and southeastern Africa. For the production of a labiodental flap, the lower lip is retracted past the upper teeth and then rapidly advanced, striking the upper teeth briefly in passing. The IPA symbol is [ⱱ] as in Mono [ávárá] 'wisdom' (the symbol [á] represents the vowel [a] spoken with a high tone; see Section 11.4.1). In American English, alveolar plosives are usually realized as flap when they follow a vowel or central approximant and precede an unstressed vowel, as in *latter* ['læɾɚ], or *party* ['paɹɾi] (see Section 3.4.1.4). In Spanish, an alveolar tap (one short closure) contrasts with an alveolar trill (several short closures) as in *pero* ['pero] 'but' and *perro* ['pero] 'dog.' While a flap requires muscle activity and involves a single movement, a trill is produced by the airflow and involves a passive repetitive motion of the trilling articulator.

The retroflex flap [ɽ] can be found in Hindi, an Indo-European language spoken in India, as in [gʰoɽa] 'horse.'

Although *laterals* are typically approximants, laterals can also be produced with different degrees of constriction. Most common among these is the **lateral fricative**. Zulu, a Niger-Congo language spoken in South Africa, contrasts the voiceless and voiced lateral fricatives, as well as the voiced lateral approximant, as in [ɬàɬá] 'cut off,' [ɮálà] 'play,' and [lálà] 'lie down.'

4.3   Vowels

Figure 4.1 shows the IPA symbols available for the transcription of vowels. They are organized in terms of the vowel quadrilateral introduced in Section 3.2. Where symbols appear in pairs, the symbol to the left represents an unrounded vowel and the symbol to the right its rounded counterpart. There are 28 vowel qualities represented on this chart, and we have discussed 13 of them in our review of the vowels of English (Section 3.2). The number of vowels in the world's languages varies tremendously, ranging from 3 to over 40. Large vowel inventories typically include sets of long and short vowels, oral and nasal vowels, or plain and pharyngealized vowels. Across the world's languages, a vowel inventory with the five vowels /i, e, a, o, u/ is most common. English thus has a relatively large vowel inventory. However, while English has high, mid, and low as well as front, central, and back vowels, it does not contrast vowels in terms of either length or lip rounding.

   We will now consider German as a language that does use length and rounding contrastively. As shown in Figure 4.2, German has 17 vowels. IPA symbols for the vowels are provided as well. As you see, German contrasts front rounded and unrounded vowels ([i, y], [ɪ, ʏ], [e, ø], [ɛ, œ]), as well as long and short vowels ([ɛ, ɛː], [a, aː]). Notice that while German has several pairs of long and short vowels (e.g. [i, ɪ], [e, ɛ], [y, ʏ], [ø, œ], [u, ʊ], [o, ɔ]), the fact that they differ primarily in quality is expressed by the use of different symbols rather than the length diacritic. The symbols for the pairs [ɛ, ɛː] and [a, aː], on the other hand, make

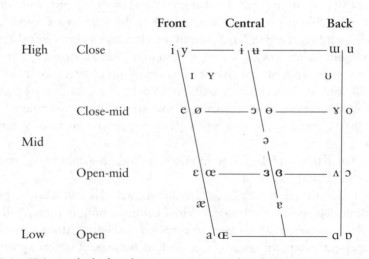

Figure 4.1   IPA symbols for the transcription of vowels (revision 2005).

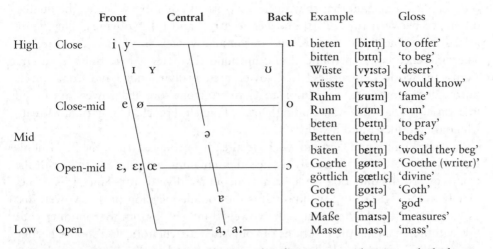

		Front	**Central**	**Back**	Example		Gloss
High	Close	i y		u	bieten	[biːtn̩]	'to offer'
					bitten	[bɪtn̩]	'to beg'
		ɪ Y		ʊ	Wüste	[vyːstə]	'desert'
					wüsste	[vʏstə]	'would know'
	Close-mid	e ø		o	Ruhm	[ʁuːm]	'fame'
					Rum	[ʁʊm]	'rum'
					beten	[beːtn̩]	'to pray'
Mid			ə		Betten	[bɛtn̩]	'beds'
					bäten	[bɛːtn̩]	'would they beg'
	Open-mid	ɛ, ɛː œ		ɔ	Goethe	[gøːtə]	'Goethe (writer)'
					göttlich	[gœtlɪç]	'divine'
			ɐ		Gote	[goːtə]	'Goth'
					Gott	[gɔt]	'god'
					Maße	[maːsə]	'measures'
Low	Open		a, aː		Masse	[masə]	'mass'

Figure 4.2 Words exemplifying the vowels of German and IPA symbols for their transcription (note that [a/aː] is usually placed in a central or even back position in German IPA charts although the symbol is that of the front vowel).

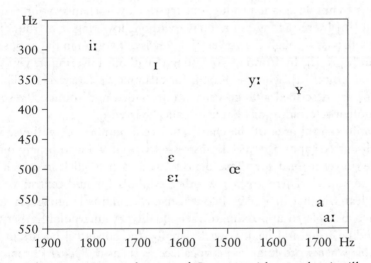

Figure 4.3 The acoustic vowel space of German with vowel pairs illustrating differences in vowel length and lip rounding.

it clear that their primary distinction is indeed one of length rather than quality. This is also clear when considering the acoustic vowel space of German, as shown in Figure 4.3. These data are obtained through acoustic analyses (the relation between articulatory and acoustic descriptions of vowel quality is discussed in Section 9.5.1). The vowels [ɛ] and [ɛː], and [a] and [aː], are very close to each other, indicating again that they differ very little in quality. Whereas the quality difference between [iː] and [ɪ] and between [yː] and [y] is obvious. This figure also displays the front rounded and unrounded vowels [i, y], [ɪ, ʏ], and [ɛ, œ]. The difference between rounded and unrounded vowels is here quite apparent. Across the world's languages, back vowels are usually rounded and front vowels unrounded. However, in addition to German, front rounded vowels are found in a variety of languages, including Dutch, Finnish, French, Hungarian, Korean, Mandarin Chinese, and Swedish.

Between English and German, we have already introduced 18 of the 28 symbols from Figure 4.1. We will briefly discuss the remaining vowels. Starting with the front vowels, the only one we have not encountered yet is [ɶ]. Since it is immediately to the right of [a], we know it is the rounded version of that vowel. Just as you should be able to change the vowel [i] into [y] by simply rounding your lips without changing the positions of your other articulators, you should be able to change [a] into [ɶ]. The latter vowel can be found in the Bavarian dialect of Amstetten (Traunmüller 1982) but seems generally quite rare.

The high central area of the chart shows the vowels [ɨ] and [ʉ]. The high central vowel [ɨ] can be found in certain dialects of American English, in plurals such as 'houses' [ˈhaʊzɨz]. Exploiting the fact that vowel articulation is much more continuous than consonant production, try to slowly change your articulation from [i] to [u] by retracting your tongue without lowering it or rounding your lips. You will pass through the vowel [ɨ]. Likewise, if you go in the opposite direction, from [u] to [i], by fronting your tongue without lowering it, you will pass through the vowel [ʉ], which is found, for example, in Norwegian. The vowels [ɨ] and [ʉ] are described as high central unrounded and rounded, respectively. They are often referred to as "barred i" and "barred u."

In the mid central area of the chart, you see a number of symbols. We have already discussed [ə] as a reduced, unstressed vowel. We also briefly mentioned [ɜ] as the vowel in *bird* for those dialects of British English in which the "r" is not pronounced. There are a few other symbols for mid-central vowels but it is not clear whether they play a contrastive role in any language. In any case, you should be able to approximate their quality by interpolating between the corresponding front and back vowels. Finally, the vowel [ɐ] occurs in German for example when word-final [əʁ] is vocalized as [ɐ] as in *Becher* [ˈbɛçɐ] 'beaker.' The quality of this sound is actually very similar to the American English [ʌ] as in the word *but*.

For the back vowels, we first encounter [ɯ]. Its position to the left of [u] indicates that it is a high back unrounded vowel, that is, [u] without lip rounding. This vowel is quite common and can be found in languages such as Japanese and Korean. A little lower, we find the unrounded counterpart of [o], the high mid back unrounded vowel [ɤ], which is found in languages such as Thai and Vietnamese. Finally, the low back rounded vowel [ɒ] is the rounded counterpart of [ɑ] and is the vowel in the British pronunciation of words such as 'pot.'

4.4   Secondary Articulations

So far, we have described sounds that are characterized by a single constriction. However, sounds can be produced with two simultaneous constrictions at two places of articulation. When that occurs, a distinction is made between sounds in which the degree of the two constrictions is considered equal (primary), and sounds in which one constriction is more prominent than the other (secondary) articulation. We have already discussed the labial-velar [w] as an example of a consonant for which the labial and velar constrictions are considered equal. Sounds like this involve a double articulation with two primary articulations (see Section 3.1.5). An example of a consonant with a **secondary articulation** is the rounding of the initial sound in the word *soup*. The primary constriction for the initial fricative is at the alveolar ridge but the rounding of the lips in anticipation of the rounded [u] constitutes a secondary articulation, resulting in a labialized fricative [sʷup]. Since secondary articulations are typically described as the superimposition of a vowel-like articulation on top of a consonantal articulation, we discussed the description of vowels first. It can be difficult to distinguish a secondary articulation from a sequence of two segments as in, for example, *soup* [sʷup] versus *swoop* [swup]. The difference concerns the relative timing of the articulation of the [s] and [w]. In a secondary articulation, the two articulatory gestures occur simultaneously. In a sequence of two segments, the articulation of [w] starts much later, toward the offset of (but still partially overlapping with) the articulation of [s].

Four types of secondary articulation are generally recognized:

1 **Labialization** is the type discussed above. Labialization, indicated by the diacritic [ʷ], can be thought of as the superimposition of a [u]-like or [w]-like articulation on the primary articulation. It is often conditioned by adjacent segments as in [sʷup]. However, labialization can occur contrastively, as in Twi, a Niger-Congo language spoken in Ghana: [àkʷá] 'a round about way,' and [àká] 'somebody has bitten.'
2 **Palatalization** involves the superimposition of an [i]- or [j]-like articulation by making a secondary constriction with the tongue body at the palate. Russian contrasts plain and palatalized consonants at several places of articulation as in [sok] 'juice' versus [sʲok] 'he lashed.'
3 **Velarization** requires the superimposition of an unrounded high back vowel [ɣ]-like articulation, raising the back of the tongue toward the velum. Velarization is indicated by the diacritic [~] as in the English postvocalic "dark l" [ɫ] or by the diacritic [ˠ]. Velarization has a contrastive function in Marshallese, an Austronesian language spoken in the Marshall Islands: [mˠatʲ] 'eel' versus [matʲ] 'eye.'
4 **Pharyngealization** involves a lowering of the back of the tongue and a retraction of the tongue root toward the back wall of the pharynx. Pharyngealization

is often indicated by the same diacritic as velarization, since languages do not seem to use these two secondary articulations contrastively. Alternatively, the symbol for the voiced pharyngeal fricative is sometimes used as a diacritic [ˤ] to indicate pharyngealization. Many dialects of Arabic distinguish a series of plain consonants from a series of pharyngealized consonants known as **emphatic consonants**. For example, Jordanian Arabic distinguishes [tuːb] 'to repent' from [tˤuːb] 'bricks.' While emphasis is considered an attribute of the consonant, it seems to be primarily audible as a change in the quality of adjacent vowels.

Of these four types of secondary articulation, labialization is the most common across the world's languages. While secondary articulations are phonemic in certain languages, they are represented by means of diacritics in IPA.

In this chapter, we have tried to illustrate the great variety that exists in terms of place and manner of articulation in consonants and vowels of the world's languages. Needless to say, this is not a complete listing of all sounds in the languages of the world. But this chapter should enhance the appreciation of the many different ways in which speech sounds are produced in languages other than English. Which sounds are perceived as more or less "exotic" will of course for a large part depend on the native language of a speaker. The next chapter describes the airflow from the lungs to the lips and nostrils in detail. Chapter 6 then describes additional consonants that are produced with an airstream that does not originate in the lungs.

Exercises

1 Choose several of the shaded cells from the IPA chart, and try to explain why these articulations are considered impossible.
2 In what way could the production of [m] in *emphasis* differ from the one in *empire*? Why?
3 Why are dental, alveolar, and postalveolar combined into one column in the IPA chart?
4 Explain how taps and trills are produced differently, and give one example of each.
5 Why are some vowels that contrast length transcribed with diacritics ([ɛ] and [ɛː]) while others are transcribed with separate symbols ([ɪ] and [i])?
6 What is a secondary articulation? Summarize and give examples of four types of secondary articulation.

5 Physiology of the Vocal Apparatus

As mentioned in Section 1.1, the lungs are the main source of energy for speech and the larynx is an important sound source. Articulation of speech sounds is mostly performed in the vocal tract. These organs are now described in more detail to understand their function and their impact on speech production.

5.1 The Subglottal System: Lungs, Bronchi, and Trachea

Most of the sounds of the world's languages and all the sounds of English are produced with an airstream from the lungs. To understand how this **egressive pulmonic airstream** is produced, we treat the anatomy and the function of the lungs first.

5.1.1 Anatomy of the subglottal system

The subglottal system (see Figure 5.1), which we use for breathing, consists of two **pulmones (lungs)**, located in the **thorax (chest)**. They are linked to the **trachea (windpipe)** by means of the left and right **bronchi**. The bronchi split up inside the lungs into smaller branches, the **bronchia**, and further into approximately 300 million **alveoli pulmonis** (Weibel 1984). Here, the vitally important exchange of gas between air and blood takes place. To do so, the alveoli have very thin membranes to separate the blood (outside the alveoli) from the air (inside the alveoli).

The lungs consist of a spongy, elastic fabric, without any muscles. About 25 percent of the elasticity of the lungs is due to the elasticity of the tissue itself, comparable, for example, to the elasticity of a sock. The remainder of the elasticity is the result of the **surface tension** of the water molecules in the blood around the alveoli, which draws the lungs together. The elasticity of the lung tissue and the surface tension of the alveoli together form the **elastic recoil force**, which contracts the lungs.

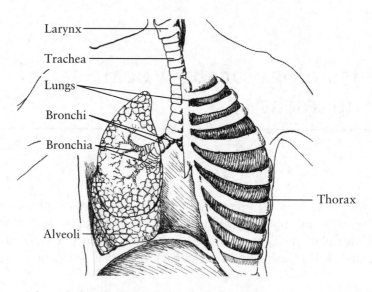

Larynx

Trachea

Lungs

Bronchi

Bronchia

Thorax

Alveoli

Figure 5.1   The subglottal system. On the left, tissue and ribs have been omitted to expose relevant structures.

   Since the lungs themselves do not have muscles, how are we able to breathe, or – in other words – how is air forced into and out of the lungs? Breathing implies expanding the lungs, so that the air pressure inside them becomes lower than the air pressure outside the body, causing air to enter the lungs through the trachea (breathing in). The physical reason for this is known as **Boyle's Law**, which states that the product of the pressure of a gas multiplied with its volume is constant for a given temperature:

volume × pressure = constant.

Or, in other words, the pressure is inversely related to its volume:

$$\text{volume} = \frac{\text{constant}}{\text{pressure}} \quad \text{(or, shorter: } V = \frac{\text{const.}}{p}\text{).}$$

This implies that *in*creasing the volume of the lungs (i.e. V becomes larger) *de*creases the (air) pressure inside them (i.e. p becomes smaller), which, in turn, leads to the inward (**ingressive**) airflow (breathing in). Conversely, contraction of the lungs leads to an outward (**egressive**) airflow (breathing out). That is, decreasing the lung volume increases the air pressure in the lungs and consequently, air flows outward. The lungs thus alternately expand and contract for breathing in and breathing out – but they cannot do this themselves, since they do not have any muscles.
   The important factor enabling the lungs to expand and to contract is the way they are suspended in the thorax (see Figure 5.2). Both lungs are surrounded by

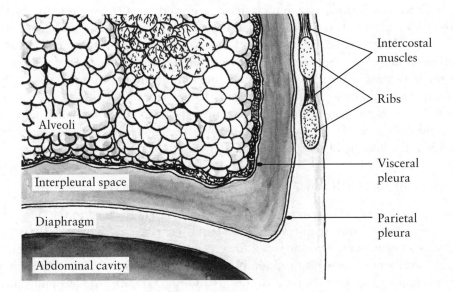

Intercostal
muscles

Ribs

Alveoli

Visceral
pleura

Interpleural space

Diaphragm

Parietal
pleura

Abdominal cavity

Figure 5.2 Close-up of a lung with details of the lung membranes and adjacent structures.

their own **visceral pleura (lung membrane)**. Through the **interpleural space**, these membranes are linked to the **parietal pleura,** adjacent to the ribs and just above the **diaphragm.** Visceral and parietal pleura consist of very smooth and almost airtight tissues, which is essential for their proper functioning in breathing and speaking.

5.1.2   Movements of the lungs

The cavity formed by the ribs and diaphragm is known as the **thoracic cavity.** The movements of the thoracic cavity are transmitted to the lungs through the visceral and parietal pleurae and the interpleural space. The interpleural space between the visceral and parietal pleurae is filled with a lubricating liquid. Special cells in the pleurae continuously withdraw gas from this space, thus keeping the pressure in the liquid lower than in the lungs. This leads to the **pleural linkage** between visceral and parietal pleurae, which makes the lungs move along with the movements of the thorax and diaphragm. This system can be illustrated by putting a few drops of water between two glass plates (the two pleurae): the two plates can be rubbed against each other but it is very hard to separate them.

5.1.2.1   BREATHING IN (INSPIRATION, INHALATION)

The thoracic cavity can be made larger or smaller by muscle activity. By means of the **external intercostal muscles**, the ribs can be slightly turned outwards, which makes the thorax larger. This happens when a person applies **thoracic breathing**.

The diaphragm, which is a muscle itself, can additionally or alternatively be used for breathing. It is slightly domed upwards when at rest. When tensed, the diaphragm is flattened, and enlarges the lung cavity downwards, resulting in **abdominal breathing**. There appear to be individual differences, independent of gender, in the way people breathe: some favor thoracic breathing, others have a preference for abdominal breathing (Zemlin 1998, p. 93). In speech production, typically both movements occur: activating the inspiration muscles, that is, turning the intercostals outwards and tensing the diaphragm, expands the chest cavity and consequently the size of the lungs.

5.1.2.2   BREATHING OUT (EXPIRATION, EXHALATION)

During expiration, the movements just described are performed in the opposite direction. This hardly requires any muscle power, since the lungs tend to contract as a result of their elastic recoil force. Since the ribs and/or diaphragm have been forced out of their rest position by muscular power during inspiration, they passively move back into that position. In addition, gravity tends to pull down the chest cavity, making it smaller. Thus, breathing out or passive expiration does not require any muscle activity, until the rest position is attained, that is, up to the position where the contracting force of the lungs and the expanding force of the chest cavity are equally large. If the lungs are contracted beyond this rest position, the **internal intercostal muscles** must be activated to pull the ribs together. This active form of expiration by means of the internal intercostal muscles is not as finely controlled as the passive expiration regulated by the external intercostal muscles. Since the loudness of speech depends on air pressure in the lungs (see Section 5.1.4), this predicts that loudness can be more precisely controlled during passive expiration than during the active expiration phase.

As we described, breathing out occurs automatically. It is therefore not surprising that the lungs can be compared to a balloon: after a balloon is inflated, and the air is then allowed to leave the balloon, the balloon empties itself quickly, and in fact rather abruptly. The same would happen to the lungs, but during expiration, the *inspiration* muscles can hold back the lungs until the rest position is attained, in order to prevent the lungs from emptying themselves too quickly. This means that the *inspiration* muscles remain active during *expiration* as well. The expiration muscles only become active if air has to be squeezed out of the lungs past the rest position. Together, the inspiration and expiration muscles obtain a relatively stable air pressure during the production of speech.

5.1.3   *The volumes of the lungs and their control over time*

Both lungs together have a maximum volume of about 6 liters ($\approx$ 1.6 gallons). At rest, they are filled with about 3 liters of air. During quiet respiration, an additional volume of about half a liter (1 pint) is actively inhaled (**tidal volume** or (**at**)

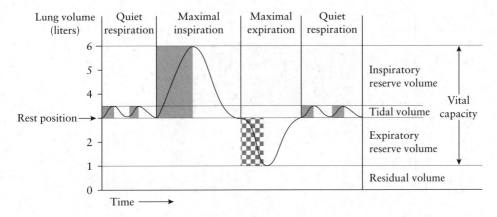

Figure 5.3   Air volume in the lungs during breathing cycles. The gray areas indicate activity of the inspiration muscles (external intercostals and diaphragm); the checked area indicates activity of the expiration muscles (internal intercostals).

rest capacity; see Figure 5.3). During a deep breath the lungs can be maximally increased by the **inspiratory reserve volume** with the inspiration muscles. Expiration occurs passively up to the resting position, under the influence of the elastic recoil forces, although it can be actively restrained by the inspiration muscles. Air may be actively evacuated from the lungs beyond the rest position so that the lungs can be maximally depleted by the **expiratory reserve volume** with the expiration muscles. The **residual volume** of about one liter cannot be exhaled and is always present in the alveoli. The difference between the volume at maximum inspiration and maximum expiration is called the **vital capacity**.

During quiet respiration, about half a liter of air is breathed in and out at a rate of 10 to 20 times per minute. This rate is reduced during speech. However, the essential difference between breathing during quiet respiration and speaking does not reside in its frequency, but rather in the planning of the breathing sequences. During quiet respiration, about 40 percent of the breathing cycle is reserved for breathing in, the remaining 60 percent for breathing out. During speech, however, only about 10 percent of the time is used for breathing in, against 90 percent for breathing out (see Figure 5.4). The respiration musculature thus extends the expiration phase when a person is speaking.

5.1.4 Loudness and the air pressure in the lungs

As mentioned earlier, air pressure inside the lungs is kept relatively constant during speech. Irrespective of the speech sound, the different muscle groups keep the air pressure in the lungs at approximately the same level. This is very important, because the sound pressure level of the speech signal (see Section 7.3.2), a

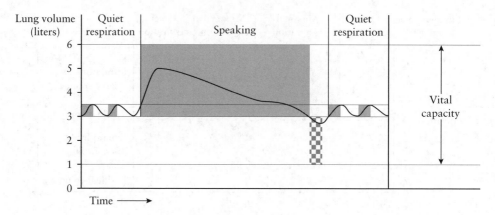

Figure 5.4   Air volume in the lungs during breathing and speaking. The gray areas indicate activity of the inspiration muscles (external intercostals and diaphragm); the checked area indicates activity of the expiration muscles (internal intercostals).

parameter that is to a great extent responsible for the loudness of speech, increases roughly by the square of the increase in subglottal air pressure. In other words, doubling the subglottal air pressure amounts to multiplying the sound pressure level by four. A high level of control with regard to the air pressure is therefore required to regulate the loudness of speech. This control is mainly achieved by the external intercostal muscles.

This state of affairs has direct consequences for theories about stress on syllables in speech (see Section 11.1). It seems that stress is not simply realized by an increase in muscular tension to increase the loudness of a syllable, but that it may involve, among other things, an increase in the closing speed of the vocal folds, which leads to a speech signal that is perceived as "louder" by the listener (see Section 5.2.3). Expiration is a complex interaction between the inspiration muscles, which are activated during the expiration phase up to the rest position, and the expiration muscles, which are activated beyond the rest position. What are the consequences of simply increasing muscle activity? During the first phase of expiration, a higher muscular activity increases the tension of the *inspiration* muscles, which expands the lungs. This *reduces* the air pressure in the lungs instead of increasing it, which makes the produced sound softer. Only beyond the rest position are the expiration muscles activated, which causes an increase in loudness. That is, a phenomenon like "stress" is not simply a one-to-one projection of a concept (stress) onto a physiological reality (heightened muscular tension). Instead, the simple abstract concept implies a highly complex motor activity with deactivation or activation of different muscle groups, depending on whether the lungs are above or beyond rest position.

To summarize, during inhalation, the thoracic cavity is actively extended, which causes airflow through the trachea, bronchi, and the bronchial ramification into the two lungs. Although some interjections are sometimes produced with an ingressive air stream (more to express surprise or confirmation than to convey linguistic meaning), in running speech no sounds are produced during this inhalation phase. During speech, air flows out of the lungs through the trachea and the larynx and into the vocal tract. This process is passive in the sense that the air flows out of the lungs by itself until the lungs reach their rest position. It requires active force to restrain this passive airflow during speech production. Only beyond the rest position is active force needed to exhale. Precise control of the air pressure in the trachea is required because the intensity of the speech signal depends on this parameter. As already mentioned, the role of the larynx is essential for speech production, and is treated in detail in the next section.

5.2   Structure and Function of the Larynx

The larynx, which is located inside the neck on top of the trachea, contains the vocal folds. Speech sounds are called voiced when the vocal folds vibrate during their production. Speech sounds are called unvoiced or voiceless when the vocal folds do not vibrate (see Section 2.1, but see Section 6.3 for an alternative definition of voicing for plosives in several languages). The vibration of the vocal folds attributes a quality to the speech which is perceived as **pitch**, giving a certain "melody" to a word or sentence. The next sections cover the anatomy of the larynx and the principles of vocal fold vibration.

5.2.1   Anatomy of the larynx

The larynx is an adjustable cartilage tube through which air flows with each breath. It is located on top of the trachea and is suspended from the **hyoid bone**, a horseshoe-shaped ring bone located in the upper part of the neck, which supports the tongue root (see Figure 5.5a and b).

The trachea consists of cartilage rings with an opening at the back, making them look like small horseshoes. The back part of the half-rings directly touches the **esophagus (gullet)** and is made airtight by its tissues and the **trachealis muscle**. Between the cartilage rings, a series of ligaments surround the entire trachea, enclosing it airtight.

Like the trachea, the larynx on top of it consists of cartilage, muscles, and ligaments. Its skeleton is formed by the **thyroid cartilage**, consisting of two cartilage plates that are fused together at the front. For women, they are at an angle of 90°, whereas for men, they form an angle of 80° (Zemlin 1998, pp. 176–177; see Figure 5.5c). The front (anterior) part of the thyroid can be visible, particularly in men with the sharper angle between the plates, as the **Adam's apple**. Between

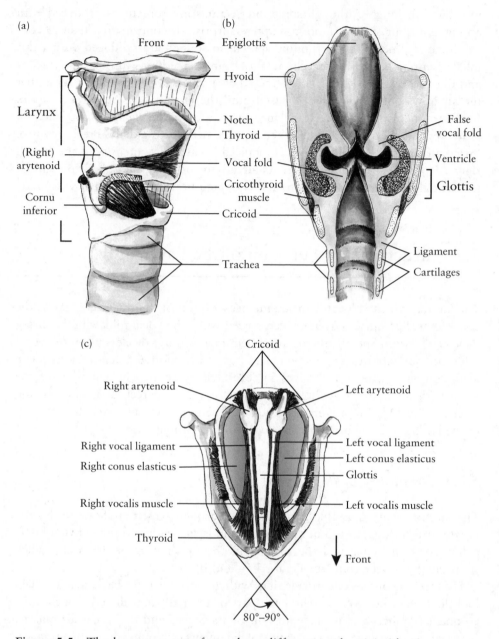

Figure 5.5 The larynx as seen from three different angles: (a) side view (sagittal view) from the right, (b) frontal cross-section (anterior view), and (c) view from above (coronal view). In (a), the vocal folds and the arytenoid are visible inside the thyroid, which is drawn semi-transparently.

the plates of the thyroid is a triangular notch which can be felt from the outside (see Figure 5.5a). The vocal folds, which through their vibration produce the voicing of speech sounds, are attached at the inside, just below this triangular notch.

The second cartilage of the larynx is the **cricoid cartilage**, which looks like a signet ring: a ring with a flat plate at the back (see Figure 5.5a). It has extensions on each side (not visible in Figure 5.5), which join with the **cornu inferior** of the thyroid, thus providing a horizontal axis around which the thyroid and the cricoid cartilages can rotate relative to each other. This rotation (produced by the **external laryngeal muscles (cricothyroid muscles)**) is a swing-like movement that causes the vocal folds to be more or less stretched, which is important for controlling the rate of vocal fold vibration (which is responsible for our perception of pitch).

The two **arytenoid cartilages**, which are attached like two pyramids on top of the cricoid (see Figures 5.5a and c), are the third group of cartilages of the larynx. Each of them has an extension, called **vocal process**, to which one of the vocal folds is attached. By tensing the **posterior cricoarytenoid muscles**, the arytenoids can be tilted, which has the effect of moving the two vocal folds apart, upwards, and to the sides, a process known as **abduction**. This can produce a complete opening of the vocal folds, for example during breathing, or while producing voiceless speech sounds. By tensing the **lateral cricoarytenoid muscles** the vocal folds can be moved together (**adducted**), by means of a downward and inward movement of the arytenoids. If the vocal folds are slightly open and under tension, they may start to vibrate in the pulmonic airstream for the production of voiced sounds. Tensing the **transverse and oblique arytenoid muscles** closes the vocal folds completely, for example, when a person swallows, in order to prevent food from entering the trachea. A complete closure of the vocal folds may occur during speech production, for example to produce a glottal plosive (see Section 3.4.1.5) or a glottalic airstream (see Section 6.1.1).

The epiglottis (see Figure 5.5b) is a cartilage shaped like a shoehorn, located in the hyoid bone, on top of the entrance to the larynx. While its function is not entirely clear (Zemlin 1998, pp. 107–108), some authors (for example, Moore and Dalley 1999, p. 1054) claim that the epiglottis prevents food from entering the trachea when a person swallows. This is motivated by its position like a trapdoor on top of the larynx. This "trapdoor" can be closed passively, by the pressure of the food particles themselves when they approach the larynx, and actively, by a contraction of the thyroepiglottic muscle that pulls the epiglottis down.

Inside the larynx, the two **vocal folds**, sometimes called the *vocal cords*, play an essential role in speech production. At the front, each of them is attached to the junction of the two thyroid plates below the triangular notch. From there, each of them reaches to its corresponding arytenoid (see Figures 5.5a and c). Each vocal fold consists of the **vocalis muscle**, attached to the **vocal ligament** that stretches from the thyroid to one of the arytenoids. The vocal ligament is the upper part of the airtight **conus elasticus** that stretches to the inner side of the cricoid and separates the upper, superior part of the larynx from its lower, inferior part.

The muscles of the vocal folds can contract to change the elastic tension, but they can additionally change the shape of the vocal folds from fleshy lips into tense, thin bands, which is another means of influencing their vibration properties.

In the past it has been assumed that the vocal folds vibrate just like the strings of a violin (that is, like two cords under tension). But current research assumes a more complex movement, which is based on the properties of the muscular tissue. The term *vocal folds* is therefore preferred over the more common term *vocal cords*, since both in their appearance and in their mechanical properties, they are closer to "flaps" or "folds" rather than to "cords."

The **false vocal folds** are situated above the true vocal folds, separated from them by the space of the **ventricles** (see Figure 5.5b). These false vocal folds cannot be stretched, and it is assumed that they have a protective function. In some pathological speakers, they may flutter like sheets in the wind, resulting in a rough voice quality.

The space between the vocal folds, reaching from the bottom side of the vocal folds to their top, is called the glottis. People often speak about the glottis as if it were an organ, as in, for example: "opening the glottis"; it is not. The glottis is essentially the whole area of the vocal folds that is involved in sound production. It should be pointed out that even with maximal glottal opening, the vocal folds still block about 50 percent of the diameter of the trachea, which makes humans not very efficient in terms of the respiratory process.

To summarize, the larynx is located on top of the trachea. It is partly suspended by ligatures and muscles from the hyoid, which is itself attached by ligatures and muscles to the tongue root. The thyroid, which forms the main body of the larynx, is located above the cricoid. The thyroid and the cricoid can rotate relative to each other. The vocal folds can be tensed and released by the rotating movement of the thyroid and the cricoid. The positioning of the vocal folds can be changed by the arytenoids. The arytenoids, which are located on top of the cricoid, can be tilted. Tilting the arytenoids downwards and inwards adducts the vocal folds, causing them to close. Tilting the arytenoids upwards and outwards abducts the vocal folds, causing them to open. Tensing and releasing the vocal folds influences their rate of vibration (see Section 5.2.2), which is the result of an interaction between the pulmonic airstream and the glottis. The glottis can be open (for example, during breathing or the production of voiceless sounds), it can be closed (for example, during swallowing or the production of ejectives; see Section 6.1.1), or it can be partially open with the vocal folds abducted halfway to a point where they start vibrating in the pulmonic airstream. This vibration (or oscillation) is described in detail in the next section.

5.2.2 Vocal fold vibration

The vibration of the vocal folds is a very complex movement. Generally speaking, the vocal folds open up from bottom to top and from back to front. The closing of the vocal folds also proceeds from bottom to top, but along the horizontal axis it starts from the middle, closing forwards and backwards at the same time. The closure of the vocal folds is often incomplete, especially for women, since a small triangle next to the arytenoids, at the posterior (back) end of the vocal folds, remains open.

A number of different theories have been proposed to explain the vibration of the vocal folds during speech. While many are no longer supported by recent evidence, we present these arguments in some detail to show how the present theory about vocal fold vibration has developed. Various researchers have assumed that voicing is the result of one of the following:

1 *Vibrating string theory*: the vocal folds oscillate in the airstream just like strings.
2 *Neurochronaxic theory*: neural impulses of the central nervous system directly control the vocal folds.
3 *Aerodynamic theory*: a sucking pressure drop of the streaming air.
4 *Myoelastic theory*: the elasticity of the vocal folds.

The **vibrating string theory** (Ferrein 1741) assumes that the vocal folds vibrate just like the strings of a violin, and that the vibrating vocal folds produce a tone. This assumption is not plausible, for an oscillating string needs a resonance body in order to be clearly audible. For example, the string of an electric guitar, which does not have a resonance body, can hardly be heard without amplification. On an acoustic guitar an oscillating string can be clearly perceived because it does have a resonance body. As we will see in Chapter 9, the vocal tract has resonating qualities, but it is a rather poor resonator and it needs the large energy of the air puffs going through the vocal folds to make this quality audible. The vibrating vocal folds alone (without air flowing through them) are inaudible.

The **neurochronaxic theory** (Husson 1950) assumes that the vibration of the vocal folds is realized by rapidly contracting and relaxing muscles. But this theory is not plausible either, since no muscle group in the human body is able to execute movements as fast as the vocal folds, which open and close during speech between 100 and 400 times per second. During singing, this may happen even faster, while the vocal folds of a crying baby may oscillate up to 2,000 times per second. No muscle can be actively moved fast enough to attain such high oscillation rates. In addition, even the nerves which activate muscles can only generate up to 1,000 impulses per second. The fast vibration of the vocal folds during the production of voiced sounds thus requires still another explanation.

We now know that the vocal folds do not oscillate by contracting and relaxing of muscles requiring a resonance body, but rather act more as the mouthpiece of a woodwind instrument, for example, like an oboe: a stream of air is periodically interrupted, and the resulting impulses of air are perceived as a tone. It is not the vibration of the vocal folds themselves which leads to a sound, but the effect on the air that passes through, as in the case of an oboe, where the interruptions of the airflow make the vibration audible.

5.2.2.1 THE BERNOULLI EFFECT AND THE AERODYNAMIC THEORY

Imagine the vocal folds as two swinging doors in a drafty corridor. They can be locked shut (adducted), permanently wide open by being hooked to the wall (abducted), or move freely in the draft. The stronger the draft, the further the doors open. We reported in Section 5.1.4 that the air pressure in the lungs is kept at a relatively constant level. This implies that the airflow through the trachea and the larynx is relatively steady as well. If the airstream is constant, swinging doors (the vocal folds) could be expected to open to a certain degree, but there is no reason for them to start swinging back and forth. For this reason, it has long been unclear why the steady stream of air should make the vocal folds oscillate between opening and closing, instead of simply keeping them slightly open. This question was answered by van den Berg and his colleagues (1957), who suggested an explanation based on the **Bernoulli effect**. This effect is now explained in detail.

When a liquid or a gas (for instance, air) flows steadily and without turbulence through a tube, all the molecules move along at approximately the same speed in the direction of the stream. This is known as **laminar flow**. To be precise, the molecules still execute a number of movements back and forth, but the steady forward movement in one direction predominates. This is comparable to a carnival procession in which the participants are continuously dancing and moving in all directions but, on the average, move along with the parade.

What happens if the tube is narrowed (see Figure 5.6)? This is comparable to the situation between the vocal folds in the larynx. The flow entering and exiting the tube remains constant. Since the air molecules have the same speed before and after the narrow passage, the molecules must move faster while they are passing through the narrow passage.

This is represented more accurately in Figure 5.7. In this "snapshot," four molecules (represented by four black footprints) are moving along in a single row

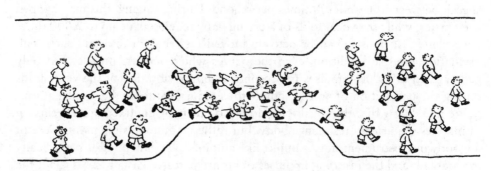

Figure 5.6 Molecules in a laminar stream. In the narrow passage, the molecules must move faster than before and after the constriction, in order to avoid congestion.

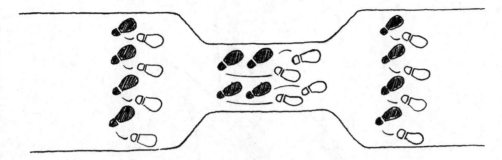

Figure 5.7 The speed of air in a laminar flow through a narrow passage. The footprints represent molecules.

of four, both before and after the narrow passage. Within the passage, there are also four molecules, but this time grouped into two rows of two because the passage is only half as wide in this part. Now consider the situation a moment later, as represented by the white footprints. The two rows of four molecules before and after the narrow passage have advanced by one step. Within the passage, the four molecules must have advanced as well, since there is no congestion in the steady stream. This means that the molecules within the passage, which are grouped into rows of two, must have advanced by *two* steps. In other words, a steady forward movement requires that the same number of molecules advance both before and after the narrow passage. But within the passage, the molecules *must* move faster. The speed of the air is therefore higher when it flows through a narrow passage than before or after it.

This phenomenon is relatively straightforward to explain and understand. It may seem a bit of a paradox, however, that the pressure is lower *within* the narrow passage than before or after. This is counterintuitive, for everybody knows from traffic congestion that the jam (and therefore the pressure) seems to be the highest within the narrow passage.

But this comparison does not hold. When observing the congestion in traffic going from, for example, two lanes to one lane and back again to two lanes, the congestion arises *before* the narrowing, and the jam is at its maximum *before* the narrow passage. *Within* the passage the traffic does move along, although the cars move slowly and are close together. After the narrow passage, the traffic is more spread out and moves fast. The situation is different in a laminar stream, since the density before, within, and after the narrow passage is the same, and the speed is higher *within* the passage than before or after. Thus, the experience that congestion arises in a narrow passage, and therefore the pressure within the passage must be at its highest, does not correspond to the behavior of air flowing through the narrow part of a tube. How can this be explained?

We already mentioned that the molecules move on average with a certain speed in one direction, although their movements are actually rather disordered. They move back and forth, left and right, up and down. Their speed and direction

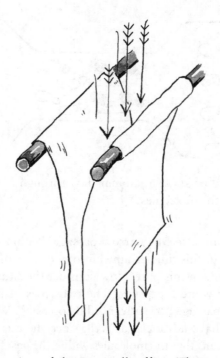

Figure 5.8   Demonstration of the Bernoulli effect. The two sheets of paper move toward each other when air is blown between them.

is only given by the sum of these movements. We compared this to a carnival procession moving through the streets: the individual participants walk freely about, they may even jump in the air, and still continue to move together in one direction. Some participants at the edges of the parade may accidentally bump into spectators; this is the pressure which they exert upon the borders of their path. In the same way, the air molecules bump against the walls of the tube, thus exerting a pressure on the inside of the tube. When the carnival procession moves faster, the individual participants have less time to move to the left or to the right, and therefore bump less often into spectators at the edges of the parade. Exactly the same happens to the airstream going through a narrow passage: the individual molecules move faster in one direction, and less often up and down or left and right. They therefore bump less often against the walls of the tube and the resulting force that they exert on the walls is lower. The air pressure is therefore lower *within* the narrow passage, where the molecules move faster forward, than before or behind it (or below and above the vocal folds). In other words, instead of *in*creasing the pressure, the narrow passage actually *de*creases the pressure of the air flowing through. This phenomenon is known as the Bernoulli effect. Since it is a characteristic of flowing air, it is called an **aerodynamic** effect. As a result of this relatively lower pressure in the passage between the vocal folds, the folds are sucked together instead of being forced apart.

A simple demonstration of the aerodynamic Bernoulli effect can be seen in Figure 5.8, where two sheets of paper are attached loosely to pencils and hang next to each other. If one blows in between, the two sheets of paper approach each other. This shows that the air pressure in the passage decreases as a result of the air flowing through at greater speed. The sheets are *not* forced apart, as is the case when the air pressure increases.

5.2.2.2   THE MYOELASTIC THEORY OF VOCAL FOLD VIBRATION

Using the aerodynamic Bernoulli effect to explain the behavior of the vibrating vocal folds was an important breakthrough toward understanding the mechanism responsible for vocal fold vibration. The application of the Bernoulli effect made it possible to explain why the vocal folds close so quickly, even though the air pressure from the lungs should push them apart. An aerodynamic account of vocal fold vibration thus involves the following: the vocal folds are initially closed; they are then blown apart by the subglottal air pressure, and, finally, sucked together because of the Bernoulli effect. Once they are closed, the cycle starts all over again. This account nevertheless has at least one shortcoming: under this view, the rate of vocal fold vibration depends on the speed of the flowing air – in other words, it depends on the relation between subglottal and supralaryngeal air pressure. Since the subglottal air pressure is relatively constant, the rate of vocal fold vibration should remain constant as well. However, this rate continuously changes during speech production. Additional mechanisms are therefore required to explain all aspects of vocal fold vibration.

A first, important, factor influencing the rate of vocal fold vibration is the *length* of the vocal folds: long vocal folds oscillate at a slower rate than short ones. This is comparable to string instruments: a cello, having longer strings than a violin, produces lower tones. And since the vocal folds of men are usually longer than those of women, male voices are usually lower than female voices. An example of the influence of the length of the vocal folds can be observed during puberty, when the length (and thickness, see below) of the vocal folds of boys change rather quickly. This leads to the so-called "voice mutation" during which the speaker has not yet learned to correctly control the changed anatomical structure.

A second factor determining the rate of vocal fold vibration is the *elasticity* of the vocal folds. Even without the Bernoulli effect, the vocal folds, after being opened, are pulled back together by their own elastic recoil force. This is comparable to a guitar string that swings by plucking it: once the string is moved away from its rest position, it returns to it due to the elastic recoil force and overshoots it to the other side – and so forth. This type of oscillation (without Bernoulli effect) occurs during vocal fold vibration when the folds are very tense and a speaker uses a very high-pitched *falsetto voice*.

In addition, the rate of vocal fold vibration depends on their elastic tension: tense folds oscillate faster than slack folds, because they are pulled back to the rest position with more force. The same is true of a guitar string: if the tension is increased, the string oscillates faster (that is, more often per time unit), thus producing a higher tone – this effect is actually used to tune a guitar. Vocal fold tension may be changed by a movement of the cricoid and the thyroid relative to each other caused by the cricothyroid muscles. The vocal folds become slightly longer (since the distance between the notch on the thyroid plates and the arytenoids increases), which causes a drop in frequency. However, the increase in tension predominates, so that the net result of this rotating movement of the two cartilages is a higher rate of oscillation. The fine adjustment of the oscillation rate during speech is essentially achieved by means of this mechanism.

A fourth factor influencing the rate of vocal fold vibration is their *mass*, which is linked to their "thickness." This too can be related to string instruments: keeping length and tension equal, a thick guitar string produces a lower tone than a thin string. In the same way, thick vocal folds oscillate at a lower rate than thin vocal folds. The thickness of that part of the vocal folds which participates in the vibration is to a certain extent determined by anatomical factors, but can additionally be adjusted by the muscular tissue of the vocal folds themselves. They can change their form from fleshy lips to thin bands, thus changing the rate at which they vibrate.

These four effects, relating the vibration of the muscular vocal folds to their length, elasticity, tension, and mass, are called **myoelastic** effects.

Our account of vocal fold vibration so far includes the following four factors:

1   The Bernoulli effect enables the vocal folds to close during normal oscillation. This aerodynamic effect depends on the speed of the airstream. As this speed increases, the pressure in the direction perpendicular to the airflow decreases. Since this speed in turn depends on the air pressure difference between the subglottal and supralaryngeal systems, the rate of vocal fold vibration is influenced by this difference in air pressure across the vocal folds.
2   Long vocal folds vibrate at a lower rate than short ones. Length differences between vocal folds are mostly determined by anatomical factors.
3   Vocal folds oscillate faster when they are tense than when they are relaxed. The tension of the vocal folds is determined primarily by the rotating, swing-like movement executed by the thyroid and the cricoid. This factor is used to fine-tune the rate of vibration in normal speech production.
4   Vocal folds with a large mass oscillate slower than thin vocal folds. The thickness of the vocal folds is partly determined by anatomical factors, but can additionally be adjusted by the muscles themselves.

Treating the vocal folds as an aerodynamic and myoelastic system provides a reasonable explication for the oscillation of the vocal folds and the changes in their oscillation rate. However, no fewer than three additional principles are needed in order to fully explain the actual oscillation characteristics (Broad 1973). Imagining the vocal folds as an elastic system submitted to the aerodynamic forces of the Bernoulli effect, they are comparable to a pair of swinging doors in a drafty corridor, as mentioned before: the draft causes them to swing back and forth, and the tension in the hinges as well as the mass and size of the doors determine the rate of their vibration. Such swinging doors in a drafty corridor could only close entirely if the tension of the springs in the hinges is very high; instead, both panels of the door move back and forth periodically, without ever fully closing the passage. But this is not the behavior of the vocal folds: when they are vibrating, the left and right vocal folds do touch each other for a relatively long time and over a relatively long distance. Swinging doors never do so. The next sections introduce additional effects to explain this difference.

5.2.2.3 TWO-MASS THEORY OF VOCAL FOLD VIBRATION

More recent research has shown that the vocal folds can only oscillate because they do not constitute an indivisible unit, unlike swinging doors; instead, the upper and lower parts of the vocal folds may execute separate, but related, movements. This can be seen in Figure 5.9: first, the lower parts of the vocal folds are forced open by the pressure from the lungs, but the upper parts still remain closed (Figure 5.9b). Only at a later stage are the upper parts opened as well (Figure 5.9d) – partly as a result of the air pressure, partly because they are pulled along by the tissue of the lower parts. As a result of the acceleration of their mass, the upper parts continue to move apart, but at the same time the lower parts are already

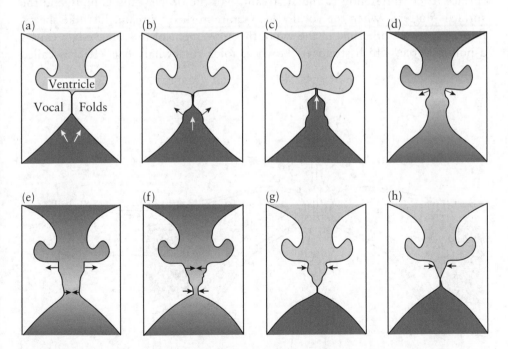

Figure 5.9 Different phases of vocal fold vibration, shown by means of simplified cross-sections of the larynx (see Section 5.2.2.5 for details). In each panel, the trachea is on the bottom, and the pharynx on the top.

starting to close again (Figure 5.9e). Somewhat later, the lower parts of the vocal folds are already entirely closed, but the upper parts are still in their closing stage (Figure 5.9g). Both the upper and lower parts of the vocal folds thus execute an opening and closing movement, but they are not in the same phase: the upper parts of the vocal folds follow behind the lower parts. It is precisely this lag between the movement of the upper and lower parts of the vocal folds that enables them to form a complete closure of the trachea. This principle is called the **two-mass theory** of vocal fold vibration (Ishizaka and Flanagan 1972). This does not mean that only two masses are involved; it can be any number, but two masses are the minimum to explain this behavior.

5.2.2.4 MUCO-VISCOSE, COVER BODY, AND FLOW-SEPARATION THEORY

The different mechanisms that have already been described explain the vocal fold vibration to a considerable extent. However, mathematical modeling has led to the insight that the aerodynamic and myoelastic effects occurring at the vocal folds, combined with the phase difference between two masses, cannot explain all the details of the vibration. Two additional characteristics have been identified. First, the outer edges of the vocal folds consist of many layers of different kinds of tissue, which together form viscous surfaces (see Figure 5.10). As a result, the surface reacts differently to the airstream than the deeper muscle body and the surface "flutters" when the vocal folds vibrate in the airstream. Just like sheets, fluttering on a clothesline in the wind, this movement of the outer edges causes a pulling force, which stretches the vocal folds somewhat. This effect is called

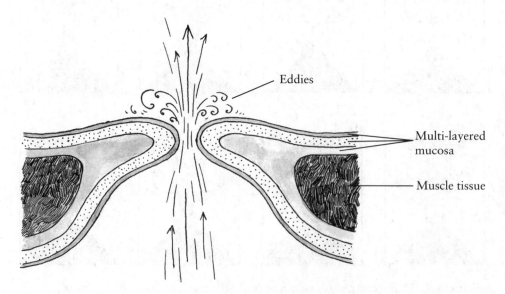

Figure 5.10   Close-up of the tips of the vocal folds showing the airflow through the glottis.

muco-viscose by Broad (1979), and is described by the **cover body** theory of Hirano (1974).

Second, the **flow-separation theory** (Ishizaka and Matsudaira 1968) states that the abrupt change of the airstream that occurs at the edges of the vocal folds leads to a certain amount of turbulence (so-called **eddies**). They are comparable to the eddies that can sometimes be observed in the fall at corners of a house, where fallen leaves start moving around in circles. These small whirlwinds influence the movements of the vocal folds by forcing the tips of the vocal folds apart (see Figure 5.10). Without these additional forces, the vocal folds would not be able to vibrate as they do.

5.2.2.5   ONE CYCLE OF VOCAL FOLD VIBRATION

To summarize, the following factors provide a complete account of vocal fold vibration:

1   The aerodynamic effect explains why the vocal folds are able to close as quickly during normal oscillation.
2   The myoelastic effect explains why the vocal folds can be forced open in the first place, and why they are able to oscillate even when the Bernoulli effect does not apply.
3   The two-mass theory explains why the vocal folds are able to achieve complete closure.
4   The muco-viscose and flow-separation theories explain the details of the oscillation characteristics of the vocal folds.

In sum, one cycle of vocal fold vibration can be described as follows (see Figure 5.9): initially, the vocal folds are fully closed by adducted arytenoids (a). The vocal folds are slightly tensioned by their own muscular force and the position of the cricoid relative to the thyroid. The pulmonic air pressure pushes the lower parts of the vocal folds apart while their upper parts are still together (b). When the vocal folds are forced to open at their upper end (c), air starts passing through them. This initiates the Bernoulli effect that pulls the folds together but the inertia of mass of the folds continues to open the upper parts (d). The Bernoulli effect together with the elastic recoil forces of the folds causes the lower parts to move together, while the upper parts are still moving apart as a result of the inertia of mass and their muco-viscose structure that pulls the peripheral parts of the folds apart supported by the eddies of the flow-separation (e). The lower parts of the vocal folds finally are almost together (f), which means that the Bernoulli force is particularly strong, pulling them firmly together. The upper parts are moving together as a result of the elastic recoil forces and the pulling forces of the lower parts (g). (Note that this cannot be the result of the Bernoulli effect, since the airflow has stopped.) Eventually, the upper parts close as well and the next cycle begins (h).

5.2.3   *Loudness and larynx signal*

The airstream coming from the lungs is interrupted repetitively at the vocal folds as a result of the mechanisms described above. The resulting laryngeal signal is the basis of all voiced sounds. In other words, it is a **source signal**, which is subsequently modified by the vocal tract, which filters parts of it similar to the way colored glass filters sunlight. The loudness of a speaker's voice depends, among other things, on the larynx signal. It can be increased in two ways: first, by widening the opening of the vocal folds, which increases the amount of air flowing through; second, by increasing the pressure of the airflow, so that more air molecules are pushed through the glottis during one glottal cycle. Most speakers probably choose the second option to become louder. These methods of increasing loudness have two main disadvantages. First, more air and energy are used up. And second, since more air flows through the vocal folds at a high level of pressure, the vocal folds are put under more strain, which dries them out more quickly, leading to a hoarse voice. But there is a more efficient way of increasing the loudness of speech.

The loudness of speech also depends on the vigor with which the vocal folds open and close. This can be compared to the action of a water tap to which a hose is connected. If the tap is slowly closed, the amount of water flowing through gradually becomes less, until the tap is completely closed. But if the water flow is abruptly interrupted (as some washing machines do), the hose executes a sudden movement. This movement is not determined by the quantity of water, but by the suddenness with which the water flow is changed, often changing faster

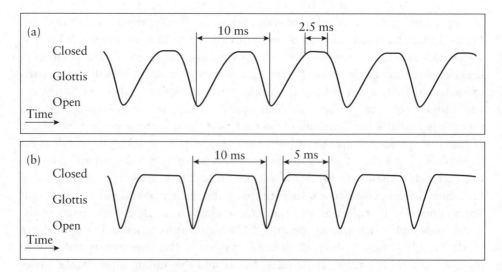

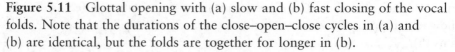

Figure 5.11   Glottal opening with (a) slow and (b) fast closing of the vocal folds. Note that the durations of the close–open–close cycles in (a) and (b) are identical, but the folds are together for longer in (b).

with stopping than starting. This is actually the case for the glottal signal: the largest peaks in the waveform of a speech signal are caused by the rapidly closing vocal folds, not by their (slower) opening. The vigor with which the vocal folds open and close during oscillation can influence the loudness of speech. The vigor of closing can be increased by stronger elastic forces of the vocal folds. This greater vigor of closing does not necessarily lead to more vibration cycles per second, since the folds can remain closed longer, which does not alter the time of one full closed–open–closed cycle (see Figure 5.11).

Thus, a higher speed of opening and closing of the vocal folds (not their *rate* of vibration) results in an increase in perceived loudness and seems to be used by trained speakers and singers. Their larynx signal therefore does not look like Figure 5.11a, but is similar to Figure 5.11b. As an additional result, the vocal folds are open for shorter periods. This means that less air (and therefore less energy) is needed, even though the loudness increases. This effect can be used unconsciously by speakers when they stress individual syllables of a word (Sluijter 1995). And, the amount of stress can be regulated much more finely by adjusting the speed of opening and closure of the vocal folds.

5.2.4 Register

The concept of **register** refers to different ways in which the vocal folds may vibrate. A large number of different and sometimes contradictory categorizations and descriptions have been proposed to cover this concept (see Laver 1980, pp. 93–95). In this book, we only describe three **types of phonation** which are relevant for speech production (see Section 6.2).

First, the "normal" vocal fold vibration is called the **chest register** or **modal voice**. This kind of vibration was described in the previous pages.

If the arytenoids are not fully adducted, the vocal folds do not close along their entire length during a glottal cycle and a narrow passage remains always open. This narrow passage leads to a fast airstream caused by the Bernoulli effect and a frication noise emerges at the glottis, giving the speech a rough and husky, or **breathy voice** quality. This voice quality can be speaker-specific or caused by a cold, but it is applied in some languages for certain speech sounds (see Section 6.2).

When the vocal folds are fully relaxed and thick they hang like two sacks against each other. In this state, the vocal folds do not really vibrate. Instead, air "bubbles" through the loosely adjoined vocal folds, producing a **creaky voice** with a very low rate of vibration (30–50 times per second). No Bernoulli effect occurs in this mode of vibration, since the vocal folds do not separate. This creaky voice occurs in some speakers and dialects more or less regularly at the end of voiced utterances, while some languages use it as part of their phonetic inventory.

To summarize, the vibration of the vocal folds can be described as a complex, three-dimensional movement. The vocal folds move apart in an undulating movement from bottom to top and from back to front, and close again from

bottom to top and from the middle to the back and front. The following parameters are essential for the vibration:

1   The arytenoids open and close the vocal folds, so that voiced and voiceless
    sounds can be produced during speech production. For the vocal folds to vibrate,
    they must be adducted.
2   The swing-like movement of the cricoid and the thyroid relative to each other
    changes the tension of the vocal folds. This makes it possible to adjust their
    rate of vibration quickly and accurately.
3   Changes in the mass and tension of the vocal folds lead to different types of
    vibration.

Babies' vocal folds vibrate (open and close) about 400 times per second, young
women's about 220 times, and young men's about 130 times. With age, the
vibration rate decreases for women, and increases for men, so that the gender
difference becomes less.

The movement of the vocal folds is rather complex, and this complexity is
important for the production of speech. The problem is that this complex signal
can be altered in loudness and pitch but it has only one sound *quality*: it is a
"snaring" sound that does not resemble the quality of any speech sound. Still,
this source signal produced at the vocal folds is the acoustic raw material for all
voiced sounds. Only because this raw material is so "rich" can it be subsequently
filtered, that is, specifically enhanced or dampened, by the supralaryngeal system,
and finally projected from the lips and/or from the nose. The anatomical properties of the vocal tract are treated in the next section.

5.3   Vocal Tract

The vocal tract can be roughly divided into the three parts: pharynx, nasal
tract, and oral tract (see Figure 2.1 on p. 10). Each of these can be divided into
several subdivisions, which are described in the next sections. The vocal tract has
many more bones, ligaments, and muscles than the lungs and the larynx, resulting in a long list of names that does not help to understand their function. Therefore,
we have included these details in compressed form to provide a reasonably complete picture of the structures involved in the production of speech.

5.3.1   *Pharynx*

The top of the larynx joins with the esophagus at the **laryngopharynx**, which
is the area above the larynx. An important structure here is the epiglottis (see

Section 5.2.1), which forms the upper part of the larynx. The most superior part of the epiglottis marks the upper end of the laryngopharynx where it becomes the **oropharynx**, which forms the back oral tract. The **nasopharynx**, finally, is the area above the velum, the posterior part of the nasal tract. In a way, the pharynx is a four-way crossing in the form of a stretched "X" where the passages from the nasal and oral tract join and then split into larynx and esophagus. All four passages can be open at the same time; the velum and back of the tongue can open the nasal and oral tract, and the epiglottis and the vocal folds can open the passage through the larynx into the trachea. The esophagus is open only during food swallowing. Swallowing is actually a complex process, especially because food has to be transported across the pharyngeal crossing from the oral tract into the esophagus. Normally, the passage from the nasal tract to the larynx is open for breathing. Transporting the food and closing the laryngeal passage is performed by three **constrictor muscles**, which lie around the pharynx (but leaving the oral tract open) and the three muscles palatopharyngeus, stylopharyngeus, and salpingopharyngeus, which form an internal, longitudinal layer of the pharynx. The latter three muscles raise the larynx and shorten the oropharynx during swallowing and speaking. This is particularly important for the production of the glottalic airstream (see Section 6.1.1) for certain stop consonants.

Lengthening the oropharynx automatically makes it narrower. This is accomplished either by pulling the tongue root back or by tensioning the constrictor muscles. The passage becomes so narrow that fricatives can be produced at this position. As mentioned in Section 4.1.4, few languages use these sounds but pharyngealization as secondary articulation is more common.

5.3.2   Nasal tract and velum

The upper part of the pharynx is formed by the nasopharynx, which merges into the nasal tract. This tract exhibits large individual differences in size and shape (Bjuggren and Fant 1965; Dang et al. 1994), is rather immobile, and can hardly serve to produce a sound by itself. But by being connected to or disconnected from the rest of the vocal tract by a lowered or raised velum, respectively, it can alter the acoustic properties of the speech signal considerably (see Section 10.2.4). Nasal sounds occur as nasal (stop) consonants (see Section 2.3.2), as nasal vowels (see Section 3.4.2.2), or as nasalized vowels (see Section 3.4.1.2).

The nasal tract is a bony structure covered by mucous lining. The **nasal septum** separates the pathway into two **nares**, which eventually emerge at the cartilaginous **nostrils** into the open air. The septum is often buckled, which leads to an asymmetry between the two nares. Posteriorly, the two tubes end as **choanae** into the nasopharynx. The posterior part of the nares is each divided into three channels (**meati**), which are separated by the bony **concha**. Most of the air streams to the lowest of these channels, which are separated by the inferior concha. This concha is covered by many layers that contain blood vessels. The covering mucosa of the concha can swell when they become infected, for example by a cold, which leads to the "stuffed nose." All surfaces are covered by mucous membranes, which are kept moist by several glands, which are partly located in several paired cavities that can resonate during the production of nasal sounds. One biological function of this twisted pathway is the warming of the inhaled air when we breathe. In a way, the nasal cavities form a sort of air-conditioning system that prevents dry, cold, hot, or dirty air from reaching the sensitive small alveoli pulmones. The nasal cavity is connected to the oral cavity but its highly dampened acoustic system does not allow much sound energy to be emitted from the nostrils.

The nasal tract can be connected to the oropharynx by lowering the velum (soft palate), which opens the **velopharyngeal port**. This movement of the velum cannot be compared to a simple "gate" that is lowered or raised. In fact, it is a complex process, as can be seen by looking in a mirror when producing alternating oral and nasal sounds (e.g. [a] and [ã]). The velum bulges forward, changes it thickness, and is raised (or lowered), usually in combination with the sidewalls of the oropharynx and the back of the tongue.

In sum, the size and shape of the nasal tract differ considerably between individuals, the passages can be narrowed by blood vessels or by swollen mucosa, and side cavities can be open or filled with phlegm. Additionally, the velopharyngeal port can be opened to different degrees by lowering the velum, which in turn affects the shape of the velum and pulls up the back of the tongue.

As mentioned earlier, speech sounds are commonly called *nasal* when the velum is lowered and air streams through the nose. Consequently, it seems simple to measure the airflow through the nose or to measure the opening of the velopharyngeal port to determine the amount of "nasality" in a speech signal. But a speaker with a blocked nose (either due to a cold or by closing the nostrils with the fingers) sounds extremely "nasal." This is a situation where there is no airflow through the nasal tract at all. Likewise, certain speech sounds sound *less* nasal than others even though their velopharyngeal port is *more* open than for more nasal-sounding speech (Maeda 1993, p. 156). Thus, a definition of "nasality" needs a somewhat different measure than the amount of opening of the nasal tract or the amount of nasal airflow.

A first modification is the consideration of the *relation* of airflow though the nasal and oral tract. If the oral tract is rather open, an airflow through the nasal tract has less impact than when the oral tract is more closed, simply because more sound energy is emitted from the oral tract in the former case. By computing the relation between nasal and oral airflow, the percentage of airflow through the nasal tract in relation to the oral airflow can give an estimate of the **nasalance** of a signal:

$$\% \text{ nasalance} = 100 \times \frac{\text{nasal airflow}}{\text{nasal airflow} + \text{oral airflow}}.$$

This explains why a low vowel, like the vowel [ɑ], can be produced with a reasonably large velopharyngeal opening and nasal airflow without sounding "nasal" (since the oral airflow is large) whereas a high vowel, like [i], can have a smaller oral opening and less nasal airflow, but sound more "nasal."

The second effect, that a blocked nasal passage leads to nasal-sounding speech, can be explained by taking the coupling of the nasal cavity to the oral pathway into account (see Section 10.2.4). The large nasal cavities alter the system of the resonating cavities of the vocal tract considerably, even when no air escapes from the nostrils. A certain amount of "sound energy" that is emitted from the larynx moves into the nasal cavity instead of leaving the vocal tract through the oral tract. Even when no air is emitted from the nasal cavity, the nasal cavity draws energy away from the sounds emitted through the oral tract, which together leads to a less oral and more nasal sound quality. In sum, it is the opening of the velopharyngeal port which causes speech to sound nasal, but it must be seen in relation to the overall configuration of the vocal tract. If the nasal pathway is not blocked, measuring the nasal airstream can be used to estimate the size of this opening and, hence, the nasality of a speech signal as long as the rest of the vocal tract is not changed. For example, measurement of the airstream of multiple productions of [i] can establish which is more nasal, but the airstream measures of an [i] cannot be easily compared with those of an [a].

5.3.3   Oral Tract

We introduced in Section 2.2 the active and passive articulators of the speaking apparatus. We now add some anatomical facts about the oral tract that contribute to the production of speech sounds.

The mouth with its lips is a very mobile three-dimensional muscular structure – at least 12, partly paired, muscles are involved in the shaping of the facial area around the mouth. We do not list the individual muscles and their activities but repeat the observation that lips can change their shape from more protruded, rounded lips to more spread lips. What should be kept in mind is that any lip gesture involves the coordination of several muscles, some of which are rather large. As a consequence, the movement of the lips can be slower than that of other muscles of the vocal tract involved in the production of speech, simply because a larger mass of tissue has to be moved.

The next important structure of the oral tract is the lower jaw (mandible), which performs a sliding-rotating movement at the **temporomandibular joint (TMJ)**. This joint is located in front of the ear lobes, as can be felt with the fingers while opening and closing the mouth. Doing so, it can be felt that the opening of the jaw is not simply a rotation at the joint but that the jaw moves forward and downward. Inside this joint sits the **articular disc**, which divides the joint into an upper part that performs mostly the gliding movements, and a lower part that performs the elevation of the joint.

Opening the mouth by lowering the jaw is mostly done by gravity: its own weight pulls the jaw down. This action is actively supported by the **suprahyoid muscles** above the hyoid bone and the **infrahyoid muscles** below the hyoid on each side of the cheek. As a consequence, the active opening of the jaw with these muscles may pull the larynx upwards because the hyoid muscles shorten to reduce the distance between jaw and larynx.

Closing of the mouth is mostly performed by the muscles **masseter, temporal,** and **lateral pterygoid**. The masseter, which reaches from the lowest part of the mandible to the chin, and the temporal, which stretches from the TMJ across the entire side of the skull, are sizable muscles on each side of the head: when closing the mouth firmly, their movements can be easily seen and felt. The asymmetry of large (and strong) muscles to close the mouth and gravity to open the mouth indicates the primary function of the jaw: to bite and crunch food. For the purpose of speech production, this asymmetry does not seem to play a role. That is, there is no difference in timing that can be related to the strength of the muscles for transitions from a closed articulatory position to an open one and for the other way round. Or, in other terms, in a C_1VC_2 sequence (i.e. any consonant followed by any vowel, which again is followed by any other consonant), the transition from C_1 to V (closed to open) is not longer than from V to C_2 (open to closed). This lack of asymmetry is due to another factor, which is that the opening and closing of the oral tract itself is mostly performed by the tongue, rather than by the jaw.

The tongue is the most important muscular system for speech production in the oral tract. The tongue is a very complex system of many muscles covered by a mucous membrane that act synergistically so that the impact of a single muscle can hardly be described on its own. Roughly speaking, there are two muscle groups: (a) the extrinsic muscles (**genio-, hyo-, stylo-,** and **palatoglossus**), and (b) the intrinsic muscles (**superior longitudinal** and **inferior longitudinal, transverse,** and **vertical**). Both sets of muscles exist in pairs at the left and right part of the tongue. Simplistically speaking, the extrinsic muscles are relatively large muscles that move the tongue by depressing and retracting it whereas the smaller intrinsic muscles change the shape of the tongue by curling the tip and sides of the tongue (longitudinal muscles), narrowing and elongating it (transverse), and flattening and broadening it (vertical).

One consequence of the different masses of the extrinsic and intrinsic muscles is the speed with which different parts of the tongue can be moved, with the tongue-tip being the fastest and the root the slowest. Consider the following example of the articulatory movements involved in producing an alveolar plosive at fast and slow speech rates. For fast speech, the tip of the tongue curls first slightly backwards and then moves forwards for the production of an alveolar plosive. In slow speech, the tip moves in a nearly straight line towards the alveolar ridge. This difference in articulatory movement has led to a discussion of a possible difference in motor planning for fast and slow speech (e.g. Payan and Perrier, 1997;

McClean, 2000), which has far-reaching consequences for the mental representation of speech. That is, if different motor-command sequences are needed for different speaking rates, then "speech" must be stored with great articulatory detail, including different motor commands for fast and slow speech. If different motor planning is not needed, it may be possible that "speech" could be stored in a more abstract form without specific articulatory details. Some researchers, for example, argue that the source for the different trajectories for fast and slow speech can be explained by different moved masses: the tip of the tongue is light and can be moved quickly while the body of the tongue is heavier. To reach the alveolar ridge, the tongue must move forwards and the tip must be raised. For slow speech, these activities are performed slowly so that body and tip move with the same speed to the target position. In fast speech, the lighter tip reaches its target position much faster (slightly curled backwards and up) than the more heavy tongue body that shifts the tongue tip in this (target) position slowly forward. In other words, the different trajectories are not a consequence of different motor activities but follow simply from the inertia of accelerated masses of the tongue. Whether there is a different articulatory planning for fast and slow speech or whether the different trajectories are simply a consequence of the involved moving masses has not yet been settled. But the investigation and interpretation of articulatory movements can have implications for models of how speech is stored and processed in the brain.

Similar to the nasal cavity, we should point out that the oral tract itself can differ considerably among speakers. The size of the oral cavity can vary between speakers and the hard palate can be flat or domed and differ noticeably in shape. Additionally, the mobility of the tongue is not the same for all speakers: some can easily make a groove in the middle, which is impossible for other people. This has consequences for how speech sounds are produced. What may be a "comfortable" position to produce a certain sound for one speaker, might be a very "unnatural" position for another person. Both may produce the same sound but may accomplish this with different articulatory positions.

In sum, seemingly simple articulations, like lowering the velum, may involve a complex interaction of muscular systems and can lead to rather complicated acoustic consequences. And what might be a "natural" articulation for one speaker can be a very difficult setting for another.

Having presented the physiology of the vocal apparatus, we now investigate its function for speech production. Similar to the presentation in this chapter of airstream, larynx, and vocal tract, we first treat different airstream mechanisms in Chapter 6. Chapter 9 focuses on the interaction between larynx and vocal tract, based on the concepts introduced in this chapter. To understand the effects of the larynx and vocal tract, we need more knowledge about acoustics, how acoustic effects can be measured, and the cause and consequences of resonance. Chapters 7 to 9 provide this knowledge before we return to a more detailed description of speech sounds.

Exercises

1   Describe the role played by the external intercostal muscles, internal intercostal muscles, diaphragm, and elastic recoil force during inspiration and expiration.
2   What role do the posterior and lateral cricoarytenoid muscles play in vocal fold vibration and the production of speech sounds?
3   Why are the vibrating string theory and the neurochronaxic theory inadequate explanations of vocal fold vibration?
4   What are the four factors that contribute to the myoelastic effect? How do these impact the rate of vocal fold vibration?
5   What are three different ways to increase loudness? Which is the most effective and why?

6 Airstream Mechanisms and Phonation Types

Now that the basics of the respiratory and laryngeal systems have been introduced, we can describe classes of speech sounds that involve these systems in a different way than English sounds do. In particular, some languages have sounds with non-pulmonic airstreams and some languages have additional types of phonation, expanding the sound inventory beyond sounds that are either voiced or voiceless.

6.1 Airstream Mechanisms

In the production of speech sounds, three basic airstream mechanisms are distinguished: **pulmonic airflow, glottalic airflow**, and **velaric airflow**. Pulmonic airflow, generated by the lungs, is basic to speech production. During regular breathing, inward (ingressive) and outward (egressive) airflow alternate (see Section 5.1.2). For the production of speech, the most common mode is an outward flow of air generated by the lungs, known as an egressive pulmonic airflow. Recall that an egressive airflow does not require muscular effort after inhaling: the elastic recoil forces will automatically operate to reduce the lung volume and, consequently, air will start to flow from the lungs to the air outside the vocal tract.

Oral stop consonants produced with an egressive pulmonic airstream are also known as plosives. However, stop and other obstruent consonants can also be produced with other airstream mechanisms. Typically in these cases, a constriction is formed in the oral cavity, as is the case for plosives, but the airstream is generated and modified in a different way. As we will see, the use of a glottalic airstream mechanism results in two additional types of obstruents while a third additional type involves the use of a velaric airstream mechanism. We now describe these mechanisms in more detail.

6.1.1 Glottalic airstream mechanisms

In the production of a glottalic airstream, the larynx is the energy source (and not the lungs). The glottis is closed, so that the air in the lungs remains below

Table 6.1 IPA symbols for non-pulmonic consonants: ejectives, voiced implosives, and clicks

Ejectives		Voiced implosives		Clicks	
[']	as in:				
[p']	bilabial	[ɓ]	bilabial	[ʘ]	bilabial
[t']	dental	[ɗ]	dental/alveolar	[ǀ]	dental/alveolar
				[ǃ]	(post)alveolar
				[ǂ]	palatoalveolar
				[ǁ]	alveolar lateral
[c']	palatal	[ʄ]	palatal		
[k']	velar	[ɠ]	velar		
[q']	uvular	[ʛ]	uvular		
[s']	alveolar fricative				

the glottis. The air in the vocal tract above the glottis now functions as a body of air that can be moved by either raising or lowering the larynx.

Raising of the larynx produces obstruents known as **ejectives**. In the production of an alveolar ejective stop, for example, the glottis is closed and a constriction is formed at the alveolar ridge. The larynx is raised like a piston, thereby compressing the air in between the larynx and the alveolar constriction. Retraction of the tongue root may further compress the air. This compressed air is then released by relaxing the alveolar constriction, resulting in an alveolar ejective stop [t'] (as shown in Table 6.1; ejectives are indicated by means of the diacritic ['] in addition to the symbol for the pulmonic obstruent). Ejectives thus are produced with an egressive glottalic airstream. After release of the alveolar constriction, the glottal constriction is released and vocal fold vibration resumes. Ejectives occur primarily in many African, Caucasian, and North, Central, and South American languages. Ejective fricatives and affricates have also been reported in several languages.

Lowering the larynx produces stops known as **implosives**. The initial stages are the same as for the production of ejectives: the glottis is closed and a constriction is formed in the oral cavity. Then, instead of raising the larynx as in the case of ejectives, the larynx is lowered. Since this increases the volume between the glottis and the constriction, Boyle's law predicts that the air pressure decreases, such that air is sucked into the mouth upon release of the oral constriction. This results in an ingressive glottalic airstream. However, it is quite difficult to maintain a tightly closed glottis while lowering it against the pressure of the air below the larynx. As a result, the larynx is usually lowered by allowing some air to leak through a glottis that is not entirely closed, which often leads to vocal fold vibration. Because of this leakage, the increase in volume does not really change the air pressure in the cavity between larynx and constriction very much.

Table 6.2 Voiced and voiceless implosives in Seereer-Siin (from McLaughlin 2005)

	Bilabial	Alveolar	Palatal
Voiced	[aɓira] 'he milked'	[adega] 'he cut'	[aʄaxa] 'he crunched'
Voiceless	[aɓ̥ira] 'they milked'	[ad̥ega] 'they cut'	[aʄ̥axa] 'they crunched'

Contrary to the term, then, implosives do not really involve an implosive action. Instead, the implosive sound quality arises from "the complex changes in the shape of the vocal tract and in the vibratory pattern of the vocal folds" (Ladefoged 2006, p. 117). Since the vocal folds are not tightly closed and vibrate as air leaks through, implosives are typically voiced. As shown in Table 6.1, the IPA symbol for voiced implosives consists of the addition of an extended hook (as in [ɗ], for example) to the symbol for the corresponding pulmonic stop ([d]). Notice that the current version of the IPA does not have a symbol for voiceless implosives. Instead, voiceless implosives can be indicated by the addition of the diacritic indicating voicelessness, [̥], as in [aɓ̥a] (alternatively, the extended hook can also be attached to the symbol for the voiceless plosive as in [ƥ]). Implosives are primarily found in languages of West Africa, with Seereer-Siin, a Niger-Congo language spoken in Senegal, contrasting voiced and voiceless implosives at three places of articulation, as shown in Table 6.2.

6.1.2 *Velaric airstream mechanism*

The velaric airstream mechanism is involved in the production of **clicks**. Clicks can be found in many of the languages spoken in Southern Africa. The velaric airstream is generated entirely within the oral cavity, which is why it is also known as an **oral airstream** mechanism. It always involves a complete posterior constriction, usually at the velum, although it can also be at the uvula. In addition to the posterior constriction, a more anterior constriction is formed as well, trapping a body of air between them. The tongue body is then lowered to increase the volume between the two constrictions. Upon release of the anterior constriction, outside air rushes in, yielding a click-like quality. Then, the posterior closure is released. The location of the anterior constriction determines the place of articulation of the click, and Table 6.1 shows the IPA symbols for clicks. Any articulatory activity in the posterior part of the oral cavity, as well as the exact location of the posterior constriction, provides what are known as click accompaniments (Ladefoged and Maddieson 1996). For example, a click may be accompanied by a posterior velar articulation and voicelessness, aspiration, or breathy voice (see Section 6.2 for a discussion of breathy voice). A dental click [ǀ] and each of these accompaniments would then be represented as [kǀ], [kǀʰ], and [gǀ], respectively.

Table 6.3　Taxonomy of the five different types of plosives based on source and direction of airflow

	Airflow source	Direction of flow	Airstream mechanism
Plosive	Lungs	Egressive	Pulmonic egressive
Nasal	Lungs	Egressive (through nasal cavity only)	Pulmonic egressive
Ejective	Glottis	Egressive	Glottalic egressive
Implosive	Glottis	Ingressive	Glottalic ingressive
Click	Tongue	Ingressive	Velaric ingressive

In addition, the velopharyngeal port may be open, providing a nasal accompaniment, as in [ŋǀ].

In sum, there are five kinds of stops that are distinguished in terms of the source and direction of the airflow, as shown in Table 6.3: plosives (or oral stops), nasals (or nasal stops), ejective stops, implosives, and clicks.

6.2　Phonation Types

The term phonation refers primarily to vocal fold vibration. Due to the complex laryngeal musculature discussed in Section 5.2, the vocal folds can be manipulated in many different ways. Moreover, there are more factors than simply the position of the vocal folds that determine a particular phonation type, including the shape and area of the glottal opening, the rate of airflow, and whether or not the vocal folds are vibrating. While there are many possible laryngeal settings, five of these settings are used distinctively across the world's languages. These five phonation types or states of the glottis are shown in Table 6.4.

Voice is produced with normal vibration along most or all of the length of the vocal folds. This is also known as *modal* voice. Modal voice, used in all languages of the world, is described in detail in Section 5.2.2. Briefly, the vocal folds are initially brought together in loose contact, and vocal fold vibration results from the combination of pulmonic airflow, which blows the folds apart, and elastic and aerodynamic forces that bring the folds back together.

Voicelessness refers to the absence of any vocal fold vibration. The vocal folds are sufficiently far apart to allow a non-turbulent (laminar) flow through the glottis. The opening of the glottis in the production of voiceless sounds is usually greater than for any other phonation type. It is similar to the glottal opening for normal breathing.

Table 6.4   Overview of different phonation types and their corresponding vocal fold position

	Position of the vocal folds	*Vocal fold vibration*
Voicelessness	Far apart	No
Whisper	Less far apart	No
Breathy voice	Slightly apart	Yes
Voice	Closely together	Yes
Creaky voice	Posteriorly: tightly together	No
	Anteriorly: slackly together	Yes

Whisper requires a closer approximation of the vocal folds. The vocal folds are partially adducted, with a posterior opening near the arytenoids. Passage of high airflow through this narrow opening produces turbulent noise. This noise becomes the sound source for whisper, exciting the resonances of the oral cavity. Because whisper requires high airflow, it is an inefficient way of speaking. A person who whispers a long sentence will run out of breath quite quickly. Whisper is produced without vocal fold vibration and is transcribed using a filled dot as a diacritic [̣], as in [ạ]. (Note that in older IPA transcriptions, the dot is used for retroflex sounds; see Section 4.1.2.) Distinctions that are typically signaled by means of the presence and absence of vocal fold vibration are not available. This can be tested easily: can your partner distinguish your whispered versions of minimal pairs such as *Sue* (with a voiceless fricative) and *zoo* (with a voiced fricative)? If so, it is probably because the whispered fricative in *Sue* is longer than that in *zoo*. Several South Asian and Native American languages do make a phonemic distinction between "normal" (modal) and whispered vowels.

Whispered vowels are also referred to as devoiced or voiceless vowels. Well-known examples of context-conditioned devoiced vowels are found in Japanese and Korean. In these languages, "devoiced," "voiceless," or "whispered" vowels occur in the context of voiceless obstruents. Specifically, high vowels become voiceless in between voiceless obstruents. For example, Japanese distinguishes [ki̥ka] 'vaporization' from [kiga] 'hunger.' However, it is not entirely clear whether the vowel is devoiced or deleted altogether and "filled in" by the listener on the basis of coarticulatory information in adjacent segments.

In the production of *breathy voice*, also known as murmur, the vocal folds are only slightly separated (see Section 5.2.4). They do vibrate but are never completely adducted. This incomplete glottal closure means that airflow from the lungs is never interrupted, providing sounds produced this way with a breathy or husky quality. This breathy quality can sometimes be heard in the production of intervocalic voiced [ɦ] in English words such as *ahead*. The diacritic for breathy voice consists of two dots under the "breathy" sound, as in [a̤]. Certain

South Asian languages distinguish modal voice from breathy voice. For example, Chanthaburi Khmer, spoken in southeastern Thailand, distinguishes clear (plain) and breathy vowels, as in [kat] 'cut' and [ka̤t] 'he, she.'

Finally, the production of *creaky voice*, also known as **laryngealization, glottalization, creak,** or **glottal or vocal fry** (see Section 5.2.4), requires the vocal folds to be tightly together along their posterior section. At the same time, the anterior portion of the folds is slack, resulting in low-frequency vibration. Creaky voice occurs when phonating at the lowest possible pitch and can often be observed at the very end of a long utterance. Creaky voice is transcribed using the diacritic [̰] as in [a̰]. Several South Asian and Central American languages distinguish creaky voice from modal voice. For example, Jalapa Mazatec, an Otomanguean language spoken in Mexico, has a three-way distinction between modal, breathy, and creaky voice, as in [já] 'tree,' [ja̤] 'he wears,' and [ja̰] 'he carries' (Kirk et al. 1993; the symbol [á] represents the vowel [a] spoken with a high tone; see Section 11.4.1).

6.3 Voicing, Voicelessness, and Aspiration in Plosives

Consider a vowel–plosive–vowel (VCV) sequence. A number of articulatory events play a major role in the production of plosives, including the formation of the oral constriction, the degree and duration of glottal aperture, the subsequent release of the oral constriction, and the onset of vocal fold vibration for the following vowel. The temporal relationships among these events largely determine the degree of voicing, voicelessness, and aspiration of the plosive. Three types of plosives can be distinguished in terms of the timing of these gestures: voiced plosives, voiceless plosives, and voiceless aspirated plosives. We will consider each in turn.

- **Voiced plosives.** Voicing is continuously present during the entire VCV sequence. That is, the vocal folds are vibrating during the initial vowel, throughout the consonantal closure and release, and during the second vowel. The vocal fold vibration only ceases if the closure duration is too long to keep up an airflow to maintain the vibration, but the vocal folds remain in the same position and vibration continues after the release. The voiced closure duration is typically short, and there is no delay between the release of the constriction and the onset of the following vowel (see Figure 6.1a). These plosives are also known as **fully voiced plosives.**
- **Voiceless plosives.** There is an absence of voicing during closure after the end of the initial vowel. The vocal fold vibration ceases, usually because the vocal folds separate or because they close completely and produce a glottal stop. However, at (or very shortly after) the release of the constriction, the vocal folds are back in their vibrating position and voicing resumes. The voiceless

closure duration is typically long, and there is little or no delay between the release of the constriction and the onset of the following vowel (see Figure 6.1b).
These plosives are also known as **voiceless unaspirated plosives** or **plain plosives**.

- **Voiceless aspirated plosives.** Again, there is an absence of voicing during
  closure. Just as in the case of voiceless unaspirated plosives, the vocal folds
  separate and vocal fold vibration ceases at the end of the vowel. However,
  in the production of aspirated plosives, the vocal folds are not together at
  the release of the constriction. Since the vocal folds are not yet back together
  when the closure is released, there is a period when air flows through the
  open glottis and through an unconstricted oral cavity. This unobstructed flow
  of air results in aspiration noise, similar to that in the production of [h].
  This period of aspiration is characteristic of voiceless aspirated stops. The
  voiceless closure duration is generally long, and there is a substantial delay
  between the release of the constriction and the onset of the following vowel
  (see Figure 6.1c).

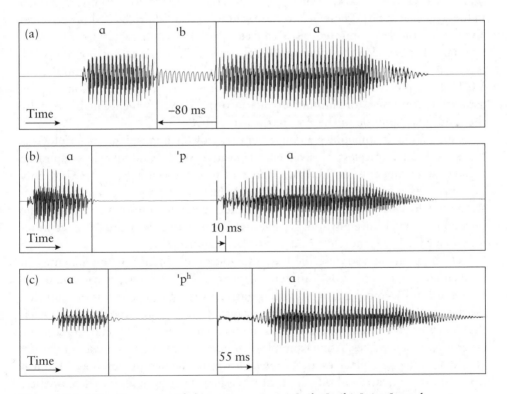

Figure 6.1   Oscillograms of the utterances (a) [ɑ'bɑ], (b) [ɑ'pɑ], and
(c) [ɑ'pʰɑ]. In each panel, the leftmost marker indicates the onset of the
consonantal closure portion and the rightmost marker shows the onset of
vocalic voicing. The middle markers in (b) and (c) indicate the release of
the consonantal constriction. VOT measurements are indicated below each
waveform.

The parameter **voice onset time (VOT)** is a convenient way of quantifying some of the voicing and aspiration patterns described above. VOT refers to the temporal interval between the release of the consonantal constriction and the onset of voicing, and is expressed in milliseconds (ms). VOT relates two articulatory gestures: an oral gesture, namely the release of the consonant, and a laryngeal gesture, namely the onset of vocal fold vibration. Although VOT was originally defined only for initial plosives (Lisker and Abramson 1964), we will use it for plosives more generally, as is current practice.[1]

In terms of VOT, for fully voiced plosives (see Figure 6.1a), the onset of voicing *precedes* the release of the consonant. By convention, this is represented with a negative value and it is said that the sound has "a negative VOT" or "lead VOT." For example, the VOT of the plosive in [aˈba] in Figure 6.1a is −80 ms. This interval is also known as a period of **prevoicing**, if it occurs in word-initial position. For voiceless unaspirated plosives (see Figure 6.1b), the release of the consonant and the onset of voicing occur nearly simultaneously (within approximately 20 ms of each other), so that these plosives have a VOT below 20 ms, as shown in the sequence [aˈpa]. These plosives are said to have a "short lag" (short positive) VOT. For voiceless aspirated plosives (see Figure 6.1c), characterized by a substantial delay between the consonantal release and the onset of voicing, the VOT is said to have a positive or "long lag" (long positive) VOT. For example, the VOT of the plosive in [aˈpʰa] shown in Figure 6.1c is 55 ms. Additionally, the aspiration continues for another 20 ms into the vowel, which can be seen by the reduced amplitude of the first part of the vowel.

In sum, VOT is sometimes a convenient way of distinguishing voiced plosives (negative VOT), voiceless plosives (short positive VOT), and voiceless aspirated plosives (long positive VOT). It is important to keep in mind that VOT is only one of a series of parameters that all contribute to the voicing and aspiration status of plosives. Most notably, VOT rarely provides information about the duration of the closure portion. Plosives with a negative VOT are the exception, in which case VOT and closure duration are identical.

VOT is often used to describe how the voicing distinction is implemented in a given language and across different languages. For example, many languages distinguish fully voiced plosives, with negative VOTs, from voiceless unaspirated plosives (with VOTs around 0 ms). However, phonological oppositions between the classes of voiced and voiceless consonants do not necessarily refer to the same criteria across languages. As an example, compare the way in which *phonologically* voiced and voiceless plosives are *phonetically* implemented in Dutch and English (for a short motivation about the difference between phonology and phonetics, see Chapter 3, page 24). In Dutch (and many other languages, including Spanish and French), the phonological voicing distinction is represented by the presence or absence of vocal fold vibration during the consonant closure (see Figures 6.2a and b). In contrast, when considering English plosives in word-initial position, the phonological voicing distinction is typically between voiceless unaspirated plosives, with a short positive VOT, and voiceless aspirated plosives, with a long

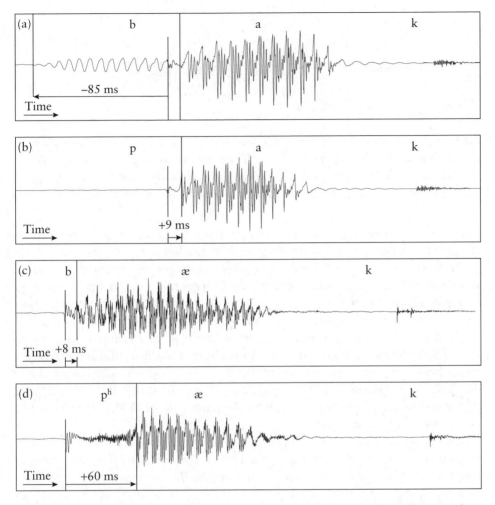

Figure 6.2 Oscillograms and VOT measurements for phonologically voiced and voiceless plosives in syllable-initial position for a male speaker of (a, b) Dutch and (c, d) English. In (a), three vertical markers are shown. The leftmost marker indicates the onset of consonantal voicing, the middle marker indicates the release of the constriction, and the rightmost marker shows the onset of vocalic voicing. In (b, c, d), the leftmost vertical marker indicates the release of the constriction while the right marker indicates the onset of vocalic voicing.

positive VOT (Figures 6.2c and d). Thus, while Dutch and English both have *phonologically* voiced and voiceless plosives, they differ in the way in which this distinction is *phonetically* implemented. Dutch does it in terms of the presence/absence of vocal fold vibration during the closure, while English does it in terms of the length of the VOT. In fact, a plosive with a short positive VOT would correspond to a voiceless plosive in Dutch but to a voiced plosive in English. This

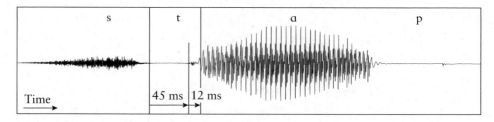

Figure 6.3 Oscillogram of the word *stop* spoken by an English speaker. The leftmost marker indicates the onset of the closure portion, the middle marker indicates the release of the constriction, and the rightmost marker shows the onset of vocalic voicing. Closure duration is 45 ms and VOT is 12 ms.

can often lead to voicing confusions in perception when native speakers of a language such as Dutch speak a language such as English.

There are contexts in English and other languages where there is a long, voiceless closure and a short (positive) VOT; typically in a fricative+oral stop sequence in word-initial position (e.g. *stop*; see Figure 6.3). If the transcription sticks to the presence or absence of voicing, this sound ought to be transcribed as [t]. If the transcription uses the length of the VOT as a criterion to separate voiced and voiceless plosives, then the transcription of this sound should be [d]. Nevertheless, even in these cases the transcription is [t] since the long closure duration leads to the perception of a "voiceless" sound. In a way, listeners compute the "voicelessness" from both the closure duration and the VOT in the signal and do not use only one criterion.

Some languages have a three-way distinction between fully voiced, voiceless unaspirated, and voiceless aspirated plosives, as illustrated by the Thai minimal triplet [dam] 'black,' [tam] 'to pound,' and [tʰam] 'to do' (see Figure 6.4a–c). Korean also has a three-way distinction but it is different from that in Thai. Korean distinguishes what are called lax, aspirated, and tense (or reinforced) plosives (see Figure 6.4d–f). This distinction occurs at the bilabial, alveolar, palatal, and velar places of articulation. The voiceless lax plosives [p, t, c, k] exhibit a moderate to strong degree of aspiration, with VOT values ranging from 20 to 70 ms in word-initial position. The aspirated plosives [pʰ, tʰ, cʰ, kʰ] are always voiceless and strongly aspirated, with VOT values that range from 70 to 140 ms. Finally, the tense or reinforced plosives [p*, t*, c*, k*] are voiceless and unaspirated, with a short VOT ranging from 5 to 25 ms. These plosives are produced with a greater degree of muscle activity and build-up of pressure than the lax plosives (see Cho et al. 2002, for details). The greater laryngeal tension often lends a laryngealized tense quality to the following vowel. Notice also that the aspirated and tense consonants have substantially longer closure durations than the plain consonants.

There are two additional types of plosives for which VOT is not a very insightful measure:

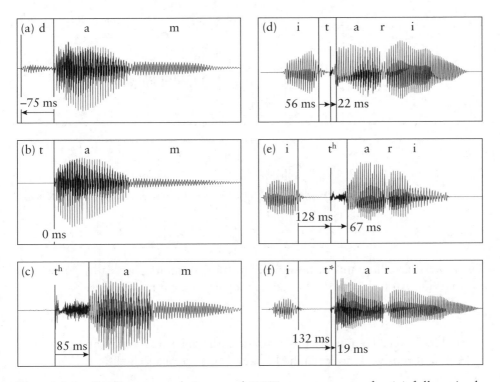

Figure 6.4 Oscillograms, closure, and VOT measurements for (a) fully voiced, (b) voiceless unaspirated, and (c) voiceless aspirated plosives in Thai, and for (d) lax, (e) aspirated, and (f) tense plosives in Korean.

- **Voiced aspirated plosives.** The vocal folds are vibrating during the initial part of the closure portion, just as in the case of the voiced plosives. When the constriction is released, the vocal folds then start vibrating in a slack manner while allowing a high rate of airflow through the glottis. As a result, the vowel consists of a mixture of voicing and aspiration, as in the case of a breathy voiced vowel (see Figure 6.5a). The voiced aspirated plosive is transcribed by a diacritic that is the voiced counterpart of the diacritic for (voiceless) aspiration, [ʰ], as in [ɑˈbʱɑ]. Unfortunately, VOT is not a very useful parameter in the description of voiced aspirated plosives since their distinctive characteristic is the combination of voicing and aspiration, which cannot be captured by a temporal measure.[2]
- **Voiceless pre-aspirated plosives.** Pre-aspiration occurs in sequences in which a vowel is followed by a voiceless plosive and refers to the early offset of vocalic voicing in anticipation of the voicelessness of the final plosive. A measure to describe pre-aspirated plosives is known as **voice offset time**. It refers to the interval between the offset of vocalic voicing and the onset of the silent interval related to the closure of the final plosive (see Figure 6.5b). Pre-aspirated plosives occur in several Northern European languages, including Finnish, Gaelic,

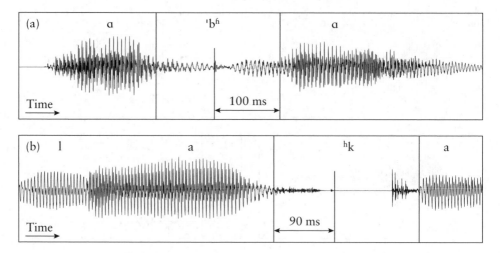

Figure 6.5 Oscillograms of (a) Bengali [ɑˈbʰɑ] containing a breathy voiced plosive, and (b) Icelandic [ˈlaʰka] containing a pre-aspirated plosive.

and Icelandic. To indicate pre-aspiration, the diacritic for aspiration precedes the final plosive as in Icelandic [ˈlaʰke] 'brine' versus [ˈlage] 'to make.'

Bengali is an example of a language that uses aspiration as an additional way to separate plosives. Bengali has fully voiced (negative VOT) and voiceless (positive VOT) plosives, with short (singleton) and long (geminate) closure durations, with and without aspiration. Nearly all these modes can be combined and give a total of eight different plosives for most places of articulation. With plosives at four places of articulation, West-Bengali has 32 different plosives (see Table 6.5).

6.4   Common and Rare Sounds

In this chapter, as well as in Chapters 3 and 4, a great variety of speech sounds has been introduced. The IPA consonantal chart includes a total of 83 symbols, representing 59 pulmonic, 14 non-pulmonic, and 10 "other" consonants. It is important to realize that this is a total inventory across the languages of the world documented so far. No single language will have all, or even most, of these phonemes in its inventory. To provide a perspective on the probability of encountering a particular phoneme, UPSID (UCLA Phonetic Segment Inventory Database, 1984) is a valuable source of information. The most detailed description and analysis of UPSID can be found in Ian Maddieson's 1984 book *Patterns of Sounds*. At the time of the book's publication, UPSID contained information about 317 languages.[3] These languages were sampled using genetic criteria, such that only

Table 6.5 Plosives in Bengali. Bengali uses aspiration, length, and voicing to distinguish plosives at four places of articulation

| Aspiration | Length | Plosives (voiceless/voiced) | | | |
		Bilabial	Dental	Retroflex	Velar
Unaspirated	Singleton	p / b	t̪ / d̪	ʈ / ɖ	k / g
	Geminate	pː / bː	t̪ː / d̪ː	ʈː / ɖː	kː / gː
Aspirated	Singleton	pʰ / bʱ	t̪ʰ / d̪ʱ	ʈʰ / ɖʱ	kʰ / gʱ
	Geminate	pʰː / bʱː	t̪ʰː / d̪ʱː	ʈʰː / ɖʱː	kʰː / gʱː

one language from each family grouping was included. This information is based on reference grammars, and, for a few languages, on phonetic fieldwork.

The modal consonant inventory – that is, those consonants that occur most frequently in this database – is shown in Table 6.6.

This table provides a sense of the common consonants. English has quite a few of them and lacks only the postalveolar nasal and glottal plosive. Ejectives, implosives, and clicks are not among the most common consonants of the world's languages. In terms of plosives, 92 percent of the languages in UPSID have plain voiceless plosives, 67 percent plain voiced plosives, 29 percent voiceless aspirated plosives, 16 percent voiceless ejectives, and 11 percent voiced implosives, followed by a smattering of other types. The most common places of articulation for plosives are bilabial, dental/alveolar, and velar (all around 99 percent), followed by postalveolar (19 percent) and uvular (15 percent). Of the languages in UPSID, 93 percent have one or more fricatives, most likely a form of /s/, which is present in 84 percent of the languages, followed by /ʃ/ (46 percent) and /f/ (43 percent).

Maddieson's book contains a wealth of information for people who are interested in a detailed analysis of these sound patterns. While Table 6.6 shows which

Table 6.6 The most frequently occurring consonants in UPSID (after Maddieson 1984)

	(Bi)labial	Dental/ alveolar	Postalveolar/ palatal	Velar	Glottal
Plosive	p b	t d		k g	ʔ
Nasal	m	n		ŋ	
Fricative	f	s	ʃ		ɦ
Affricate			t͡ʃ		
Approximant		ɹ, l	j	w	

consonants are most common across the world's languages, the chance of these sounds occurring in a given language varies as a function of the language family. For example, while /s/ is one of the 20 most common consonants and occurs in 84 percent of the UPSID languages, the vast majority of Australian languages do not have any fricatives at all. Finally, it is important to emphasize that UPSID tabulates the frequencies of phonemes, not sounds. That is, while many of the sounds of the world's languages do not occur in English *contrastively* (e.g. nasal or creaky-voiced vowels), they do occur quite frequently in the language.

This chapter concludes our introduction to the articulation and transcription of speech sounds. While the initial focus was on English, subsequent chapters surveyed additional places and manners of articulation as well as phonation types and airstream mechanisms to illustrate the richness of sounds found across the world's languages. The next chapters of the book will introduce basic concepts in acoustics and hearing to set the stage for a discussion of the acoustics and perception of speech.

Exercises

1 What two types of stops are produced using a glottalic airstream? Describe how each is produced.
2 What type of stop is produced using velaric airstream? How are these stops produced and how is their place of articulation determined?
3 Briefly describe the following phonation types: voice, voicelessness, whisper, breathy voice, and creaky voice.
4 Why do voiced stops have a shorter closure duration than voiceless stops?
5 Explain how VOT measurements can distinguish fully voiced, voiceless unaspirated, and voiceless aspirated stops. Use examples to illustrate your answer.

Notes

1 Mikuteit and Reetz (2007) suggested the more generally applicable terms ACT (After Closure Time) and SA (Superimposed Aspiration) that capture a wider range of plosives. While it is as yet unclear whether this terminology will be adopted by the scientific community, we stick to the traditional term VOT in this book, although it is not entirely appropriate for non-inital plosives, and does not cover aspiration in all cases.
2 Again, the ACT and SA terminology mentioned before captures these cases.
3 The web page for this book provides a link to this database.

7 Basic Acoustics

We have described speech sounds in terms of the way they are produced and how they can be transcribed by phonetic symbols on paper, and we have described in detail the organs and mechanisms by which they are produced. Eventually, all these activities lead to the production of speech *sounds*. The science to describe sound is known as acoustics. This chapter describes the basic concepts of acoustics, focusing on sound waves. It introduces the concepts of *frequency*, *amplitude*, and *phase*, and ways of measuring and representing them.

7.1 Sound Waves

Sound waves are the means of acoustic energy transmission between a sound source, such as a human speaker or loudspeaker, and a sound receiver, such as a human listener or microphone. The next section describes what sound waves are, how they arise, and how they spread.

7.1.1 Sound waves are variations in air pressure

Sound waves are small differences in air pressure which diffuse in all directions. Air pressure is a familiar concept from weather forecasts, where it indicates the presence of areas with high or low atmospheric pressure (the H and L on the maps of weather reports) measured, for example, in hectopascals (hPa), millibars (mb), millimeters of mercury (Torr), or inches of mercury (insHg), where the average air pressure of 1,013 hPa corresponds to 1,013 mb, 760 Torr, or 29.92 insHg.[1]

Atmospheric air pressure and sound waves are essentially the same. Whereas changes in atmospheric air pressure may take hours or days, the changes in air pressure caused by sound waves take place many hundreds or thousands of times per second. Atmospheric air pressure variations occur at levels in the range of ±50 hPa (= 5,000 Pa) around 1,013 hPa. Sound waves perceived by the human ear consist of fluctuations in air pressure ranging from 20 μPa to 20 Pa (for normal speech signals, they range from 600 μPa to 2 Pa). Finally, atmospheric air pressure remains stable across many kilometers and miles, but the pressure in a sound wave only varies within a few meters or centimeters (i.e. a few feet or inches).

Variations in air pressure, as caused by sound waves, are always added to the current atmospheric air pressure. Suppose, for instance, that the atmospheric air pressure is 1,010 hPa (= 101,000 Pa), and that the sound pressure, that is, the range of the oscillations in the sound wave, is eight millipascal (8 mPa = 0.008 Pa). The air pressure in the sound wave oscillates then between 100,999.996 Pa and 101,000.004 Pa. When looking at the air pressure variations caused by the sound waves, the sizable meteorological air pressure is ignored, because the sound waves oscillate fast around the nearly static meteorological air pressure, and we have a variation of the air pressure by ±4 mPa.

7.1.2   *Origin and propagation of sound waves*

Imagine a closed space filled with air, for example a living room. The air molecules in this room can be represented by a large number of dots, distributed at random on a sheet of paper (see Figure 7.1a). On paper, the dots do not move, of course, but the actual air molecules do. The air molecules inside the room are constantly moving around, bumping into each other and rebouncing – many million times each second. The general result is an average air pressure. This air pressure can be affected in two ways. If the room becomes smaller but the number of air molecules stays the same, then the pressure increases because the molecules have to squeeze into a smaller volume. Likewise, if the same number of dots were to be displayed on a smaller piece of paper, the density of the dots would increase. Alternatively, the air pressure increases when more air molecules are present in the same space (see Figure 7.1b). That is, increasing the number of dots on a page increases their density. Both instances illustrate Boyle's Law (see Section 5.1.1), which states that pressure and volume are inversely related for a given temperature.

Now imagine an empty balloon in the center of the room (see Figure 7.1c). As this balloon is inflated with air from a gasholder, it starts to occupy a certain amount of space, pushing air molecules out of its way. Since air is elastic, the molecules that are pushed aside move to neighboring regions, thus increasing the air pressure at their new location (see Figure 7.1d), although in the rest of the room the air pressure is still the same as before. This in turn causes air molecules to move from this region with higher pressure to the surrounding space, where the pressure is lower (see Figure 7.1e). Very quickly, this results in an increase of air pressure further and further away from the balloon, although the balloon itself has never been at that particular position.

If the air is now released from the balloon (see Figure 7.1f), an empty space emerges which does not contain any air molecules (as it was occupied by the balloon). The molecules from the surrounding area hurry to occupy this space. Thus,

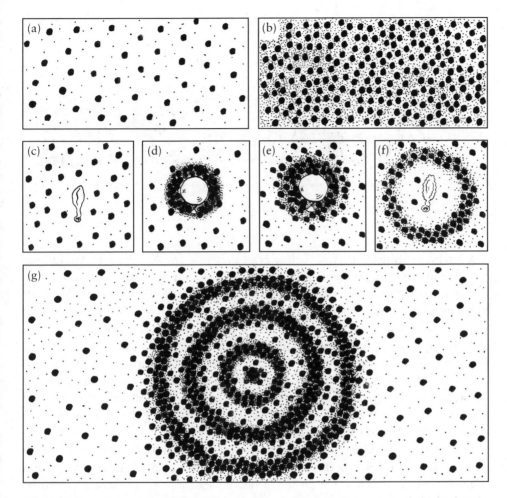

Figure 7.1 Air molecules in a room with (a) low air pressure and (b) high air pressure. Inflating and deflating a balloon in very rapid succession could lead to a pressure wave (c–g).

just like the high-pressure area, a decrease in pressure spreads through the whole room. If the balloon is inflated and deflated repeatedly, then the air molecules are moving back and forth all the time, each time the balloon is inflated and deflated (see Figure 7.1g). These oscillations in air pressure not only occur next to the balloon, but also further away, as illustrated above.

The oscillation of air molecules is comparable to a traditional German type of party behavior called *schunkeln* ['ʃʊŋkl̩n], which consists of people lining up and rhythmically swaying from left to right while singing songs (see Figure 7.2). If the first person bends sideways to the right, his right neighbor does the same thing a few moments later, followed by the next right neighbor, and so on. After a while, the first person bends back to the left, followed by the second, the third, and so on.

Figure 7.2 Party guests swaying from left to right.

The participants do not leave their places; they just sway to the right and to the left. But the swaying movement itself spreads through the whole line of people.

This activity has other characteristics in common with the movement of air molecules in a sound wave. For example, the participants may choose to sway only across a small distance, just as if the balloon is inflated and deflated only slightly, and individual air molecules may only move across small distances. But the partygoers may decide to bend further aside, just as if the balloon is inflated more, and the air molecules may be forced to move across longer distances. In addition, people may sway rapidly or slowly, independent of how far they bend sideways. In the same way, the movements of the air molecules may be rapid or slow, independent of the range of their movement.

But there is a correlation between the distance covered by the oscillating movement of the molecules, and their own speed:[2] in order to move further away within a given time, a molecule has to move faster, since a longer distance has to be covered in the same time span. The speed of the oscillating molecule therefore depends on the distance covered. This correlation is important when calculating the "energy" of a speech signal, as is done in Section 7.3.2.

In sum, we have discussed three independent characteristics of sound waves: the differences in air pressure spread much further than the range of movement of a single molecule, this range may differ in magnitude, and the rate of change may differ.

7.1.3 The Speed of Sound

The dispersion of the movement of the air molecules (in other words, the propagation of the sound wave) takes time: one molecule bumps into its neighbor, which then bumps into its neighbor, and so forth. And as for anything moving across a distance over time, its speed can be calculated. This speed of sound is a third characteristic that can be measured, in addition to the size and rate of the air pressure differences.

Speed is measured according to physical standards in meters per second, and calculated by dividing the distance traveled by the time needed to do so:

$$\text{speed} \left[\frac{\text{m}}{\text{s}} \right] = \frac{\text{distance [m]}}{\text{time [s]}}.$$

It is important to remember that the speed of the spreading sound wave is not the same as the speed of the molecules themselves, which is related to the rate of their oscillating movement (the number of movements of the molecules to and from their rest position). In fact, the traveling speed of a sound wave depends only on the property of the medium (air, gas, or solid matter) and is entirely independent of the property of the wave (size and rate of the molecules' oscillation).

The sound wave thus consists of air pressure variations. The speed at which these air pressure variations spread through a space is called the **speed of sound**. The speed of sound depends on the density and the elasticity of the medium (usually air), and is around 344 m/s ($\approx$ 1,238 km/h or 770 mph) in dry air of 21 °C ($\approx$ 70 °F).[3] The term "breaking the sound barrier" is used for exceeding this particular speed. The speed of sound through a gas increases with an increase in temperature (since molecules move faster at higher temperatures) and when the molecules are lighter (since lighter molecules are easier to move, and therefore faster), but it is independent of the air pressure.

7.1.4 *Relative positions within a sound wave*

Since it takes time for a sound wave to move from one place to another, two different points in a room through which a sound moves need not have the same air pressure at the same time. To understand why, remember the swaying example: at any moment some persons are close together (see Figures 7.2 and 7.3, point A), while others are further apart (see Figures 7.2 and 7.3, point B). This means that the pressure at point A is higher (more persons per unit of space) than at point B (fewer persons per unit of space). The difference between two particular states in the same sound wave is called **phase**.

While we do not consciously hear the phase difference of sound waves – after all, we can only be in one place at one time – our ear does perceive the phase information of sound waves. Although we are in one place, our two ears are separated in space. The distance between the left and right ear can be treated as the distance between points A and B in Figure 7.3. The brain can analyze this phase difference between the signal as received by each ear. This information helps to determine the direction from which a sound arrives.

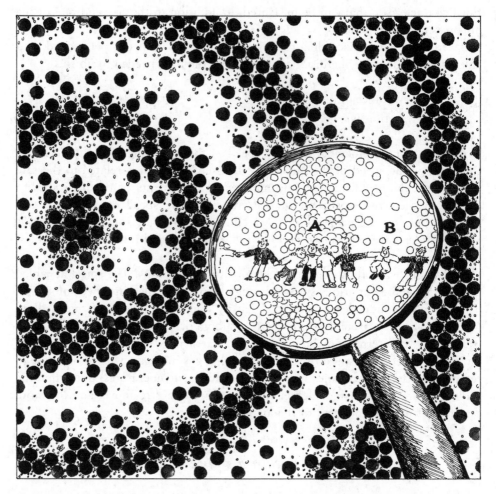

Figure 7.3 The air pressure in a sound wave is higher at point A than at point B.

7.1.5 *Longitudinal waves and transverse waves*

The sound waves just described belong to the group of **longitudinal waves**. In this type of wave, the direction in which the molecules oscillate is the same as the direction of the wave itself. This is clearly demonstrated by the swaying example (see Figures 7.2 and 7.3): the participants move horizontally to the right and to the left, and the wave travels horizontally in the same direction. Another type of wave exists, in which the direction of movement of the individual molecules is perpendicular to the direction in which the wave itself travels. Such waves are known as **transverse waves**. An example is the so-called *La Ola* or Mexican wave, which is sometimes practiced by spectators at sporting events (see Figure 7.4). In this type of wave, one person stands up and lifts his arms. One moment later, his

Figure 7.4 The *La Ola* (*or Mexican*) *wave* as an example of a transverse wave, where participants stand up and sit down one after another.

neighbor stands up to lift his arms, followed by the next neighbor, and so on. In the meantime, the first person sits down again, followed by the second, the third, and so on. As a result, each person moves *vertically* up and down, but the wave itself moves *horizontally*, that is, perpendicular to the movement of its participants. Transverse waves play an important role in the internal ear, where sound waves are transformed into neural impulses (see Section 12.3.5).

Now that we have presented the principles of the propagation of sound waves, the next question is: how can sound waves be measured? In acoustic phonetics, we want to describe and analyze speech signals, which, physically speaking, are sound waves.

7.2   Measuring Sound Waves

Sound waves are small, fast radiating air pressure variations. To investigate such waves, they need to be measured. A well-known device to convert variations in air pressure to an electrical signal is the microphone (see Section 7.2.1). Once an acoustic signal is registered with a microphone, it may be graphically represented in an *oscillogram* (see Sections 1.1 and 7.2.2).

7.2.1   *The microphone*

A **microphone** transforms air pressure variations of a sound wave into electrical signals, which are then available for further processing. In principle, a microphone consists of a membrane stretched over a closed compartment which is almost airtight (see Figure 7.5a). As such, it is essentially built like a drum. When a sound

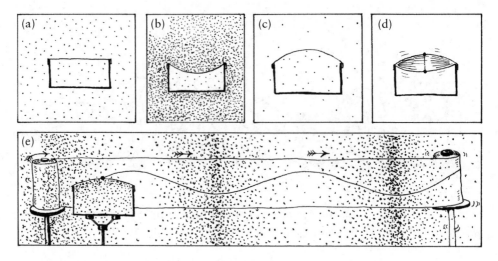

Figure 7.5 The principle of a microphone (see text for details).

wave – that is, a succession of areas with higher and lower air pressure – reaches a microphone, its membrane is forced inwards or outwards, because the air pressure inside the closed compartment behind the membrane remains stable. If the air pressure outside is higher, the membrane moves inwards (see Figure 7.5b); if it is lower, the membrane moves outwards (see Figure 7.5c). How can these variations be measured? If a small pencil were attached to the center of the membrane, for example, and a sheet of paper were next to it, the up and down movement of membrane and pen would draw a line on the paper (see Figure 7.5d). The further the membrane moves away from its rest position, the longer the line would be. In other words, the length of the line would correspond to the maximum size of the air pressure variations.

As the membrane moves back and forth, the pencil would draw a single line. This would be an important shortcoming of such a drawing device: it could only show the *size* of the deviation from the rest position, and not register *when* a particular deviation had occurred. But by moving the paper along with constant speed, the pencil draws a continuous line on the paper (see Figure 7.5e). This line now not only shows the size of the air pressure variations, but makes it possible to determine at which moment a specific air pressure occurred.

Of course, a microphone does not use paper and pencil to record the movements of its membrane. Instead, the movements generate small electrical signals. These electrical signals are amplified, and can then be registered by means of a flash or hard disk recorder, computer, or any other recording device. The electrical signals are transformed back into sound waves, and thus made audible again, by means of a playback device, connected to an electronic amplifier and speakers or headphones.

The closed compartment under the microphone membrane should not be completely airtight, because otherwise the membrane would undergo the influence of atmospheric air pressure differences. Atmospheric air pressure variations (±5,000 Pa) are very large compared to the air pressure variations of sound waves (max. ±20 Pa). This means that any change in the atmospheric air pressure would have a considerable effect on the microphone membrane. Therefore, the compartment under the membrane contains a very small hole, which allows the air pressure in the compartment to adjust to the large but slow atmospheric air pressure changes. During the very fast air pressure variations of a sound wave, almost no air molecules have a chance to pass through this narrow hole. Thus, for the purpose of the sound wave, the air pressure in the closed compartment remains practically constant. A comparable mechanism can be found in the human ear, as is described in Section 12.2.3.

7.2.2   *The oscillogram*

The electrical signals generated by a microphone can be represented in a graph. The resulting image is comparable to the drawing of the pencil attached to the membrane (see Figure 7.5e). This type of representation, where the sound pressure is plotted vertically against a horizontal time axis, is called an oscillogram or **waveform** (see Figure 7.6). In an oscillogram, acoustic events can be *seen* which normally are only *heard*.

Oscillograms are a way of graphically representing the acoustic signal. Although an oscillogram is a faithful representation of the air pressure variations in a sound wave, further phonetic analyses and representations are needed to isolate important characteristics of a signal. These methods are the subject of Section 8.3. In the remainder of this section, we describe which parameters can be read directly from an oscillogram.

The possibility of registering sound waves and seeing them represented in an oscillogram is very important for the study of phonetics. A sound, such as an act of speaking, is temporary by nature and only exists during the act itself. Once a sound wave has been generated, it spreads and gradually disappears. Before Edison invented the phonograph in 1877, phonetic researchers could only listen once to a particular utterance or try to repeat the same utterance as closely as possible. However, two separate repetitions of a single utterance are never exactly the same.

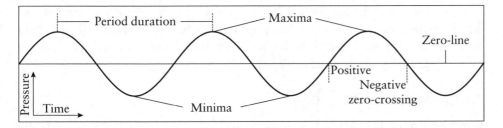

Figure 7.6   An oscillogram of a simple, symmetrical signal.

One had to "be there," attending a concert or a public speech, in order to hear a particular singer, orchestra, or speaker. However, sound recording makes it possible to play the same acoustic event over and over again, reproduce it, and store it.

Even when an acoustic event is recorded, it only exists temporarily each time it is reproduced. Unlike an image, which can be observed and studied for as long as necessary, an acoustic event disappears in time. An oscillogram is a graphical representation of an acoustic event that can be watched like an image. The possibility of graphically representing speech has enabled certain phonetic investigations that are not possible by listening to the transient sound signal.

7.3   Acoustic Dimensions and their Units of Measurement

This section introduces the principal dimensions used to define acoustic signals, which are *frequency*, *amplitude*, and *phase*, with their respective units of measurement *hertz*, *decibel*, and *degree*.[4] In Section 7.1, in which the basic concepts of acoustics were introduced, we already saw that sound waves are characterized by:

1 the rate of the changes in air pressure;
2 the magnitude of these changes;
3 the relative position of points within a sound wave or between sound waves (i.e. the phase);
4 the speed at which a sound wave travels.

These characteristics are treated in more detail in the following sections.

7.3.1   *Frequency*

On an oscillogram, the points with minimum or maximum air pressure have the largest deviation from the middle value (zero-line), which represents the average air pressure (see Figure 7.6). Whether a deviation from atmospheric air pressure in an oscillogram is drawn upward or downward is arbitrary since the same sound wave produces two mirror images depending on whether the microphone is held up or down in a given location. We will represent an air pressure maximum in an oscillogram by an upward deviation.

7.3.1.1   PERIOD DURATION

Consider the oscillogram in Figure 7.6, where the distance between two maxima can be easily measured. The horizontal axis represents time. If the oscillogram is a periodic wave – that is, if the same air pressure changes occur repeatedly over and over again (like the oscillation of a pendulum) – the interval between two maxima is called the **period**.

It is not really necessary to take the distance between two maxima in order to measure a period duration. It works just as well with two minima, or two positive or two negative zero-crossings, that is, the points at which the signal, while going upward or downward, crosses the zero-line. The only requirement is that the points have the same phase position within the wave. In other words, they must be at comparable points in relation to their respective periods.

If the air molecules oscillate at a higher rate (i.e. more often in the same time span), the maxima in Figure 7.5e are closer together (as long as the "paper speed" remains constant). If they oscillate more slowly, the maxima are further apart. In other words, slow oscillation corresponds to a long period duration (see Figure 7.7a), whereas fast oscillation corresponds to a short period duration (see Figure 7.7b).

To measure time intervals in an oscillogram, it is not sufficient to measure the distance on the paper: the speed of the paper has to be taken into account as well. This can be seen in Figure 7.7. The waveforms in Figure 7.7a and c look the same, but they represent two different signals. On the other hand, Figure 7.7b and c look different, but they represent the same signal. In fact, Figure 7.7a and Figure 7.7b differ from Figure 7.7c with regard to the time scale – that is, the speed with which the paper was moved.

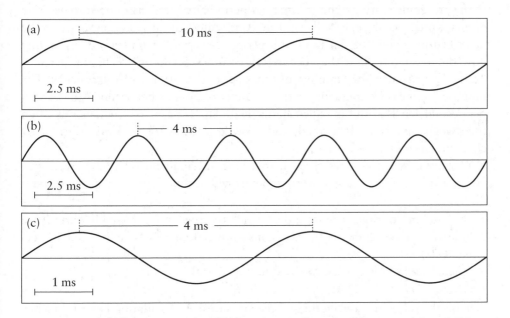

Figure 7.7 Oscillograms with different time-scales. Oscillograms (a) and (b) represent two different signals, but oscillograms (b) and (c) represent the same signal. The time-scale is identical in (a) and (b), but differs in (c). Figures (a) and (c) *look* alike, but this is only the result of the different time-scales.

In Figure 7.7a and b, 1.5 cm represents 2.5 milliseconds, but in Figure 7.7c, 1.5 cm represents only 1 millisecond. This means that in Figure 7.7a, the 6 cm that separate the maxima represent a time interval of 10 milliseconds (distance of 6 cm × scale of 2.5 ms/1.5 cm = time interval of 10 ms). But in Figure 7.7c, the 6 cm represent 4 ms (6 cm × 1 ms/1.5 cm = 4 ms). The important message is that when studying an oscillogram, the scale with which something is represented is critical.

What is the ideal scale for drawing speech signals? There is no single answer to this question, as the correct scale depends on the purpose. For some purposes, longer time window representations are needed where an entire word or phrase is visible in the same display, whereas for other purposes short time window oscillograms, which show more details of part of a sound wave, are needed. This is similar to the use of road maps when traveling by car. To find the direction to travel from one place to another, a driver chooses a map with a large scale. On such a map, the starting point and the destination can be distinguished, but not the details of how to drive. For that purpose, another map with a smaller scale must be chosen. On such a map individual streets, for example, can be recognized, but the overview of the main directions is lost. By using both maps together, a driver is well equipped. The same applies to oscillograms.

7.3.1.2 PERIOD DURATION AND PERIOD FREQUENCY

In the preceding sections, the concept of "periodicity" was introduced to describe events which occur repeatedly and at equal intervals. Periodic events may be described by giving the duration of a period ("every 20 minutes") or by stating how often per time unit they occur ("three times per hour"). This property of "rate of occurrence" or "number of times per time unit" is called **frequency**. The unit used to measure frequency is the "number of periods per second" (or "cycles per second [cps]"), and is called **hertz [Hz]**. The concept of frequency is often used when signals are described, and provides a basis for understanding many characteristics of sound waves.

We have now encountered three methods for describing the relation between two air pressure maxima, or any other two points with identical phase, in a sound wave:

1 the number of times per second at which they occur, expressed in hertz (Hz);
2 the time interval between two consecutive occurrences, expressed in seconds (s);
3 their (spatial) distance, expressed in meters (m).

What is the relation between these three measures? An oscillation has a frequency of one hertz (1 Hz) if something swings back and forth once a second, as for example the pendulum of a clock. In this case, one period of the oscillation lasts one second (1 s). If an oscillation has a frequency of 10 periods per second (or 10 Hz), one period lasts a tenth of a second (1/10 s = 0.1 s). If it has a frequency of 1,000 Hz, one period lasts a thousandth of a second (1/1,000 s = 0.001 s). The relation between frequency (in hertz) and period duration (in seconds) is expressed by the formula:

$$\text{Frequency [Hz]} = \frac{\text{number of periods}}{1 \text{ [s]}}$$

$$= \frac{1}{\dfrac{1}{\text{number of periods}} \text{ [s]}} = \frac{1}{\text{period duration [s]}}.$$

Or, written shorter as a formula where "frequency" is represented by f and the time of one period by T:

$$f = \frac{1}{T}.$$

In order to avoid writing too many zeros when describing high frequencies, the factor "1,000" is abbreviated to "kilo"; 1,000 Hz can thus be written as 1 kHz (read: "one kilohertz"). Likewise "milli" is a convenient abbreviation for "thousandth." Instead of saying: the period is one thousandth of a second (0.001 s) long, one can say: the period duration is one millisecond (1 ms). In other words, in a periodic oscillation with a frequency of 1 kHz, each individual period lasts 1 ms. A mistake that is sometimes made is thinking that when a 100 Hz signal has a 10 ms period duration, a 200 Hz signal must have a 20 ms period duration. This is wrong since an *in*crease in period duration leads to a *de*crease in period frequency. For the example of 200 Hz we get:

$$200 \text{ [Hz]} = \frac{200}{1 \text{ [s]}} = \frac{1}{\dfrac{1}{200} \text{ [s]}} = \frac{1}{200 \text{ [s]}} = 0.005 \text{ [s]} = 5 \text{ [ms]}.$$

The frequencies which are relevant for speech range from approximately 30 Hz to 8 kHz (i.e. the period durations range from 33.3 ms to 0.125 ms).

7.3.1.3 PERIOD FREQUENCY AND WAVELENGTH

In the previous section, we saw that the period duration (in seconds) relates to the period frequency (in Hz). We now calculate the distance between two air pressure maxima in a sound wave (i.e. the "length" of one period) that is moving through a room.

In a signal with a frequency of 100 Hz, each period lasts 10 ms. In Section 7.1.3 (on the speed of sound), we mentioned that speed is simply the relation between distance (in meters) and time (in seconds):

$$\text{speed} \left[\frac{m}{s} \right] = \frac{\text{distance [m]}}{\text{time [s]}}.$$

In this formula, the speed of sound is known (around 340 m/s). In this example, the duration of a period is known as well, it is 10 ms = 0.01 s. The unknown factor is the distance between two pressure maxima in the sound wave. By transforming the formula, this distance can be calculated:

$$\text{speed} \left[\frac{m}{s} \right] \times \text{time [s]} = \text{distance [m]}.$$

This formula expresses in general that traveling further away means traveling longer or faster: the distance that is crossed depends on how fast and how long somebody travels. Applying this formula to the speed of sound, that is, replacing "speed" by "speed of sound", "time" by "period duration", and "distance" by "length of a wave", we obtain:

$$\text{sound speed} \left[\frac{m}{s} \right] * \text{period duration [s]} = \text{wavelength [m]}.$$

Or, by using c as a symbol for the speed of sound, T for the duration of one period, and for wavelength the Greek letter λ (['læmdə]), we get:

$$c \times T = \lambda.$$

By putting in the numbers of the example above (340 m/s for the speed of sound and 10 ms for the duration of one period for a frequency of 100 Hz) we obtain:

$$340 \frac{m}{s} \times 0.01 \text{ s} = 3.4 \text{ m}.$$

The distance between two pressure maxima in a room is therefore 3.4 meters ($\approx$ 11 ft) for a frequency of 100 Hz. If it were possible to "freeze" the air and visualize the pressure, then pressure maxima could be seen every 3.4 meters for a frequency of 100 Hz. Following the same principle, the distances are 34 cm ($\approx$ 1 ft) for 1 kHz, and 6.8 m ($\approx$ 22 ft) for 50 Hz, as can be calculated with the formula.

We can additionally transform the formula $f = 1/T$, which states the relation between frequency and period duration (see Section 7.3.1.2), into $T = 1/f$. This allows us to compute all relations between speed of sound (c), period duration (T), period frequency (f), and wavelength (λ):

$$c \times T = c \times \frac{1}{f} = \frac{c}{f} = \lambda, \quad \frac{c}{\lambda} = f, \quad \text{and} \quad \lambda \times f = c.$$

The distance between maxima is called the **wavelength** of an oscillation. As shown in the formula, the wavelength depends on the speed of a sound and its frequency. For high frequencies the wavelength is small; for low frequencies the wavelength is large – assuming that the sound speed remains constant, which implies constant temperature, constant air humidity, etc.

7.3.1.4 REPRESENTING F_0 OVER TIME

Until now, we have talked about "the" frequency of a signal. A very simple signal, as in Figure 7.6, has only one frequency. Speech, on the other hand, is a complex signal and looks rather different, as we have already seen in Section 1.1, and consists of many signals, each with their own frequency. Nevertheless, even in a complex signal there is one "period" which repeats itself again and again. Rather than a simple "up-and-down-and-up" pattern as in Figure 7.6, a periodic speech signal can have a complex shape. Still, this shape appears repetitively and we can speak of "a (complex) period." The "period frequency" of a complex signal is a "basic" frequency called **fundamental frequency** or F_0 (read: "f zero"). For a voiced speech signal, this **fundamental period** ($T_0 = 1/F_0$) is caused by the periodically opening and closing vocal folds.

This fundamental frequency of a (speech) signal is what we perceive as its pitch.[5] Variations in pitch across an utterance give rise to intonation in phonetics, so tracking F_0 over time is important and is expressed with F_0 **contours** or **pitch contours** (see Figure 7.8b). The horizontal axis represents time, as in an oscillogram (see Figure 7.8a), whereas the vertical axis gives the frequency in hertz. Figure 7.8b shows the F_0 contour of a question uttered by an English speaker who raises his voice toward the end of the phrase. Notice that the individual periods in the oscillogram become shorter and are therefore closer together in the oscillogram – resulting in the rise in frequency.

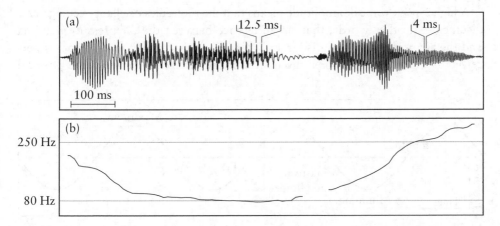

Figure 7.8: (a) Oscillogram and (b) F_0 contour for a question uttered by a male speaker of English.

It seems straightforward to compute the fundamental frequency of a signal because a computer program would only have to measure the period durations and express their duration in hertz. Unfortunately, the individual cycles of the vocal fold vibration are not perfectly periodic; that is, each cycle differs a bit in length and shape from the preceding and following cycles. For this reason, the vibration is called **quasi-periodic**, even if we speak – somewhat sloppily – of the "periodic vocal fold vibration." These small irregularities make it surprisingly complicated to compute the F_0 or pitch of a speech signal. Many different methods have been proposed but there are no ideal procedures that compute "the" pitch of a signal. All methods are contaminated with some error, which might either result in wrong F_0 values, computing no values at all, or computing values for voiceless stretches of a signal. Even though computer programs calculate F_0, it is advisable to consult the speech waveform to verify the accuracy of the F_0 contour.

7.3.2 Amplitude

In Section 7.3.1, we saw that the frequency with which the air molecules oscillate is the period frequency of the sound wave. This frequency is indirectly represented in an oscillogram as the distance between two comparable points (that is, as the duration of one period). In addition, the oscillation of the individual air molecules is directly related to the movements of the microphone membrane. If the microphone membrane is at its rest position (i.e. its equilibrium), that is, if no sound waves affect it, the corresponding oscillogram remains at the **zero-line** (see Figure 7.9). A deviation from this zero-line is called **displacement** and the distance between the zero-line and the maximal displacement is called amplitude. This shows up in the vertical range of the oscillogram. The distance between a maximum (above the zero-line) and the next minimum (below the zero-line) is called **peak-to-peak amplitude**.

A higher peak-to-peak amplitude means that the molecules oscillate over a greater distance – in other words, that the difference between the air pressure maxima and the air pressure minima is larger. This means that the acoustic signal is perceived as being louder. (For a discussion of the difference between the physical

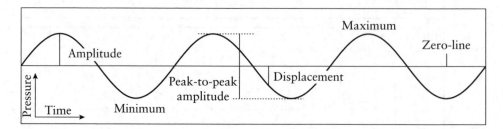

Figure 7.9 Amplitude terms illustrated with the oscillogram of a simple, symmetrical signal.

"amplitude" of a signal and the subjective impression of "loudness," see Section 12.6). Note that a signal has a displacement at each moment. It can be above the zero-line ("positive"), below the zero-line ("negative"), or "zero." Note further that an amplitude or displacement of "zero" does not mean that there is no air pressure; instead, it means that the ambient air pressure has been reached (e.g. 1,013 hPa).

In the oscillograms discussed so far, we have always used the horizontal axis to display the time so that we could compute the period duration and hence the period frequency (see Section 7.3.1.2). But we have indicated neither the dimension nor the unit of the vertical axis for the amplitude. We mentioned that sound waves are small fluctuations in air pressure that can be measured in pascals. These fluctuations are picked up by a microphone, which converts them into electric voltage or current. If we had a calibrated microphone and calibrated electrical amplifiers, we could simply write "pressure" as dimension and "pascal" as unit on the vertical axis of an oscillogram.

However, recordings are not typically made with calibrated microphones. Moreover, during recording sessions the recording level is frequently adjusted, either manually or automatically, so that relations between the incoming signal of a microphone and what is stored on a recorder are anything but constant. And on playback we usually adjust the loudness by turning the "volume" control of the amplifier. In sum, the original pascal values of the signal as it was picked up by the microphone are not available when the signal is stored, displayed, or reproduced.

Nevertheless, the relation in a signal between higher amplitude portions and lower amplitude portions remains the same, as long as the recording level or volume settings are not changed in that stretch of speech. In other words, the absolute amplitude values are not known but the relation between amplitudes in a signal can always be computed. Usually some reference value is chosen to compute such a relation.

There is a second problem with registering actual pressure values of sound waves: the pressure values in sound waves cover a very large range, from 20 μPa to 20 Pa – that is, the largest amplitude is a million times larger than the smallest one. Surprisingly, our ear can easily hear an amplitude difference of a few micropascal but cannot hear the same small difference when the signal is several millipascal large. In other words, we can hear a needle falling when it is quiet but not at a rock concert.

This ability to perceive small changes for small signals and only large changes for large signals exists in other modes of human perception and holds for brightness and force as well. This relation is approximated very well by the "logarithm" of the relation of the values. The relation between two sound pressures can simply be computed as:

$$\log\left(\frac{\text{amplitude}}{\text{reference amplitude}}\right).$$

The logarithm expresses ratios between values rather than absolute differences. The logarithm captures the observation that small differences at low amplitude are perceptually equal to larger differences at higher amplitude. Appendix A.3 gives a much more elaborate explanation for this formula and ways to compute the "loudness" of a signal.

Calculation of the relation between two amplitude values by means of the formula above results in a measure called the **bel**. Since bel values are often very small, the obtained values are multiplied by 10. A bel is thus equivalent to 10 **decibels** (**dB**) (that is, 6 bels are 60 decibels).

Thus, to compute the relative amplitude of a signal, the formula:

$$10 \times \log\left(\frac{\text{amplitude}}{\text{reference amplitude}}\right) [\text{dB}]$$

is used. Note that the (deci-)bel is not a unit (i.e. there are no pascals or volts or other things involved along some dimension) but only a formula to compute a value. This is actually a great advantage since pressure, voltage, current, numbers in a computer or values from any other dimension can be compared easily by using (deci-)bels.

As mentioned in Section 7.1.2, in sound signals with high amplitude, the air molecules have to cross a larger distance in the same time than in signals with low amplitude (if the frequency stays the same). This leads to a higher speed of the air molecules in their oscillation (which is independent of the speed of sound; see Section 7.1.3). This is comparable to the pendulum of a clock: whether it is moved only a bit from its equilibrium point (= low amplitude) or far away from it (= high amplitude), it swings with the same frequency. However, the weight of the pendulum that was dragged far away moves much faster. As a consequence, the wider-swinging pendulum has a much higher energy, which can be easily felt by stopping it at the lowest point of the pendulum. This energy is known as the "kinetic energy" of the swinging pendulum.[6]

In general, the energy of the pendulum (or the oscillating air molecules) increases with the square of its speed. For this reason, the amplitude values are squared whenever a loudness is being calculated (Appendix A.2 treats the relations between energy, intensity, and power in more detail). This applies to the calculation of dB values as well. The formula to calculate sound *energy* from the pressure values is:[7]

$$10 \times \log\left(\frac{\text{amplitude}^2}{\text{reference amplitude}^2}\right) = 20 \times \log\left(\frac{\text{amplitude}}{\text{reference amplitude}}\right).$$

If the dB calculation is performed on sound pressure values, and if the reference amplitude is set to be the lowest perceivable amplitude by humans (20 μPa), then the formula is said to express the **sound pressure level (SPL)**, as indicated by **dB$_{\text{SPL}}$**.

If the lowest perceivable amplitude of a specific listener is used as reference value, then the formula expresses **sound level (SL)** and the related term is **dB$_{SL}$**. On a CD or sound file the smallest value is "1" unit of the digital recording (see Section 8.1.3) and the reference amplitude for the dB formula is simply "1." In this case, dB is either written without an index, or the highest possible level ("full scale") is used as reference and the values are given in negative **dB$_{FS}$**.

A common method to compute amplitude values over time is the **root mean square (RMS)** amplitude, which expresses the perceived loudness of a signal reasonably well. The way to compute the RMS amplitude is presented in detail in Appendix A.3.1. It would be most correct to indicate both the computing method (e.g. RMS) and the reference used (e.g. SPL), as in "dB$_{RMS-SPL}$." In practice, however, since instantaneous dB values are computed for a single value and dB values of a time stretch are usually based on RMS amplitudes, the computing method is not indicated in the index (i.e. it is usually written "dB$_{SPL}$" and not "dB$_{RMS-SPL}$").

The existence of different dB scales may seem confusing, but it has an important advantage. Since dB values express a proportion between two values whose units of measurement disappear during the calculation of the ratio, it is easy to compare dB values obtained from different physical domains (pascal, volts, centimeters, numbers in a computer, etc.). These scales differ in terms of what the unit of measurement is, but the relations in the domains are the same.

To summarize, the formula for computing the **intensity level** is:

$$10 \times \log\left(\frac{\text{intensity}}{\text{reference intensity}}\right) [\text{dB}_{IL}]$$

and the formula for computing the sound pressure level is:

$$20 \times \log\left(\frac{\text{amplitude in Pa}}{20\,\mu\text{Pa}}\right) [\text{dB}_{SPL}].$$

Since most of the time the amplitude is not measured with calibrated devices, the sound pressure level is often given relative to some arbitrary reference, which can be the smallest unit of a system (e.g. one bit on a computer) and the formula collapses to:

$$20 \times \log(\text{amplitude}) [\text{dB}]$$

where the amplitude is usually the RMS amplitude.

Using proportions rather than absolute values has another advantage. As mentioned before, someone who makes a recording first selects an appropriate recording level by turning a knob. Then, during playback, the person turns the volume control in order to obtain a comfortable listening level. This process of setting recording and playback levels alters of course absolute loudness values, but it does not change the relation between loud and soft passages. Thus, the dB scale makes it possible to calculate relative amplitude characteristics of a signal, without any reference to the setting of recording and playback levels.

Furthermore, since the relation of two values is computed, the dB values can be computed in relation to the maximal possible amplitude a system can tolerate (until now, we have always used the minimal possible value a system can handle). The effect is that "amplitude" in the formulas given before are smaller than the "reference amplitude," which leads to negative dB values. This representation is often used to report dB levels on professional equipment. A value of "-3dB," for example, indicates that the amplitude is 3 dB below the maximal capacity of the system.

Finally, it is important to recognize that a value of "0 dB" does not mean that there is no amplitude (like 0 °C does not mean that there is no temperature). It only indicates that the "reference amplitude" has been reached:

$$20 \times \log\left(\frac{\text{reference amplitude}}{\text{reference amplitude}}\right) = 20 \times \log(1) = 0.$$

Second, doubling the amplitude leads to an increase of 6 dB and not to a doubling of the dB value, since:

$$20 \times \log\left(\frac{2 \times \text{amplitude}}{\text{amplitude}}\right) = 20 \times \log(2) \approx 20 \times 0.3010 \approx 6 \text{ dB}.$$

7.3.2.1 REPRESENTING AMPLITUDE CHANGES OVER TIME

The RMS amplitude of a speech signal provides a rough measure of the overall loudness of a signal. But often the changes of loudness during an utterance are of interest, for example to investigate whether one syllable is louder (or more stressed) than another. To this end, instead of obtaining a single value for the signal as a whole, the changes in RMS amplitude over time need to be investigated. It is therefore useful to have a graph that represents the changes in signal level over time.

This can be achieved by a simple method. First, a short stretch of signal is selected and its RMS amplitude is calculated. One then moves a little further along the signal, selects a second stretch of equal size, and repeats the procedure until the end of the signal (see Figure 7.10a). In other words, instead of using the "whole" signal at once, a **window** is moved along the signal, and at each position of the window, the RMS amplitude is calculated and plotted. This is like sitting in a train and seeing the landscape through a train window from some distance: only a certain stretch of the landscape can be seen, but because the train moves, the whole landscape will be covered. The plotted amplitude values form a curve, called an **amplitude contour**.

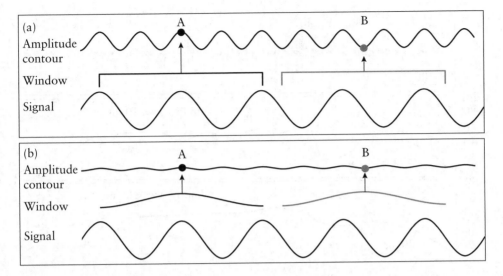

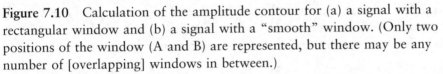

Figure 7.10 Calculation of the amplitude contour for (a) a signal with a rectangular window and (b) a signal with a "smooth" window. (Only two positions of the window (A and B) are represented, but there may be any number of [overlapping] windows in between.)

The shape and length of the window have consequences for the computed amplitude contour. As shown in Figure 7.10a, the use of a square window leads to a wavy amplitude contour, because sometimes five maxima and minima (point A in Figure 7.10a) and sometimes four maxima and minima (point B) are included in the computation. Thus, although the amplitude of the signal is constant, the calculated dB values vary according to the relative position of the window (that is, its phase) in the signal. This effect can be reduced by "flattening" the window at its edges, which decreases the influence of the amplitude at the edges of the window, as shown in Figure 7.10b.

But even the use of flattened windows cannot always prevent the calculated amplitude contour from being irregular. If the window becomes too large,[8] it is not possible to trace rapid changes in amplitude, since the mean values are taken over a longer stretch. If the window is too small, it moves up and down with the waveform, like a small boat on a wavy sea. Normally, a compromise can be found between a high resolution in time (a small window) and a good smoothing effect (a large window). As a rule of thumb, the window size is essentially determined by the period duration of the signal: to obtain a useful amplitude contour, the window should cover two to three periods.

Figure 7.11 illustrates these considerations. Figure 7.11a shows an oscillogram of the English word *stair* and Figure 7.11b the corresponding amplitude contour calculated with a small window; it represents the low amplitude of the signal at point A, just before the release of a closure, and the increase in amplitude at point B, where the closure is released. But the representation of the RMS amplitude

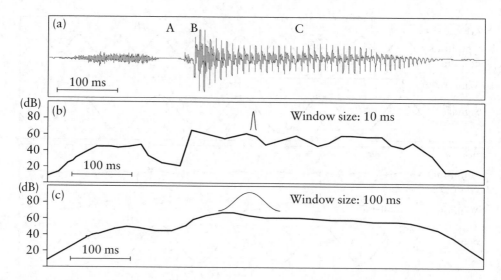

Figure 7.11   (a) Oscillogram and (b, c) two amplitude contours of the word *stair* [stɛɹ]. In (b) the amplitude has been calculated with a window size of 10 ms; in (c) it has been calculated with a window size of 100 ms.

of the vowel (point C) shows variations that are not present in the signal itself. These variations are only due to the small window size. The variations seem to occur at random, caused by small changes in the duration of the period of the signal. If a larger window is used (see Figure 7.11c), these amplitude changes are not observed. But with a large window, the silence at point A and the sudden rise in amplitude at point B are no longer visible. There is no "best" window size – window size has to be chosen according to the needs of an investigation. The situation is similar to the road map example given in Section 7.3.1.1.

7.3.3   *Phase*

Frequency and amplitude are essential characteristics of a waveform. But an additional dimension is needed to determine the exact position of a specific point in a waveform, or to compare the position of two waveforms in relation to each other. This dimension is *phase*. In a sense, the phase provides information about where specific points in time are located within a period. The location of these points is indicated in geometric **degrees** (°). What is the relation between a period and a geometric angle?

Recall that a waveform is a sequence of periods that repeat themselves over and over again. This is comparable, for example, to the hand on an analog watch, which moves in circles over and over again. The position of the minute hand is indicated by a value between 0 and 60 (with 60 being the same as 0). In geometric degrees, this is a value between 0° and 360°. In order to indicate a particular point

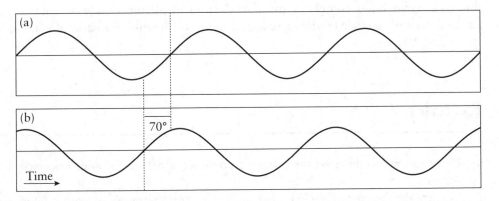

Figure 7.12   A relative phase shift of two signals with identical amplitude and frequency. Note that there is no time scaling, since a phase shift exists independently of the frequency of a signal.

on the circle, the number of degrees from the beginning of the circle is used, known as the **phase angle**. Likewise, the position in a period can be expressed by its phase angle, which is a value between 0° and 360°.

Degrees cannot only be used to express the position of points within a period, but can also be used to compare the relative position of two waveforms with respect to each other. Figure 7.12a and b show two waveforms which share the same amplitude and frequency. They are not entirely identical, however, since there is a **phase shift** between the two signals: the waveform in Figure 7.12b precedes the one in Figure 7.12a by 70°, since the waveform in Figure 7.12b crossed the zero-line earlier than the waveform in Figure 7.12a.

A full description of two (simple) waveforms requires information about their frequency, amplitude, and phase. These three parameters are sufficient for a complete mathematical description of simple waveforms.

In sum, the (fundamental) frequency of a signal (measured in hertz) is given by its period duration (usually measured in ms) and is perceived as the pitch of a signal. Period duration and period frequency are inversely related, with a decrease in period duration leading to an increase in frequency. The amplitude of the signal is usually perceived as its loudness. Because the absolute determination of an amplitude in pascal values is difficult, amplitude is usually measured in relation to reference values. Since loudness perception is related to the logarithm of amplitude relations, dB scales are often used to express amplitude values. And finally, the phase relations of signals (measured in degrees) are a third dimension to describe signals.

The next chapter introduces methods to analyze signals in terms of amplitude, frequency, and phase. Since these operations are performed on a computer, we describe how computers represent signals. This also helps to understand what happens when a signal is recorded with a digital recorder, since it operates on the same principle as a computer to represent signals. A final section presenting different signal types completes the introduction of all the elements required for analysis and acoustic modeling of speech signals – the subject matter of Chapters 9 and 10.

Exercises

1 Using examples, describe the difference between longitudinal and transverse waves.
2 You are the director of a science fiction movie. Your heroine's spaceship floats in space and its crew has just blown up a planet that is 100 km away. You show this with a large flashing explosion. How many seconds later must the detonation become audible to make the film realistic?
3 Insert the missing values:

Period duration		Frequency	
(ms)	(s)	(Hz)	(kHz)
1	0.001	1000	1
	0.05		
10			
			0.05
		1	
4			
		400	
			3
	0.1		

4 What is fundamental frequency and how is it perceived by listeners? Why is it difficult to compute the F_0 of a speech signal?
5 How is amplitude represented on an oscillogram? How is it perceived by a listener?
6 How is the dB scale different from a scale measuring absolute amplitude values? What are the advantages of the dB scale?
7 What are the three dimensions needed to describe a sine signal? How is each measured?

Notes

1 The use of abbreviations like "h" for *hundred*, "m" for *thousandth*, and "μ" for *millionth* is explained in Appendix B.

2 Note that the speed of the movement of molecules in a wave from and to their rest position is different from the speed of the travelling of this change through space, i.e. the speed of sound (see Section 7.1.2), and that the term "rate" refers to the number of occurrences of this change per second (see Section 7.3.1).

3 For convenience, we use a value of 340 m/s in subsequent computations.

4 A *dimension* is something that is measured. A *unit of measure* is a value by which the measurement in a certain dimension can be expressed. For example, the dimension *length* can be measured using the unit of measure *meter*, *inch*, or *yard*. A dimension is a property that exists in an absolute way (that is, each object has a length), whereas a unit is a more or less arbitrary figure attributed to this dimension (for example, a length may be measured in meters, inches, ells, etc.).

5 There is a technical distinction between *fundamental frequency* (defined in physical terms as the frequency at which the vocal folds vibrate), and *pitch*, which is a subjective perception of tonal height. Fundamental frequency and pitch are not distinguished in this textbook.

6 kinetic energy $= \frac{1}{2}$mass $\times$ velocity^2 or $E_{\text{kin}} = \frac{1}{2}mv^2$.

7 Without going into the mathematical rules for calculating powers and logarithms, it is sufficient to know that $(a^2/b^2) = (a/b)^2$, and $\log(a^2) = 2 \times \log(a)$.

8 The "window" is a stretch of time, which can be shorter or longer. But it is usual to speak of a "small" or "large" window size.

8 Analysis Methods for Speech Sounds

In this chapter, we present a number of common analysis methods used in phonetic research, with reference to the different acoustic parameters that are used in phonetic description. Since these analyses are typically done with the help of a computer, we first discuss the transfer of the acoustic signal into a digital computer.

8.1 Digitizing Acoustic Signals

As we explained in the previous chapter, sound is a sequence of air pressure variations spreading over time. The air pressure variations may present *any value* within a large range, and do so at *any time*. This means that there are an infinite number of possible air pressure values that may occur at an infinite number of points in time. This is why the signal is called **continuous**. In recording a signal, the membrane of a microphone moves along with the sound pressure of a sound signal, thus generating an electrical signal that is **analog** to the air pressure. The movement of the membrane and the ensuing electrical signal are both continuous. A digital computer, on the other hand, can only represent a finite number of **discrete** states. When read into a computer, the computer translates the continuous signal into a finite number of **digital** values. The distance between these values may be extremely small, but in principle a digital computer cannot represent *all* possible values. Thus, the continuous, analog signal is transformed by the computer into a digital signal with discrete values.

The same distinction between analog and discrete states can be found in the case of clocks (see Figure 8.1): an analog clock has hands which go continuously through *every* point of the circle, thus representing *any* possible time. Consequently, even the slow-moving minute hand represents every second by its position. But since *every* position of the hands represents a different time, a (slightly) wrong time is read by someone who is looking at the clock from an angle. There is no "safe area" where a slightly changed position still represents the same time.

A digital clock has individual digits to indicate a time. Only those points in time that can be represented by the digits can be indicated by the digital clock.

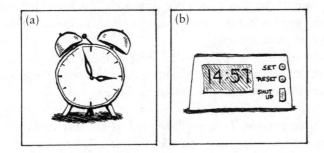

Figure 8.1 (a) Analog clock and (b) digital clock.

For instance, the digital clock in Figure 8.1b cannot display subdivisions of minutes. But the numbers are easy to read even when looking at them from an angle. This high level of reliability to present values is one of the main advantages of a digital representation. It makes up for the disadvantage that not *all* values can possibly be represented, and that intermediate values may be lacking. There is one inherent risk with digital data: if they deteriorate so that they cannot be read any more, they are lost completely (for example, if the middle horizontal segment of a digital display is out of order, an "8" may appear as a "0").

8.1.1 *Digitizing in the time and amplitude domains*

When speech signals are digitized by a computer, two dimensions of the analog world are transformed into discrete values. First, air pressure values that change continuously are translated into discrete numbers. Second, this is done at separate points in time. This can be illustrated by the work of a meteorologist, who notes the outside temperature over a month. She does so by using an (analog) mercury thermometer, a pencil, a sheet of paper, and a watch. Every minute she looks at the thermometer and writes down the time and the temperature on the sheet of paper. This is an example of digitization: time runs continuously, but the meteorologist only registers the measurements once a minute. Furthermore, although the thermometer indicates temperature values analogically by means of the height of the mercury column, the meteorologist only writes down discrete numbers. With such a method, some information is lost, because she cannot write down *every* possible height of the mercury column at *every* moment. But, in turn, she may easily store, copy, or transmit the registered values. Once digitized, the data are more accessible and can be processed and stored in many different ways.

There are two different ways to improve the quality of the digitization: first, measuring more often, or second, measuring more accurately. The example of the meteorologist may serve to show the advantages and drawbacks of both methods. If the meteorologist measures more frequently, the representation of the temperature contour becomes more complete, but it requires more paper to be copied and stored. If she measures more accurately, the individual values become longer, with the same result that more paper is needed. A balance has to be found between frequency and accuracy.

The same considerations apply to digitizing speech signals on a computer. We would like to take as many measurements as possible with the greatest accuracy in order to obtain a faithful representation of the signal. But this leads to large amounts of data. The main question is how often and how accurately should a speech signal be measured? We will see that it actually can be a drawback if measurements are taken too often (see Section 8.3.5).

8.1.2   Sampling rate

Consider again the example of the meteorologist. If she takes only a few measurements, then changes in temperature in between measurements are not recorded. On the other hand, if she measures very frequently, few temperature changes escape recording, but the number of data values is unnecessarily large. How often should measurements be taken in order to be sure that no change is missed?

Let us examine this question on the basis of a very simple acoustic signal. Consider that ten thousand times per second a **sample** is taken from a signal (i.e. the **sampling rate** is 10,000 Hz or 10 kHz):

$$\frac{10,000 \text{ samples}}{1 \text{ [s]}} = 10,000 \text{ [Hz]} = 10 \text{ [kHz] sampling rate.}$$

That means that every 100 μs a sample of the signal is taken (i.e. a value is measured):

$$\frac{10,000 \text{ samples}}{1 \text{ [s]}} = \frac{1 \text{ sample}}{\dfrac{1}{10,000} \text{ [s]}} = \frac{1 \text{ sample}}{0.0001 \text{ [s]}} = \frac{1 \text{ sample}}{100 \text{ [μs]}}.$$

Now we apply this **sampling** to the 200 Hz signal in Figure 8.2. A 200 Hz signal has a period duration of 5 ms or 0.005 s (see Section 7.3.1.2). Since the signal is sampled every 100 μs, one 5 ms period of the signal is sampled 50 times (in other words, 50 samples fit into one period of the signal), which results in a very accurate digital representation (see Figure 8.2a):

$$\text{measurements per period} = \frac{\text{period duration [s]}}{\text{interval between two samples [s]}};$$

$$\text{here: } \frac{5 \text{ ms}}{100 \text{ μs}} = \frac{0.005 \text{ s}}{0.0001 \text{ s}} = 50.$$

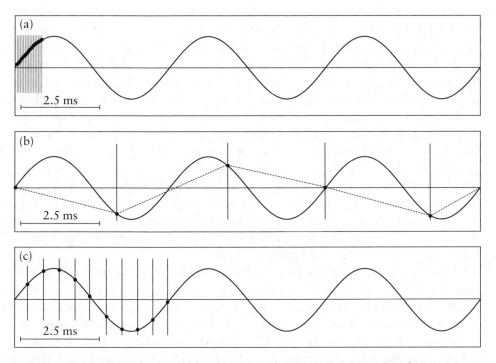

Figure 8.2 Digitizing a signal in the time domain. A 200 Hz signal is digitized with a sampling rate of (a) 10 kHz, (b) 300 Hz, and (c) 2 kHz. In (b), the individual measurements are connected with a dotted line to show the alias signal.

But if the signal is measured only 300 times a second (i.e. the sampling rate is 300 Hz and two samples are 3.33 ms apart), the waveform can no longer be reconstructed from the digitized signal (see Figure 8.2b): connecting the individual samples does not obtain the original signal (see dotted lines in Figure 8.2b). Finally, if the sampling rate is 2 kHz, each period of the signal is measured ten times (see Figure 8.2c) – the digital representation is therefore less accurate than the one based on a 10 kHz sampling rate, but the waveform is still fairly well represented. And by connecting the individual samples, the original waveform can be reconstructed reasonably well.

Theoretically, a signal can be correctly digitized if the sampling rate is at least two times the highest frequency contained in the signal. This is called the **Nyquist criterion**, and the **Nyquist frequency** is exactly half the sampling rate. For the present 200 Hz example, a sampling frequency of at least 400.1 Hz is therefore theoretically sufficient to digitize the signal. In practice, however, the sampling frequency should be higher than this theoretical minimum.

The previous discussion has shown that the sampling rate depends on the frequency of the signal to be digitized. If the signal contains frequencies above the Nyquist frequency, "fake" signals may occur. This effect, called **aliasing**, is illustrated in Figure 8.2b, where a signal of 200 Hz is digitized with a sampling rate of 300 Hz. The signal obtained after reconstruction does not look like the original signal any more, but like a signal with a lower frequency (represented by the dotted lines in Figure 8.2b). The latter signal becomes audible in the reproduction of the digitized signal, although it was not part of the original signal. It is not possible to identify this frequency as an erroneous signal, because nothing in the digital data suggests that it was not originally there. In other words, the reproduced signal does not sound distorted like some badly tuned radio; it sounds as clear and normal as any signal, except that it never was part of the original signal. To prevent this **undersampling** from happening, an **anti-aliasing filter** is used *before* signals are digitized. This filter serves to suppress any frequencies above the Nyquist frequency, that is, higher than half the sampling rate. Often, this anti-aliasing filter is integrated into the audio hardware of a computer and is automatically controlled by the software; that is, the anti-aliasing filter is "invisible" to the user of a computer.

Theoretically, the sampling rate should be just more than double the highest frequency component contained in the signal. Unfortunately, no simple criterion exists for determining exactly how high the sampling rate should be to obtain a faithful representation of speech data. In a phonetics lab, most often sampling frequencies of 10, 11.025, 16, 20, 22.05, or 44.1 kHz are used. In the case of the compact disc (CD), the sampling rate is 44.1 kHz. A digital audio tape (DAT) recorder samples at 48 kHz, and for the super audio CD (SA-CD) and the audio digital versatile disc (Audio-DVD) the sampling rate is as high as 96.2 kHz. These sampling rates are partly the result of historical developments in computer science. The 22.05 kHz sampling rate is half of 44.1 kHz and 11.025 kHz is a quarter of it. While it may seem advantageous to use the highest available sampling rate for all analyses, this requires additional memory and results in unnecessarily high processing times for many calculations without gaining any accuracy for the results.

8.1.3   *Quantizing resolution*

The second parameter which plays a role in digitization is the resolution in the amplitude domain. Ideally, the value should enable us to provide a good representation of the lowest amplitude perceivable by the human ear, and at the same time represent extremely loud signals as well. Amplitude is conveniently measured by means of the dB scale (see Section 7.3.2). So, how large should the amplitude range be (in dB) for a speech signal to be properly represented?

In modern phonetic practice, signals are digitized with the amplitude range divided into 65,536 steps. This value looks strange but is achieved by multiplying 2 by itself 16 times, which in mathematics is written as $2^{16} = 65,536$. This is the largest integer value that can be represented with a binary 16-bit number (which can easily be handled by a digital machine) and this is the reason why people sometimes speak of a "16-bit resolution." This gives a total range of 96 dB, as can be computed with the dB formula for amplitude values given in Section 7.3.2:

$$20 \times \log\left(\frac{65{,}536}{1}\right) \approx 20 \times 4.816 \text{ dB} \approx 96.3 \text{ dB}.$$

This is entirely sufficient for most purposes. Indeed, hardly any microphone or recording situation ever covers this entire range and most of the time a recording spans a range of 35 to 50 dB.

Figure 8.3 shows how a signal is digitized. The signal is measured at discrete points in time, as represented by the vertical lines in Figure 8.3a. At those points, the displacement of the signal is measured. This gives only values as represented by the horizontal lines in the same figure. At each time measurement, the nearest horizontal line is taken as the measurement value. Only these measurements or samples appear as data in the computer (see Figure 8.3b). When the signal is reproduced, the measured values of the individual samples are reproduced one after another. In a graphical representation on a computer screen, the measured value points are often linked by lines (the solid lines in Figure 8.3c), making the signal look more like a continuous analog signal. However, it should be kept in mind that the digitized signal only consists of separate data points.

The complete process of the analog-to-digital conversion (A/D conversion) of (speech) signals is represented in Figure 8.4. As a first step in the digitizing, the anti-aliasing filter makes sure that the signal contains no frequencies above the

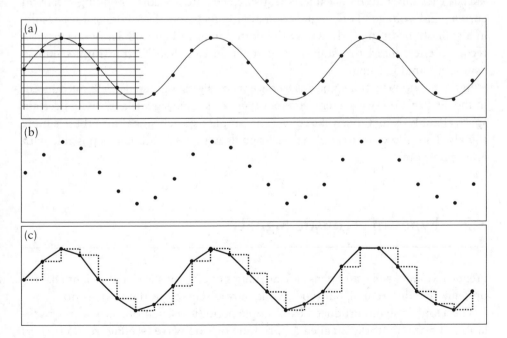

Figure 8.3 Digitizing a signal in the amplitude and time domain.

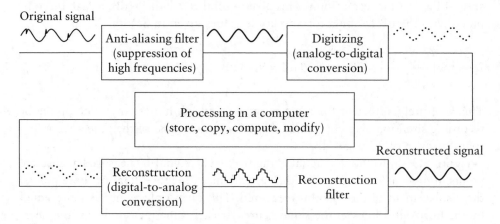

Figure 8.4   The recording and reproduction of signals by a computer.

Nyquist frequency. At discrete points in time, the filtered signal is then transformed into discrete sample vales (quantified). This step is the actual digitizing process, resulting in the (speech) samples. The *sampling rate* (e.g. 22.025 kHz) indicates the degree of detail in the time domain, whereas the *quantizing resolution* (e.g. 16-bit resolution) indicates the number of possible amplitude displacement values. The samples thus obtained are just a sequence of numbers, which can be copied, transmitted, or stored for any amount of time. Each time the digital signal is reproduced, each discrete data value is transformed into its corresponding electrical current and voltage. This digital-to-analog conversion (D/A conversion) results in a stair-shaped signal, shown by the dotted lines in Figure 8.3c. By means of a **reconstruction filter**, this stair-shaped function can then be transformed into a "smooth" analog signal.

In the previous sections, the basic concepts of digitizing signals were introduced. In the next section, we present different types of simple signals and discuss certain spectral analysis methods that convert a complex speech signal into these simple signals. This allows us to study speech signals in more detail than is possible with an oscillogram.

8.2   Types of Acoustic Signals

Frequency, amplitude, and phase are attributes of all acoustic signals. Figure 8.5a–e presents five different signal types, which are discussed in the next section.

The acoustic signal produced by a simple periodic oscillation, such as the oscillation of a tuning fork, is called a **pure tone** or **sine wave** (see Figure 8.5a). This type of acoustic signal is referred to as pure, since from a physical point of view

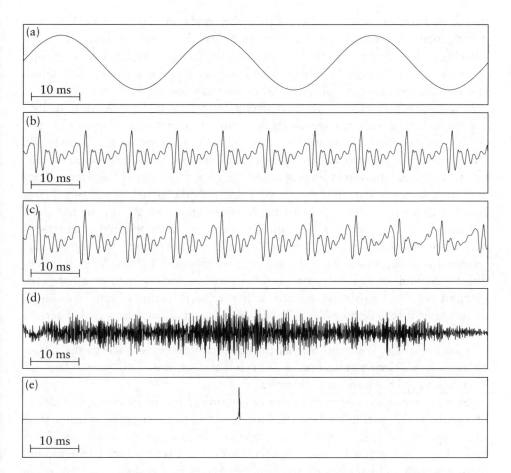

Figure 8.5   Five different types of signals: (a) pure tone, (b) periodic signal, (c) quasi-periodic signal, (d) noise, and (e) impulse. Only (a) and (b) are purely periodic signals; (c) is quasi-periodic, and (d) and (e) are non-periodic signals.

it is the simplest signal possible. Each oscillating tuning fork or each clockwork pendulum executes a movement that can be described by a sine function which is completely defined by its frequency, amplitude, and phase. As shown in Section 8.3.1, all signals can be approximated as a combination of many sine functions.

Many existing signals, including speech, are not pure sine signals, but are **complex signals** (see Figure 8.5b). A complex signal is periodic; in other words, the signal shape repeats itself each cycle. Moreover, complex signals can be formed by adding up a number of sine signals, as is described in detail in the next section.

In addition to frequency, amplitude, and phase, sounds have a fourth determining characteristic: the quality of a sound, which is called **timbre**. The timbre of a sound distinguishes two sounds with identical pitch and loudness. The difference between musical instruments is an example of "timbre": the "middle C" played on a trumpet sounds different from the same note played on a piano, even if both sounds are equally loud. In the same way, the vowel [ɑ] differs from the vowel [i]. The difference in timbre between two complex signals is due, among other things, to the sine signals (or sine components) that make up the sound, and to their frequency, amplitude, and phase relations (see Section 8.3.1).

Voiced speech signals are not as perfectly periodic as the signals we have considered so far. In reality, a speech signal continuously undergoes small changes, so that no two periods are ever exactly the same in terms of the frequencies, amplitudes, and phase relations of their sine components. For this reason such signals are called **quasi-periodic signals**. A quasi-periodic signal (see Figure 8.5c) may look and sound identical to a complex periodic signal (see Figure 8.5b), but it is characterized by the presence of continuous changes. In the left parts of Figure 8.5b and c, for example, both signals are identical, but in the right parts, only a few milliseconds later, they start to differ. This change arises gradually, so that it is difficult to determine exactly at which point it starts. Since it is very difficult to find an exact description of a quasi-periodic signal, small sections of quasi-periodic signals are treated as if they were periodic. This decision is discussed further in Section 8.3.3. In the case of a quasi-periodic signal, a certain periodicity can be detected; that is, a part of the signal looks similar to its surrounding parts. A period frequency may therefore be assigned to the signal, although in a strictly physical sense this is not correct, since two "quasi-periods" of such a signal are never fully identical.

A period frequency, however, cannot be determined for the following two classes of signals: **noise**, exemplified by the hissing sound of air escaping when a soda can is opened (see Figure 8.5d), and **impulse**, for example the sound produced by hitting a nail with a hammer. In these cases, the sound is very irregular, and there are no signal stretches that repeat themselves in a periodic or even quasi-periodic way. A noise can be said to have a certain amplitude and timbre, but no periodic frequency – the only thing in common between separate stretches of the signal is their irregularity. An impulse is even more aperiodic, without any separate stretches that are similar. It consists of a sudden irregularity with a relatively high amplitude, preceded and followed by silence. Thus, an impulse does not have a period frequency either.

The oscillogram of a speech signal (see Figure 8.6) shows that it consists of complex periodic and quasi-periodic stretches, as well as noises and impulses. In Figure 8.6a, the oscillogram of the sentence *Almost everyone knows Belinda hasn't found out yet* ([ʔʌ̃mɔstɛʊɟʌnoʊs bəlĩnɾʌɦæzn̩faʊ̃ndaʊjeː]), which is 2.4 seconds long, is given. There are stretches with higher amplitude and quasi-periodic spikes, which stem from the glottal pulses of voiced sounds, most probably vowels. There are stretches where the amplitude is low, which could be pauses, stops or sounds that are produced with lower energy. One part of the signal is enlarged (in the time domain) in Figure 8.6b, where only 0.5 seconds are displayed. This part actually relates to the phrase *hasn't found* [ɦæzn̩faʊ̃nd]. On the left, the glottal fricative [ɦ] merges with the low front back vowel [æ] and appears

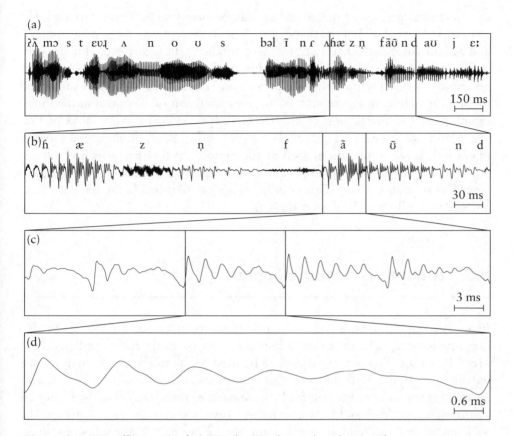

Figure 8.6 Oscillograms of a speech signal: (a) the phrase *Almost everyone knows Belinda hasn't found out yet*, length: 2.5 s, (b) the phrase *hasn't found*, length: 500 ms, (c) the vowel [ã] from the diphthong [ãʊ̃], length: 50 ms, and (d) one period from the vowel [ã], length: 10 ms. The vertical lines indicate the position of the enlarged (zoomed-in) segments. The vertical scale is the same in all four panels.

as the lowered amplitude and the slight blackness on the waveform from the frication. The voiced fricative [z] can then be seen as a rather black stretch (from the frication) that still shows the modulation of the vibrating vocal folds (from the voicing). After the syllabic nasal [n̩] there is no closure or plosion, which indicates that the speaker has dropped the plosive [t] altogether and produces the labiodental fricative [f], which shows up as a low-amplitude stretch. The diphthong [ãʊ̃] has an [ã] with a slightly higher amplitude than the [ʊ̃] and the [n] shows a less "jaggedy" waveform (and looks similar to the [n] of *hasn't*). The final [d] is completely reduced and the plosion can only be made visible with a resolution as in Figure 8.6d, which we do not display here for lack of space. All these details are even more difficult to see when looking only at Figure 8.6a. In Figure 8.6c, 50 ms of the first part of the diphthong [ãʊ̃] are enlarged and the individual periods of the voiced sounds become visible. These periods look somewhat "irregular" but the shape of each period is repeated very similarly again and again, which is the nature of (quasi-)periodicity. In Figure 8.6d, finally, one 10 ms long period is stretched out. In this display, the periodicity can obviously not be seen (since there is only one period) and the signal looks much smoother than, for example, in Figure 8.6b. What these different oscillograms of the same signal display is that choosing a different time-scale changes the looks of the signal and can reveal certain details. On the other hand, looking too closely might hide some information, such as the periodicity that becomes invisible in Figure 8.6d. Note, that the amplitude of the diphthong [aʊ̃] seems to decrease from Figure 8.6b to 8.6d. This is only an optical illusion, as the peak-to-peak amplitude in all three displays is the same.

8.3   Analyzing Acoustic Signals

In an oscillogram, the five types of signals (pure tones, complex periodic signals, quasi-periodic signals, noises, and impulses) can be easily recognized (see Figure 8.5). An oscillogram can therefore be used for simple acoustic analyses, as we did in Section 2.3.3, and to measure durations, as we did in Section 6.3. But an oscillogram is not very helpful if, for example, the speech sound [ɑ] should be distinguished from an [i]. Although these vowels sound different, both sounds look suspiciously alike in an oscillogram (see Figure 8.7). The oscillogram does contain this distinctive information, because it is a complete representation of the acoustic signal, but the information is not visible as such. This section presents and discusses the most important methods that can be used to trace and quantify this kind of information that is not easily visible in an oscillogram.

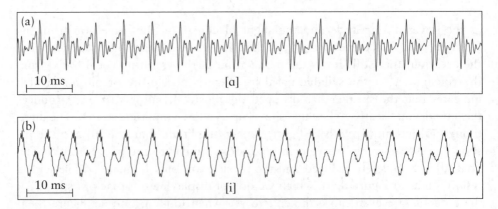

Figure 8.7   Waveforms of the vowels (a) [ɑ] and (b) [i].

8.3.1 *Fourier transformation*

In Section 8.2 we mentioned that complex periodic signals may be constructed by adding up pure tones. In 1822, Fourier proved that *any* periodic signal, no matter how complex, may be decomposed into a combination of sine signals. In the following section, we first describe how sine signals are summed and how their sums can be used to construct any periodic signal.

8.3.1.1   SUMMING UP SIGNALS: FOURIER SYNTHESIS

An acoustic signal is a continuously changing sequence of air pressure values. When two waveforms occur simultaneously, for example coming from two separate loud-speakers, their air pressure values are added up. This means that two oscillograms may be combined by simply adding up the displacements of both signals.

The sum of two signals is a new signal with the sequence of the sums of the displacements of both signals at each point in time (see Figure 8.8). If, at a given point in time, both displacements are on the same side of the zero-line, their sum is greater than each of the separate displacements (point A in Figure 8.8). If the

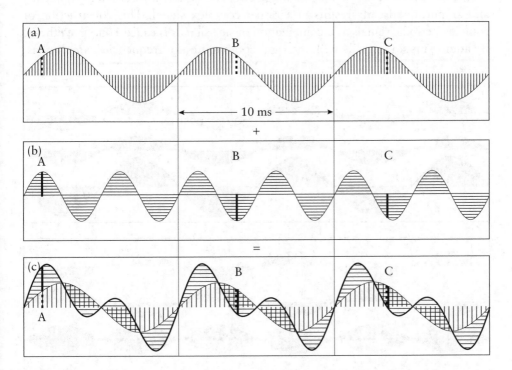

Figure 8.8   The sine signal in (a) has a frequency of 100 Hz; the one in (b) has a frequency of 200 Hz. Both signals have identical amplitude and start with equal phase. In (c), their sum is represented by a dark line; the shading expresses the individual contribution of each signal.

two displacements are on opposite sides of the zero-line (one being positive, the other negative), then their sum is smaller than each of the separate displacements (point B in Figure 8.8). If the two displacements are on opposite sides of the zero-line and have exactly the same size, their sum is "0" (point C in Figure 8.8).

It follows from the previous paragraph that the peak-to-peak amplitude of the combined signal is *not* necessarily the sum of the peak-to-peak amplitudes of the two signals. This is shown in Figure 8.9. In Figure 8.9a, two sine signals with identical frequency, amplitude, and phase have been added up. Since the maxima and minima in both signals occur at identical points in time, their summed amplitude has twice the amplitude of the separate signals.

But in Figure 8.9b, the same signals have been shifted in phase by 180° with regard to each other. Now the displacements of both signals are equal in size but at opposite sides of the zero-line, so that their sum is always "0". As a result, the sum signal results in the zero-line: the two signals have canceled each other out. This effect is used in "noise canceling headphones." These headphones have microphones that pick up the surrounding noise and play this noise with a phase difference of 180°. Since both noise sound waves cancel each other, the noise becomes (under ideal circumstances) inaudible.

As can be seen in Figure 8.8, summing two sine signals with different frequency and amplitude already results in a rather complex signal. This construction of complex periodic signals as a combination of sine signals is called **Fourier synthesis**. By adding up sine signals with the right combination of frequencies, amplitudes,

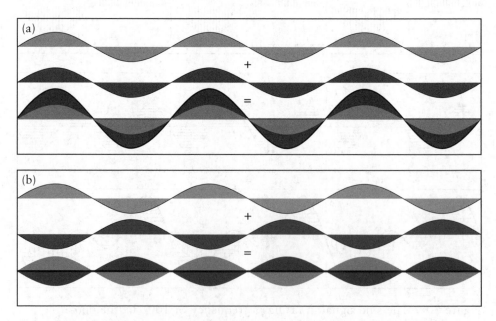

Figure 8.9 Adding up two sine signals with equal frequency and amplitude. In (a), two signals with identical phase are added up, whereas (b) shows the addition of two signals with opposite phase.

and phases, *any* periodic signal may be constructed. This indicates the importance of sine signals in acoustics, since they may serve as the basis for all complex acoustic signals.

8.3.1.2 DECOMPOSING SIGNALS: FOURIER ANALYSIS

The procedure just outlined is particularly interesting because it can be reversed: by means of the **Fourier analysis**, any periodic signal can be decomposed into separate sine signals which are uniquely defined by their frequencies, amplitudes, and phases. In other words, for any given periodic signal, only a unique combination of sine signals produces exactly the same signal, and Fourier analysis is able to find this combination.

This process is represented in Figure 8.10. The signal in the "foreground" has been decomposed by Fourier analysis into four sine signals. (That is, if these four sine signals are added, the signal on the "front" of the display is generated.) At the "front" of this graph, time is represented horizontally from left to right, and amplitude vertically from bottom to top. Thus, the "front" represents an oscillogram. The frequencies of the sine signals are represented as going from front to back "into the image." The *length* of each vertical line on the left side, perpendicular to the frequency axis, indicates the amplitude of the corresponding sine component, and the *position* of each vertical line indicates the period frequency of the associated sine signal.

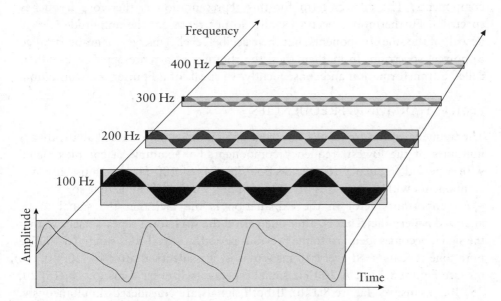

Figure 8.10 Four sine signals with increasing frequency and decreasing amplitude are added up. In this three-dimensional representation the resulting signal is represented "in the foreground" of the graph, whereas the individual sine signals and their frequencies are represented "going deeper into the picture."

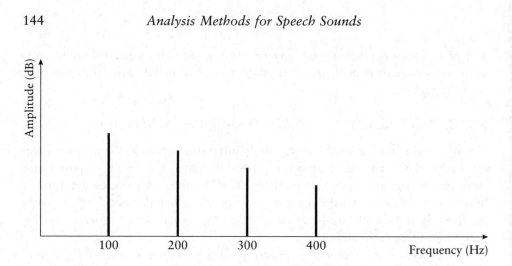

Figure 8.11 The individual frequencies with their amplitude values, which were represented as "going deeper into the picture" in Figure 8.10, are drawn from left to right in a frequency power spectrum.

In Figure 8.11 this representation of the sine frequencies and their amplitudes has been rotated so that the frequency axis now goes from left to right. In this graph, the amplitude is represented vertically and the frequency horizontally. Notice that a spectrum does not show the phase relations between the individual sine components. The correct term for this representation is therefore **frequency spectrum**. Furthermore, spectra usually do not represent the amplitude (e.g. in pascal) of the sine components, but their decibel level. This type of graph is called a **(power) spectrum**. In mathematics, the rotation of a representation by 90° is called a transformation and consequently we speak of a **Fourier transformation**.

8.3.1.3 HARMONIC FREQUENCIES

The frequencies in a frequency spectrum of a complex periodic signal are always multiples of the lowest frequency component. For example, a complex signal with a period frequency (F_0; see Section 7.3.1.4) of 100 Hz, contains only sine components with frequencies of 100, 200, 300 Hz, etc. Why is that so?

An important factor in the explanation is the fact that the signal to be analyzed is periodic. That is, after one period the waveform repeats itself, so that the signal becomes identical to the previous period. A signal consisting of a 100 Hz pure tone repeats itself every 10 ms – that is, it is identical after 10, 20, 30, . . . ms (see Figure 8.12a). A 200 Hz signal repeats itself every 5 ms (5, 10, 15, 20, 25, 30, . . . ms; see Figure 8.12b). If both signals are considered simultaneously, it can be seen that they "meet" every 10 ms. That is to say, they have the same phase relative to multiples of the duration of a period of the 100 Hz signal. This duration is the duration of one period of the sum signal (see Figure 8.12c). The fundamental frequency ($F_0 = 1/T_0$) of this fundamental period (T_0) is called the **first harmonic** (H1) of the complex signal. The 200 Hz component is called the

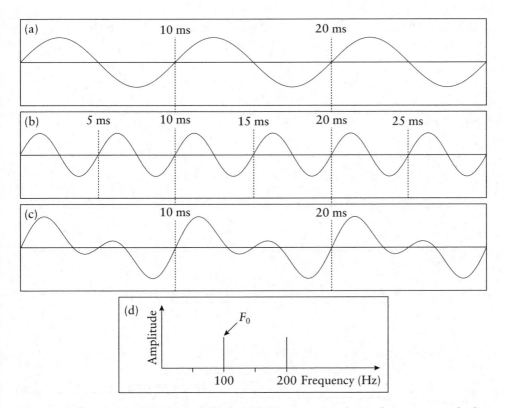

Figure 8.12 A (a) 100 Hz and (b) a 200 Hz sine signal, (c) their sum, and (d) its spectrum.

second harmonic (H2), and so on. That is to say, all frequency components of a complex signal are the harmonics of the fundamental frequency, with $F_0 = $ H1 and $n \times F_0 = $ Hn. As a general law, the fundamental frequency is the greatest common denominator (GCD) of all harmonics, and the duration of a period of the fundamental frequency is the least or lowest common multiple (LCM) of the durations of the periods of the harmonics. Figure 8.12d shows the individual spectral components of the complex signal in Figure 8.12c as lines. Therefore, this special sort of frequency spectrum is called a **line spectrum**.[1]

Consider the sum of a 100 Hz and a 150 Hz sine signal (see Figure 8.13). The 100 Hz signal repeats itself every 10 ms (10, 20, 30, . . . ms; see Figure 8.13a), whereas the 150 Hz signal does so every 6.7 ms (6.7, 13.3, 20, . . . ms; see Figure 8.13b).[2] The 100 Hz and 150 Hz signal "meet" every 20 ms – that is, they have the same phase position at 20 ms intervals, corresponding to a frequency of 50 Hz.[3] We thus obtain a period frequency of 50 Hz, although the signal consists of sine components with frequencies of 100 and 150 Hz. A Fourier analysis of this signal shows sine components at 100 and 150 Hz (see Figure 8.13d). However, the GCD is 50 Hz although this frequency is entirely absent from the

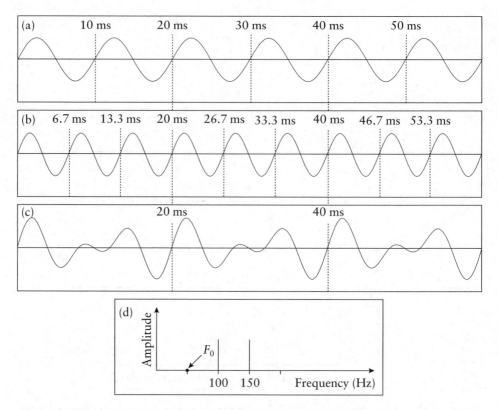

Figure 8.13 A (a) 100 Hz and (b) a 150 Hz sine signal, (c) their sum, and (d) its spectrum. Note that listeners perceive this signal to have a pitch of 50 Hz although this frequency is not present in either the signal or its spectrum.

spectrum itself. Interestingly, listeners, on the other hand, *do* perceive the F_0 of 50 Hz as the pitch of the signal. For example, we can "hear" the pitch of a speaker over a telephone that only transmits frequencies above 300 and below 4,000 Hz and, hence, does usually not transmit the fundamental frequency of a speaker. This is because our auditory system re-computes the F_0 from the higher harmonics of the signal and perceives that frequency as its pitch.

It should be stressed that a spectral analysis, such as the Fourier transformation, does not *add* any information about a signal. At its best, all information in the signal is preserved. For example, a Fourier transformation provides information about the sine components *and* their phase relations in a given complex signal. If the output of a Fourier transformation is represented in a frequency spectrum, the phase information is lost. In other words, this representation contains *less* information than the signal itself. A Fourier transformation only changes the *representation* of the information contained in a signal. Some things may be easier to see in a spectral representation than in the time-based representation of an oscillogram, but no information is ever *added* to the signal.

8.3.1.4 DISCRETE FOURIER TRANSFORMATION AND "FAST FOURIER TRANSFORMATION"

Strictly speaking, the Fourier transformation can only be applied to continuous signals. A computer-based analysis uses a form of Fourier transformation based on discrete time values, which is called **discrete Fourier transformation (DFT)**.

When the DFT was first implemented on a computer, it took a long time to compute. Soon a method was developed to reduce the calculation time. This method is known as the **fast Fourier transformation (FFT)**, and is a particular form of DFT. The essential characteristic of an FFT is the fact that the number of points on which the calculation is based is always a power of two. An FFT can therefore be based on 16, 32, 64, 128, 256, 512, 1,024, 2,048, 4,096 . . . points. Although the processing capacities of modern computers have increased so much that even a proper DFT can now be performed with acceptable calculation times, the FFT is still used by many computer programs.

To summarize, the Fourier transformation is just *one* possible form of spectral analysis, although most commonly used. The DFT is a Fourier transformation performed on discrete data (for example, by a computer). And an FFT is just an efficient way of implementing a DFT on a computer. Furthermore, the term *FFT* or *FFT spectrum* is often used when referring to a power spectrum.

8.3.1.5 FOURIER TRANSFORMATION FOR NON-PERIODIC SIGNALS

In our discussion of the Fourier transformation, we have assumed that the signal to be analyzed is periodic, so that the application of a Fourier transformation is theoretically justified. But what happens when an acoustic signal is not perfectly periodic, but only quasi-periodic or non-periodic, as is the case for the speech signal? Real periodicity never occurs in speech signals, so how can Fourier analysis be applied to them at all? This question is answered in this section.

In periodic signals, the fundamental frequency is the greatest common denominator (GCD) of all the sine components contained in the signal. The fundamental frequency itself is not necessarily visible in the spectrum of a complex signal (as shown in Section 8.3.1.3). For instance, if two sine signals with frequencies of 100 and 101 Hz are added up, the fundamental frequency of the sum signal is 1 Hz, but this fundamental frequency is not one of the sine components of the signal. Theoretically, the sine components may lie as close together as possible, making the fundamental frequency infinitely low. As a result, *any* frequency may appear in a spectrum, as a multiple of an infinitely low fundamental frequency. The spectrum then consists of an infinite number of harmonics lying infinitely close together. Thus, instead of a line spectrum (see Figure 8.14a and b) we now obtain a **continuous spectrum** (see right panel of Figure 8.14c).[4] Every signal may therefore be considered to be periodic with an infinitely low fundamental frequency,

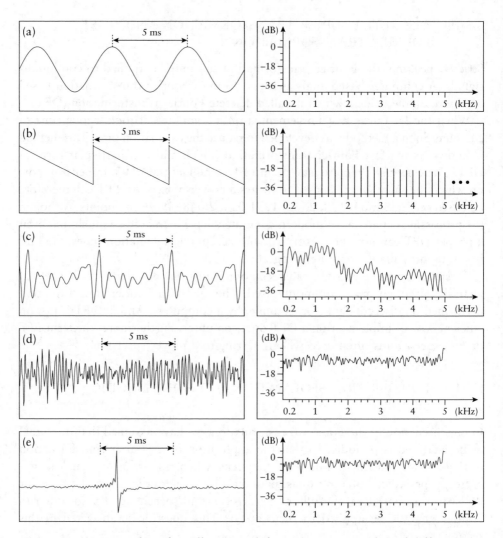

Figure 8.14 Examples of oscillograms (left) and spectra (right) of different signal types. (a) A sine signal (tone), which always has one single spectral line, (b) a saw-tooth signal as an example of a complex periodic signal, whose sine components can be seen in a line spectrum, (c) the vowel [ɑ] as an example of a complex, quasi-periodic signal, characterized by a continuous spectrum showing the (quasi)-harmonics, (d) the voiceless fricative [s] as an example of a non-periodic signal (noise) whose spectrum is continuous, and (e) the plosive [t] as an example of an impulse; like a non-periodic signal its spectrum is continuous, but the two signal types differ in the phase relations between their frequency components (which do not appear in a frequency spectrum).

which justifies the application of the Fourier transformation. (This argument may look like a "trick" to overcome the problem but it is indeed the standard way of arguing in mathematics. There is nothing wrong with it except that in real life we never encounter anything that is infinitely small.)

In a quasi-periodic signal, or in a non-periodic noise or impulse, all frequency components may occur. The spectrum of a quasi-periodic signal does have a structure in which the harmonics are visible (see Figure 8.14c), but noises or impulses have no harmonic structure at all (see Figures 8.14d and 8.14e).

A frequency spectrum does not show the difference between a noise and an impulse: in both types of signal, the distribution of the frequencies may be the same. Their difference lies in their phase characteristics. In the case of an impulse, all frequency components (i.e. all sine signals) are "in phase" at a single point in time (in the oscillogram) where all the maxima occur simultaneously; after that point all frequency components cancel each other out. But in noise, all frequency components have random phase in relation to each other, so that an oscillogram of the signal looks like an entirely random sequence of displacements.

8.3.2 What information can be seen in a spectrum?

A frequency spectrum clearly indicates *which* frequencies are present in a signal, and *how prominent* they are. Figure 8.14 shows a number of oscillograms, along with their corresponding spectra. Figure 8.14a is an example of a sine signal. In the spectrum only a single line appears, representing exactly the frequency of the sine signal. Figure 8.14b shows a periodic saw-tooth signal. The spectrum shows the fundamental frequency of the signal and the higher harmonics, which decrease in amplitude toward the higher frequencies. They appear as single lines in the spectrum, because the signal is perfectly periodic. The saw-tooth spectrum is actually a very simplified but reasonably good approximation of the spectrum of vocal fold vibration. Figure 8.14c shows the vowel [ɑ] (taken from the English word *cot*). This sound is a quasi-periodic signal, and therefore has a continuous spectrum. Figure 8.14d shows the sound [s], characterized by a high level of energy in the high frequencies, and a lower energy level in the low frequencies. In addition, since the signal is non-periodic, the spectrum does not show any harmonics. Finally, Figure 8.14e represents a sound like [t] from the word *cot*, which is a non-periodic signal as well, but an impulse. Unlike for the [s]-noise, the individual frequency components of the impulse [t] are in phase, so that their maxima occur simultaneously – something that is not visible, however, in the frequency spectrum.

The basic elements of a speech signal have now been presented. Some speech signals are easier to distinguish in an oscillogram than in a spectrum, such as the distinction between [s] (noise) and [t] (impulse), while others are easier to recognize in a spectrum than in an oscillogram, such as different vowels.

8.3.3   *"Windowing" in spectral analysis*

In our discussion of the Fourier transformation we started with periodic signals and extended the transformation to quasi-periodic and non-periodic signals. In a perfectly periodic signal, all periods are identical and, therefore, a single period is sufficient to describe the entire signal. In Figure 8.15 such a period is first selected (Figure 8.15a), then cut out of the signal (Figure 8.15b) and copied (Figure 8.15c), resulting in a reconstructed periodic signal which is identical to the original signal. That is, by taking one period from the original signal, it becomes possible to calculate its spectrum by means of a Fourier transformation. The spectrum (Figure 8.15d) shows that the complex signal consists of components at 100, 200, 300, and 400 Hz. Cutting out a short time stretch is called **windowing**, as we introduced it in Section 7.3.2.1, and the analysis yields a **short time spectrum**.

   The spectrum of exactly one period shows the fundamental frequency and its harmonics as separate lines (see Figure 8.15d). In a speech signal, however, it is impossible to determine the duration of exactly one period since the signal is at

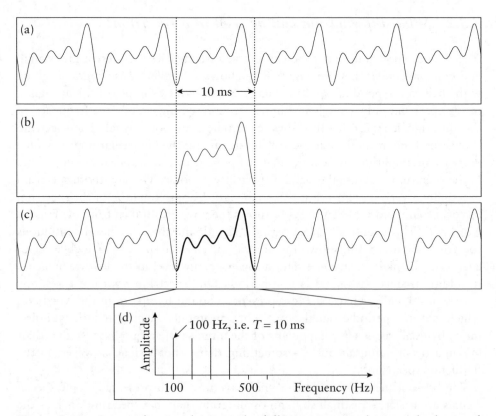

Figure 8.15   A periodic signal (a) can be fully reconstructed (c) on the basis of a single period (b). The spectrum (d) shows the harmonics of the signal in (c), which are identical to those of the original signal (a).

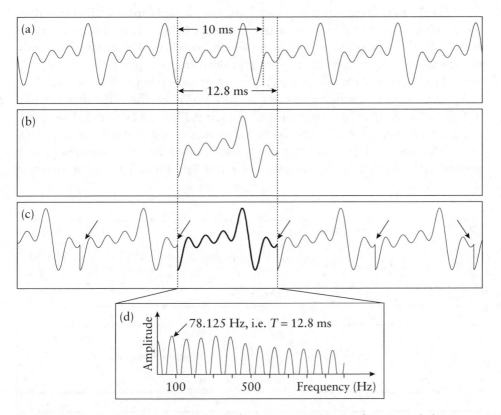

Figure 8.16 A signal stretch, which does not exactly match a period (b), is cut out (excised) of a periodic signal (a). If this stretch is replicated, the periods of the resulting signal (c) have the duration of the excised segment.

its best only quasi-periodic. Furthermore, an FFT can only be performed on signal stretches with a specific length (see Section 8.3.1.4), which usually does not correspond to the period duration of a signal. What happens if the window does not cover exactly one period?

Figure 8.16a displays the same signal as Figure 8.15a, with a 10 ms period duration. In Figure 8.16b, a 12.8 ms window was cut out of this signal. This stretch is subsequently replicated as described above. The reconstructed signal is periodic (see Figure 8.16c), but it is not identical to the original signal. In the reconstructed signal, the duration of a period is the length of the window (12.8 ms), since it is replicated. The reconstructed signal contains additionally a period of the original signal (10 ms), and many additional frequency components appear in the spectrum (see Figure 8.16d), which are not part of the original signal. The harmonics appear at multiples of the window size (12.8 ms, i.e. 78 Hz) and the spectral lines are slightly higher in the vicinity of the harmonics of the original signal (100, 200, 300, and 400 Hz). In other words, the windowing has led to a distortion of the spectrum. Can this effect be avoided?

The problem is caused by the sudden jumps in the replicated signal at the edges of the window (indicated by the arrows in Figure 8.16c). This distortion can be reduced by decreasing the amplitude of the windowed signal at its edges, and only keeping the full amplitude in the middle of the window (see Figure 8.17). (We already applied such a window in the computation of amplitude contours in Section 7.3.2.1.)

Application of this window function (Figure 8.17b) results in the signal shown in Figure 8.17c, which is then replicated (Figure 8.17d) and analyzed. The resulting spectrum (Figure 8.17e) shows the harmonics of the original signal at 100, 200, 300, and 400 Hz, and the distortions caused by other frequencies are greatly reduced (compare the spectra in Figures 8.16d and 8.17e). The shape of

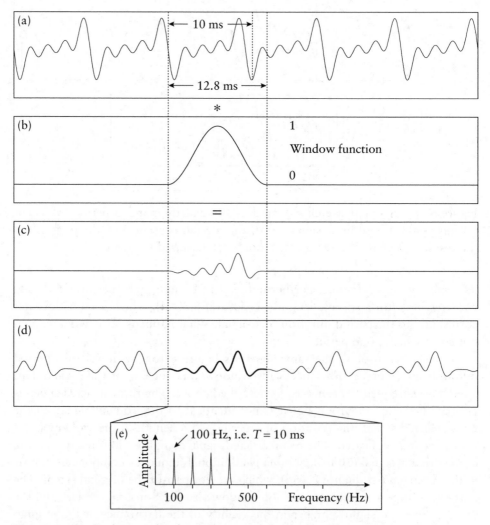

Figure 8.17 Reducing the distortions in the signal analysis by choosing an appropriate window function.

the window has an influence on the quality of the emerging spectrum and is always a compromise: if the window shape increases too steeply at its edges, sudden jumps occur in the signal. On the other hand, if the window increases too slowly, too much of the signal is suppressed and only a short stretch enters into the calculations with its original amplitude. The ideal window type increases slowly enough at its edges, while still maintaining the signal for a long time at almost its original amplitude.

There are many window types (Harris 1978), named after their shape or inventor. Most common in speech analysis are Hann, Hamming, Blackman, and Kaiser windows, which work well for most speech signals. In general, somewhat broader windows (like Hann and Hamming) give slightly narrower frequency bands around the "correct" frequencies but introduce more artifacts, whereas the more slender Blackman and Kaiser windows introduce fewer distortions. In practice, however, for speech signals these windows produce very similar results.

The use of windows in spectral analysis can solve an additional problem, especially for FFTs. After the application of a window, the signal at its edges is reduced to zero or almost zero level, so that additional "zero samples" may be added at the edges. This does not essentially affect the calculation of the spectrum, since the periodicity of the windowed signal is preserved. This trick enables us to use an FFT (see Section 8.3.1.4), which may only be applied to powers of two (... 512, 1024, 2048, ...), with windows of any possible size. For example, if a Hamming window of 300 samples has been extracted (see Figure 8.18b), the window may be supplemented by 212 "zero samples" to obtain a size of 512 samples (see Figure 8.18c), to which an FFT can be applied (see Figure 8.18d).

It should be kept in mind that a properly selected window reduces, but never entirely suppresses, the effects of sudden amplitude jumps.

8.3.3.1   THE RELATION BETWEEN WINDOW SIZE AND SPECTRAL RESOLUTION

The Fourier transformation actually takes the window size as the duration of one period (which is inversely related to its frequency; see Section 7.3.1.2) and "subtracts" this period from the signal, computing thereby amplitude and phase of this period, which is the information about the first harmonic (of the window size). Then this process is repeated for two, three, etc. periods, giving the amplitudes and phases of the second, third, etc. harmonic. Consequently, the **spectral resolution** – that is, the spacing between the frequency values – is inversely proportional to the window size (in ms): a 10 ms window has a spectral resolution of 100 Hz, a 20 ms window of 50 Hz, etc. Hence, the spectral resolution depends solely on the window size in milli*seconds*, and not on the sampling rate of the digitized signal. A higher sampling rate leads to information about higher frequencies, up to the Nyquist frequency (see Section 8.1.2), but does not increase the spectral resolution. This can only be increased (i.e. more closely spaced frequency values) by increasing the window size.

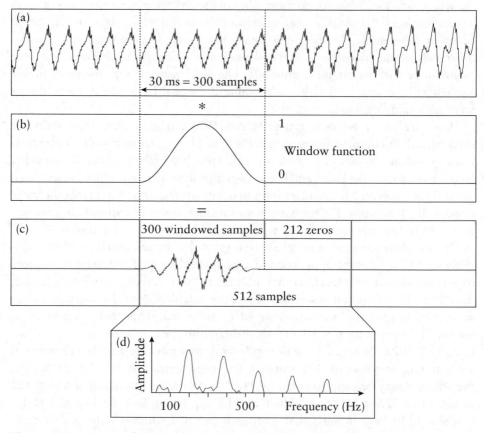

Figure 8.18   A speech signal, sampled at 10 kHz (a), has been multiplied by a Hamming window of 30 ms (b). This produces a windowed signal with 300 samples (c). Zero samples are then added to the signal in order to obtain the nearest power of two (here: 512 points). A fast Fourier transformation (FFT) is then performed on this data set, and its result represented in a frequency spectrum (d).

8.3.3.2   THE RELATION BETWEEN RESOLUTION IN THE TIME AND FREQUENCY DOMAINS

If the window is short, it represents the spectrum of a short stretch of speech, which seems appropriate, since the speech signal changes continuously. Unfortunately, a small window has a low frequency resolution (large spacing between frequency values). With a window size of 1 ms, for example, the distance between the frequencies represented in the spectrum is 1 kHz. By increasing the size of the window, a better spectral resolution is obtained. But since a speech signal changes continuously, a large window probably includes different parts of the signal, for example, part of a vowel and plosive, resulting in a spectrum that is averaged

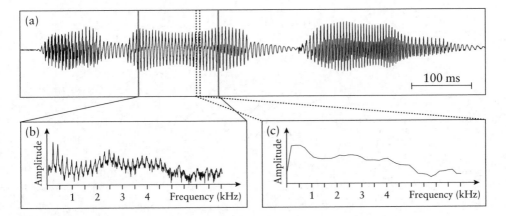

Figure 8.19   The influence of window size on the spectral (frequency) resolution. The spectrum to the left (b) is calculated with a window of 102.4 ms. The spectrum to the right (c) has been calculated with a window of 2.56 ms.

across these different parts. As a general rule, a small window (that is, a *high temporal* resolution) has a *low spectral* resolution, and a large window (that is, a *low temporal* resolution) has a *high spectral* resolution.

This principle is illustrated in Figure 8.19, where the same speech signal has been analyzed twice. The spectrum in Figure 8.19b has been calculated with a large window, resulting in a very detailed representation of the individual frequencies. However, different parts of the signal have been included in the calculation, which distorts the information about the individual parts inside the window. On the other hand, while the spectrum of Figure 8.19c has been calculated with a small window, this means that only a few frequency values can be distinguished in the representation. Usually, a window size of 20 ms gives a good compromise between good temporal and spectral resolutions.

8.3.4   *Other spectral representations: Waterfall and spectrogram*

To investigate longer stretches of speech with high temporal resolution, large window sizes are not appropriate, because the temporal resolution is lost. Instead of choosing a large window size, other approaches may be taken. In Figure 8.20, for example, a sequence of separate short time spectra have been arranged as slides one after another. In this representation, frequency is represented horizontally, amplitude vertically, and time as going "deeper into the picture." It shows quite clearly how the spectrum changes over time. As it is a kind of three-dimensional representation, it is called a **3D-representation** or **waterfall display**, since the sequence

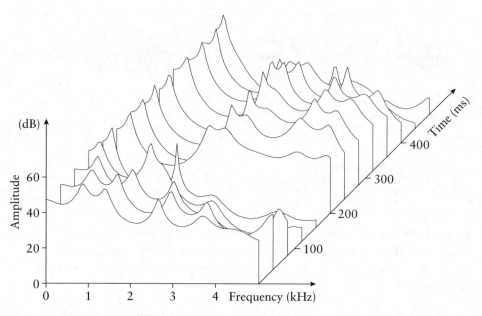

Figure 8.20 A *waterfall display* of a sequence of spectra. Each individual "slice" represents the spectrum of a single time window.

of spectra looks like a waterfall. Although it is a striking way of representing the development of spectra over time, it is not very well suited for finding the amplitude of a single frequency at a given time. In addition, if a waterfall display contains too many detailed spectra, it becomes difficult to read and some parts may be covered by other "slides." For these reasons, a different representation is usually chosen, where changes in the distribution of energy in different frequency regions can be clearly followed across time. This representation is presented now.

The sequence of spectra in Figure 8.20 looks like a kind of "mountain range." By looking at this "mountain range" from above, like a topographical map, a **sonagram** or spectrogram is obtained (see Figure 8.21). In this representation, time is displayed horizontally from left to right (as in an oscillogram). Frequency is represented vertically from bottom to top, and amplitude is represented by different shades of gray: higher amplitudes being darker, lower amplitudes being lighter. By using a spectrogram, the changes in the speech signal across time may be observed easily. A spectrogram simultaneously provides information about frequency, amplitude, and time.

With regard to the resolution in the time and frequency domains, the conclusions of Section 8.3.3.2 are true for spectrograms as well: *either* a good temporal resolution with a poor spectral resolution is obtained, *or* the spectral resolution is good but the temporal resolution is bad. This leads to a distinction between two types of spectrogram: the **narrow-band spectrogram** (see Figure 8.21b), which has good frequency resolution, and the **wide-band spectrogram** (see Figure 8.21c),

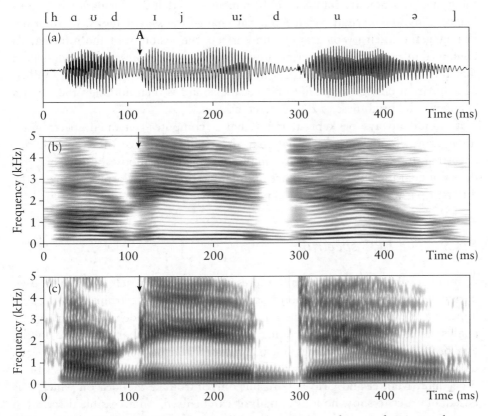

Figure 8.21 (a) The speech signal of the phrase *How do you do?* (note that the speaker does not round the lips in the first *do* and realizes the word with a high front unrounded vowel), with a (b) narrow-band and (c) wide-band spectrogram.

which has good temporal resolution.[5] In a narrow-band spectrogram, the individual harmonics are clearly visible as dark horizontal lines in the spectrum. In the same spectrogram, however, the release of [d] (point A in Figure 8.21b), which is visible in the oscillogram, only appears as a vague transition. In a wide-band spectrogram, on the other hand, this event is clearly marked (see the arrow in Figure 8.21c), but the individual harmonics are less visible. Additionally, the individual glottal pulses show up as vertical striations in the wide-band spectrogram due to the high temporal resolution.

Both the spectrogram and the oscillogram represent information present in the acoustic signal, but they do so in different ways. It is sometimes claimed that a spectrogram contains more information than an oscillogram. But the discussion in Section 8.3.1.3 has shown that no representation can contain *more* information than the acoustic signal itself – and an oscillogram already is a complete representation of the signal. It just looks *as if* a spectrogram shows certain things more accurately, but it should be remembered that the calculation of a spec-trogram involves certain parameters that change the way it looks. In addition, changing the intensity of gray-shading affects the visibility of the information contained in a spectrogram. Certain low values might be represented as white (and therefore not be visible) in one representation, and as light shades of gray in another. The apparent change in quality of a vocalic sound is then nothing other than a change in the brightness of the representation.

It should always be kept in mind that a computer-generated spectrogram involves a set of parameters that may drastically influence the way it looks. Spectrograms can be obtained by simply clicking on a mouse button, but this does not guarantee that the data are optimally represented. Correct setting of the different parameters requires care and experience.

8.3.5   *The LPC spectrum*

A number of additional spectral representations exist, each with their own parameter settings to determine the calculation of the spectrum as well as its appearance. We present here one representation that is widely used in phonetic analyses: the **linear predictive coding (LPC)** spectrum. Linear predictive coding is a procedure that determines linear estimation factors (*predictors*) by means of mathematical methods. We will not go into the complex mathematics of this procedure (Markel and Gray 1976), but only introduce the idea on which it is based, in order to show how LPC analysis can be used. An accessible description of the procedure itself can be found in Ladefoged (1996, pp. 181–214). This procedure was originally developed as an attempt to reduce the amount of data transmitted for a telephone conversation, and thus to exploit telephone lines more efficiently. It is easy to see that speech signals could be more efficiently encoded (see Figure 8.22): any reasonably small part of the speech signal looks very much like the next part, which in turn looks like the next one, and so on. On the basis of one part of a signal, it is possible to predict more or less what the next part looks like. This kind of prediction can be mathematically defined as a linear sys-tem of equations, which can be solved. Once this has been done, it is sufficient to transmit the encoded mathematical parameters required to solve the equation system, instead of the speech signal itself.

In simplified terms, this LPC spectrum intends to remove the periodicity of the vocal fold vibrations from the spectral display. In articulatory terms, it tries to separate the larynx from the vocal tract and displays only the effect of the vocal tract in the spectrum. (In this sense, the LPC procedure implements aspects of the source-filter theory of speech production; see Section 9.4.) As an outcome, the LPC spectrum does not show all detail of an FFT spectrum, which shows the influ-ence of both the vocal fold vibrations and the vocal tract on the speech signal. Instead, only the information about the vocal tract is represented. A simplified way of conceptualizing this is that instead of describing the spectrum mountain

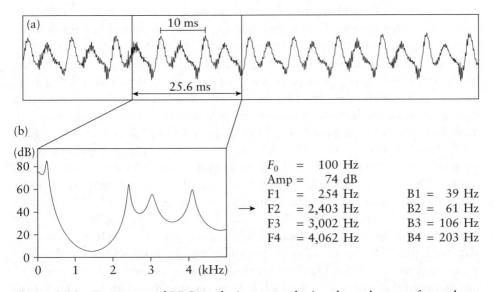

Figure 8.22   By means of LPC analysis, a speech signal can be transformed into information about the frequency of the vocal fold oscillation (F_0), a set of parameters describing the vocal tract (F1, B1, F2, B2, etc.), and the amplitude of the signal (Amp). The parameters can be used to estimate a spectrum of the vocal tract (b) by which the sound has been produced.

range in detail, only the location and "peakedness" of the mountain tops is used to describe the spectrum. These "mountain peaks" are parameterized by their location (which is called the "center frequency"; i.e. where the highest point of the "mountain" is on the frequency scale) and broadness of a peak (which is called "bandwidth"). For example, a sharp peak at a low frequency has a low center frequency and a small bandwidth, whereas a rather shallow peak at a low frequency has a low center frequency as well but a large bandwidth.

This LPC analysis procedure is interesting for phonetic purposes, because it aims to separate information about the vocal tract from information about vocal fold vibration. The procedure thus provides a simple way of making "clean" spectra of the vocal tract, and is particularly well suited for the representation of vowels. An additional advantage of this method is that it can be "reversed." Instead of analyzing speech, the LPC method can be used to synthesize speech. By means of **LPC re-synthesis**, a speech signal can be constructed on the basis of the parameters used to describe the vocal tract with the addition of amplitude and F_0 parameters. The individual parameters can be adapted to create different (artificial) speakers.

An important parameter in the computation of an LPC is, next to the window size, the "number of poles." This parameter determines the number of spectral "peaks" that can be computed. The locations of these "peaks" are an estimation of the "formants" that are an important concept in the source-filter theory of speech (see Section 9.4.1), which, in short, can be used to acoustically characterize vowels and other sounds. The number of these "peaks" is always half the number of poles, that is, with 10 poles there are maximally 5 peaks in the spectrum. The LPC procedure tries to distribute these peaks along the frequency axis according to the presence of energy in a particular frequency band. This introduces a relation between the number of poles and the sampling frequency, since digitizing the signal limits the highest frequency component to the Nyquist frequency (see Section 8.1.2). For example, if the sampling rate was 10 kHz, maximally 5 peaks are located between 0 and 5 kHz, which is an important range for speech sounds, especially vowels (see Section 10.1). If the sampling rate is 44.1 kHz, the 5 peaks are spread between 0 and 22.05 kHz. Consequently, only few or even no peaks might be located in the important range for vowels below 5 kHz. Therefore, it is advisable to increase the number of poles for higher sampling rates. As a rule of thumb, the number of poles should be the sampling rate in kHz plus two, but not larger than 24; that is, 12 poles for 10 kHz and 24 poles for 44.1 kHz. For a sampling rate of 10 (or 11.025) kHz this works reasonably well, since most of the energy in this frequency range stems from the speech signal. For a high sampling rate, most of the energy below 8 kHz is from the speech signal and the rest is only background noise. Unfortunately, it is hard to predict how many poles are needed for this "non-speech" part in the spectrum. It is essentially easier to analyze a signal that was digitized with a sampling rate not higher than 16 kHz or even 10 kHz. In other words, for some analyses, a high sampling rate might be worse than a lower rate, as we briefly mentioned at the beginning of this chapter.

We introduced different ways to represent and analyze speech signals in this chapter. An oscillogram displays all air pressure variations of a sound wave. This representation contains all information about the speech signal as it enters the ear. However, the distribution of energy in the high and low frequencies, for example, is not easily obtained from an oscillogram. The representation of the same signal in a Fourier spectrum is an improvement, since it allows the observation of individual frequency components. A drawback is the presence of information about the vocal tract and the vocal folds in the Fourier spectrum. The LPC spectrum can represent the vocal tract, especially for vowels, reasonably well, but involves the adjustment of certain parameters. The spectrogram allows the temporal investigation of frequency components, but also requires the adjustment of certain parameters. All these spectral analysis methods can provide a balance between good time and good frequency resolution, which is usually achieved with a 20 ms window size.

The previous chapter described basic acoustic terms that can be applied to any acoustic signal, and speech signals in particular. The next chapter investigates the acoustic consequences of speech articulations.

Exercises

1   What is the sampling rate? In the process of analog-to-digital conversion, how does one determine the minimum sampling rate necessary to uniquely reconstruct the original waveform without aliasing?
2   What is aliasing, why does it occur, and how can it be avoided?
3   What is the relationship between fundamental frequency and harmonic frequencies? If the F_0 of a signal is 150 Hz, what are the frequencies of H1, H2, and H3?
4   Why is the selection of a proper window shape and size important for a spectral analysis?
5   How is F_0 represented in (1) a wide-band spectrogram, (2) a narrow-band spectrogram, (3) a power spectrum, and (4) an oscillogram?
6   How many samples are in a 25 ms window if the sampling rate is 16 kHz?

Notes

1   Figure 8.11 is a line spectrum as well.
2   $150 \, \text{Hz} = \dfrac{150}{1 \, \text{s}} = \dfrac{1}{0.006666\ldots \text{s}} \approx \dfrac{1}{6.7 \, \text{ms}}.$
3   $\dfrac{1}{20 \, \text{ms}} = \dfrac{1}{0.020 \, \text{s}} = 50 \, \text{Hz}.$
4   A "continuous spectrum" on a computer consists of discrete frequency and amplitude values, and is not continuous in the mathematical sense. But the term "continuous spectrum" is used for computer-based analyses, in order to distinguish it from a line spectrum, where spectral lines only occur at multiples of the fundamental frequency.
5   The naming follows from the technology used at the time, which was directly related to the technical properties of filters (see Section 9.3). In order to produce a narrow-band spectrogram, a filter was used which only allowed a narrow range of frequencies to pass through. For a wide-band spectrogram, another filter was used which let through a wide range of frequencies.

9 The Source-Filter Theory of Speech Production

Chapters 3 and 4 described how speech sounds are produced with the speaking apparatus and how they can be transcribed. Chapters 5 and 6 presented the production of speech sounds in detail. Chapters 7 and 8 introduced the basic elements of acoustics and how sound can be analyzed. We now apply this knowledge to the acoustics of speech sound production. An important concept is the separation of speech sounds into one or more *source* signals and the modification of these signals by a *filter*.

Sound sources for speech are rather limited. The sources are either the vocal folds for voiced speech sounds or a constriction that generates a noise somewhere along the vocal tract. Such a noise can be produced either continuously as in fricatives or only as a transition as for plosives. Another possible source is "jiggling" articulators, as in trills. For example, in a trilled [r], the vibrating tip of the tongue is a sound source. More than one sound source can exist at the same time, as, for example, in the case of a voiced fricative, which has a laryngeal source at the glottis and an oral source at the constriction at the place of articulation. Despite the small number of sound sources, a great range of speech sounds can be produced by filtering. This is what the vocal tract does to the sound source(s) at the larynx or in the vocal tract itself: it filters the sound sources and gives the speech sounds their characteristics.

This situation is similar to a trumpet player who produces a louder or softer tone with lower or higher pitch but the sound always has a characteristic trumpet "sound." To change the sound quality, a trumpet player can use a mute at the opening of the trumpet and move it during playing. This does not change the pitch of the trumpet sound, and varies the loudness only to some degree, but more importantly, it changes the quality of the sound. What actually happens is that the sound source, here the trumpet tone, is *filtered* by the mute. Something similar can be done with a stereo set by turning the "bass" and "treble" controls: this does not change pitch or rhythm, but it changes the sound quality by increasing or attenuating the low-frequency or the high-frequency regions.

In this chapter we discuss how articulation leads to the acoustic characteristics of sounds. The acoustic characteristics of speech sounds are seen to arise from the combination of a source signal and the filtering properties of a given vocal tract configuration. We first introduce some additional concepts that are relevant for the description and analysis of speech signals, which are *resonance*, *damping*, and *filtering*.

9.1   Resonance

When tapping a wine glass with a fork, the glass starts to oscillate and produces a sound. If the fork is quickly moved close to your ear, the sound of the oscillating fork can be heard, although it fades away much quicker than the sound of the glass. Instead of tapping the glass, one could sing a note at the same pitch that the glass produces. In that case, the glass may start oscillating with that frequency. This oscillation of an object along with, and in reaction to, another object, is called **resonance**. Each object has a preferred frequency with which it oscillates when it is set into vibration, which is its **resonance frequency**. The resonance frequency is the frequency at which the glass or the fork oscillates best after being tapped and it depends on the characteristics (e.g. material, size) of the object.

Not only objects have a resonance frequency. The same is true for columns of air contained within a tube. This can be demonstrated by blowing across the opening of a bottle. A long air column (an empty bottle) has a low resonance frequency, and a short air column (a short or a full bottle) a high resonance frequency. Just as the resonance frequency depends on the characteristics of an oscillating object, the resonance frequency of an air column depends on the speed of sound and on the shape and length of the tube in which the air column oscillates. Since the vocal tract is such a tube that resonates with the source signal, and since the resonance frequencies of tubes play an important role in the production of speech sounds, they are treated in detail. We start with the simplest shape of a resonator, a cylindrical tube, which roughly resembles the vocal tract when it produces a schwa ([ə]).

9.1.1   *Resonating frequencies of cylindrical tubes*

Imagine a cylindrical tube which is open at one end and closed at the other (Figure 9.1). What are its resonance frequencies? At the open end of the tube, the air pressure is identical to the air pressure of the surrounding air (point A in Figure 9.1). The further one moves into the tube, the more the air pressure can increase (or decrease). The air pressure maximum (or minimum) therefore occurs at the closed end of the tube (point B in Figure 9.1). This increase and decrease in air pressure is represented with the graph in the bottom panel of Figure 9.1. The zero-crossing in this graph corresponds to the atmospheric air pressure, and the greatest (peak-to-peak) amplitude of the waveform corresponds to the maximal change of air pressure (difference between maximum and minimum) in

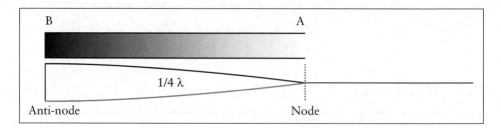

Figure 9.1 Air pressure change in a resonating cylindrical tube open at one end. Top panel: darker grays indicate larger changes of air pressure; bottom panel: the dark line indicates a pressure maximum and the lighter line a pressure minimum.

the tube. This point of maximal change is called the **anti-node** of the oscillation and the point of minimal change (at the atmospheric air pressure) is the **node**. Examining the graph, the tube fits one quarter of the wavelength of a single oscillation from the maximum of a sine-wave to its zero-crossing. In other words, the length of one wave is four times the length of the tube. As discussed in Section 7.3.1.3, the wavelength and the frequency of a waveform are related ($c/\lambda = f$). This enables us to calculate the resonance frequency of the tube, where the wavelength is four times the length of the tube:

$$\frac{\text{speed of sound [m/s]}}{4 \times \text{length of tube [m]}} = \text{resonance frequency [Hz]} \quad \text{or} \quad \frac{c}{4l} = f.$$

Thus, on the basis of the speed of sound (about 340 m/s in air) and the length of the tube, it is possible to calculate the frequency at which the air column in a cylindrical tube resonates. For example, if the length of a tube is 20 cm ($\approx$ 8 inches), its resonance frequency is:

$$\frac{340 \text{ m/s}}{4 \times 0.2 \text{ m}} = \frac{340}{0.8 \text{ s}} = 425 \text{ Hz}.$$

The production of sound in wind instruments follows the same principle. Again, the length of the tube determines the frequency of the sound. For example, a flute player produces low notes by closing holes in the flute, thereby increasing the length of the tube and thus the wavelength of the resonance frequency, which leads to the lower frequency produced. An instrument like the French horn, however, is nothing but a single, long tube. Unlike the flute, the French horn does not have any holes. This seems to imply that only a single note can be produced, but horn players nevertheless manage to produce several tones on their instrument. This implies that a tube may have other resonance frequencies. How do these arise?

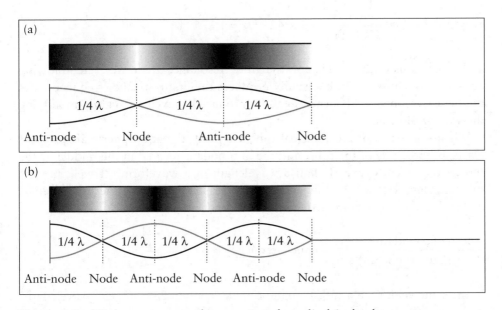

Figure 9.2 Higher resonance frequencies of a cylindrical tube open at one end.

Until now, the existence of a node (atmospheric air pressure) at the open end of the tube and an anti-node (maximal change of air pressure) at its closed end has led to the conclusion that exactly one fourth of the wavelength can fit into the tube. However, this combination of a node at the open end and an anti-node at the closed end can additionally be achieved by putting not only 1/4 of the wavelength into the tube but also 3/4 of the wavelength (see Figure 9.2a), 5/4 of the wavelength (see Figure 9.2b), etc. In other words, frequencies whose wavelengths are 4 times, 4/3 times, 4/5 times, etc. the length of a given tube fit well. Since the (odd) multiples of the quarter wavelength match the length of the tube, the tube resonates with these wavelengths and is called a **quarter-wavelength resonator**.

The corresponding resonance frequencies must be 3, 5, etc. times higher when 3, 5, etc. times a quarter-wavelength fits into the tube, since wavelength and frequency are inversely related ($c/\lambda = f$). A convenient way of calculating the corresponding resonance frequencies consists of multiplying the tube's first resonating frequency by the (odd) multiples:

$$f_k = (2k - 1) \times \frac{c}{4l}$$

(where 'f_k' denotes the k-th resonance frequency and '$2k - 1$' gives just the odd numbers "1, 3, 5 ..." when "1, 2, 3 ..." is inserted for "k").

In the example above, with 425 Hz as the first resonance frequency, this formula gives for the second resonance frequency (i.e. $k = 2$, $c = 340$ m/s, and $l = 0.2$ m):

$$f_2 = (2 \times 2 - 1) \times \frac{340 \text{ m/s}}{4 \times 0.2 \text{ m}} = 3 \times 425 \text{ Hz} = 1{,}275 \text{ Hz},$$

and, analogously, 2,125 Hz for the third resonance frequency, etc. Blowing across the opening of a tube usually produces the first resonance frequency, but the higher resonance frequencies can be produced as well by slightly modifying the way of blowing.

When both ends of a cylindrical tube are open, the atmospheric air pressure exists at both ends of the tube, and the anti-node is located in the middle of the tube. Consequently, exactly half a wavelength of a waveform fits well into the tube (see Figure 9.3a). Following the same reasoning as with the tube open at one end, the resonance frequency of a tube open at both ends is:

$$\frac{\text{speed of sound [m/s]}}{2 \times \text{length of tube [m]}} = \text{resonance frequency [Hz]} \quad \text{or} \quad \frac{c}{2l} = f.$$

In the same vein, such a tube can additionally contain 2/2, 3/2, etc. wavelengths (see Figure 9.3b and c) and we speak of a **half-wavelength resonator**. In other

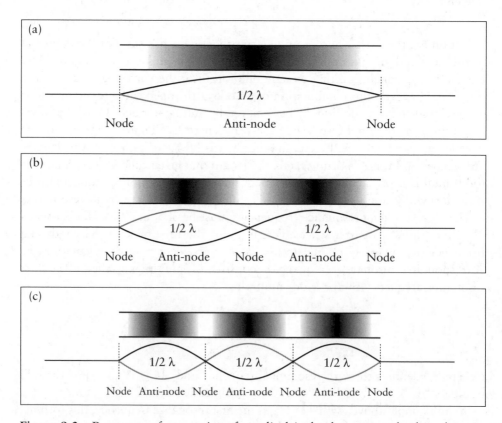

Figure 9.3 Resonance frequencies of a cylindrical tube open at both ends.

words, frequencies whose wavelengths are 2/1, 2/2, 3/2, etc. the length of a given tube fit well. Thus, the frequencies of this resonator can be computed with the formula:

$$f_k = k \times \frac{c}{2l}.$$

Tubes that are closed at one end and open at the other (quarter-wavelength resonators) as well as tubes that are open at both ends (half-wavelength resonators) are relevant for speech production. In addition, a tube closed at both ends is relevant, as shown in Section 10.2.2. Such a resonating tube closed at both ends has the same properties as a tube open at both ends and is therefore also a half-wavelength resonator.

9.1.2 Resonating frequencies of non-cylindrical tubes

The resonance frequencies not only depend on the length of the tube and the speed of sound, but also on the shape of the tube. To understand this, we investigate the behavior of the air molecules in more detail. When a sound wave oscillates in such a tube, the same principles apply as laid out in Section 7.1.2: the individual molecules swing back and forth, but do not necessarily move in and out of the tube. This can again be compared to the behavior of swaying people, which behave like oscillating molecules in a tube closed at both ends (see Figure 9.4). Persons at the anti-nodes "B" are alternatively compressed and stretched (i.e.

Figure 9.4 Molecules swinging in a tube closed at both ends (the pressure situation is opposite to the case illustrated in Figure 9.3b).

experience the maximal change in "neighbor density"), but they do not have to move. Only the persons in between have to sway back and forth, and those at the nodes "A" (i.e. in the middle between the anti-nodes) have to move the most.

If there is a constriction at a node, the movement of people (or molecules) is perturbed, and the swaying (or oscillation) takes longer; that is, the resonance frequency is lower. If there is a widening at a node, it is easier to move, and the resonance frequency is higher. If there is a constriction at an anti-node, fewer people (or molecules) are needed to reach the maximal or minimal density, and the oscillation is faster and hence the frequency higher. Likewise, a widening at the anti-node requires more people (or molecules), and the resonance frequency is lower. These conditions apply for any of the resonance frequencies at the open and closed ends of a tube, as illustrated in Figure 9.5a–d, since all have an anti-node at the closed end and a node at the open end.

If, on the other hand, a constriction occurs somewhere along the tube, the influence on the different resonance frequencies is different, as illustrated for the first and second resonance of a tube open at one end. A constriction in the middle of the tube (see Figure 9.5f) does not change the first or second resonance

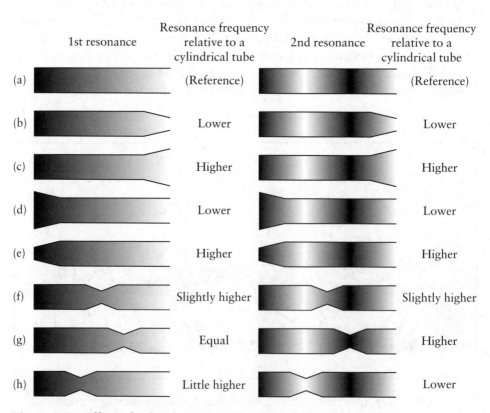

Figure 9.5 Effect of tube shapes on resonance frequencies.

frequency considerably since the constriction is halfway between a node and an anti-node.[1] A more anterior constriction (see Figure 9.5g) decreases the first resonance slightly since the constriction is closer to a node, but increases the second resonance, since the constriction is at an anti-node. If, on the other hand, the constriction is further back (see Figure 9.5h), the first resonance is slightly increased (the constriction is closer to an anti-node) whereas the second resonance becomes lower (at a node).

Likewise, the influence on the third or higher resonance frequencies can be computed, and this can be done for tubes open or closed at both ends as well. This way of explaining the change in the resonance frequencies is called the **perturbation theory** (Chiba and Kajiyama 1941) and is a convenient way to compute whether the resonance frequencies for an arbitrarily constricted tube are higher or lower than those for the unconstricted cylindrical tube. Applied to the production of vowels, if the location of the constriction is known, perturbation theory predicts for each resonance frequency whether it will increase or decrease compared to that for the neutral vowel schwa (see Section 9.5.1).

Another way to compute the resonance frequencies of a constricted vocal tract is by constructing it piece-wise from a combination of simple cylindrical tubes that are open or closed at one or both ends. This method is used in Section 10.2 to compute resonance frequencies for several vocal tract configurations for consonants.

It is precisely the dependency between the shape of the vocal tract and the resonance frequencies that allows a human speaker to produce a wide variety of speech sounds. In the process of speaking, we continuously move mouth, jaw, and tongue, thus modifying the shape of the oral cavity to change its resonance frequencies. This filters the source signal in different ways and hence allows us to produce different speech sounds.

We mentioned at the beginning of this chapter that the wine glass and the fork oscillate for different durations. In the next section we introduce the concept of *damping*, which is closely related to the concept of resonance frequency, to describe this behavior.

9.2 Damping

Each object has specific resonance frequencies. Two objects may not only differ in the frequency at which they resonate, but also in the time during which they continue to oscillate after being excited to the same extent. A wine glass, for example, continues to oscillate for a long time. But the fork with which it was tapped oscillates only briefly. We therefore need another parameter to describe this particular characteristic of resonance: **damping**. It provides information about the duration of the oscillation.

Damping constitutes a measure of how rapidly a waveform fades away, and is determined by the material of the vibrating object. For example, when a wine glass is tapped, the energy of the tap is converted into an oscillation of the glass. Since the elastic properties of the wine glass allow it to oscillate only at one frequency, this oscillation continues for a long time until the energy of the tap is converted into acoustic energy. A fork, on the other hand, oscillates at several frequencies, which are distributed around a "natural" or "center frequency" (see Section 9.3). The energy is distributed across these frequencies, which partly cancel each other out, and the oscillation quickly fades away. That is, there is an inverse relation between the damping (how fast the oscillation dies out) and the precision with which an object oscillates at its resonance frequency. Low damping is always accompanied by a precise resonance frequency and a persistent oscillation whereas high damping goes along with a less precise resonance frequency and a short oscillation time.

Objects (or columns of air) may be made to oscillate not only by tapping them, but also by exposing them to other oscillations. A trained singer may cause a wine glass to oscillate by singing a note at the resonance frequency of the glass. The almost perfectly periodical sound waves of the singing voice cause the wine glass to oscillate, which is called **sympathetic resonance**. The frequency of the singer's voice and the resonating characteristics of the wine glass can be used to increase the amplitude of those frequencies that are close to the resonance frequency of the glass. The same principle applies to the vocal tract, which can be thought of as a tube with one or more resonance frequencies and a degree of damping which depends on the shape of the tract. Frequency components from a sound source that are close to the resonance frequencies of the vocal tract pass the vocal tract relatively unhindered compared to those that are further away from them. This *filtering* is described in the next section.

9.3 Filters

When a sound consisting of a large number of different sine frequency components travels through a tube, only those frequencies which correspond to the tube's resonance frequencies are maintained; all other frequencies are weakened. The tube does not generate a frequency by itself (as happens when blowing across a bottle), but instead **filters** certain frequencies from the existing (source) signal. The filter is comparable to a sieve that only allows fine sand to pass through, and stops the larger stones, which remain behind in the sieve. Similarly, in the vocal tract, the filter lets certain frequencies pass through and makes this difficult or impossible for other frequencies.

In Section 5.2.2, we mentioned that the vocal folds in the larynx perform a complex oscillation and, hence, produce a complex signal. In Section 8.3.1.3 we saw that a complex signal consists of a large number of higher harmonic frequencies in addition to its fundamental frequency. The shape of the vocal tract allows some frequency regions to pass through easily, while others are filtered from the signal. This explains why the larynx signal can be modified so that it sounds like an [ɑ] or an [i]. The source signal in the larynx is the same for both sounds, but the shape of the vocal tract is different, due to changes in the position of the articulators. Thus, the filter – that is, the tube system formed by the vocal tract – is changed, allowing some frequencies to pass through easily, others less easily. This determines the signal as it is projected from the lips.

To understand how this can be described with an acoustic theory, we discuss the acoustic properties of filters in more detail and present complex tube systems that can be used to approximate the acoustic behavior of the vocal tract. In Chapter 10, this knowledge is applied to describe speech sounds acoustically.

Since filters affect the amplitude (and hence, the intensity) of different frequency regions in the signal, a spectral representation is particularly well suited to describe their properties (i.e. their resonance frequencies and damping behaviors).

Figure 9.6 shows the spectrum of a filter that suppresses high frequencies and allows low frequencies to pass. This type of filter is called a **low-pass filter**. This filter is essentially characterized by two parameters, its *cut-off frequency* and its *steepness*. The **cut-off frequency** is the boundary above which frequency components are dampened. The filter displayed in Figure 9.6 has its cut-off frequency at 100 Hz, but any other frequency is possible as well. The **steepness** is the rate at which the intensity of the frequency components above the cut-off frequency is **attenuated** (dampened).

For physical reasons, no low-pass filter lets through all frequency components up to the cut-off frequency to their full extent, while entirely eliminating all frequency components above the cut-off frequency. The transition between the **pass-band** of a filter, where the frequency components pass through practically

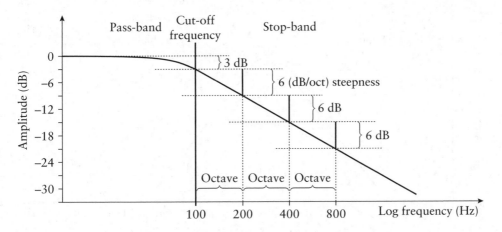

Figure 9.6 A low-pass filter with a slope of 6 decibels per octave. The frequency is plotted on a logarithmic scale (see Section 12.5.2).

unhindered, and the **stop-band**, where the frequencies are attenuated, is gradual. For that reason, the cut-off frequency of a filter is defined as the frequency at which a filter attenuates the intensity of frequency components by 3 dB (for the difference between amplitude and intensity, see Section 7.3.2 and Appendix A.2). Filters attenuate a signal beyond their cut-off frequency not with a certain amount per hertz but with every doubling or halving in frequency. Since "doubling" or "halving" in frequency is the same as going one octave up or down a musical scale, the steepness of the slope above the cut-off frequency is measured in **decibels per octave [dB/oct]**. In other words, for each octave (i.e. each time the frequency is doubled, in the case of a low-pass filter, or halved, in the case of a high-pass filter) the amplitude of the signal is reduced by this decibel value. The filter in Figure 9.6 has a steepness (or slope) of 6 dB per octave.

For a **high-pass filter**, the picture is reversed: above the cut-off frequency, the frequency components pass through almost unhindered (in other words, the high frequencies pass the filter), whereas the frequencies below the cut-off frequency are attenuated according to the steepness of the filter. In other words, a low-pass filter attenuates high frequencies and a high-pass filter suppresses low frequencies.

A combination of a low-pass and a high-pass filter is called a **band-pass filter** (see Figure 9.7 for a band-pass filter with a center frequency of 800 Hz).[2] In such a filter, the high-pass filter attenuates the low frequencies, while the low-pass filter attenuates the high frequencies. Only those frequency components in the area of overlap between both filters pass through a band-pass filter. For this type of filter, the width of the area between both cut-off frequencies is an important characteristic. As the filter attenuates the amplitude by 3 dB at the cut-off frequencies, this characteristic is called the **3 dB bandwidth**. It is expressed in hertz, because it indicates the "width" of the filter as measured in the spectrum on the hertz scale (see Figure 9.8). A large bandwidth means that a filter lets through frequencies

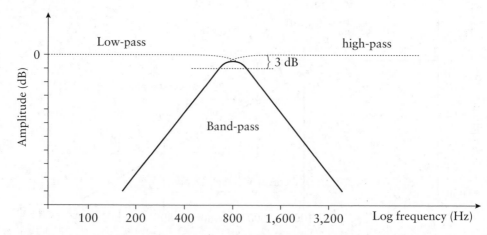

Figure 9.7 A band-pass filter (solid line) made from overlapping low- and high-pass filters (dotted lines).

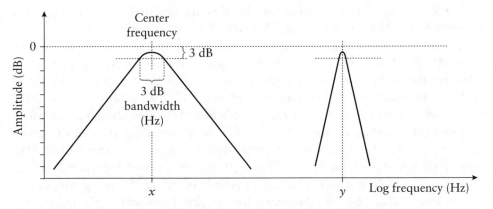

Figure 9.8 Two band-pass filters, each with its own center frequency and 3 dB bandwidth. The filter to the left has a relatively large 3 dB bandwidth at its center frequency *x* and the filter to the right has the center frequency *y* and a relatively small 3 dB bandwidth.

within a relatively large range. A small bandwidth, on the other hand, means that the filter attenuates nearly all frequencies, with the exception of a very small frequency range. Another important parameter of a band-pass filter is its **center frequency**. This is the "center" of the filter, where the frequencies are least attenuated, being allowed to pass through the filter as freely as possible. In Figure 9.8, the band-pass filter with its center frequency at *x* has a rather wide 3 dB bandwidth, whereas the filter with its center frequency at *y* has a narrow 3 dB bandwidth.

All components necessary to describe the vocal apparatus with an acoustic model have now been introduced, at least for voiced sounds with a relatively open vocal tract and a closed velopharyngeal port. (1) The complex vibration of the vocal folds generates a source signal with many harmonics. (2) The source signal has to pass through the vocal tract where, due to the resonance frequencies and damping characteristics of this system, certain frequencies are less attenuated than others. In other words, the source signal is filtered by the vocal tract. (3) The signal finally dissipates from the lips into the air, where it is transmitted as pressure variations through space. We now investigate these three parts in more detail.

9.4 Source and Filter of the Vocal Apparatus

The egressive airstream causes the vocal folds to vibrate if they are brought into an appropriate position. The vibrating vocal folds generate a waveform as displayed in Figure 9.9a. The spectrum of this signal is characterized by harmonics that decrease in altitude at a rate of about 12 dB/oct; that is, every octave the amplitude of the harmonic is 12 dB lower. Remember that the amplitude of a signal expressed in dB is in relation to a reference value, in this case the airflow behind fully closed vocal folds, which is close to zero. As a result, the relation between the airflow with an open glottis and a closed glottis can lead to a signal with an amplitude of the first harmonic of 164 dB.[3] If we assume that the vocal folds vibrate with a frequency of approximately 250 Hz, then the harmonic which is one octave higher, at about 500 Hz, has an amplitude that is 12 dB lower, i.e. 152 dB. Another octave higher (at the fourth harmonic at about 1,000 Hz), the amplitude is 140 dB, etc. (see Figure 9.9b). As a result, a harmonic with a frequency as high as 16 kHz has an amplitude of 92 dB. Even if a sound level much lower than 164 dB is assumed for the first harmonic at the larynx, the intensity is 66 dB lower at 16 kHz for a signal with a spectral decay of 12 dB/oct. In other words, the larynx signal carries considerable energy at high frequencies despite the fact that the fundamental frequency is 250 Hz. It is the complex movement of the vocal folds (see Section 5.2.2) that leads to a complex signal, which carries energy at frequencies far above the fundamental frequency. This "richness" of the source signal allows us to produce many different speech sounds from the same source signal by filtering it with the vocal tract.

9.4.1 Vocal tract filter

The vocal tract of the vowel schwa [ə] can be approximated by a cylindrical tube, which is open at one side (the lips) and virtually closed at the glottis. The length and width of the tube determine its acoustic properties. The vocal tract serves in this way as a quarter-wavelength resonator (see Section 9.1.1). The bending of the tube has little effect on the acoustic properties: whether the tube is a long straight cylinder or coiled up does not affect its acoustic properties. Assuming a vocal tract length (= tube length) of 17 cm and a speed of sound of 340 m/s, we can compute the resonance frequencies of the vocal tract producing the schwa:

$$f_k[\text{Hz}] = (2k - 1) \times \frac{340 \text{ m/s}}{4 \times 0.17 \text{ m}} = (2k - 1) \times 500 \text{ Hz}.$$

In other words, the resonance frequencies of the vocal tract with this shape are at 500 Hz, 1,500 Hz, 2,500 Hz, 3,500 Hz, 4,500 Hz, etc. These resonance frequencies of the vocal tract are very important and are called **formant frequencies**. The formant frequencies are numbered and are named F1, F2, F3, etc. Note, however, that this numbering sequence has *nothing* to do with the fundamental frequency F_0: F_0 is a property of the vocal fold vibration (the voice source) and the formant frequencies (F1, F2, F3, etc.) are properties of the vocal tract (the filter).

From an acoustical point of view, the vocal tract, containing the soft tissues of the oral and nasal cavities, is a "bad" tube since the energy across the *whole* frequency range is dampened. Only the resonance frequencies themselves are dampened to a lesser extent, which makes them appear as maxima in the spectrum. And, as said before, a high level of damping implies a large bandwidth; in other words, each resonance frequency of the vocal tract covers a large range. In acoustic terms, the vocal tract is a system of band-pass filters that can be described by their center frequencies and 3 dB bandwidths.

9.4.2 Radiation at the lips and nostrils

Once the air molecules leave the mouth and the nose, their movement encounters the giant air mass in the room. This phenomenon can be compared to a group of people walking through a long corridor (the trachea). This corridor contains a door (the glottis), which is alternately opened and closed. This causes the people, once they have passed the door, to walk in groups, the size of which depends on how long and how wide the door was opened. They continue to walk, through narrower and wider corridors (the vocal tract), until the end of the corridor (the lips), where they encounter a large, immobile crowd of people (the mass of air in the room). Upon entering the crowd, they bump into several people standing there, who in turn bump into their neighbors, etc. As a result, a small movement spreads through the crowd. When encountering a large crowd, a small group easily merges into the crowd. A larger group has more trouble entering the crowd. In this example, small crowds correspond to high frequencies and large crowds to low frequencies.

Exactly this phenomenon is expressed by the fact the high frequencies are "favored" by 6 dB per octave when the signal leaves the vocal tract and enters the open air. In other words, at the projection of a sound from the mouth, the higher frequencies undergo an increase in amplitude relative to the lower frequencies by roughly 6 dB/oct.

Figure 9.9 is a schematic representation of how the vocal tract acts as a filter upon the laryngeal signal. As can be seen, the laryngeal signal (see Figure 9.9a) has many higher harmonics, which decrease at a rate of 12 dB/oct (see Figure 9.9b). This signal passes through the vocal tract, which has (assumed) resonance frequencies at 1,500 and 3,500 Hz (that is, the vocal tract is represented as a system of band-pass filters with these particular center frequencies; see Figure 9.9c). The signal which finally leaves the vocal tract at the lips is increased by 6 dB/oct for higher frequencies (Figure 9.9d), and finally transmitted by the air as a sound wave (Figure 9.9e). By altering the center frequencies and bandwidths of the filter, which is accomplished by changing the shape of the vocal tract "tube," different frequency regions are attenuated. Thus, the distinction between individual speech sounds is the result of the characteristic resonance frequencies of the vocal tract, which determine the specific spectral shape of the speech signal.

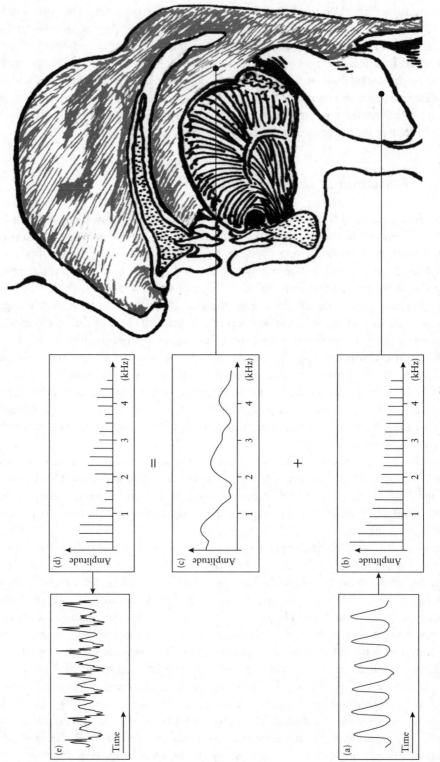

Figure 9.9 (a) Larynx signal, (b) its spectrum, (c) vocal tract filter spectrum, (d) speech spectrum, and (e) speech signal.

9.5   Formants

Formants (see Section 9.4.1) are a property of the vocal tract itself, independent of whether a laryngeal source signal is present or not. This can be demonstrated by a small experiment. Move your articulators into the position for an [o], for example, but without letting any air flow from the lungs. Now tap with your finger on the larynx or the lower jaw, and you hear an [o]. If you form the sound [a] with your articulators and then tap on the larynx, you hear an [a]. The shape of the vocal tract determines the formants, independent of whether there is a source signal or not. This sound source can be the oscillation of the vocal folds, or the tapping of a finger on the larynx.

Even when a source signal is present, the position of the formants is independent of the fundamental frequency of the vocal fold vibration. Since formants are caused by the position of the articulators, and do *not* constitute a property of the speech signal itself, the formant frequencies do not always correspond to the harmonics of the laryngeal signal, as can be seen in Figure 9.10. For example, a formant may occur at 400 Hz, while the laryngeal signal has a fundamental frequency of 90 Hz. The harmonics (F_0 = H1, H2, H3, H4, etc.) of the fundamental frequency are therefore 90, 180, 270, 360, 450, 540, 630, . . . Hz, but no harmonic occurs exactly at 400 Hz (Figure 9.10a). However, the frequency of the first formant *is* at 400 Hz, since it is only determined by the shape of the vocal tract. For a signal with harmonics closer together (lower F_0), there is a greater probability of an individual harmonic being close to or coincident with a formant. For a higher F_0 it is less likely that a formant frequency is close to a harmonic and the formant frequency might not be available in the acoustic signal. This is the reason why it can be difficult to distinguish the vowels from each other when listening to high voices (for example, female singers or children; see Figure 9.10b), since the formants are more difficult to identify in the projected signal.

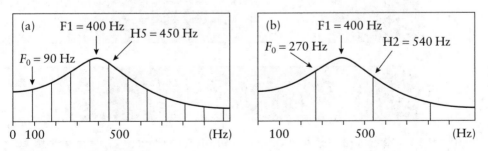

Figure 9.10   Harmonics and vocal tract spectrum of a signal with (a) low F_0 and (b) high F_0.

9.5.1   *Formant frequencies*

The position of the articulators determines the locations of the formants. Since the formant frequencies depend on the shape of the vocal tract, it is possible to formulate some general rules about how the position of the articulators influences the formant frequencies on the basis of perturbation theory (see Section 9.1.2).

We consider a few vowels to demonstrate this. The constriction for the vowel [ɑ], for example, is in the pharynx near point A in Figure 9.11. For F1, this constriction is closer to a pressure anti-node than a node, and perturbation theory predicts that [ɑ] has a high F1 since a constriction near an anti-node raises the formant frequency (relative to schwa, indicated by a "+" in the figure). For F2, however, the location of this pharyngeal constriction is very close to a node, and perturbation theory predicts that [ɑ] has a low F2 since a constriction near a node lowers the formant frequency (indicated by a "−"). The constriction for the vowel [i] is near the palate, near point B in Figure 9.11. For F1, this point is closer to a node (at the lips) than to an anti-node and F1 is predicted to be lower. For F2, this point is very close to an anti-node and F2 is predicted to be higher. You can verify these predictions by comparing the formant frequency values of [ɑ] and [i] (or any other vowel) to those of [ə] (see Appendix C.1 for a table with average formant frequency values for the English vowels). In this way, Figure 9.11 indicates the predictions of perturbation theory about where and to what extent a constriction would raise or lower F1, F2, and F3 relatively to a schwa-like sound produced by a cylindrical unconstricted tube.

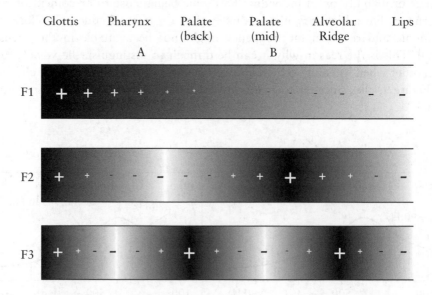

Figure 9.11   Effects of constriction location on the frequency of the first three formants, F1–F3. As the constriction is moved along the length of the vocal tract, each formant is raised (+) or lowered (−), relative to that for schwa.

As a rule of thumb, *low* vowels in the vowel quadrilateral have a high F1 and *high* vowels have a low F1. Likewise, *front* vowels have a high F2 and *back* vowels have a low F2. Note that the terms *low, high, front,* and *back* refer to positions in the vowel quadrilateral that reflect idealized tongue positions, that is, an articulatory description. The low and high frequencies of the formants, on the other hand, reflect acoustical measures – that is why a *low* vowel can have a "high" formant frequency.

Formant frequency values can serve as a basis for a rough classification of different vowels, which holds across different speakers, languages, and dialects. Studies conducted by Peterson and Barney (1952) of a large sample of men, women, and children, and a replication by Hillenbrand et al. (1995), have shown that there is quite a consistent formant pattern for different vowels. The average formant frequencies of these two studies for men, women, and children are listed in Appendix C.1 and the data of male speakers of the Hillenbrand et al. study is graphically represented in Figure 9.12. The principles given above about vowel types and their formant positions can be clearly recognized. It is evident, however, that individual differences among speakers do exist and that the formant values alone are not always sufficient to determine the quality of a vowel.

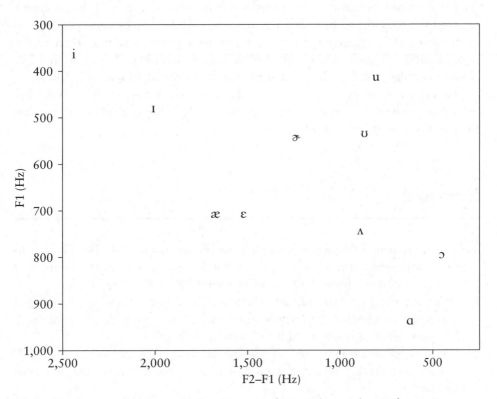

Figure 9.12 Average formant frequencies of 50 male speakers of American English plotted in a F1 versus F2–F1 plane.

Now that we have laid out the relation between the position of the articulators and the resulting formant frequencies, we can return to a discussion of vowels. In Section 2.4, we discussed vowels in terms of the three articulatory dimensions height, frontness, and lip rounding. While the vowel quadrilateral introduced in Section 3.2 is a convenient way of discussing the vowels of English or any other language, it should be kept in mind that its dimensions and labels do not directly relate to the dimensions of height and frontness. For example, for the height dimension, the description of the vowels [i] and [u] as high implies that the highest point of the tongue is equally close to the roof of the mouth for both vowels. However, as pointed out repeatedly by Ladefoged (1967, 2006) and others, this is not the case. The highest point for [u] is more similar to that of the high front lax vowel [ɪ]. In fact, vowel descriptions may at least in part be based on auditory impressions. Indeed, as early as 1928, the American phonetician Russell referred to this fact by stating that "Phoneticians are thinking in terms of acoustic fact, and using physiological fantasy to express the idea."

Nowadays, the vowel quadrilateral is considered to be more closely related to acoustic or auditory than articulatory properties of vowels. Figure 9.12 shows the pure vowels of American English plotted in what is known as an acoustic vowel space. As you see, the dimensions are acoustic in nature, with the location of the first formant frequency (F1) plotted along the vertical axis and the difference between the second and first formant frequencies (F2–F1) plotted along the horizontal axis. This representation, based on acoustic properties rather than articulatory position, is quite similar to that of the vowel quadrilateral from Section 3.2. A more detailed acoustic description of vowels is provided in Section 10.1.

In the next chapter, we discuss the acoustic characteristics of vowels and extend the source-filter theory of speech production to consonants in order to review their acoustic properties as well.

Exercises

---

1 The fundamental frequency of a glottal source spectrum is 125 Hz. The amplitude of the first harmonic is 62.5 dB. What is the frequency of the component that is an octave above the fourth harmonic? What is its amplitude?

2 Calculate the first, second, and third resonance frequencies of a quarter-wavelength resonator with a tube length of 25 cm. Now do the same for a half-wavelength resonator with the same tube length.

3 What happens when sounds are passed through a low-pass filter? Through a high-pass filter? Through a band-pass filter? How is this related to speech production?

4 Does the fundamental frequency or the vocal tract shape affect formant frequencies? Explain your answer.

5 What vowel could have a high F1 and high F2? A high F1 and low F2? A low F1 and high F2? A low F1 and low F2?
6 What is the difference between an acoustic and an articulatory description of vowels?

Notes

1 "Halfway" between node and anti-node is a phase angle of 45° but the difference between the pressures (or speeds) of node and anti-node is reached at 30°, since $\sin(30°) = 0.5$.
2 Note the difference between a "pass-band" of a filter, which marks the range where frequencies pass a filter unhindered, and a "band-pass" filter, which describes the shape of a filter.
3 This value might seem excessively high, considering that a normal conversation is carried out at a loudness of about 65 dB and a starting jet-plane has a loudness of about 120 dB. The reason is that dB values for loudness are normally measured at 1 meter distance from the source, and since intensity reduces with the square of the distance (see Appendix A.2), values are much higher directly at the source.

10 Acoustic Characteristics of Speech Sounds

This chapter discusses the primary acoustic characteristics of a variety of speech sounds and illustrates them by means of spectrograms and spectra. We start with vowels and subsequently discuss consonants.

10.1 Vowels

Vowels are produced with a relatively open vocal tract and the airstream is not severely impeded. The resulting acoustic signal is therefore relatively loud. In addition, vowels are usually produced with vocal fold vibration. The primary acoustic characteristic of vowels is the location of the formant frequencies, specifically, the first three formants (F1–F3). As discussed in Section 9.5.1, the shape of the vocal tract determines the location of the formant frequencies. Changes in the position of the articulators will modify the shape of the vocal tract and, as a result, the location of the formant frequencies. Since the same formant frequencies can be generated with a variety of articulatory positions, formant frequency location is a critical determinant of vowel quality rather than the positions of the articulators. For a given speaker or for a group of speakers with the same vocal tract length, each vowel is associated with a distinct acoustic formant frequency pattern. As an example, Figure 10.1 shows spectrograms and linear predictive coding (LPC) spectra of the vowels [i] and [ɑ] spoken by a male English speaker.

As on any spectrogram, frequency is plotted along the vertical axis, and time along the horizontal axis. Intensity is represented by the darkness of the display. The darker a particular area, the greater its intensity. The spectrograms of the two vowels have several things in common. They are both characterized by the presence of a number of dark bands along the frequency scale. These dark bands correspond to the formant frequencies that reflect the resonances of the vocal tract and appear as "peaks" in the LPC spectrum.

The crucial difference between the two vowels is of course the exact location of the formant frequencies. As indicated in Figure 10.1, the vowel [i] has a first formant frequency around 240 Hz, a second formant frequency around 2,450 Hz,

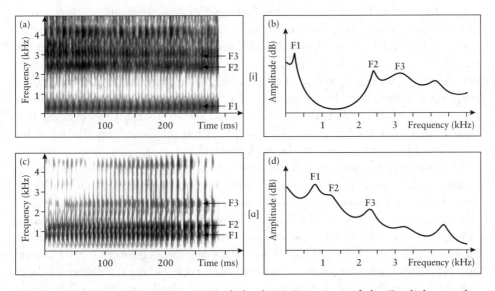

Figure 10.1 (a, c) Spectrograms and (b, d) LPC spectra of the English vowels [i] and [ɑ] produced by a male speaker.

and a third formant frequency around 3,200 Hz. In contrast, the vowel [ɑ] has a first formant frequency around 810 Hz, a second formant frequency around 1,250 Hz, and a third formant frequency around 2,400 Hz. This difference reflects the different vocal tract shapes involved in the production of the two vowels. Figure 10.2 shows the stylized frequencies of the first three formants for all monophthongal vowels of American English, averaged over a group of 50 male speakers (Hillenbrand et al. 1995).

The vowels along the horizontal axis are organized from front to back. In addition, the front vowels are ranked in descending order of height, from high [i] to low [æ], and the back vowels in ascending order of height, from low [ɑ] to high [u]. When the vowels are arranged this way, it is apparent that the two

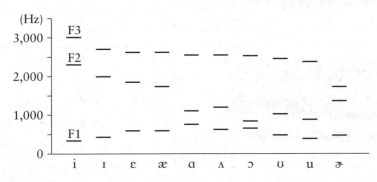

Figure 10.2 Average and stylized formant frequencies (F1–F3) of the monophthongal vowels of American English produced by 50 male speakers.

major dimensions for describing vowels, height and backness, have clear acoustic correlates. Vowel height is inversely correlated with the frequency of the first formant: the higher the vowel (and the higher the tongue position), the lower the F1. This is true for both the front and back vowels. Moreover, vowels of comparable height, such as [i] and [u], have comparable first formant frequencies. Vowel backness is reflected in the frequency of the second formant frequency, or more precisely, in the distance between the first and second formant frequencies. It is clear from Figure 10.2 that the difference F2–F1 is relatively large for the front vowels and relatively small for the back vowels.

As vowel quality changes, the frequency of the third formant does not change nearly as much as that of F1 and F2, with the possible exception of the vowel [i], for which F3 is quite high. Overall, then, F3 does not provide much information about the quality of the English vowels, which is why many acoustic descriptions of these vowels consist only of the first two formant frequencies. However, there are languages in which F3 does provide an important cue to vowel quality. For example, languages such as Dutch, French, German, and Swedish have both front unrounded and front rounded vowels. The lengthening of the vocal tract due to lip rounding lowers all formants (see Section 9.5.1), and moves F3 close to F2, which distinguishes between front unrounded and front rounded vowels, as illustrated in Figure 10.3 for German.

Formant frequencies higher than F3 are not considered important cues to the identity of a vowel because they hardly vary as a function of vowel quality. Instead, for vowels, the frequencies of higher formants such as F4 and F5 seem more speaker-specific and may therefore provide information about the identity of the speaker rather than the vowel itself. Therefore, for vowels, F1–F3 provide **acoustic cues**

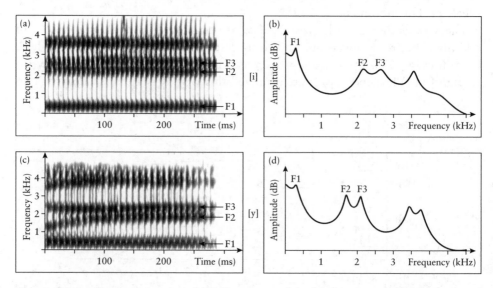

Figure 10.3 Spectrograms and LPC spectra of (a, b) the unrounded high front vowel [i] and (c, d) its rounded counterpart [y] spoken by a native male speaker of German.

to vowel quality. An acoustic cue consists of one or more acoustic properties that are considered to provide unique information about the identity of a particular segment such as the height, frontness, or rounding of a vowel.

The production of nasal and nasalized vowels requires two resonators, the oral and the nasal cavity. The complex interaction between these two resonators and the heavy damping of the nasal cavity result in several differences between oral and nasal(ized) vowels. Compared to an oral vowel, a nasal vowel typically shows greater formant bandwidths, lower overall amplitude, a low-frequency nasal formant, and one or more anti-formants (see Section 10.2.4 for a more detailed discussion of the acoustic correlates of nasalization). Figure 10.4 shows spectrograms of the oral vowel [ɑ] and the nasal vowel [ɑ̃] spoken by the same speaker. Notice in Figure 10.4b the increased energy in the second harmonic around 200 Hz and the dip in the spectrum around 450 Hz.

Duration can also be a cue to a vowel's identity. Many languages have vowel distinctions that are primarily based on duration. For example, the German vowels [ɪ] and [iː] differ in terms of duration and their spectral properties. And Estonian distinguishes short, long, and very long vowels. And in English, tense vowels tend to have a longer **steady-state** portion than lax vowels. The steady-state portion is the stretch of the vowel during which the formant frequencies are relatively stable, usually toward the middle of the vowel, away from the influence from surrounding segments. In English, [æ] is an exception, in that it is a lax vowel (it does not occur in open syllables) but has a long duration. It has been observed

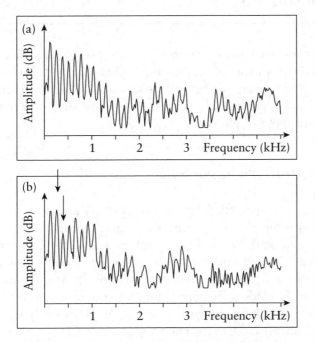

Figure 10.4 FFT spectra of (a) the oral vowel [ɑ] and (b) the nasal vowel [ɑ̃] spoken by the same speaker as in Figure 10.3. The arrows in (b) indicate the increase in energy around 200 Hz and decrease in energy around 450 Hz.

that when tense vowels are flanked by consonants, the formant transitions into and out of tense vowels are relatively symmetrical while lax vowels have slightly longer transitions into, and much longer transitions out of, the vowel. In general, though, the primary difference between the English tense and lax vowels is one in terms of quality (formant pattern) rather than duration. A shortened [i] still sounds like an [i] just as a lengthened [ɪ] still sounds like an [ɪ], which is why, as mentioned in Section 3.2, the symbols [i] and [ɪ] are more appropriate to represent the tense and lax vowel in English, respectively, than the symbols [iː] and [i] or [ɪː] and [ɪ].

Diphthongs (see Sections 2.4 and 3.2) are characterized by a change in formant pattern due to a change in articulatory shape during their production. This changing formant pattern primarily involves the first two formants and is very noticeable on spectrograms. Figure 10.5 shows spectrograms of the English diphthongs [aɪ], [ɔɪ], and [aʊ]. Acoustically, diphthongs are usually described by specifying their onset and offset frequencies. Notice that the formant frequency values at offset match those of the corresponding monophthongs ([ɪ, ʊ]) shown in Figure 10.2, as do the values at onset for [ɔ]. The onset of the diphthongs [aɪ] and [aʊ] is a vowel that is more central than the monophthong [ɑ], with F2 onset values that are slightly higher.

10.2   Consonants

All consonants involve a modification of the airstream, ranging from mild in the case of approximants to severe in the case of plosives. Our overview of acoustic characteristics of consonants is organized in terms of manner of articulation, beginning with those of approximants, since they are most similar to those of vowels, and ending with those of plosives.

10.2.1   (Central) Approximants

In the production of approximants, two articulators approach each other without severely impeding the flow of air. The acoustic properties of approximants are therefore quite similar to those of vowels produced at a comparable location in the vocal tract. Their formant pattern is clear but somewhat weaker than for the vowels because of the approximants' slightly greater constriction, which results in a shorter steady-state portion and lower acoustic energy. For example, the articulation of the palatal approximant [j], in which the blade of the tongue is positioned relatively close to the palate, is quite similar to that of the vowel [i], the main difference being that the blade is closer to the palate for [j] than for [i]. The frequency spectrum of [j] therefore resembles that of [i], except that [j] is less

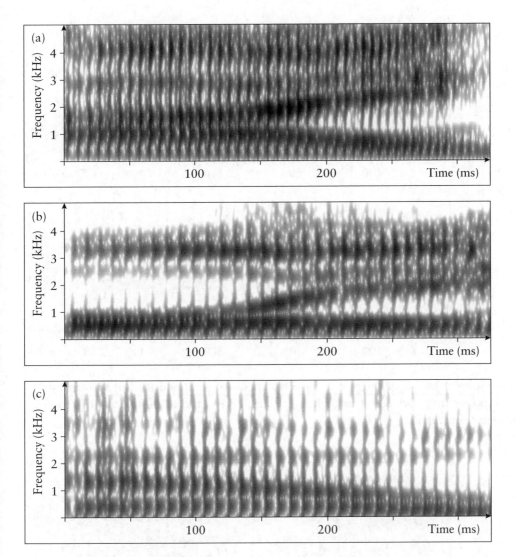

Figure 10.5 Spectrograms of the English diphthongs (a) [aɪ], (b) [ɔɪ], and (c) [aʊ] spoken by a male speaker.

intense since the airflow is impeded more than for [i]. Figure 10.6a shows a spectrogram for the utterance [ɑjɑ]. The palatal approximant is characterized by a low F1, and high F2 and F3, similar to the vowel [i]. The transitions into and out of the approximant are quite pronounced, both in terms of frequency range and duration. Of course, the extent of the transition in the frequency domain depends on the vowel context. As illustrated in Figure 10.6b, when [j] is flanked by vowels with a similar formant pattern, as in [iji], the transitions are small.

During the production of the labial-velar approximant [w], the back of the tongue is brought closer to the velum and the lips are rounded. It is in that sense quite

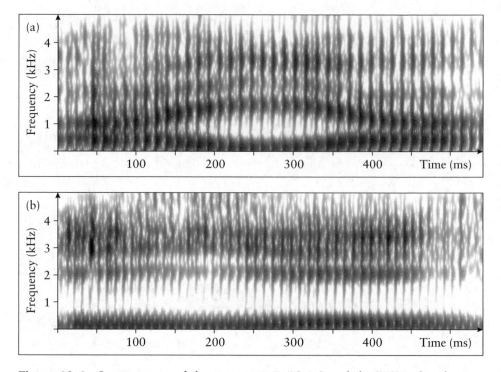

Figure 10.6 Spectrogram of the utterances (a) [ɑjɑ] and (b) [iji] spoken by a male native speaker of English. Note that F3 is almost "on top of" F2 during the consonant.

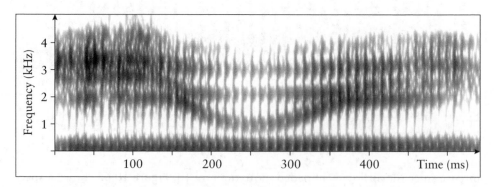

Figure 10.7 Spectrogram of the utterance [iwi] spoken by a male native speaker of English.

similar to the production of the vowel [u]. Figure 10.7 shows a spectrogram for the utterance [iwi]. During the labial-velar approximant, F1 and F2 are low and close together while F3 remains relatively steady at approximately 2,300 Hz, similar to the vowel [u]. Again, formant transitions depend on vowel context.

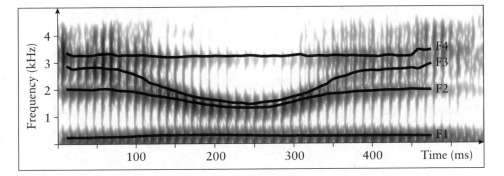

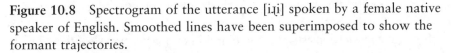

Figure 10.8 Spectrogram of the utterance [iɹi] spoken by a female native speaker of English. Smoothed lines have been superimposed to show the formant trajectories.

The retroflex approximant [ɹ] is typically produced with three simultaneous constrictions, all of which serve to lower F3: lip rounding, a narrowing near the alveolar ridge involving the tip of the tongue, and a narrowing in the pharynx because of retraction of the tongue root. As a result, [ɹ] is characterized by a very low third formant frequency, which comes close to F2. This is illustrated in Figure 10.8, where F3 during the approximant is around 1,800 Hz. In fact, [ɹ] has the lowest F3 of all English speech sounds, often dipping below 2,000 Hz even for female speakers.

In summary, approximants are distinct by being shorter and weaker than vowels and by having longer formant transition durations than vowels.

10.2.2 *Fricatives*

Fricatives are produced with a narrow constriction in the oral cavity. The turbulence resulting from air passing through this constriction (the position of which depends on the particular fricative) is the typical sound source for all fricatives (in addition to the voice source at the glottis for voiced fricatives). Fricatives can be characterized in terms of four attributes: spectral properties of the friction noise, amplitude of the noise, duration of the noise, and spectral properties of the transition into and out of the surrounding vowels.

The overall spectral shape of each fricative is mostly determined by the size and shape of the oral cavity in front of the constriction. The source-filter theory of speech production, introduced in Chapter 9, and illustrated by means of the acoustic characteristics of vowels, also explains the acoustic characteristics of consonants. Since obstruents are produced with a severe constriction, their resonant frequencies can be calculated for the front and back cavities separately, without having to consider complex interactions between the two. The simplest model for representing the articulatory configuration of these consonants is shown in

Glottis   Lips

Figure 10.9   Vocal tract model representing the articulatory configuration for obstruents by means of three tubes corresponding, from left to right, to the back cavity, constriction, and front cavity, respectively

Figure 10.9. It requires three tubes, one for the front cavity, one for the constriction itself, and one for the back cavity.

The three-tube model consists of a combination of quarter-wavelength and half-wavelength resonators (see Section 9.1.1). The back cavity can be considered closed at both ends: one end is the glottis; the other end is the constriction in the oral cavity, which makes it a half-wavelength resonator. The short tube representing the constriction is also a half-wavelength resonator since it is open at both ends: both openings are large relative to the small area of the constriction. Finally, the front cavity is closed at one end at the constriction and open at the lips, making it a quarter-wavelength resonator.

We will use this model to calculate the formant frequencies. We will not consider the first formant here, which results from a **Helmholtz resonator**, a resonant system formed when a relatively wide back cavity is completely closed at one end (the glottis) and has a narrow constriction at the other end. The resonant frequency of this Helmholtz resonator is determined by the relative volumes of air in the back cavity and constriction, and is typically very low (below 1 kHz).

As an example, consider the alveolar fricative [s]. Based on X-ray and MRI studies of the vocal tract, we will assume a total vocal tract length of 16 cm, a back cavity length of 11 cm, a constriction length of 3 cm, and a front cavity length of 2 cm. Since the back cavity is a half-wavelength resonator, we will use the formula from Section 9.1.1:

$$f_k = k \times \frac{c}{2l}.$$

Using $l = 11$ cm $= 0.11$ m and 340 m/s for the speed of the sound, this tube model predicts the following back cavity resonances:

$$f_k = k \times \frac{340 \text{ m/s}}{2 \times 0.11 \text{ m}} = k \times \frac{340}{0.22 \text{ s}} = k \times 1{,}545 \text{ Hz},$$

which yields 1,545 Hz, 3,090 Hz, 4,635 Hz, 6,180 Hz (for $k = 1, 2, 3, 4$), etc., as resonance frequencies.

For the front cavity, a quarter-wavelength resonator, we will use the formula from Section 9.1.1:

$$f_k = (2k - 1) \times \frac{c}{4l}.$$

Using $l = 2$ cm $= 0.02$ m, the following front cavity resonances are predicted:

$$f_k = (2k - 1) \times \frac{340 \text{ m/s}}{4 \times 0.02 \text{ m}} = (2k - 1) \times \frac{340}{0.08 \text{ s}} = (2k - 1) \times 4{,}250 \text{ Hz},$$

which yields 4,250 Hz, 12,750 Hz (for $k = 1, 2$), and so on, as resonance frequencies.

When assigning formant frequency numbers, the lowest resonance frequency that we calculated for fricatives is labeled F2 (F1 is from the Helmholtz resonator), the next one F3, etc. Thus, for [s], this model predicts F2 to be 1,545 Hz, F3: 3,090 Hz, F4: 4,250 Hz, F5: 4,635 Hz, etc. However, it is important to know whether a given formant frequency is associated with the back or the front cavity. This is because obstruent spectra are dominated by front cavity resonances. Friction noise or burst friction generated at the constriction primarily excites the cavity in front of the constriction. Since our calculations above showed that F2 and F3 are back cavity resonances, their influence is not as great as that of F4, which is a front cavity resonance. Thus, we expect the spectrum of [s] to show a concentration of energy at (and above) 4,250 Hz.

In general, it is the case that the longer the anterior cavity, the more distinct the resulting spectrum is since it operates as a resonating "chamber," which contributes more when it is larger. In addition, the spectral shape is more pronounced for the fricatives [s, z, ʃ, ʒ] because the airstream also hits the teeth. As a result, the alveolar and postalveolar fricatives are characterized by clear, distinct spectral shapes while labiodental and (inter)dental fricatives display a relatively flat spectrum. In particular, [ʃ, ʒ] typically exhibit a mid-frequency spectral peak around 2,500–3,500 Hz. Alveolar [s, z] are produced with a shorter anterior cavity than [ʃ, ʒ] and therefore display a primary spectral peak at higher frequencies, ranging from 4,000 to 7,000 Hz. In addition, since for these four fricatives the airstream hits the teeth, the high-frequency turbulence is very intense. In contrast, both [f, v] and [θ, ð] are characterized by a relatively flat spectrum, although recent research suggests that labiodentals may have a slightly higher spectral peak frequency (close to 8,000 Hz) than interdentals.

For more posterior constrictions (and longer front cavities), such as velar, uvular, and pharyngeal fricatives, the dominant energy is concentrated at lower frequencies, in the area of the first two formants. Velar fricatives have a concentration of energy in the region corresponding to F2 of the adjacent vowel and very little energy in the higher frequencies. The primary difference between uvular and pharyngeal fricatives seems to be in terms of the first formant frequency. Consistent with their more posterior constriction, pharyngeal fricatives have a higher F1 than uvular fricatives.

Voiced fricatives have two energy sources: in addition to the turbulent noise generated by the constriction, the vibrating vocal folds provide low-frequency energy. Spectrograms of the voiced fricatives are similar to those of their voiceless counterparts, except that they contain additional low-frequency energy corresponding to vocal fold vibration and slightly less intensity in the higher frequencies because part of the energy of the airstream serves to make the vocal folds vibrate.

In terms of amplitude of the friction noise, [s, ʃ] have a substantially greater (10–15 dB) amplitude than [f, θ], which is why [s, ʃ] and their voiced counterparts [z, ʒ] are sometimes referred to as strong or sibilant fricatives in contrast to the weak or non-sibilant fricatives [f, θ, v, ð]. Within each of these two groups, measures of **relative amplitude** distinguish all four places of articulation. Relative amplitude is the difference between amplitude of the fricative and that of the following vowel measured in a specific frequency range (corresponding to F3 for alveolars and postalveolars and to F5 for labiodentals and interdentals). This relative measure of amplitude indicates that postalveolars have a concentration of energy in the region corresponding to F3 of the following vowel while alveolars have their major energy in a much higher region. In addition, for the non-sibilants, fricative amplitude in the F5 region is greater for the labiodentals than the interdentals.

Noise duration also serves to distinguish sibilant from non-sibilant fricatives, with [s, ʃ, ʒ] being longer than [f, θ]. Noise duration also distinguishes voiced and voiceless fricatives, with voiceless fricatives having longer noise durations than voiced fricatives.

Finally, it has been suggested that the formant transitions between fricative and vowel, especially the second formant transition, may cue place of articulation. Recent research indicates that F2 at the onset of the vowel tends to increase as place of articulation moves further back in the oral cavity.

In sum, fricatives have a relatively long noise portion with reasonably stable acoustic characteristics.

10.2.3 Plosives

During the production of plosives, the airstream is momentarily blocked by a complete constriction in the oral cavity. As discussed in Section 2.3.2, air pressure builds up behind the constriction. The release of the constriction and the subsequent movement of the articulators toward the next speech sound result in two primary cues to the place of articulation of the plosive, burst frequency and formant transitions. Figure 10.10 provides spectrograms of intervocalic plosives and illustrates a number of their distinctive acoustic characteristics. The closure interval between the initial vowel and the release burst of the plosive is a primary characteristic of plosives and is of course due to the complete constriction in the vocal tract. This "gap" in the spectrogram corresponds to what is known as the closure portion of the consonant and contains no energy in the case of the voiceless plosives and only very low-frequency energy (called **voice bar**) in the case of fully voiced plosives.

Burst frequency – that is, the frequency spectrum of the release burst – varies as a function of the length of the vocal tract in front of the constriction, much as the dominant frequency of the friction noise for fricatives. Burst frequencies can be estimated with the same formulas used for the calculation of resonances for fricatives in the preceding sections, with a few modifications. Bilabials are formed at the lips without any appreciable portion of the vocal tract in front of the constriction. Since any constriction at the lips typically lowers the formant frequencies (see Section 9.1.2), bilabial bursts tend to have a concentration of energy in the lower frequencies (500–1,500 Hz). The short portion of the vocal tract in front of the alveolar constriction results in relatively higher burst frequencies for alveolars, ranging from about 2,500 to 4,000 Hz. Velars are characterized by a lower burst frequency than alveolars since the portion of the vocal tract in front of the velar constriction is substantially longer. The burst frequency for velars usually lies in between that of bilabials and alveolars, ranging from approximately 1,500 to 2,500 Hz. Release bursts are clearly visible in Figure 10.10 and their frequency can be seen to match our general description. Little is known about the acoustic differences between velar and uvular plosives. Consistent with their more posterior articulation, uvular plosives have a lower burst frequency.

Transitions of the second and third formants from the initial vowel into the closure gap and from the release burst into the following vowel can also provide cues to place of articulation. Formant transitions are the acoustic consequences of articulatory movement between adjacent vowels and plosives and are typically completed within 50 ms. All plosives share a low F1 because F1 during the constriction is at about 200 Hz. Since bilabials are characterized by low-frequency energy during the release, F2 and F3 transitions from vowel to plosive may descend into the closure gap and rise from the low-frequency burst toward the formant frequencies of the next vowel. Analogously, since alveolars typically have high-frequency energy during the release, F2 and F3 of the preceding vowel may rise into the closure gap and fall from the high-frequency burst into the following vowel. Finally, velar plosives with their mid-frequency bursts are often found to have an F2 and F3 that are close together in the mid-frequency range (2,000–2,500 Hz). That is, F2 rises and F3 falls into the closure portion; and F2 falls and F3 rises from the burst into the vowel. The proximity of F2 and F3 during the velar plosive is known as the **velar pinch**. While formant transitions provide cues to place of articulation, their extent is dependent on the quality of the adjacent vowel. For example, in the case of the sequence [ɑtɑ], the second formant transition is much steeper (since [ɑ] has a low F2) than in the sequence [iti] (since [i] has a high F2 that is closer to the high-frequency energy concentration of [t]).

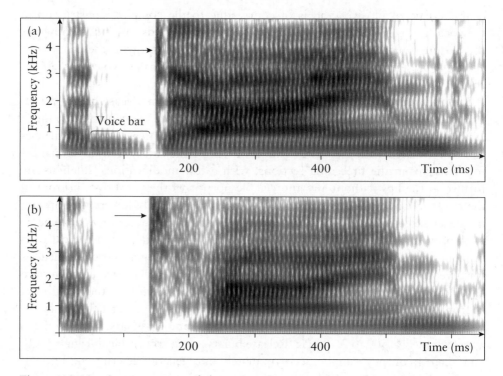

Figure 10.10 Spectrograms of the utterances (a) *a dime* with a voiced and (b) *a time* with a voiceless intervocalic plosive spoken by a female native speaker of American English. Arrows indicate the highest concentration of burst energy.

Finally, amplitude and duration provide information about consonant voicing but not place of articulation. A voiceless plosive in English typically has a longer closure duration, a stronger burst, and a longer (positive) VOT than a voiced plosive.

In sum, plosives are distinct by having a closure interval, a release burst, and rapidly changing formant transitions.

10.2.4 Nasals

For the production of nasal stop consonants the oral airflow is temporarily blocked by means of a complete constriction in the oral cavity. However, the velum is lowered such that air can escape only through the nasal cavity. The resulting sound is known as **nasal murmur**. Nasals require the use of two resonance cavities, oral and nasal, which are combined in a complex way. As a class, nasals are characterized by several properties. The first formant is very low because the total cavity length of all branches (pharyngeal, nasal, and oral) is longer than

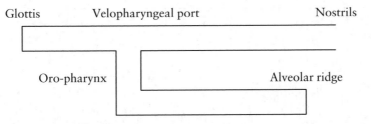

Figure 10.11 Schematic representation of the vocal tract configuration for an alveolar nasal stop consonant.

that for oral sounds. This low F1 is sometimes referred to as the **nasal formant**. The formants are weak (low in amplitude) because the airflow is impeded by a relatively narrow opening into the nasal cavity. The formants have an increased bandwidth, due to absorption of sound energy by the walls of both the oral and nasal cavities. And, finally, nasals are characterized by the presence of **anti-formants** due to the interaction between the oral and nasal cavities (see below).

For a given place of articulation, the oral cavity during the production of oral and nasal stops is very similar. For example, alveolar [d] and [n] both require a complete constriction at the alveolar ridge. As a result, the acoustic characteristics of [d] and [n] share certain properties. However, the only articulatory difference between the two sounds, the lowered velum for [n], turns out to have major acoustic consequences. Because of the open nasal cavity, the vocal tract needs to be modeled by means of a two-tube model (see Figure 10.11). One tube is closed-open and begins at the closed glottis and ends in the nasal cavity, which opens into the atmosphere. The other tube can be viewed as a side tube, open at one end – the uvula – and closed at the other – the point of constriction in the oral cavity.

Resonances of the oral cavity cannot be seen directly in a nasal's spectrum because the oral cavity has no opening to the atmosphere. Instead, the coupling or inter-action between the oral and nasal cavities results in the presence of anti-formants. That is, those resonant frequencies in the nasal that are close to the resonances of the oral cavity are absorbed or canceled and "subtracted" from the overall spectrum because part of the acoustic energy of the pulsating airflow from the larynx causes resonance in the oral cavity. These anti-formants show up as conspicuous valleys in the spectrum, and their frequency varies as a function of place of articulation. The shorter the posterior part of the oral cavity – that is, the further back (more posterior) the place of articulation – the higher the resonances and, therefore, the higher the anti-formants in the output spectrum. In general, the anti-formant is located in the low-frequency range for bilabial [m] (750–1,250 Hz), in the mid-frequency range for alveolar [n] (1,450–2,200 Hz), and in the high-frequency range for velar [ŋ] (above 3,000 Hz). These charac-teristics are shown in Figure 10.12.

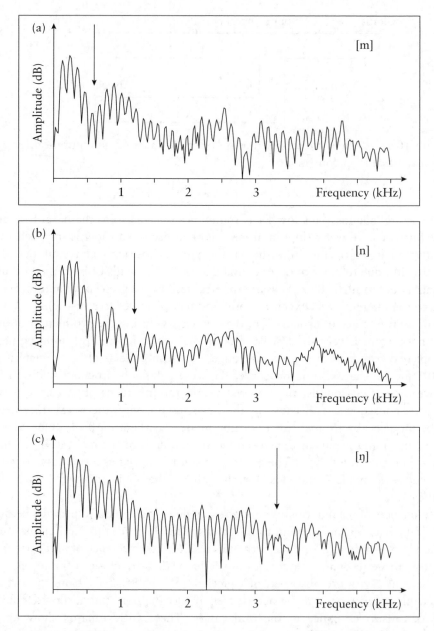

Figure 10.12   FFT spectra from the center of the nasal consonants in the utterances (a) [ɑmɑ], (b) [ɑnɑ], and (c) [ɑŋɑ]. The arrows indicate the locations of the anti-formants, which show up as dips in the spectra.

It would be unfair to conclude this section on cues to nasal place of articulation without mentioning that it is often very difficult to measure or even locate anti-formants. Moreover, individual variation in the size and shape of the nasal cavity increases the already substantial inter-speaker variability due to variation in oral tract size. However, the formant transitions from preceding and into following segments may also contain information about place of articulation. The characteristics and interpretation of these transitions for nasal consonants are very similar to those for plosives produced at the same place of articulation (see Section 10.2.3).

10.2.5   *Lateral approximants*

Finally, the acoustic characteristics of the lateral alveolar approximant [l] are quite similar to those of nasals. In the production of [l], part of the tongue makes contact with the upper part of the mouth. Specifically, the tip of the tongue touches the alveolar ridge, while one or both sides of the tongue are lower and thus only approximate the roof of the mouth. [l] has a steady-state portion with a spectrum characterized by formants. Average adult male formant frequencies (F1 to F3) for [l] are approximately 340 Hz, 1,200 Hz, and 2,800 Hz, respectively. These characteristics are shown in Figure 10.13. For lateral alveolar approximants, a small pocket of air remains above the tongue body while air escapes on either side of the constriction. This situation is analogous to that for nasals in that the vocal tract can again be considered as consisting of a main tube and a side tube. The main tube extends from glottis to mouth opening while the pocket of air is modeled as a short side tube.

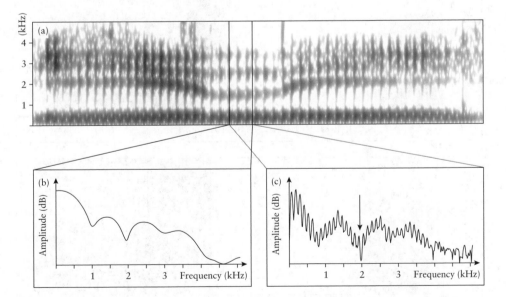

Figure 10.13   (a) Spectrogram of the utterance [ili] together with (b) LPC and (c) FFT spectra of the central part of [l], spoken by a male native speaker of English. The arrow in the FFT spectrum points to the anti-formant at 2,000 Hz.

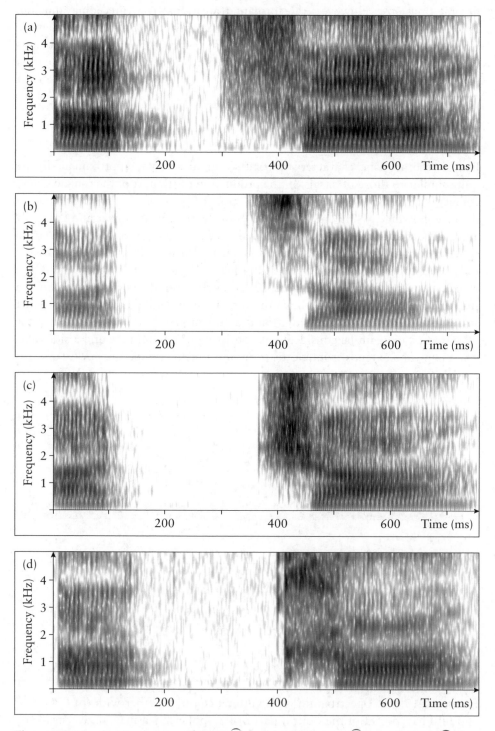

Figure 10.14   Spectrograms of (a) [ap͡fa], (b) [at͡sa], (c) [at͡ʃa], and (d) [ak͡xa] spoken by a Swiss German speaker.

The coupling between these two tubes again results in anti-formants. Formants from the side tube will cancel out formants from the main tube. Since the side tube is short, the anti-formant will be relatively high, at approximately 2,000– 2,300 Hz for an adult male.

10.2.6　*Affricates*

Affricates combine aspects of plosive and fricative and their acoustic character-istics are similar to those of plosives and fricatives at the same place of articula-tion, except for the duration of the friction portion, which is shorter than for fricatives. Spectrograms of the utterances [ap͡fa], [at͡sa], [at͡ʃa], and [ak͡xa] are shown in Figure 10.14.

As a class, affricates can be distinguished from fricatives in terms of **rise time**, the temporal interval from the onset of the consonant until the maximum ampli-tude of the friction noise. Fricatives have a relatively long rise time since their amplitude builds up in a gradual manner. In contrast, affricates have a short rise time, reflecting the fact that following the plosive portion, the friction noise rapidly reaches maximum amplitude.

10.3　Summary

Our discussion of the acoustic characteristics of speech sounds suggests that it is easier to identify cues to manner of articulation and voicing than to place of articulation. In terms of manner of articulation, vowels and approximants stand out by the absence of any noise (burst or friction) portion. Vowels are distinct from approximants by having relatively intense and long steady-state portions. Plosives and affricates are both characterized by the presence of a closure gap without any (high-frequency) energy. Oral stops have a faster increase in energy following release than affricates, which in turn have a shorter rise time than fricatives. Finally, nasals are characterized by a very low first formant frequency and the presence of anti-formants.

Voiced speech sounds have low-frequency energy due to the vibrating vocal folds. For vowels, approximants, fricatives, and nasals, this voicing is usually present throughout the sound. For plosives, the voicing is most clearly observed during the closure portion.

For sounds with a substantial constriction, such as oral stops and fricatives, cues to place of articulation are largely determined by the length of the vocal tract in front of the constriction (i.e. the anterior part of the vocal tract). Therefore, oral stops and fricatives at the same place of articulation share certain acoustic properties. Bilabials are generally characterized by a predominance of energy in the low-frequency range, alveolars by a predominance of high-frequency energy, while velars fall in between. Nasals are slightly different, in that the location of the characteristic anti-formant is determined by the length of the vocal tract between the uvula and oral constriction, which results in velars having the highest anti-formant frequency.

It should be kept in mind that while the acoustic properties discussed here are characteristic of the different manners of articulation, places of articulation, and voicing properties, they may not always be present for a given speech sound. The extent to which each or all of these properties occur depends on a variety of factors, including speaker, phonetic context, and speaking rate. This observation has led researchers to debate the extent to which the acoustic properties associated with a particular speech sound are invariant or context-dependent. The final section of this chapter is meant to provide a flavor of the kinds of data that researchers use to address the nature of the mapping between the physically continuous signal and discrete linguistic categories.

10.4   Variability and Invariance

As discussed earlier in this chapter, the most challenging aspect of consonants, particularly plosives, concerns cues to their place of articulation. While cues to plosive place include the frequency of the release burst and characteristics of the formant transitions, the role of each of these properties has been the topic of intense debate. Consider Figure 10.15.

This classic figure from Delattre et al. (1955) displays schematic spectrograms (of synthetic English speech) that are perceived by English listeners as [di] and [du], respectively. (Notice that these are simplified relative to natural speech tokens

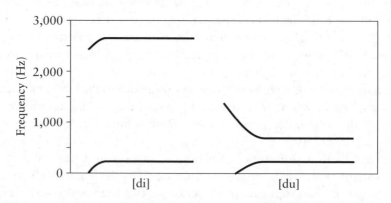

Figure 10.15   Stylized F1 and F2 pattern for [di] and [du] (after Delattre et al., 1955).

in that they do not have a release burst.) What is it in these two spectrograms that makes listeners perceive both syllables as starting with an alveolar plosive? Considering only [di] for the moment, the spectrogram can be decomposed into a number of components. The rising F1 transition indicates that it is a plosive. The location of the steady-state F1 and F2 indicates that the vowel is [i]. The only component left to indicate the place of articulation of the consonant is the rising F2 transition. However, consideration of [du] immediately suggests that a rising F2 transition is not likely to be a consistent cue to the alveolar place of articulation. While the rising F1 transition again indicates a plosive and the steady-state formants correspond to [u], the component that apparently indicates place of articulation is now a falling F2 transition in quite a different frequency range.

These kinds of observations led to the claim that most acoustic cues are highly *context-dependent*. According to this claim, there are no (or few) acoustic cues that are stable, consistent, or invariant. In this case, F2 transition as a cue to place of articulation varies drastically as a function of vowel context. That is, the same percept [d] is represented by two different acoustic cues, depending on the following vowel. These kinds of observations led Liberman and colleagues to claim that there is a "lack of invariance" in the speech signal, meaning that there is no simple one-to-one mapping between acoustic properties and phonetic percepts. Instead, different acoustic cues may yield the same phonetic percept (as in the [di–du] example).

It is important to note that this lack of invariance refers specifically to the acoustic domain. The issue is not whether or not there is invariance in the process of speech perception. Invariance clearly plays a role given that listeners map a variety of acoustic cues onto invariant phonological categories. Rather, the question is at which level this invariance resides. Demonstrations of the context-dependent nature of acoustic cues suggested that the invariance did not reside in the acoustic signal itself.

10.4.1 A Theory of acoustic invariance

In contrast to Liberman's conclusion, other researchers (most notably, Stevens and Blumstein 1981) claim that invariant acoustic properties do indeed exist. One of the reasons why Blumstein and Stevens found invariant acoustic properties while Liberman and colleagues did not may have to do with how researchers analyzed the speech signal.

When Liberman started his quest for invariant acoustic properties, the best way to visualize and analyze the speech signal was the spectrogram. As discussed in Section 8.3.4, the spectrogram represents changes in frequency over time. When considering plosive-vowel syllables, three properties stand out on such spectrograms: release bursts, formant transitions, and formant steady-state portions. It is therefore tempting to treat each of these attributes as independent cues to consonant perception. Indeed, early studies in the 1950s did exactly that. For example, the frequency location of the release burst was systematically manipulated to evaluate its role as a cue to place of articulation. The bursts were followed by combinations of steady-state two-formant patterns corresponding to different vowel qualities. Results failed to show a consistent mapping between burst frequency and perceived place of articulation. These kinds of findings reinforced the notion that the cues used in speech perception were highly context-dependent.

In their study of plosive-vowel syllables, Stevens and Blumstein used a spectral analysis technique that had not become generally available until the late 1960s, namely LPC analysis. As discussed in Section 8.3.5, in this analysis, spectral information is integrated over a time window. An LPC spectrum thus does not represent bursts, formant transitions, and steady states as separate events. Instead, the spectrum provides a single "snapshot" in which that information is integrated over time. The typical analysis window used in the study of plosive spectra is on the order of 10–25 ms. It is believed that this kind of representation is more like that derived by the auditory system.

Analysis of LPC spectra computed over only the first 25 ms of CV sequences suggested that the global shape of the spectra contained cues to place of articulation that were invariant across such sources of variability as phonetic context and vocal tract size. Templates representing the global shape associated with each place of articulation are shown in Figure 10.16. Bilabial consonants were found to be consistently associated with either a falling spectrum, indicating a predominance of energy in the lower frequencies, or a relatively flat spectrum without any clear concentration of energy. The rising spectrum for the alveolars reflected the predominance of energy in the higher frequencies, while the velar spectrum indicated that velars typically have a concentration of energy in the mid-frequency region, a spectral shape labeled "compact."

LPC spectra were then computed for CV and VC syllables produced by a new set of speakers and the templates were used to classify the consonants in terms of place of articulation. Results showed that place of articulation was classified with 85 percent accuracy for 1,800 tokens produced by four male and two female speakers (Blumstein and Stevens 1979).

Subsequent research on invariance focused on a more *dynamic* cue, namely the change in distribution of high-frequency energy as compared to low-frequency energy between consonant onset and the onset of the following vowel. This approach was a refinement of the earlier research in that it still captured the basic notion that bilabials are characterized by a relative predominance of energy in the lower frequencies while alveolars showed a predominance of energy in the higher frequencies. Using this dynamic criterion, 91 percent of the labial, dental, and alveolar plosives in English, French, and Malayalam were correctly classified (Lahiri et al. 1984; see also Kewley-Port 1983 for a dynamic approach).

Integrated dynamic invariant acoustic cues have also been documented for place of articulation in nasals. This research focused on the spectral change surrounding the nasal-vowel boundary in nasal-vowel syllables. Spectra were computed for the last two glottal pulses of the nasal murmur and the first two of the release into the vowel. A metric was established that captured the relative energy changes

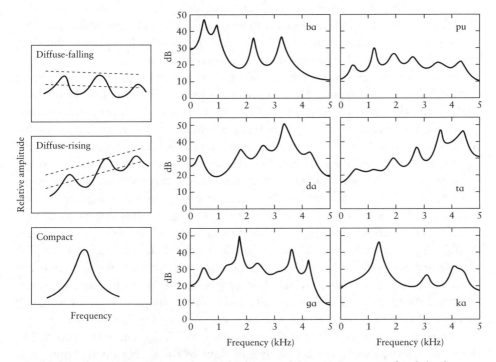

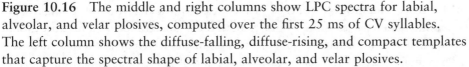

Figure 10.16 The middle and right columns show LPC spectra for labial, alveolar, and velar plosives, computed over the first 25 ms of CV syllables. The left column shows the diffuse-falling, diffuse-rising, and compact templates that capture the spectral shape of labial, alveolar, and velar plosives.

Reused with permission from Sheila E. Blumstein and Kenneth N. Stevens, *The Journal of the Acoustical Society of America*, 66, 1001 (1979). Copyright 1979, Acoustical Society of America.

in a low and high frequency range, corresponding to those reported as the location of the anti-formant for [m] and [n], respectively. This metric revealed that [m] was characterized by a rapid increase in energy in the lower frequencies while [n] showed a rapid increase in the higher frequencies. Classification of nasal place of articulation reached 89 percent accuracy across three speakers and five vowel contexts (Kurowski and Blumstein 1987).

Finally, invariant acoustic cues have also been reported for the manner distinction between plosives and approximants, specifically the glides [w] and [j]. In addition to differences in formant frequency onset values and formant transition duration, plosive-vowel and glide-vowel syllables such as [ba] and [wa] also differ in terms of the relative change in energy between the release of the consonant and the onset of voicing in the following vowel. Since plosives are produced with a complete constriction followed by a release, the change in energy from plosive to vowel is relatively large, certainly larger than that for approximants, which have only a moderate constriction. Taking the ratio of the energy in the first pitch period after the release and the energy in the period containing the release, Mack and

Blumstein (1983) found that plosives had consistently larger ratios than glides. Specifically, the adoption of a cut-off ratio of 1.37 allowed classification of consonants as either plosive or glide with 92 percent accuracy. In addition, the same metric distinguished [d, g] from [j] with 90 percent accuracy.

In sum, the studies summarized in this section suggest that invariant patterns corresponding to place and manner of articulation may be found in the acoustic signal. Crucially, these patterns do not focus on a single acoustic property, because, as Liberman and colleagues clearly showed, individual properties are usually highly context-dependent. Instead, dynamic cues that integrate several properties over a brief period seem to be much less affected by variations in speaker and phonetic context.

More recently, several statistical approaches to the classification of consonants in terms of place of articulation have been proposed. In an attempt to accommodate context effects, Forrest et al. (1988) used **spectral moments** to classify word-initial voiceless obstruents. To do this, a series of fast Fourier transforms (FFTs) was calculated every 10 ms from the onset of the obstruent. Each FFT was treated as a random probability distribution (i.e. as a set of values that can be statistically analyzed) from which the first four moments (mean, variance, skewness, and kurtosis) were computed. The mean of the frequency values weighted by their amplitude reflects *where* energy is concentrated on the frequency scale. The variance gives a measure for the range over which this energy is spread. The skewness refers to spectral tilt (the overall slant of the energy distribution), and the kurtosis is an indicator of the "peakedness" of the distribution. Using a spectral moments metric thus incorporates both local (spectral peak) and more global (spectral shape) information. The spectral moments were entered into a statistical discriminant analysis for classification in terms of place of articulation.[1] Correct classification of place based on the first 20 ms of the plosives (produced by five females and five males) averaged 89 percent.

A different statistical approach is exemplified by the use of **locus equations**. Locus equations provide a way of quantifying the fact first observed by Lindblom (1963) for voiced plosives that F2 frequency at the onset of the vowel following a voiced plosive is correlated with its frequency in the vowel midpoint of a plosive-vowel syllable. A locus equation can be defined as "a straight-line regression fit to coordinates formed by plotting onsets of F2 transitions in relation to their coarticulated F2 midvowel 'target frequencies'" (Sussman et al. 1993, p. 1256). In other words, each production of a CV syllable yields one datapoint consisting of an F2 value measured at vowel onset and an F2 value measured in the middle of the vowel. When all these points are plotted in an F2(onset) by F2(middle) space, a best-fitting line is drawn through this cloud of points such that each point is as close to this line as possible. Locus equations can be considered as indicators of the degree of coarticulation between a plosive and following consonant. If there were maximal coarticulation, the target F2 of the vowel would already be reached during the preceding plosive. The F2 at the middle of the vowel would therefore determine the F2 at the onset of the vowel and the locus equation would have a slope of 1, as illustrated in Figure 10.17. If, however, there were

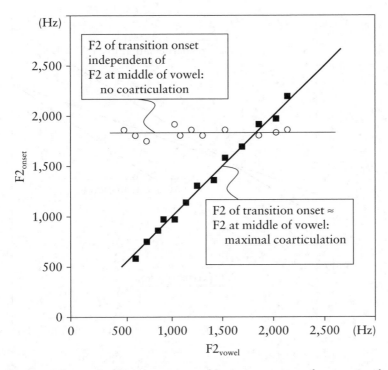

Figure 10.17 Schematic representation of locus equations for maximal and minimal consonant-to-vowel coarticulation.

no coarticulation, the F2 of the consonant would remain the same, regardless of the quality of the following vowel, and the locus equation would have a slope of 0, as shown in Figure 10.17.

Locus equations indicate that bilabials show the greatest degree of coarticulation, with steep slopes, velars an intermediate degree, and alveolars exhibit the smallest degree of coarticulation with relatively shallow slopes, as shown in Figure 10.18.

Locus equations constitute a dynamic representation of speech sounds since they express a relation between F2 at different points (vowel onset and midpoint) in the speech signal. In their study of English voiced plosive consonants, Sussman et al. (1991) found that discriminant analysis (based on the slope and *y*-intercept values) of each speaker's locus equations for each of the three places of articulation yielded a correct classification rate of 100 percent.

In conclusion, this chapter discussed the broad acoustic correlates of a number of sound classes. As shown on the spectrograms (e.g. Figure 10.6), some of these correlates vary depending on the context in which they occur. The debate about the existence and nature of invariant cues will likely continue for some time. While the classification rates of recent statistical metrics are very impressive, it remains to be determined whether human listeners base their identification of place

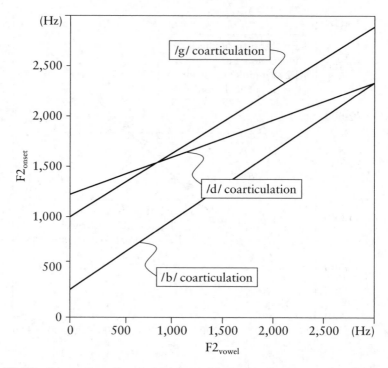

Figure 10.18   Regression lines of F2 transitions in relation to their F2 midvowel target frequencies for [p, t, k] and the three vowels [i, a, u] in German based on 10 speakers.

of articulation on similar sources of information. We will return to these issues in Chapter 13.

Exercises

1   Which formants are important for distinguishing the vowels in Dutch and German? What information does each formant provide?
2   How do oral and nasal vowels differ in spectrograms? What causes this difference?
3   How can monophthongs and diphthongs be differentiated in spectrograms?
4   What are four acoustic characteristics used to distinguish fricatives? In terms of these characteristics, how do [s, z, ʃ, ʒ] differ from [f, v, θ, ð]?
5   The acoustics of sounds with a substantial constriction can be modeled by means of a three-tube model consisting of a back cavity, a constriction, and a front cavity. Assume a model with a total tube length of 16 cm (13 cm for

the tubes, 3 cm for the constriction) and calculate F2, F3, and F4 and their cavity affiliations for the following consonants:

/s/ as in 'see' (length of the back cavity = 11 cm)
/ʃ/ as in 'she' (length of the back cavity = 10 cm)

In which frequency range do you expect the energy to be concentrated for each of these two consonants?

6   What acoustic characteristics are used to discern the place of articulation of stops? What indicates whether a stop is voiced or voiceless?

7   What is meant by the claim that the speech signal is characterized by a "lack of invariance"?

Note

1   A statistical discriminant analysis assigns cases to groups based on a number of (acoustic) parameters.

11   Syllables and Suprasegmentals

Our discussion of the articulatory and acoustic characteristics of speech sounds has until now focused on individual vowels and consonants. However, spoken language rarely consists of isolated speech sounds. Instead, vowels and consonants are combined to form larger units such as syllables, phrases, and sentences. These larger units can also be described in terms of their articulatory and acoustic properties. The examination of aspects of speech that extend beyond individual vowels and consonants is known as the study of suprasegmentals or **prosody**. The term prosody is sometimes used as a synonym only for "intonation." However, as we discuss in this chapter, intonation is only one instance of a range of phenomena properly known as "prosody," which we use as a synonym for "suprasegmentals," intonation being part of it.

The principal suprasegmental features are stress (how "prominent" a syllable is), length (or quantity), tone (F_0 level or movement in a syllable), and intonation (F_0 movement during a phrase). These features are independent of those required for the description of segmental properties. While the term *suprasegmental* implies a difference between properties of individual segments and properties over longer stretches of speech, it is important to consider prosodic structure as an integral part of the speech signal.

Before any introduction of suprasegmentals, we need to discuss the notion of the syllable since suprasegmental features such as stress and tone make reference to it. While most people have an intuitive notion of what a syllable is, it is quite difficult to define a syllable using phonetic criteria.

11.1   Syllables

While syllables most often consist of a combination of consonants and vowels, they can also consist of individual vowels (*eye* [aɪ]) or consonants (the syllabic nasal in *cotton* [kɑtn̩]). The syllable is often represented by the Greek symbol σ. For descriptive purposes, a syllable can be said to consist of, minimally, a **nucleus** and, maximally, an **onset**, nucleus, and **coda**. Typically, the nucleus of the

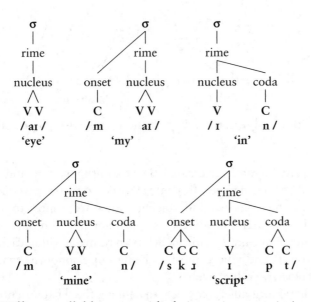

Figure 11.1 Different syllable types with their components (σ is a convenient symbol for "syllable").

syllable is the vowel, the onset is made up by the consonants preceding the vowel, and the coda consists of the consonants following the vowel. The nucleus and coda together form the **rime** (see Figure 11.1).

Most people can easily identify syllables. For example, native speakers of English generally agree that the word *yesterday* ['jɛs.tɚ.deɪ] consists of three syllables (following IPA convention, syllable breaks are indicated by the symbol [.]). However, other cases are more controversial. Words like *mirror* or *fire* will be perceived by some as having two syllables while others will hear only one syllable. A definition of the syllable should be able to account not only for the clear-cut cases but also for the "controversial" cases.

Phonetic definitions of the syllable have been proposed in both articulatory and auditory terms. Early articulatory accounts of the syllable claimed that each syllable was the result of a contraction of the respiratory muscles. However, subsequent work showed that there was no one-to-one mapping between syllables and muscle activity: certain bisyllabic (two-syllable) words were shown to involve only a single contraction of the expiratory muscles, and, conversely, certain monosyllabic (one-syllable) words were produced with two muscular contractions. (See Section 5.1.4 on the difficulty of relating muscular activity of the thorax to the loudness of speech sounds.)

Auditory definitions of the syllable make reference to the notion of **sonority**, the relative loudness of sounds. Even if all speech sounds were produced with the same length, stress, and pitch, some are louder than others. For example, vowels are louder than consonants, and within the class of vowels, [ɑ] is louder than [i]. When speech sounds are ranked in terms of their loudness, a ranking

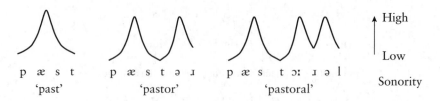

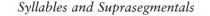

Figure 11.2   Idealized sonority levels of the words *past*, *pastor*, and *pastoral*.

known as **sonority hierarchy** is created. The two primary contributors to the perception of sonority are degree of opening of the vocal tract (the more open the tract, the louder the sound is) and voicing. Going from most to least sonorous, the order in this hierarchy is vowels → approximants → nasals → fricatives → plosives. Additional fine-grained distinctions can be made within each manner class, such as low vowels and voiced plosives being more sonorous than high vowels and voiceless plosives, respectively.

How does the sonority hierarchy help in defining the syllable? Phonologists have proposed that each syllable is associated with a peak in sonority (e.g. Selkirk 1984). The **sonority principle** stipulates that sonority increases from syllable onset, reaching a maximum at syllable nucleus, and then decreases toward syllable coda. Words such as *past*, *pastor*, and *pastoral* all fit the pattern predicted by the sonority principle, with one, two, and three sonority peaks, respectively (see Figure 11.2). Unfortunately, some English words violate the principle, most notably those beginning with [s]+plosive clusters such as *speak* [spik]. Since [s] is judged as more sonorous than all other voiceless and voiced plosives, a word such as *speak* would have two sonority peaks, yet it consists of only a single syllable. The sonority principle is perhaps best thought of as a statistical fact over many languages rather than a grammatical fact. There are violations in many languages that may have onsets like [mr,ft,rt] or codas like [rj]. Nevertheless, taking "sonority" as an ordering principle of an "idealized" prominence of sounds that roughly relates to the openness of the vocal tract and allowing for certain exceptions in a particular language gives a formal means of segmenting words into syllables.

In sum, while the notion of a syllable is intuitively straightforward and plays a prominent role in phonological theory, a comprehensive phonetic definition still remains to be formulated.

11.2   Stress

Stress is a property of a syllable that serves to make it relatively more prominent. Three levels of stress, from strongest to weakest, are usually distinguished: primary stress, secondary stress, and unstressed. For example, in the word *phonetician*

[ˌfoʊ.nə.ˈtɪ.ʃn̩], the third syllable receives primary stress (indicated by a high vertical stroke [ˈ] preceding the syllable), the first syllable receives secondary stress (indicated by a low vertical stroke [ˌ] preceding the syllable), and the second and last syllables are unstressed. Articulatorily, a stressed syllable is usually produced with greater physical effort. This may be reflected in an increase in activity of the laryngeal muscles (particularly the cricothyroid muscle), an increase in subglottal air pressure, or an adjustment in spectral tilt, that is, increasing the amount of high-frequency energy in relation to the low-frequency energy (Sluijter et al. 1997; see Section 5.2.3). Acoustically, the four main acoustic correlates of stress are fundamental frequency, duration, intensity, and formant frequency pattern. (The effect of the spectral tilt has not yet been intensively investigated and will be left out of the subsequent discussion.) Compared to an unstressed syllable, a stressed syllable in English typically has a higher fundamental frequency, greater duration, greater intensity, and a less reduced ("schwa-like") quality. Stressed syllables may be characterized by any one or more of these correlates. In some languages, stress can be indicated by means of a decrease in fundamental frequency (e.g. Bengali; cf. Hayes and Lahiri 1991) or much more complex patterns (e.g. Welsh; cf. Williams 1983).

The understanding of the acoustic correlates of English stress has benefited from a series of studies on the perception of bisyllabic minimal pairs such as *the record* [ˈɹɛ.kɚd] and *to record* [ɹə.ˈkɔɹd]. In English, bisyllabic nouns are often stressed on the first syllable (sometimes referred to as a "trochaic" stress pattern) while bisyllabic verbs are stressed on the second syllable (an "iambic" stress pattern). The transcription of the minimal pair clearly indicates that there is a difference in phonetic quality: the stressed first syllable contains a full vowel [ɛ] while the unstressed first syllable contains the reduced vowel [ə]. Figure 11.3 shows oscillograms, spectrograms, as well as intensity and pitch contours of the word *record* spoken as a noun and as a verb. In this example, all four acoustic correlates of stress are present. A comparison of the stressed syllables to the unstressed syllables shows an increased fundamental frequency, longer duration, increased intensity, and modified formant frequency pattern. With respect to the role of fundamental frequency, it is sometimes observed that rather than an increase per se in fundamental frequency, a change in any direction is a correlate of stress. That is, a stressed syllable could have either a higher or lower fundamental frequency than its unstressed counterpart. Perception experiments with synthetic speech, where the segmental content remained the same while each correlate of stress was systematically varied, suggest that fundamental frequency and duration may be stronger cues to stress than intensity. As for formant frequency, the second formant frequency (F2) of the vowel in the *first* syllable is lowered for the verb while F2 in the *second* syllable is lowered for the noun. Vowel reduction is pervasive in English. Many unstressed syllables are realized in English as [ə]. This is not necessarily the case in other languages. In Spanish, for example, the quality of the vowel /o/ does not change as a function of stress in minimal pairs such as *miro* [ˈmi.ro] ('I watch') and *miro* [mi.ˈro] ('he watched').

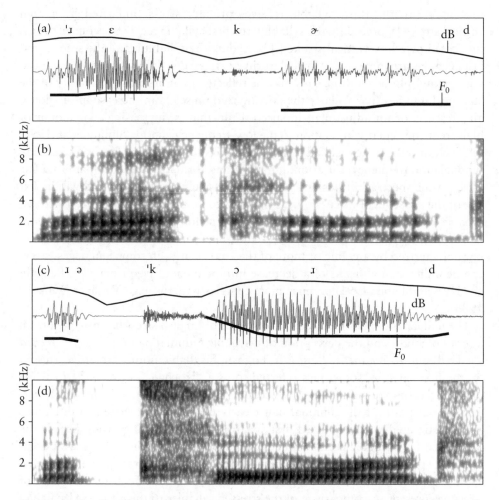

Figure 11.3 Oscillogram, spectrogram, intensity, and F_0 contours of the word *record* spoken as (a, b) a noun (['ɹɛkɚd]) and (c, d) a verb ([ɹə'kɔɹd]).

It must be kept in mind that the correlates of stress also serve other purposes. Fundamental frequency signals tone and intonation, duration is important in languages with phonemic distinctions in length, and formant frequency pattern is the primary correlate of vowel quality. The relative importance of a particular acoustic correlate of stress may in part be determined by its role in signaling other distinctions.

In addition to the syllable, the **foot** is also an important constituent in any discussion of stress. A foot can be defined as consisting of the stressed syllable and all unstressed syllables that follow it (for alternative definitions of the foot, see Hayes 1995). It is claimed that stressed syllables alternate with unstressed syllables to create a rhythm of prominence peaks. In a word such as *information*

[ˌɪn.fɚ.ˈmeɪ.ʃn̩] the stressed syllables [ɪn] and [meɪ] are each followed by an unstressed syllable. Thus, the word *information* consists of two feet, [ɪn.fɚ] and [meɪ.ʃn̩]. Languages in which more and less prominent syllables alternate in this way are known as **stress-timed** languages. Within the group of stress-timed languages, a distinction is made between *fixed* and *variable* stress. In a language with fixed stress, primary stress always falls on the same syllable. For example, in Czech stress falls on the first syllable, in Polish words are almost always stressed on the penultimate syllable, and in French it is nearly always the final syllable. In variable stress-timed languages such as English or German, stress does not consistently fall on a fixed syllable in a word; it is variable across words (cf. Hayes 1995).

At the sentence level, the alternating stress creates different rhythms. For example, the utterance *Eddy's playing a trombone* consists of three feet, *Eddy's*, *playing a trom*, and *bone*. It is claimed that in stress-timed languages like English and other Germanic languages, linguistic rhythm is based on the **isochrony** of interstress intervals. That is, in stress-timed languages, interstress intervals tend to have the same duration. In other words, in the example utterance, each foot, regardless of the number of syllables (*Eddy's*, *playing a trom*, and *bone*), is equally long. However, as illustrated by the oscillogram in Figure 11.4, the even spacing of stress has received little empirical support.

In **syllable-timed** languages like French and Spanish, *all* syllables, stressed and unstressed, are assumed to occur at regular intervals, in contrast to stress-timed languages (in which stressed syllables are claimed to occur at regular intervals). Linguistic rhythm is thought to arise from the isochrony of syllables. In other words, for syllable-timed languages, stressed and unstressed syllables do not differ significantly in duration. Indeed, it has been reported that the difference between stressed and unstressed syllables is smaller in Spanish, a syllable-timed language, than in English, a stress-timed language. The fact that unstressed syllables are not reduced in Spanish also contributes to the regular intervals. However, syllable duration was not found to be constant.

We should note here that Japanese may provide an example of a third type of timing, **mora timing**. Japanese has a unit called the **mora**. In Japanese, the

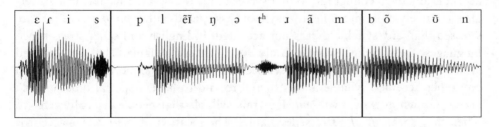

Figure 11.4 Oscillogram of the sentence *Eddy's playing a trombone*. The duration of each foot is marked and provides little support for the existence of isochrony.

difference between a syllable and a mora is that a consonant in the coda of a syllable forms a mora of its own (and so does the second half of a long vowel). According to traditional accounts, each mora takes up approximately the same duration. Consider the Japanese words /ha-ʃi/ 'edge' and /ke-k-ko-ŋ/ 'marriage.' While both words consist of two syllables, the first word has two morae and the second has four (separated by dashes for convenience). Some duration measures support a mora-based account. That is, /ke-k-ko-ŋ/ is twice as long as /ha-ʃi/. However, recent careful acoustic research has not been able to support the notion of the mora as a direct temporal unit (Warner and Arai 2001).

Depending on the structure of the sentence, a given word in a sentence can be pronounced with or without stress. In the sentence *I crave fame **and** fortune*, the word *and* receives emphasis and is produced in what is called its **strong (unreduced) form**, [ænd]. In contrast, in the sentence *I **crave** fame and fortune*, the word *and* is produced in its **weak (reduced) form** [ənd]. Function words (articles, conjunctions, prepositions, and pronouns) are usually much more prone to such strong–weak alternations than content words (such as nouns and verbs). Phonetically, this alternation can lead to changes in vowel quality, and even the loss of vowels or consonants, as in the weak forms of *and* [ənd], [ən], [n̩d], or [n̩].

At the sentence level, the stress of a word can also change as a function of the stress of neighboring words. For example, the word *fourteen* produced in the utterance *I'll turn fourteen tomorrow*, is stressed on the second syllable. However, in the phrase *I am fourteen years old*, it is typically produced with stress on the first syllable. This phenomenon is known as **stress shift** or **rhythm reversal**. Note that *fourteen* is also stressed on the first syllable in the phrase *I am fourteen semesters behind*. The fact that *fourteen* is followed by an unstressed syllable demonstrates that stress shift is not triggered by a sequence of two stressed syllables. Instead, stress shift operates at the level of the phrase. As Carr (1999) points out, stress shift "reverses a sequence of a secondary stressed syllable and a primary stressed syllable when it is followed by a primary stressed syllable within the phrase" (p. 111).

When a word occurs as part of a sentence, a **pitch accent** or **nuclear accent** can be used to make certain stressed syllables more prominent than others. A pitch accent is any pitch configuration that serves to make a specific syllable in an utterance relatively more prominent. A syllable associated with a *pitch accent* is more stressed than any syllable that is not accented. In English and other stress-timed languages, the accented syllable is always a stressed syllable. The last accented syllable of an intonational phrase (see Section 11.4.2) is also more prominent than any other accented syllable and is therefore said to have a special type of pitch accent known as *nuclear accent*. It is this syllable that people typically refer to when they speak of '*the* stressed syllable'. The location of the nuclear accent is determined by discourse properties that the speaker wants to highlight for the hearer (e.g., whether new information is brought into a conversation, or whether two items are contrasted).

11.3   Length

The acoustic correlate of length is duration. Duration is affected by many factors whose domain ranges from the segmental to the sentential level. Much of the current understanding of both local and global influences on segment duration stems from research in speech synthesis. Early attempts to synthesize speech (i.e. generate speech by computer) sounded incomprehensible at times because the synthesis rules did not adjust segment durations appropriately. This inspired researchers to conduct detailed studies to identify and quantify factors that affect duration. Table 11.1 lists some of these factors; it is based on a similar table by Klatt, one of the pioneers of modern speech synthesis.

Articulatorily, duration is determined by the timing of articulatory movements. The duration of the segment, syllable, foot, and sentence is affected by a number of both local and global factors. One factor that affects duration strongly is the presence of a phonemic length distinction, known as **contrastive length**. Many languages contrast long and short vowels. Duration seems to be the primary cue to vowel length in languages such as Arabic, Danish, Estonian, Ewe, Finnish, and Japanese, with long to short vowel duration ratios ranging from 1.3:1 to 2:1, that is, with long vowels being from 30 to 100 percent longer than their short counterparts. In these cases, the long vowel is indicated by the length mark [ː], as in [iː] versus [i]. In languages such as Dutch, English, and Swedish, however, the distinction is primarily one in terms of quality and only secondarily in terms of duration. In these cases, the contrast is represented by the use of two distinctive phonetic symbols, as in [i] versus [ɪ].

Although less common than vowel length contrasts, contrasts between long and short consonants also occur in a variety of languages. Italian is an oft-cited example with minimal pairs such as *fato* ['fato] 'fate' and *fatto* ['fatːo] 'done.' These long consonants are known as **geminates**. Other well-documented languages with a distinction between single and geminate plosives include Arabic, Bengali, Estonian, Finnish, Italian, Luganda, Swiss German, and Turkish, with long consonants generally being two to three times as long as their short counterparts. Geminate plosives can be realized by means of a longer closure duration (e.g. Swiss German) and/or a longer VOT (e.g. Cyprus Greek).

Intrinsic duration differences constitute another factor affecting length. When all other factors are held constant, low vowels are slightly longer (20–25 ms) than high vowels. This difference may be perceptible since psychophysical studies suggest that intrinsic duration differences exceed the minimal difference (**just noticeable difference (JND)**) needed by listeners to discriminate two sounds in terms of duration. Intrinsic duration differences have been reported for a variety of languages and are therefore likely to be language-universal. The most common explanation for the correlation between tongue height and duration is that low vowels involve a greater extent of articulatory movement. The tongue in a low

Table 11.1 Parameters affecting the duration of segments (after Klatt 1973). Klatt gives references for every statement, which we have omitted here

1	Pause insertion rule	Insert a brief pause before each sentence-internal main clause and at other boundaries limited by an orthographic comma.
2	Clause-final lengthening	The vowel or syllabic consonant in the syllable just before a pause is lengthened. Any consonants in the rhyme (between this vowel and the pause) are also lengthened.
3	Phrase-final lengthening	Syllabic segments (vowels and syllabic consonants) are lengthened if in a phrase-final syllable. Durational increases at the noun-phrase/verb-phrase boundary are more likely in a complex noun phrase or when subject-verb-object order is violated; durational changes are much less likely for pronouns. The lengthening is perceptually important.
4	Non word-final shortening	Syllabic segments are shortened slightly if not in a word-final syllable. (This rule is disputed.)
5	Polysyllabic shortening	Syllabic segments in a polysyllabic word are shortened slightly. (This rule is also disputed.)
6	Non-initial-consonant shortening	Consonants in non-word-initial position are shortened.
7	Unstressed shortening	Unstressed segments are shorter and more compressible than stressed segments.
8	Lengthening for emphasis	An emphasized vowel is significantly lengthened.
9	Postvocalic context of vowels	The influence of a postvocalic consonant (in the same word) on the duration of a vowel is such as to shorten the vowel if the consonant is voiceless. The effects are greatest at phrase and clause boundaries.
10	Shortening in clusters	Segments are shortened in consonant–consonant sequences (disregarding word boundaries, but not across phrase boundaries).
11	Lengthening due to plosive aspiration	A stressed vowel or sonorant preceded by a voiceless plosive is lengthened.

vowel has to move further to following consonants, which require a more closed vocal tract that usually goes along with a higher tongue position, and hence require more time. For consonants, it has been reported that labials tend to be longer than either alveolars or velars. One explanation is that the lips are less mobile (and hence, slower) articulators than the tongue.

There are additional local conditioning factors for segment duration. One such factor was discussed in Section 3.4.2.1, namely that vowels are longer when followed by a voiced as compared to a voiceless consonant. Other factors influencing segment duration include the place and manner of the consonants that either precede or follow the vowel. More global conditioning factors include the number of segments in the syllable and the number of syllables in the word. In general, segment duration is shortened as the number of segments and syllables increases. For example, the duration of the vowel [u] will be shortest in the word *fruitier*, somewhat longer in *fruity* and longest in *fruit*. This may again be an instance of isochrony, shortening longer words in an attempt to keep the intervals between stressed syllables relatively constant at the phrasal level.

In addition to local factors, global factors affecting duration include the position of the segment or syllable in the sentence. This effect can be observed by measuring the length of a syllable in running speech and comparing it to the same syllable in a different position. A syllable is substantially longer at the end of a phrase than at the beginning or middle of a phrase, a phenomenon known as **phrase-final lengthening**.

One final global factor affecting segment length is **speaking rate**. Speaking rate can be defined as the overall tempo of a speaking turn. The same sentence (*How do you do?*) can be uttered at a slow or a fast tempo. Speaking rate can be computed based on the number of phonemes or syllables per second. For English, the average speaking rate is on the order of 4–6 syllables per second. However, with an increase in speaking rate, there is often a change in the phonemes that are produced. It makes a difference, then, whether rate is computed on the basis of the idealized transcription of an utterance or on the actual produced sounds.

When calculating speaking rate, filled pauses (e.g. "um," "oh," etc.) within utterances as well as silent pauses between the utterances that make up the speaking turn must also be taken into account. Increases or decreases in speaking rate shorten or lengthen, respectively, both segment durations and pauses. However, changes in speaking rate do not affect all segment durations and pauses equally. In general, longer segments are affected more than shorter ones so that the duration of vowels, for example, changes more than that of consonants. In addition to affecting duration, variations in speaking rate can also affect F_0 range, with an increase in speaking rate typically leading to a reduction in F_0 range.

11.4   Tone and Intonation

While a change in F_0 serves as a cue to lexical stress, a number of local and global factors affect F_0 per se. As mentioned in Section 7.3.1.4, pitch is the perceptual correlate of fundamental frequency, which makes vocal fold vibration its articulatory correlate. The most obvious factor affecting fundamental frequency is gender, with average fundamental frequency values of 130 Hz for males and 220 Hz for females (although these values may vary across cultures). Another factor affecting fundamental frequency is the speaker's emotional state. For example, a substantially raised F_0 seems to be indicative of anger, fear, or happiness. Vowels also differ in terms of their **intrinsic fundamental frequency**.[1] In general, the fundamental frequency of high vowels is higher (by approximately 15 Hz) than that of low vowels. This is well within a listener's range of sensitivity since the just noticeable difference for fundamental frequency is approximately 1–2 Hz under ideal conditions and 10 Hz with speech-like stimuli. (Klatt 1973).

Intrinsic fundamental frequency differences have been observed across the world's languages. One explanation states that the effect is due to the muscular link between larynx and tongue. In this "tongue-pull" theory (Lehiste 1970), raising the tongue for the production of high vowels causes the larynx to rise as well, which leads to a tilt between cricoid and thyroid and increases the tension of the vocal folds, ultimately resulting in an increase in fundamental frequency. A general physiological "laryngeal dependency" theory has also been proposed (Ladd and Silverman 1984), according to which greater muscular tension for higher vowels leads to a greater muscular tension in the larynx. Yet another approach is "acoustic coupling" (Flanagan and Landgraf 1968), according to which the narrowed vocal tract leads to a Bernoulli effect with a higher speed of airflow, which reduces the air pressure above the larynx, which increases trans-glottal pressure, which ultimately increases the oscillation frequency of the vocal folds. Finally, the F_0 could be under "active speaker control" to enhance vowel height contrasts (Kingston & Diehl 1994).

Similar to local conditioning factors for duration, a segmental conditioning factor for F_0 is the observation that a vowel's fundamental frequency is slightly higher (approximately 5–10 Hz) when the vowel is preceded by a voiceless obstruent as compared to a voiced obstruent.

11.4.1   Tone

While gender is a major contributor to variation in fundamental frequency across speakers, the factor that affects fundamental frequency most strongly for a given speaker is the presence of a phonemic fundamental frequency distinction, known as **contrastive tone** or **lexical tone**. Tones can be defined as pitch variations that change either the lexical or grammatical meaning of a word. A language in which the meaning of a word depends on its tone is known as a **tone language**.

Tone languages can have either **register tones** or **contour tones**. In a register tone language, the relative height of each syllable's pitch within the speaker's pitch range (or register) provides a cue to word meaning. These languages typically have up to four distinctive pitch levels. The vast majority of languages spoken in Africa are register tone languages (including Igbo, Shona, Yoruba, and Zulu to name but a few). Yoruba, for example, has three register tones, high, as in the first and second syllable of [ó.bé] 'he jumped,' mid, as in the second syllable of [ó.bē] 'he is forward,' and low as in [ó.bè] 'he asks for pardon.' Notice that, following IPA convention, the high tone is marked by an acute accent [´] over the vowel, the mid tone by a macron [¯], and the low tone by a grave accent [`].

In a contour tone language, pitch movement, instead of pitch level, serves to distinguish word meaning. Each tone is associated with a particular shape and direction of the pitch trajectory. Many of the languages spoken in Southeast Asia (including Mandarin Chinese, Thai, and Vietnamese) are contour tone languages. Mandarin Chinese, for example, has four tones, high-level (Tone 1), high-rising (Tone 2), low-falling-rising (Tone 3), and high-falling (Tone 4). Figure 11.5 shows pitch contours for each of the four tones. Tone 1 is indeed at the high end of the speaker's range and remains level throughout its duration. Tone 2 starts lower but still in the speaker's upper range and rises throughout its duration. Tone 3 starts toward the speaker's lower range, dips even lower, and then rises toward the end. And Tone 4 starts about as high as Tone 1 but then shows a rather steep fall.

Table 11.2 shows sample transcriptions of the four tones. The column labeled "Pitch" indicates a common numerical representation of the tones, where 1 and 5 specify the lowest and highest points, respectively, of a speaker's pitch range, and 2, 3, and 4 are equally spaced in between (that is, "35" represents a tonal contour that starts in the middle and rises to the highest pitch of a speaker's range). IPA has two alternative sets of symbols to indicate tone, which we label as "tone markers" and "tone letters." Both sets are listed under "tones and word accents" on the IPA chart. The tone markers are placed above the vowel. In Table 11.2, the column labeled "Tone markers" shows the four markers used to indicate the Mandarin tones. Tone letters follow the syllable and consist of a vertical line with a stroke preceding it. The vertical line represents pitch range, and the stroke indicates movement and height within that range, as shown in the column labeled "Tone letters."

Historically, the process by which a non-tonal language changes into a tonal language is known as **tonogenesis**. We will focus on just one of the ways in which lexical tones may develop, having to do with a segmental conditioning factor mentioned previously, namely the fact that the fundamental frequency is higher for a vowel preceded by a voiceless as compared to a voiced obstruent. Research suggests (cf. Hombert 1978) that some tonal distinctions arose as the result of the listener's reinterpretation of a previously secondary cue after the disappearance of the primary cue. For example, in a language with voiced and

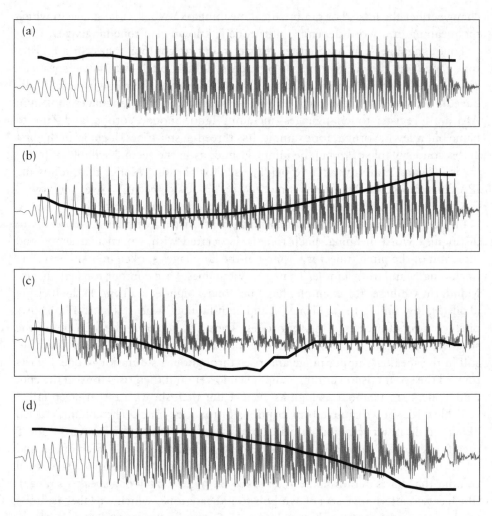

Figure 11.5   Oscillograms and pitch contours (dark lines) of the word [ma] spoken with each of the four Mandarin tones by an adult male.

Table 11.2   The four tones of Mandarin Chinese and three ways of transcribing them

	Pitch	*Tone markers*	*Tone letters*	*Gloss*
Tone 1: high-level	55	[mā]	[ma˥]	'mother'
Tone 2: high-rising	35	[má]	[ma˦]	'hemp'
Tone 3: low-falling-rising	214	[mǎ]	[ma˩]	'horse'
Tone 4: high-falling	51	[mà]	[ma˥]	'scold'

voiceless obstruents, the vowels following voiced obstruents have a slightly lower pitch. As mentioned earlier, this may be actively produced by the speakers of a language to enhance the voicing contrast. However, when the language subsequently loses its voicing contrast in the plosives, the originally secondary pitch difference now becomes the primary cue to the lexical distinction and a tone language with two tones, high and low, on the vowels, has emerged. The tone contrast, which was originally only a by-product of the voiced–voiceless distinction, has then become part of the phonemic inventory of a language.

11.4.2 *Intonation*

Intonation is the distinctive use of pitch over units larger than a single word. Intonation may convey linguistic information by marking the boundaries of syntactic units or by distinguishing different sentence types such as statements, questions, and commands. Intonation may also convey non-linguistic information such as boredom, impatience, or politeness. We will limit our discussion to the linguistic functions of intonation.

Many languages indicate the end of a syntactic unit such as a phrase or sentence by means of a falling pitch (such as in declarative sentences). Many languages mark a yes–no question (a question to which the answer is expected to be either "yes" or "no") or other requests for information with a rising intonation. Although English declarative sentences and questions usually differ in terms of word order (*This is Jane.* vs. *Is this Jane?*), the same declarative sentence could be a statement or question, depending on its intonation. For example, the statement *We've been invited to a party tomorrow.* with a falling intonation informs somebody about an invitation whereas *We've been invited to a party tomorrow?* with a rising intonation expresses surprise about the existence of such an invitation.

Pitch contours for a declarative statement and a yes–no question are shown in Figure 11.6. Notice that the declarative sentence is marked by a general lowering of the fundamental frequency throughout the sentence, a phenomenon known as **declination**. In contrast, for the yes–no question a steep rise is evident, particularly at the end of the sentence.

The declination that is often observed in English declaratives can be perturbed by local changes in emphasis. Consider the following sentences, in which the emphasized word is in italics:

a   We will buy our *first* home tomorrow.
b   We will buy our first *home* tomorrow.
c   We will buy our first home *tomorrow.*

Pitch contours for each of these three readings are shown in Figure 11.7. The intonation contours show a clear change in pitch at the **tonic syllable**, the syllable of the phrase receiving primary stress (the italicized syllable in the example sentences).

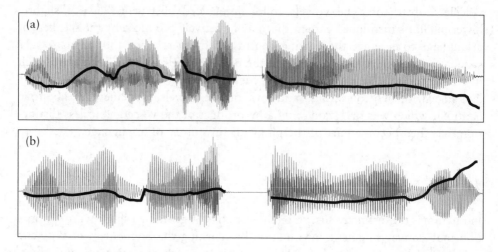

Figure 11.6 Oscillograms and pitch contours for *We've been invited to a party tomorrow* as (a) a declarative sentence, and (b) a yes–no question.

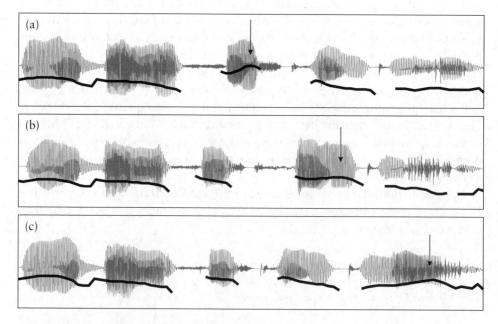

Figure 11.7 Oscillograms and pitch contours of the sentence *We will buy our first home tomorrow* with emphasis on (a) "first," (b) "home," and (c) "tomorrow" as indicated by the arrows.

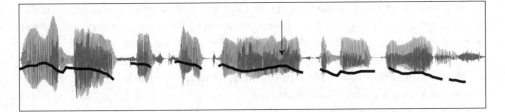

Figure 11.8 Oscillograms and pitch contour of the sentence *We will buy our first home tomorrow if the bank will let us*, consisting of two intonational phrases. The arrow marks the onset of the second intonational phrase *if the bank will let us*.

All sentences that we have considered so far consist of a single **intonational phrase**. However, a sentence such as *We will buy our first home tomorrow if the bank will let us* consists of two intonational phrases. As shown in Figure 11.8, the onset of the second intonational phrase *if the bank will let us* is marked by an increase in fundamental frequency, which indicates the existence of a second intonational phrase.

Figure 11.9 shows the pitch contours of sentences that can be considered minimal pairs in terms of their syntactic structure. The sentence *Almost everyone knows but Linda hasn't found out yet* consists of two conjoined main clauses while the sentence *Almost everyone knows Belinda hasn't found out yet* is nearly identical in terms of its segments but consists of a main clause and embedded clause. The

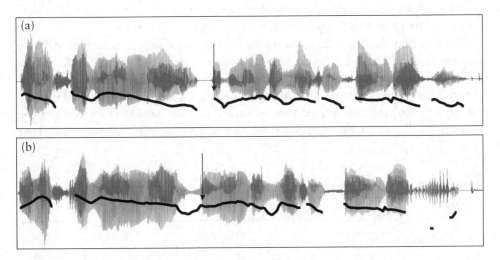

Figure 11.9 Pitch contours of the sentences (a) *Almost everyone knows but Linda hasn't found out yet* and (b) *Almost everyone knows Belinda hasn't found out yet*. The different syntactic structures of the two sentences are reflected in their distinct intonation patterns at the beginning of [lɪn], marked by the arrows.

pitch contours of these sentences are distinct in that the boundary between the two main clauses is marked by a more pronounced "fall–rise" pattern than that between main and embedded clause. While the peak value of F_0 in *knows* was the same for both sentences, the lowest F_0 value in *knows* and the peak value in *lin* were significantly lower (by approximately 5 Hz) for the sentence consisting of two conjoined clauses (Cooper and Sorensen 1977). Research also suggests that listeners can make use of this kind of information while parsing the sentence.

We have discussed stress, tone, and intonation as if they were all independent phenomena. However, as soon as the domain of investigation is larger than a single word, cues to stress, tone, and intonation begin to interact, as mentioned in our discussion of the role that intonation can play in making certain words more prominent. In addition, we do not mean to suggest that a language can use pitch for either tone or intonation only, or that a language can only be either a stress or a tone language (see Hyman 2006). In most tone languages, declarative statements are produced with a falling intonation (i.e. they use intonation). Moreover, several languages, including Pirahaã, Ma'ya, and Curaçao Papiamentu have been documented as having both stress and tone.

Finally, we end this chapter by discussing a language type that is not quite a tone language nor a stress language, again emphasizing the point that the distinctions and categories introduced in this chapter are not always clear-cut. This language type is the pitch-accent language, of which Japanese is a well-known example. Pitch-accent languages are similar to tone languages in that each syllable (or mora, in the case of Japanese) in a word is associated with a particular tone. However, unlike in a tone language, in a pitch-accent language, the entire tonal pattern of a word is known once the location of the accent of the word is known. Consider the examples from Japanese shown in Table 11.3.

The location of the accent, indicated by the diacritic ['], is not predictable and needs to be learned for each word. However, once the location of the accent is known, the entire tonal pattern follows from two simple rules. The first rule is that an accented mora and all morae preceding it receive a high tone (H) while all morae following the accented mora receive a low tone (L). The second rule is that (in the dialect spoken in Tokyo) the first mora of a word receives a low tone

Table 11.3 Words illustrating Japanese (Tokyo dialect) as a pitch-accent language

Tonal pattern	Word	Gloss
H-L	[sóɾa]	'sky'
L-H	[kawá]	'river'
L-H-L	[kokóɾo]	'heart'
L-H-H	[otokó]	'man'

when it is not accented. Once the location of the accent is known, these two rules account for all forms in Table 11.3. This is in contrast with tone languages such as Mandarin Chinese, where speakers must learn the pitch pattern of each syllable of a word.

In this chapter, we have discussed the principal suprasegmental features of stress, length, tone, and intonation and their acoustic correlates of fundamental frequency, duration, amplitude, and formant frequency patterns. Perceptually, the four dimensions available to the auditory system for differentiating aspects of the speech signal are pitch, duration, loudness, and auditory quality (= timbre). In the next chapter, we will discuss the basic structure and function of the human auditory system as well as some of the non-linear ways in which the auditory system transforms the speech signal.

Exercises

1   What is prosody? What features are used to describe prosody?
2   Why is it difficult to define a syllable? What is the sonority hierarchy and how does it help?
3   What is stress and what are its acoustic correlates?
4   Briefly explain the difference between stress-timed, syllable-timed, and mora-timed languages.
5   How do register tone and contour tone languages differ?
6   What is the difference between intonation and stress?

Note

1   Sometimes called "intrinsic pitch," although the term intrinsic fundamental frequency is to be preferred since the rate of vocal fold vibration is increased (and it is not a perception phenomenon) and the increased F_0 does not necessarily result in an increase in perceived pitch.

12 Physiology and Psychophysics of Hearing

For historic reasons, speech sounds are categorized according to the way they are produced. This approach to investigating speech, focusing on the *production* of sounds, was motivated by the limited set of methods that were available for the measurement and representation of speech. The speech production apparatus was more or less easily accessible to investigation, and the chain of events during speech production was studied by means of introspection and careful observation. The ear, on the other hand, is small and inaccessible. Examining what happens within the ear in living subjects requires advanced technical equipment. Furthermore, much of the task of "hearing" relates to processes performed in the brain, where eventually the perception of "sounds" leads to the perception of "speech." The scientific investigation of the process of hearing is therefore relatively young, and our knowledge still incomplete in many domains.

With very recent **brain imaging techniques** (including electro-encephalography [EEG], magneto-encephalography [MEG], and functional magnetic resonance imaging [fMRI]), it has become possible to observe brain activity to a limited extent when a listener hears, for example, an [ɑ] or an [i]. Other aspects of the hearing process are investigated by indirect methods, allowing only for inferences: for example, by asking a subject if she hears an [ɑ] or an [i], and relating the answer to the acoustic properties of the speech signal.

The observation that a given phoneme can be produced with different articulatory gestures suggests that, in addition to an articulatory description, auditory and perceptual descriptions of speech sounds are important as well. For example, vowels are produced with rather different tongue positions by individual speakers, and the production of "rounded" vowels (like [u]) does not necessarily require a lip gesture after all: just stand in front of a mirror and try to produce an [u] without pursing the lips. This suggests that auditory targets (for example, the distribution of energy in a spectrum) rather than articulatory targets (like the position of the tongue) play the major role in speech perception. In other words, although it is possible to describe speech sounds in articulatory terms, and although the existing articulatory categorizations are generally quite effective, it may be advantageous to use auditory or perceptual categories.

The following sections describe basic knowledge about the ear and the hearing process. The hearing organ is composed of a series of structures: the external ear, middle ear, and internal ear. The internal ear contains relatively simple sensory cells, which are surrounded by a watery liquid. The neural impulses registered by the sensory cells are then analyzed by the brain.

12.1   The External Ear

What is called the "ear" in everyday language is only a small part of the actual hearing organ. As represented in Figure 12.1, the **external ear** consists of the visible **auricle (pinna)**, the **meatus (ear canal)**, and the **tympanic membrane (ear drum)**.

The auricle helps humans to determine the origin of a sound, in particular, whether it comes from in front of or behind the head. The presence of this information can be easily demonstrated by putting on headphones. Since headphones disable the localization function of the auricles, no information is available about the location of the sound source in relation to the head. The music therefore sounds as if it comes from somewhere "inside the head."

After passing the auricle, the sound wave arrives in the ear canal (meatus). This channel is covered on the inside with a thin layer of earwax (cerumen), a noxious and sticky substance to prevent the ear canal from drying out and to keep insects out. If the ear canal is blocked, for example, by earwax, hearing capacity is considerably reduced.

The ear canal is about 2.5 cm ($\approx$ 1 inch) long and 8 mm (0.3 inch) wide, and it is closed at one end. Modeling it as a half-open tube (i.e. as a quarter-wavelength

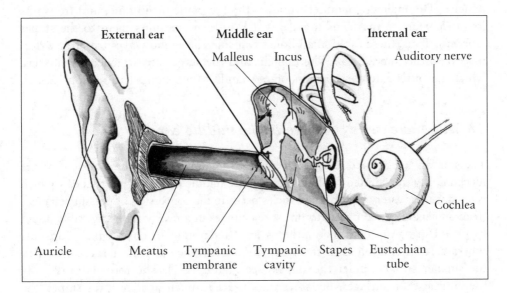

Figure 12.1   External, middle, and internal ear and their main structures.

resonator; see Section 9.1.1), it has its first resonance frequency at about 3,400 Hz.[1] But frequencies above or below this resonance frequency are transmitted as well, as the ear canal has a high level of damping. From an acoustic point of view, the ear canal is a filter that amplifies frequencies between 2 and 5 kHz by 15 dB relative to the other frequency bands. This particular frequency range is important for speech signals, as discussed in Chapter 10.

The ear canal is closed by the tympanic membrane, a thin elastic membrane which forms an airtight boundary between external and middle ear. The tympanic membrane bends inward and outward due to the air pressure variations of sound waves, just like the membrane of a microphone, as described in Section 7.2.1. These movements are then transferred to the middle ear. Under very high sound pressure levels, separate areas of the membrane may start oscillating with different phases relative to each other. Such **partial oscillations** reduce the transmission capacity of the tympanic membrane. This means that at a given point in time, the pressure variations of the sound wave move the tympanic membrane inwards in some areas and pull it outwards in others. This cancels part of the total force transferred to the middle ear. As a result, this mechanism protects the inner parts of the ear from high sound pressure levels.

12.2 The Middle Ear

The **middle ear** consists of the **tympanic cavity** (Figure 12.1), which is an almost airtight space containing the smallest moving bones of the human body: the **ossicles**. The **malleus** (**hammer**) touches the tympanic membrane, and transmits its movements to the **incus** (**anvil**), which in turn transmits them to the **stapes** (**stirrup**). Thus, these three small bones transmit the sound waves from the external ear to the internal ear. The malleus and the stapes are attached to muscles, which may attenuate the transmission of sound by these bones (see Section 12.2.2).

12.2.1　Increase in pressure in the middle ear

The sound waves which reach the tympanic membrane from the external ear are mechanically transmitted by the ossicles of the middle ear to the internal ear, which is filled with a watery liquid. The ossicles perform the conversion of pressure changes from an elastic medium (air) to pressure changes in a nearly incompressible liquid (water). During this conversion, the ossicles function like a cone, which transmits the force that is applied to the tympanic membrane, with its large surface, to the smaller surface under the stapes (see Figure 12.1). The force is practically the same at both surfaces. But since the surface is much smaller at the stapes, the pressure at the stapes is much higher than the pressure at the tympanic membrane (see Appendix A.1). The ratio of the surface of the tympanic membrane to the surface under the stapes results in an increase in pressure by a factor of about 17. In addition, the malleus is slightly longer than the anvil, so that both bones together produce a leverage effect, and the movements from the larger anvil are transmitted onto the smaller, but more powerful, movements of the stapes. In humans, the proportion between the length of anvil and stapes is about 1 : 1.3. The combination of both surface area changes and the leverage effect leads to an amplification factor of $17 \times 1.3 \approx 22$. In other words, the pressure variations that are transmitted to the internal ear are about 22 times stronger than the original air pressure variations of the sound wave. Expressed in decibels, the amplification factor is about $20 \times \log(22/1) \approx 27$ dB.

The necessity of increasing the pressure when going from air into a liquid is well known to anyone who has ever jumped into a pool. Trying to enter the water with a large surface, that is, with a belly flop, does not lead to a deep dive; in fact, the water "reflects" the diver. But diving with the fingertips first – that is, entering the water with a very small surface – leads to deep penetration. The same is true for sound waves. The large surface of the tympanic membrane is transferred to the small surface of the stapes by the middle ear. If the pressure level were not increased by the mechanics of the middle ear, sound waves would be mostly reflected by the liquid surface of the internal ear.

The leverage effect of the ossicles works most efficiently for frequencies between 800 Hz and 2,500 Hz. The system is less efficient for frequencies above 2,500 Hz, since at those frequencies the tympanic membrane executes several partial oscillations. At frequencies below 800 Hz, the transmission of sound is dampened by the mechanism which links the ossicles to their supporting ligatures and muscles.

12.2.2 Sound attenuation in the middle ear

The middle ear additionally performs a kind of "volume control." The muscles that support the malleus and the stapes can be slightly tensed, which has the effect of damping the lower frequencies in particular. While this damping mechanism (up to 20 dB) is very quick, it is not very efficient as a means of protection against sudden, loud noises. Before the muscles in the middle ear can be tensed, the brain has to send the corresponding neural impulses – but it can only do so *after* the noise has been processed in the internal ear. In other words, this type of damping of the signal can only occur once the high intensity signal has reached, and possibly damaged, the internal ear.

The sudden increase in sound level and the subsequent neural impulses issued by the brain to the muscles are represented along a time axis in Figure 12.2. As shown in Figure 12.2a, muscle tension (B) follows onset of the signal (A).

Figure 12.2b shows that the muscles of the middle ear can be tensed just *before* a person starts speaking *herself*. In this case, the muscles are activated (point C in Figure 12.2b) *before* the sound of the speaker's own voice reaches the internal

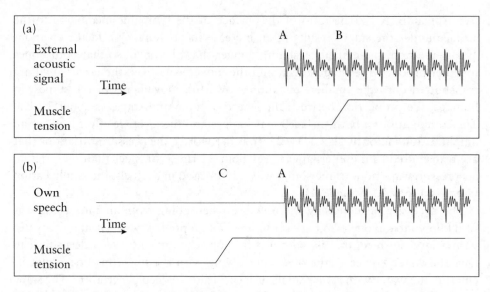

Figure 12.2   Schematic representations of how the muscles of the middle ear actively reduce the sound volume.

ear (point A in Figure 12.2b). This damping mechanism of the muscles of the middle ear forms a protection against the speaker's own voice.

Another function of the muscles of the middle ear is their capacity to dampen the lower frequencies of a signal. As a result, the listener is able to concentrate more on the higher frequencies, which are essential for the localization of sound. This is one mechanism that is helpful in listening to single out a person speaking in a noisy group.

12.2.3   Pressure equalization in the tympanic cavity

The small ossicles of the middle ear are enclosed in a germ-free space to protect them from bacterial infection. An ideal solution would be to keep the middle ear cavity airtight. However, if the tympanic cavity is completely airtight, a serious problem arises with meteorological air pressure changes, as they occur every day. For this reason, the tympanic cavity of the middle ear is linked to the nasopharynx through the **Eustachian tube** (see Figure 12.1). Although the Eustachian tube is not involved in the actual process of sound transmission from the external to the internal ear, it enables the ear to adapt to the slow changes in meteorological air pressure.

In Section 7.1.1, we explained that sound waves do not differ in principle from meteorological air pressure variations, only their amplitude is much smaller and they change much more quickly than the meteorological air pressure. If the tympanic cavity were entirely closed, the tympanic membrane would be pushed inward or pulled outward whenever the weather changes, as the variations of the meteorological pressure change are much larger than the pressure variations in a sound wave. This effect is the well-known "pressure on the ear" which is felt when rapidly changing altitude, and associated with it, air pressure, for example when driving down a hill. This is where the Eustachian tube comes into play. The Eustachian tube's walls normally lie loosely together, closing its pathway. But if a large pressure difference exists between both ends of the tube, air is forced through the tube into or out of the tympanic cavity. (The membrane can be actively opened by yawning or swallowing.) Eventually, the air pressure in the tympanic cavity adapts to the meteorological air pressure that is present in the ear canal, preventing it from bending. The air pressure variations of sound waves, which are much smaller, do not pass through the Eustachian tube. Rather, they move the tympanic membrane.

The ossicles of the middle ear serve to increase the pressure of the sound waves on their way to the **oval window** of the internal ear (see Section 12.3). The function of the oval window is straightforward: without this window, the movements of the stapes cannot be transmitted to the lymphatic fluid inside the internal ear.

12.3   The Internal Ear

The part of the internal ear that is relevant for hearing is the **cochlea**. In this bony, spiral-shaped structure, sound waves are transformed into neural impulses, which pass through the auditory nerve into the brain.

The cochlea is shaped like a snail shell. It is thicker (and more narrow) at its **base**, where it is attached to the middle ear, than at its tip, the **apex**, where it is thinner and wider. This structural characteristic is important for its function, as shown in Section 12.3.5. If it could be uncoiled (as in Figure 12.3), the cochlea of adult humans is about 3.5 cm (1.4 inch) long. Internally, it contains two passages, the upper **scala vestibuli** and the lower **scala tympani**, separated by the **basilar membrane** (or cochlear membrane), where the auditory nerve originates. These two "corridors" meet at the apex in the **helicotrema. Reissner's membrane** separates the scala vestibuli completely from the **scala media** (see Figure 12.4). Scala vestibuli and scala tympani are filled with a fluid called **perilymph**, which has a surplus of sodium (natrium ions), whereas the scala media is filled with **endolymph**, which has a surplus of potassium (kalium ions). The scala vestibuli leads to a flexible membrane in the wall of the tympanic cavity of the middle ear, located at the oval window, just underneath the stapes. The scala tympani leads

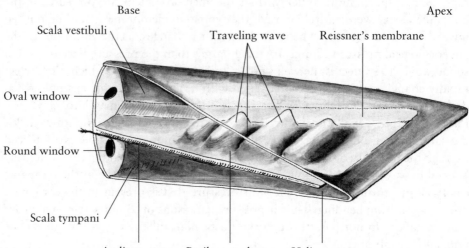

Figure 12.3 A schematic representation of an "uncoiled" cochlea and the traveling wave.

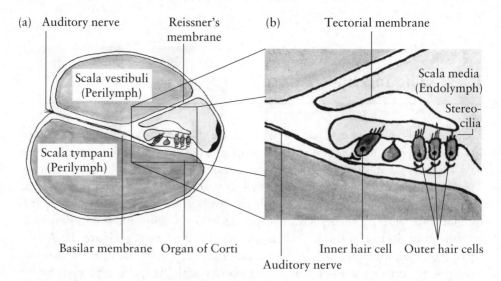

Figure 12.4 The organ of Corti, as shown in (a) a cross-section of the entire cochlea, and (b) enlarged in isolation.

to a flexible membrane, called the **round window,** into the tympanic cavity (see Figures 12.3 and 12.1).

Before the structure of the basilar membrane and the actual hearing organ are presented, the next section first describes what happens to the scalas of the cochlea and the basilar membrane when a sound wave arrives.

12.3.1 *Pressure waves in the cochlea*

The pressure variations of sound waves, after being enhanced by the ossicles of the middle ear, reach the cochlea through the oval window. Here, they move as longitudinal pressure waves in the internal ear fluid with a speed of about 1,500 m/s (see Section 7.1.5) from the base through the scala vestibuli to the apex. Sound waves spread further through the helicotrema, returning back to the base of the cochlea through the scala tympani. In parallel, the pressure waves move through the basilar membrane as well. At the base, they enter the tympanic cavity of the middle ear again through the membrane of the round window.

The function of the round window is to "release" the sound waves from the cochlea. This is necessary, since both the perilymph and the endolymph are virtually incompressible. Without this release, the lymphatic fluids of the internal ear act as a rigid substance, preventing the oval window from reacting to the sound waves, in spite of its flexibility. The round window thus serves to adjust the pressure inside the cochlea: an inward move of the oval window leads to an outward move of the round window, and vice versa.

The path through the scala vestibuli, helicotrema, and scala tympani is only taken by the relatively slow pressure changes of the lower frequencies in an acoustic signal. For the higher frequencies and their faster pressure changes, the small helicotrema acts as an impenetrable barrier. This is similar to slow and fast moving crowds of people that have to pass a narrow door: slow moving people (like low frequencies) have enough time to move through the door, but fast rushing crowds will lead to a blockage at the narrow entrance. But the opening at the helicotrema is not needed to let pressure changes pass from the oval window to the round window since the basilar membrane is an elastic structure that itself starts oscillating under the influence of the pressure waves, as described below. Thus, the basilar membrane directly transmits the pressure from the scala vestibuli to the scala tympani, bypassing the helicotrema.

The presence of the two windows is fundamental to another function of the middle ear. The ossicles of the middle ear serve not only to increase the pressure of the sound waves on their way to the oval window (see Section 12.2.1), they also transmit the pressure waves to the cochlea asymmetrically only to the scala vestibuli and not to the scala tympani. In the absence of the ossicles, the sound waves pass through the tympanic membrane and travel freely through the air in the tympanic cavity, reaching the oval *and* the round windows almost simultaneously. Both membranes would then move inward or outward equally far. This increases or decreases the pressure in the cochlea, but the pressure waves could not travel along the paths described above. The basilar membrane could not oscillate either, since the pressures in both scalas counteract each other.

Some hearing loss resulting from the absence or non-functioning of the ossicles is caused by the absence of the pressure adjustment described in Section 12.2.1. But the other major part of this hearing loss is related to the loss of the asymmetry in the transmission of the pressure between the oval and round windows in the cochlea. If the basilar membrane cannot oscillate, the internal ear cannot generate the required neural impulses as described in the next sections.

12.3.2   *The basilar membrane as an oscillating body*

The oscillation of the basilar membrane is essential for the transformation of pressure waves into neural impulses in the cochlea. Considering that the basilar membrane has the same, non-compressible fluid on both sides and that the same pressure appears nearly instantaneously above and below the basilar membrane, it cannot vibrate up and down like the membrane of a microphone. What other mechanism could govern the oscillation of the basilar membrane?

12.3.3   *Resonance theory*

In the nineteenth century, it was discovered that the basilar membrane consists of separate strips, held together by tissue. These strips are stiffer at the base than at the apex. This led Helmholtz (1863) to theorize that the basilar membrane acts as a kind of "inverted piano," with separate "strings" that resonate individually in response to the frequencies of the pressure waves. Higher frequencies cause the basilar membrane to oscillate more prominently at the base, where it is stiffer and narrower, than at the apex. Conversely, the lower frequencies cause a stronger oscillation at the apex, where the membrane is softer and wider. By simply measuring *where* the membrane oscillates, the nerve cells are able to determine the amplitude of a sound signal and which frequencies it contains. In this theory, the ear performs a kind of mechanical Fourier analysis, where the frequency is encoded by the location of the oscillation along the membrane, and amplitude by the displacement of the membrane at that point.

   At the beginning of the twentieth century, von Békésy (1928) experimentally investigated Helmholtz's theory. He did so by inserting the lens of a microscope into the cochlea of dead animals and simulating sound waves by mechanically moving the oval window. This made it possible to observe directly the movements of the basilar membrane. Since these movements are very small, Von Békésy made his measurements using high amplitudes corresponding to loudness levels between 120 and 160 dB, which caused the membrane to oscillate by about 0.5 µm, which is just observable with a microscope. He saw that the basilar membrane did indeed oscillate at different locations for different frequencies, just as Helmholtz had predicted: near the base for high frequencies and near the apex for lower frequencies. He did not, however, observe the individual strips of the membrane oscillating separately, as the resonance theory had predicted, but instead saw a **traveling wave**. This type of wave can be compared to the waves occurring in a tablecloth that is shaken out on a table (holding it by one edge and moving it quickly up and down). The oscillation runs through the whole tissue of the membrane, reaches its maximum displacement at a location that is specific to its particular frequency (the so-called **critical frequency**), and fades out again (see Figure 12.3).

These displacement maxima are caused by differences in the degree of elasticity along the membrane. This is explained in the next section. Section 12.3.5 then discusses how the traveling wave arises.

12.3.4   Objections to the resonance theory

As laid out in Section 9.2, a solid body not only has its own resonance frequency, but also a specific degree of damping. Objects, such as a wine glass, which respond only to a small range of frequencies have a low level of damping and keep oscillating for a long time. On the other hand, highly dampened objects, such as a fork, react to a greater range of frequencies, but their oscillation does not continue for a long time. The basilar membrane has a very high level of damping: as soon as a sound disappears, the basilar membrane stops oscillating and our perception of the sound disappears as well. However, with a high level of damping, there is a low degree of precision in the resonance frequencies (that is, a large frequency range may cause the object to oscillate). This does not match the capabilities of the human hearing system, which can distinguish frequency differences of less than one hertz under optimal conditions. In order to perceive such fine distinctions, the basilar membrane must have high selectivity for frequency. But that implies that it has a low damping factor and continues to oscillate for a long time – which, as we know, is not the case. This suggests that frequency selectivity along the basilar membrane is not due to resonance.

12.3.5   Traveling wave theory

The movements of the basilar membrane are not determined by the fast transmission of pressure waves through a fluid, as described in Section 12.3.1, but by the spreading of a transversal "surface wave" resembling a *la Ola wave* (see Section 7.1.5). This wave is comparable to the waves on a water surface. If you imagine a lake when there is absolutely no wind, the mirror-like surface of the water is like the basilar membrane in absolute silence. A wind starts to blow when air from an area of higher air pressure moves towards lower air pressure. This small increase in air pressure reaches water molecules closer to the wind source a little bit earlier than those further away. The molecules under higher pressure move downward to escape the pressure and the molecules under the "old," lower pressure move upward. These pressure changes lead eventually to the surface waves on the water, which then travel as transversal waves and are much slower than the longitudinal pressure waves below the water's surface. Unlike the pressure waves that have been discussed so far, the speed and amplitude of surface waves depend on the frequency of the signal and the depth of the water basin.

This effect can be observed at ocean beaches. Further out into the sea, the waves are less prominent. As they approach the beach, they become higher (until they finally break). In the open sea, where the water is very deep, the water molecules are not hindered by the bottom of the sea, so they can move up and down relatively freely. When the waves get closer to the beach, they are slowed down, since the water molecules can no longer move freely. The waves spread at lower speeds, which means that the waves themselves become shorter. However, the energy of the approaching wave remains the same, although in shallow water it moves fewer water molecules. The molecules therefore are moved across longer distances; in other words, the wave gets higher.

Near the apex, the cochlea becomes thinner, making the fluid less deep, just like the water at the beach. This has a comparable effect on the traveling wave, which is a surface wave. In addition, the basilar membrane becomes softer near the apex, which has an additional slowing effect on the wave and leads to even greater displacements. As a result of the differences in "depth" of the cochlea and the increasing "softness" of the basilar membrane, waves reach different parts along the membrane. High frequencies lead to high displacements at the base just behind the oval window, whereas lower frequencies travel further in the direction of the apex, reaching their maximum displacement somewhere along the way, depending on their frequency.

In this way, the basilar membrane acts as a mechanical Fourier transformation – but not as a result of the resonance principle, as had been suggested by Helmholtz. It should be noted, however, that in the presence of complex signals or noises, such as speech signals, the traveling waves of the individual frequency components overlap and the membrane moves in a very complex and rather unpredictable way.

The traveling wave affects the whole membrane from the base to the apex. Since the sides of the membrane are attached to the cochlea, a movement along the *longitudinal* axis from base to apex causes a movement *across* the membrane from side to side. The wave travels along the middle part of the membrane, causing the membrane tissue in the middle to move up and down. In addition, since the edges of the membrane are fixed to the cochlear walls, the membrane is twisted across its width. It is shown in the next section that this twisting movement across the membrane is finally responsible for the generation of neural impulses in the cochlear nerve.

The facts provided so far explain the existence of the traveling wave along the basilar membrane. But the observed amplitude of the traveling wave is much higher than can be expected on the basis of the mechanical properties of the basilar membrane alone. Moreover, when the loudness of a sound increases, the amplitude of the traveling wave does not increase to the same extent as the amplitude of the sound wave itself. This suggests that the movement of the basilar membrane is not just a passive oscillation, like the movement of a tablecloth that is being shaken, but rather the result of an active process. Such an active process, and the actual transformation of movement into neural impulses, can only be understood if the fine structure of the basilar membrane is known. This is treated in the next section.

12.4　The Structure of the Basilar Membrane

The basilar membrane contains the **organ of Corti,** which is linked to the auditory nerve (see Figure 12.4). The organ of Corti consists of the **tectorial membrane,** the **hair cells,** and a number of additional supporting cells. Unlike the basilar membrane, the tectorial membrane does not cover the whole width of the cochlea, but only partly overlaps the basilar membrane. One edge of the tectorial membrane is attached to the basilar membrane, close to the point of attachment of Reissner's membrane. The other edge is supported by about 20,000 **outer hair cells,** which are grouped into three rows along the basilar membrane (see Section 12.4.1). These outer hair cells rest upon the basilar membrane at their lower end, with, at their upper end, bundles of crystalline "hairs," the so-called **stereocilia,** which reach into the tectorial membrane. The body of the hair cells is almost entirely surrounded by perilymphatic fluid contained by the organ of Corti, which is linked to the scala tympani. Only the cilia themselves are surrounded by the endolymph of the scala media.

12.4.1　*Outer hair cells*

At the base of the cochlea, the outer hair cells are about 25 μm long. Those at the apex are about four times as long and more flexible than the ones at the base. In addition to the differences in elasticity of the basilar membrane, which lead to different displacements along the membrane depending on frequency, the outer hair cells thus add another, mechanical source of differentiation between frequencies. The stiffer, shorter hair cells at the base are more responsive to high frequencies, while the long, more flexible hair cells at the apex bend more easily at low frequencies. In addition to this mechanical characteristic, it appears that the electrical properties of the outer hair cells react better to high frequencies at the base and to lower frequencies at the apex.

Each time the basilar membrane moves under the influence of the traveling wave, the membrane is twisted as well, as presented in Section 12.3.5. This movement shifts the tectorial membrane against the basilar membrane, which sheers the stereocilia of the outer hair cells and causes small ion channels to open, inducing endolymph from the scala media, where the stereocilia are located, into the hair cells' bodies, which are located in the perilymph. This leads to an electrical discharge that causes the outer hair cells to contract, moving the tectorial membrane further down and leading to an amplification of the flow of the endolymph in the organ of Corti. This amplification of the outer hair cells can be regulated by about 1,800 **efferent** nerve fibers which transmit neural impulses *from* the brain.[2] The outer hair cells are like small muscles controlled by the brain, which can change the elasticity of the basilar membrane and the strength of their reaction to the sheering movement. That is, the outer hair cells act like a regulator, which *actively* changes the elastic properties of the basilar membrane under the control of the brain. The outer hair cells have only few afferent neural pathways *to* the brain, but these consist of very slow cells, and it is generally assumed that they do not transmit any detailed information about the sound signal to the brain.

The outer hair cells increase the flow of endolymph in the organ of Corti but they can additionally be used to dampen the movements of the membrane, thus reducing the oscillation of the basilar membrane. The amplitude of oscillation of the basilar membrane does not increase to the same extent as the amplitude of the sound waves. This active mechanism makes it possible to dampen selected frequency areas in a faster and more precise way than could be done by the muscles attached to the ossicles in the middle ear. The actual transmission of information to the brain is done by the inner hair cells.

12.4.2   Inner hair cells

The role of the **inner hair cells** is essential. Although their number does not exceed 3,500, inner hair cells are responsible for the conversion of the mechanical movements of the basilar membrane into neural impulses. The inner hair cells are grouped in a single row inside the organ of Corti. Unlike the outer hair cells, they do *not* touch the tectorial membrane. Instead, they react to differences in the speed with which the endolymph flows within the organ of Corti. About 30,000 afferent nerve fibers lead from the inner hair cells *into* the brain. That is, each inner hair cell is linked to about 10 nerve cells.

The inner hair cells consist also of a main cell body with thin, stalk-like stereocilia that stick out of the basilar membrane like small hairs which are located on top of the stalks. The heads of the stereocilia are linked to small fibers which, when bent aside, open small "traps" in the stereocilia, and thus bring the stereocilia into contact with the perilymph in the body of the hair cell.

Each time the basilar membrane moves under the influence of the traveling wave, the membrane is twisted as well, as presented in Section 12.3.5. The position and mechanical properties of the basilar membrane lead to movement in the endolymph in the organ of Corti, amplified by the outer hair cells, which moves the stereocilia of the inner hair cells back and forth. The upward movement to the membrane causes small ion channels to open between the perilymph, containing the stereocilia, and the hair cells, which rise from the endolymph. As a result, the concentration of sodium and potassium ions in the nerve cells changes abruptly, which in turn causes a sudden change in their electrical charge. This is the actual neural impulse, called the "firing" of the nerve cell. Unlike the case of the outer hair cells, this electrical discharge is transmitted by different types of neurons to the brain, leading eventually to the input of what we call "hearing."

When the stereocilia move back in the opposite direction, the ion channels close, allowing the cell to recharge itself. The hair cells always fire at the maximum displacement of the basilar membrane, which moves in phase with the sound wave.[3] As a result, the hair cells fire in phase with the sound wave.

Understanding the inner hair cell mechanism requires insight into how nerve cells transmit information. When at rest, nerve cells have a light electrical charge, just like small batteries. A neural impulse consists of a sudden, complete discharge of a nerve cell. In the case of the inner hair cells, this is caused by small ion channels which open up near the upper end of the stereocilia, causing a short circuit between the electrical charge of the cell and the electrical charge of the endolymph of the scala media. After a discharge, the cell gradually recovers its electrical charge and after a certain amount of time it is ready to fire again. This time lapse, called **refractory period**, depends on the type of nerve, but is never shorter than 1 ms. The cells function on an "all-or-nothing" basis, that is, they are either at rest or they fire at their maximum amplitude. In other words, they are either "on" or "off," there is no state in between. The fact that sensory impressions may be more or less strong is encoded by the rate at which the nerve cells fire, not by their intensity.

12.4.3   *Frequency coding along the basilar membrane*

It appears that frequency information, as given by the inner hair cells, is encoded in their **tonotopic** location along the basilar membrane (displacements at the base corresponding to high frequencies, displacements at the apex to lower frequencies), as well as encoded in the firing rate of the nerve cells. Different areas of the membrane reach their maximum displacement, causing the nerve cells to fire for different frequencies. In that sense, the complex and actively controlled movement of the basilar membrane can be described as a mechanical Fourier transformation. Furthermore, people with perfect pitch show a shift in the perception of the frequencies as they grow older.[4] That is, they do not perceive a frequency of 440 Hz as the reference tone a' any more, but as a lower tone. This shift could be due to an age-related increase in stiffness of the basilar membrane, so that the same frequency leads to a maximum displacement at a different area of the basilar membrane.

Alternatively, arguments for a theory that information about the pitch of a signal is transmitted by means of the firing rate of the nerve cells (rather than by their location on the basilar membrane) have been proposed. The nerve cells fire simultaneously with the maxima in the sound waves, so that the neural impulses could indicate the duration of a period. This could be taken to imply that pitch (or the frequency of a spectral component) is not encoded in the location along the basilar membrane, but in the firing rate of the nerve cells. An obvious objection is the fact that nerve cells cannot fire more often than a thousand times per second, which means that humans could not perceive any frequencies above 1,000 Hz. This objection is indeed valid, but only if a single nerve cell is taken into account. However, almost all hair cells along the basilar membrane can be stimulated by all frequencies, so that several cells fire simultaneously for the same frequency.[5] When one individual nerve cell cannot fire quickly enough because of its recovery time, another cell fires simultaneously with the maximum of the sound wave. Considering the overall pattern of all nerve cells, it follows that the neural impulses do enter the brain with the same periodicity as the sound signal. In other words, the periodicity is preserved in the collective firing pattern of many nerve cells together.

The alignment of the firing of individual cells to a maximum within a sound wave, and the collective, synchronous pattern formed by separate cells, exist up to frequencies around 5 kHz. This is in agreement with the fact that human listeners can only perceive melodies up to about 5 kHz; above 5 kHz they still perceive tones, but they can no longer arrange the separate frequencies on a tone scale. This is one of the arguments for the theory that information about the pitch of a signal is transmitted by means of the firing rate of the nerve cells (rather than by their location on the basilar membrane).

Proponents of this theory argue that the basilar membrane oscillates in a relatively uncoordinated way at sound pressure levels that occur during normal speech, so that no clear displacement can be distinguished. This implies that frequency information cannot be encoded in the location of a maximum along the basilar membrane – in other words, that it must be encoded in the periodicity of the firing nerve cells.

The internal ear essentially encodes a wide-band input signal (the sound waves, containing information between 30 Hz and 18,000 Hz) into a great number of narrow-band neural pathways. Transforming the sound waves into many parallel neural pathways has the advantage of creating a certain amount of redundancy, so that a failure of individual nerve cells does not lead to a failure of the information transmission as a whole.

Hearing is a complex process, converting a sound signal into neural impulses. The investigation of the neural information is very complicated even nowadays with advanced techniques, because the nerves of the auditory periphery are located deep inside the brain and can only be investigated in living beings.

12.4.4   Oto-acoustic emissions

It is generally assumed that the nerves first transmit the sound stimulus (the impulse projected into the ear) to the brain, and that this transmission takes place in the internal ear; the brain then tells the outer hair cells to react. As a result, the basilar membrane produces **oto-acoustic emissions**, that is, the change in the outer hair cells results in a specific movement of the basilar membrane (just like a table cloth moves when it is abruptly tightened). Signals of this type were first measured by Kemp (1978), who projected short signal impulses into the ear. With some delay, the ear produced an echo of the impulses. Interestingly, this echo occurred much later than would be expected on the basis of the time needed for a sound to travel the full distance from the external ear to the internal ear and back (that is: passing through the ear canal, through the oval window after being transmitted by the ear drum and the ossicles in the middle ear, through the cochlea, out of the round window, through the air in the middle ear to the ear drum and finally back again through the ear canal). In addition, the amplitude of the echo was higher than expected if the reflection was purely mechanical. The echo was the result of a reaction of the ear *itself*, occurring only after several milliseconds. A few years later, spontaneous oto-acoustic emissions were measured as well. This means that the basilar membrane may move by itself, even without being stimulated by a sound. In a sense, this effect is a kind of "convulsion" of the outer hair cells. Such spontaneous oto-acoustic emissions provide further support for the assumption that the membrane is actively controlled, and does not just passively react to the sound waves. Thus, the basilar membrane is partly active, so that the internal ear does more than simply transform the stimuli in a passive way.[6]

This is additional evidence against the image of the basilar membrane as a Fourier transformer, since its movements are apparently controlled by feedback processes from the brain.

In sum, the preceding sections have made it clear that the auditory system imposes many transformations on the acoustic signal, such that the representation of the signal by the firing patterns of the nerves of the auditory system may be quite different from the initial acoustic input signal. It is therefore important to make a distinction between the **physical stimulus** and the **auditory sensation**. We have so far discussed the physical properties of the acoustic waveform in terms of length, frequency, and amplitude (of the waves). However, the physical properties of length, frequency, and amplitude are not identical to the auditory sensations of duration, pitch, and loudness. For this reason, **auditory scales** are used to represent the strength of these sensations. These scales are not separate "dimensions" in the physical sense, where two dimensions are independent of each other but subjective impressions can influence each other. For example, a "louder" sound might sound "higher" in pitch even though the signal amplitude, but not its frequency, has changed.

In the next sections, we present several auditory scales that are designed to match the behavior of the auditory system better than simply linear scales. It must be noted, however, that these scales are still a crude approximation of the time-dependent and complex representation of our hearing system.

12.5   Auditory Frequency Scales

When a signal, or the results of an analysis, is plotted on a graph, the resulting image not only depends on the signal but also on the scale of the graph. There are different scales which may be used to represent frequency and amplitude. This is true for the representation of spectra, but for intonation contours as well. At first sight, it might seem strange that different scales are needed to represent the frequency of a signal, which can be unambiguously defined in physical terms. The reason lies, in fact, outside the strictly physical domain, but in the physiological basis of how people perceive frequency. The different frequency scales are used to express different properties of the perception.

12.5.1   *Linear scales*

Until now, we have represented frequency values on a **linear** scale. On this type of scale, the distance between 100 Hz and 103 Hz, for example, is equal to the distance between 500 Hz and 503 Hz. In other words, irrespective of its location on the frequency scale, an equal difference in frequency is always represented by the same distance on paper. This corresponds to everyday experience, since a human listener can perceive the difference between 100 and 103 Hz just as well as the one between 500 and 503 Hz. Unlike the perception of loudness or weight (see Appendix A.3.2), a human listener can perceive absolute differences in frequency below 1,000 Hz reasonably well. The distance between two frequencies on a linear scale is entirely determined by the difference between the two frequency values. Equal differences lead to equal distances along the scale, independent of where the value is located.

12.5.2   *Logarithmic scales*

Consider the perception of pitch. A 200 Hz tone is perceived as being "twice as high" as a 100 Hz tone. This ratio is known in music as an octave. In order to obtain a tone that is again perceived as one octave higher, the frequency has to be doubled again, from 200 to 400 Hz. Note that it is *not* increased by 100 Hz from 200 to 300 Hz. Thus, starting from 100 Hz, obtaining a signal which is perceived as *two* octaves higher requires a multiplication of the frequency by *four*.

This relation between an increase in perception by a factor of two (pitch) and an increase in the corresponding physical dimension by four (frequency) can be expressed with a **logarithmic** representation of the frequency domain for (musical) pitch, where the perceptual distance between two octaves is always the same but the physical distance is not. In such a representation, for example, the distance between 220 and 440 Hz is equal to the distance between 1,760 and 3,520 Hz, that is, one octave higher, although the difference between the frequency values is 220 Hz in the first case, and 1,760 Hz in the second case.

In western music, an octave is divided into twelve **semitones**, and the calculation of distances between two frequencies is often performed on the logarithmic semitone scale. Since octaves represent a multiplication by two, the calculation is based on the logarithm with base 2:

$$\text{distance in semitones} = 12 \times \log_2\left(\frac{\text{frequency "X" [Hz]}}{\text{frequency "Y" [Hz]}}\right) \text{[semitones]}.$$

Most pocket calculators do not contain the logarithm with base 2 ($\log_2$), but only the decimal (log or $\log_{10}$) or natural (ln or $\log_e$) variants. The following transformation formulas may therefore be helpful:

$$12 \times \log_2\left(\frac{\text{measured [Hz]}}{\text{reference [Hz]}}\right) \approx 39.863 \times \log_{10}\left(\frac{\text{measured [Hz]}}{\text{reference [Hz]}}\right)$$

$$\approx 17.312 \times \ln\left(\frac{\text{measured [Hz]}}{\text{reference [Hz]}}\right).$$

For example, the standard reference tone a' (concert pitch) has a frequency of 440 Hz, and the middle C a frequency of 261.6 Hz; their distance as expressed in semitones is therefore:

$$39.863 \times \log_{10}\left(\frac{261.6 \text{ [Hz]}}{440 \text{ [Hz]}}\right) \approx -9 \text{ [st]}.$$

Logarithmic scales have a main characteristic in common: equal proportions between physical values are represented by equal distances along the scale, irrespective of their location on the scale. Logarithmic scales are used very often, because in different domains, such as pitch or loudness, our subjective perception is structured in perceiving relations between values rather than absolute differences.

12.5.3 Mel scale

Early research into the perception of frequency differences led Stevens and Volkman (1940) to introduce the "melodic" **mel scale**. This scale was made by classifying sine tone frequencies on the basis of their perception in relation to a reference sine tone of 1,000 Hz. To this end, subjects were asked to indicate when they perceived the pitch of a sine tone as exactly twice or half the pitch of the reference tone. The tone which was perceived as half as high was set to be 500 mel, the tone perceived as twice as high was set to be 2,000 mel. By conducting further comparisons, finer distinctions along the scale were obtained. Unlike the linear or the logarithmic scales, the mel scale is exclusively based on human perception. A *mel* is defined as one thousandth of the pitch that is perceived when listening to a 1 kHz sine tone. In principle, this scale can only be obtained by collecting the impressions of individual listeners, and cannot be calculated on the basis of the physical frequency alone (in hertz). But the mel values that have been found can be approximated by the following empirical formula:[7]

$$1 \text{ mel} = \frac{1,000}{\log_2 (2)} \times \log_{10} \left(\frac{f \text{ [Hz]}}{1,000} + 1 \right) \approx 3,322 \times (\log_{10} (1,000 + f \text{ [Hz]}) - 3).$$

The concert pitch a', for example, with a frequency of 440 Hz, has a pitch of 526 mel:

$$3,322 \times (\log_{10} (1,000 + 440) - 3) \approx 526 \text{ mel.}$$

Though the mel scale is only grounded on the perceived relation between sine tones and is a sort of fine-tuned logarithmic scale, and does not reflect the auditory sensation of more complex signals, it is widely used in the area of automatic speech recognition.

12.5.4   Bark scale

Just like the mel scale, the **Bark scale** is based on human pitch perception as well. More precisely, it is based on the theory of **critical bands**, as developed by Fletcher (1940). Unlike the mel scale, which is based exclusively on the subjective impressions during the perception of sine tones, the Bark scale is based on the perception of more complex signals. It takes into account the fact that two simultaneous signals that are close in frequency are perceived as separate tones when their frequencies are low, but as a single tone when their frequencies are high. Precisely this phenomenon is described by the theory of critical bands. This theory states that in human pitch perception, the frequency range is divided into separate filter bands that are narrower for low frequencies (allowing for finer distinctions) and wider for high frequencies. All energy in one critical band is mapped onto the center of the band; that is, sound energy across a certain frequency range is integrated into one percept. Note that the critical bands do not all encompass the same frequency range. The frequency range of one critical band is much smaller for low frequencies than for high frequencies.

Because of these characteristics, the Bark scale is said to reflect human pitch perception more accurately than the mel scale. The relation between perceived pitch values (in Bark) and frequency (in hertz) can be approximated by the following formula:

$$1 \text{ Bark}_{CB} = \frac{26.81 \times f\,[\text{Hz}]}{1{,}960 + f\,[\text{Hz}]} - 0.53.$$

The concert pitch a', for example, with a frequency of 440 Hz, has a pitch of about 4.4 Bark_{CB}.

$$\frac{26.81 \times 440\,[\text{Hz}]}{1{,}960 + 440\,[\text{Hz}]} - 0.53 \approx 4.385 \ \text{Bark}_{CB}.$$

If a complete frequency spectrum (for example, the result of an FFT) is to be transformed into Bark values, the first step is to separate the (linear) frequency values into the critical bands. The critical bands are, in turn, band-pass filters, whose bandwidth and steepness depend on their center frequency and on the sound pressure level (in dB_{SPL}).

To transform a linear Fourier spectrum into a Bark spectrum requires the determination of the particular shape and width of the critical band for a given center frequency and amplitude. All amplitude values within this band enter into a calculation that results in a single amplitude value for this particular center frequency. This amplitude value is then assigned to its corresponding Bark frequency, as obtained by the formula given above. The procedure thus consists of two components: first, moving a critical band window over the spectrum and integrating the energy in each critical band, and second, transforming the distances along the frequency scale. But the Bark scale is often used by only performing the second step. It should be clear, however, that using the Bark scale in this way is different from the complete procedure described above. Transforming frequency values into Bark values only by using a formula like the one given above has the effect that separate values on the linear hertz scale (see Figure 12.5a) always remain separate on the Bark scale (see Figure 12.5b). But if the division into critical bands is included, two separate values on the hertz scale may merge into a single value on the Bark scale (see Figure 12.5c). This is in agreement with the perception data, since human listeners cannot distinguish these frequencies either. However, since the amplitude of a signal plays a role in determining exactly which frequencies are merged, the complete transformation is rather complex.

12.5.5 *Equivalent rectangular bandwidth (ERB) scale*

The **equivalent rectangular bandwidth (ERB) scale** is very similar to the Bark scale, but the procedure used to determine the critical bands is more refined to capture the nature of complex sounds (Patterson 1976). This scale seems to represent perceived frequency values in the most realistic way. Like the Bark scale, it has two components: estimating the critical bands and projecting the frequencies onto

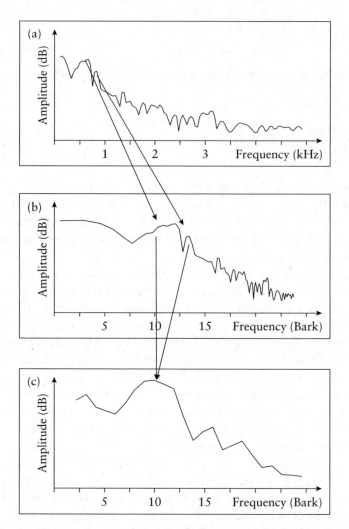

Figure 12.5   (a) Linear spectrum transformed into the Bark scale by (b) applying the frequency transformation only and (c) by taking the critical filters into account. The arrows indicate the mapping of two separate spectral peaks in (a) to (b) and the merging in (c).

the ERB scale. The following empirical formula can be used to transform hertz values into ERB values (again, without taking the distribution of energy in the critical bands into account):

$$1 \text{ Bark}_{\text{ERB}} = 25.72 \times \log_{10}\left(\frac{312 + f \text{ [Hz]}}{14{,}675 + f \text{ [Hz]}}\right) + 43; \text{ for } 100 \text{ Hz} \leq f \leq 6{,}500 \text{ Hz.}$$

According to this formula, the concert pitch a' (with a frequency of 440 Hz) has a pitch of 9.5 Bark$_{ERB}$:

$$25.72 \times \log_{10}\left(\frac{312 + 440\,[\text{Hz}]}{14{,}675 + 440\,[\text{Hz}]}\right) + 43 \approx 9.5\ \text{Bark}_{ERB}.$$

Bark and ERB scales differ only slightly in the shape of the critical bands and the transformation of the frequency scale.

The existence of different scales may seem confusing, but each has its own motivation. The linear scale expresses the fact that a human listener can perceive equal frequency *differences* (at least below 1 kHz). The logarithmic scale expresses the fact that one perceives equal semitone differences as equal musical *intervals*. The mel, Bark, and ERB scales reflect the subjective perception of frequency values. It has to be kept in mind that the Bark and ERB scales not only include a non-linear transformation of the hertz values, but also the concept of critical bands.

Auditory scales are intended to better represent the perception of sound signals by humans. Mp3 players are actually based on experiments about auditory perception. Instead of storing digitized sound samples in a linear way, these devices compute spectra and store only those parts that listeners are able to hear, based on the concept of critical bands. As a consequence, the original signal and the signal stored by such a device can be different, but they sound the same to most listeners.

In phonetics, linear (spectrographic and spectral) representations are still used, since they are well known and serve as a reliable and viable method. However, using auditory scales might change our models of the representation of (speech) signals and our assumptions about what the characteristics of speech sounds are. Unfortunately, which "auditory" spectrum might represent speech better is unknown at this time. Considering the complex transformation in the internal ear and subsequent processing by the brain, the way we look at spectrograms to represent speech might be very different from the way our hearing system perceives speech or any other acoustic signal.

12.6   Auditory Loudness Scales

For loudness, the dB$_{SPL}$ scale (see Section 7.3.2 and Appendix A, Section A.3.2) weights all frequencies equally strong, that is, it assumes a linear frequency scale. However, psychophysical experiments have shown that humans perceive very low and very high frequencies not as well as frequencies in the range of 2–4 kHz (the lower frequencies are mostly dampened by the middle ear, and the higher frequencies are attenuated by the resonance characteristics of the ear canal). Furthermore, the attenuation of the different frequency ranges depends on the

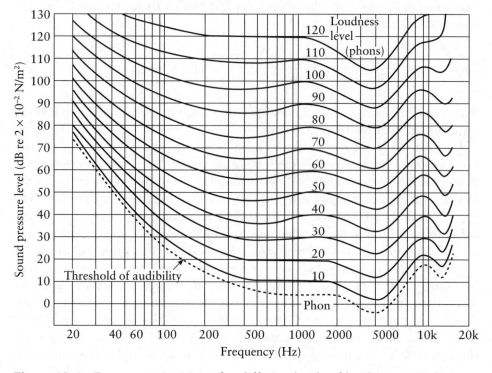

Figure 12.6 Frequency sensitivity for different levels of loudness according to the ISO 226 : 2003 standard.

Reproduced by permission of the ISO.

overall sound intensity, and leads to different curves for different intensities (see Figure 12.6). A scale that takes this effect into consideration is the **phon**-scale. Phons are defined as having the same dB_{SPL} as a sine tone of 1 kHz. Loudness at other frequencies is related to this perceived loudness at 1 kHz. For each intensity, this produces an **equal loudness scale**. Averaged over several subjects, this led to the commonly used dB_A scale that takes into account these effects. A special curve is the loudness of 40 phons, which is called one **sone** as a reference that is about as loud as normal talking at 1 meter distance. Doubling the sone values means adding 10 phons, that is 2 sones are 50 phons, 4 sones are 60 phons, 8 sones are 70 phons, and so on.

12.7 Auditory Time Scales

Many languages have short and long vowels and/or consonants, or short and long closure or VOT values, but what is perceived as short or long depends on many factors: the language itself, the position of a sound in a word (phones are lengthened at the end of a word and towards the end of a phrase), the length of a word (longer words have shorter segments), the speaking rate of a person, or even utterance context. Words in isolation are usually much longer than in the context of a phrase, but most listeners are not aware of this effect and perceive the same word as equally fast, even if a word spoken in isolation is more than twice as long. Neither is "speaking rate" easy to define, as mentioned in Section 11.3. The auditory sensation of "long" and "short" is expressed in a range of milliseconds (e.g. "a long closure duration in German is normally longer than 40 ms, while a short closure duration is shorter than 20 ms"). While absolute values differ, two-way length contrasts are common across the world's languages. Length contrasts may be different for languages that use additional means to separate "long" and "short" sounds (e.g. the "long" vowels in English are additionally diphthongized or long and short non-low vowels in German differ in their spectral properties). In sum, languages seem not to rely too much on absolute length distinctions; instead, they use relative differences in duration.

Exercises

1   Considering an articulatory description of speech sounds already exists, why might an auditory or perceptual description also prove useful?
2   What are the functions of the middle ear? Why would transferring sound from the external ear to the inner ear be less efficient without the middle ear?
3   How are the ossicles, the oval window, and the round window important to the path of sound in the inner ear?
4   Does resonance theory or traveling wave theory offer a better explanation of how the basilar membrane oscillates? Justify your answer.
5   What are the different theories of how pitch is transmitted? Provide evidence supporting and contradicting each theory.
6   How do the mel, Bark, and ERB scales differ from the linear and logarithmic scales? How do they differ from each other?

Notes

1   $f = \dfrac{c}{4l}$: $\dfrac{340 \text{ m/s}}{4 \times 0.025 \text{ m}} = 3,400$ Hz.
2   Nerves are "one-way streets" that can transmit electrical impulses either *from* the brain (efferent nerve fibers) or *to* the brain (afferent nerve fibers).

3   This does not imply, however, that the hair cells fire at the maximum of the sound pressure wave. Since the sound pressure wave is transformed into a traveling wave along the basilar membrane, it does not necessarily have an identical phase to the sound wave.

4   Perfect pitch is the ability to directly determine the musical note corresponding to a perceived tone. Upon hearing a tone of 440 Hz, for example, such a person with perfect pitch identifies it as the reference tone a'. This capacity may be developed at the ages of three to six through musical training.

5   Although the maxima of the traveling wave occur at different places along the membrane depending on the frequency components, each frequency stimulates a large area of the membrane.

6   The oto-acoustic echo is used in hospitals to investigate the hearing capacity of infants. The presence of an oto-acoustic echo in the baby's ear indicates that the middle ear, the internal ear, and the peripheral parts of the neural processing system function normally. The absence of the echo indicates a defect in one of these domains, which can then be further investigated. By means of this two-minute, entirely harmless, measurement, one can assess the hearing function of a baby of only a few days old.

7   An empirical formula describes a link between two lists of values, without making any claims about a functional relation between the two lists. In principle, one could just as well find the related values by looking them up in a table. The empirical formula is only a convenient way to replace the table by a formula.

13 Speech Perception

We have seen that articulatory gestures have acoustic consequences such that articulations lead to sounds that can be described in terms of frequency, intensity, and duration. The structure of the auditory system and the kinds of transformations that it imposes on the incoming signal have also been discussed. In addition to these factors, an understanding of the way speech is perceived requires consideration of linguistic factors that may play a role in our interpretation of a spoken message, including lexical, syntactic, semantic, and pragmatic sources of information. The study of speech perception addresses the way in which the listener analyzes the acoustic patterns and how this information is interpreted by the auditory system in order to recognize the message intended by the speaker. In this chapter, we will focus on the kinds of acoustic properties and auditory constraints that are thought to be important in the perception of individual speech sounds. It is fair to say that most of the research in speech perception has dealt with these issues at the level of individual segments or syllables. Only recently have researchers begun to investigate the perception of larger units such as words and phrases, and, consequently, to consider the role of meaning and syntactic class.

The process of perceiving speech could be thought of as the conversion of a continuous acoustic signal into a set of discrete units. Over the years, many different candidates have been proposed for these units, including features (phonetic properties which languages combine in different ways to construct their phoneme inventories), segments, syllables, and words. There is, as yet, no consensus as to what the basic unit of speech perception is, and it may well be the case that all these candidates play a crucial role at different levels of analysis. Regardless of the exact nature of these linguistic units, they are typically thought to follow each other in time. However, this *linearity* is not often observed in the acoustic signal. The linearity problem relates to the fact that the speech signal can rarely be segmented in a way that corresponds to perceived individual phonetic units. While the process of speech production at some level presumably involves a pre-planned sequence of discrete units or targets, the physiological realization of this sequence results in nearly continuous motion of the articulators. Consequently, the acoustic events that result in the perception of an ordered string of phonemes, for example, do not always occur in a sequential linear order.

While the lack of linearity provides a challenge to theories of speech perception, consensus is emerging about the nature of the acoustic properties that contribute to the perception of individual speech sounds or classes of speech sounds. We will start by discussing perceptual cues to vowels. Next, our overview of perceptual cues to consonants proceeds in terms of manner of articulation. It must be kept in mind that the literature on speech perception is vast, and a comprehensive overview could fill a complete handbook. We will focus here on major and well-established findings.

13.1   Vowels

Vowels are among the perceptually most salient speech sounds. They are typically voiced, relatively loud since they are produced with a comparatively small degree of constriction, and relatively long in duration. The most important acoustic cue to vowel quality is the location of the formant frequencies. As discussed in Section 9.5.1, each vowel is produced with a distinct position of the articulators that results in a distinct location of the formant frequencies. At first glance, vowel perception may therefore seem straightforward: In order to perceive a vowel, all the listener needs to do is extract the location of the first two or three formant frequencies and map this pattern onto an internalized vowel category. For example, based on the information that the location of the first two formant frequencies is 300 and 2,300 Hz, respectively, a native speaker of English may perceive that pattern as the vowel /i/. Likewise, formant frequency values of 800 and 1,100 Hz may be interpreted as /ɑ/.

However, phonetic context, speaking rate, and speaker size can all affect a vowel's specific formant frequency pattern. Variations in phonetic context – that is, in the actual segments that flank the vowel – and speaking rate both contribute to **vowel undershoot**. Undershoot describes a situation in which the formant frequencies do not reach their "canonical" values; that is, those values as measured in vowels produced in isolation where the articulators are in their "optimal" positions. For example, in a CVC syllable, the articulators may not reach their canonical position for the vowel due to the articulatory configuration that needs to be attained for the initial and final consonants and/or the speed with which this needs to be accomplished. That is, the articulators "undershoot" their target positions and, hence, the formant frequencies "undershoot" their canonical values. This does not mean that the formant frequencies are all too low – for example, the "undershot" F1 frequency for a high vowel (which has a low F1) is higher. That is, since the F1 target frequency is low, undershoot will result in a higher frequency value.

Vowel perception also becomes more complicated when considering vowels spoken by a variety of speakers. Since speakers vary in terms of vocal tract length and since vocal tract length is the primary determinant of formant frequency location, a given vowel will not have the same formant frequencies across a variety of speakers. For example, while a male speaker may produce the vowel /i/ with an F1 of 300 Hz and an F2 of 2300 Hz, a female speaker's /i/ may have an F1 of 400 Hz and an F2 of 2800 Hz. But even with a group of male speakers from the same dialectal area considerable variety exists in the location of formant frequencies. Figure 13.1 shows F1 and F2 values for the English monophthongs as produced by 45 males (Hillenbrand et al. 1995). If each vowel category were uniquely represented by the location of the first two formants, there should be no overlap among them. However, certain vowel categories can clearly be seen to show overlap.

The listener must assign these different acoustic patterns to the same phonemic category, a process that psychologists refer to as **equivalence classification**. The

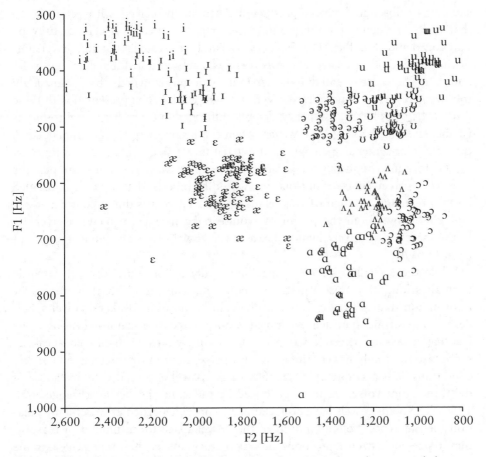

Figure 13.1 Vowel space of Hillenbrand et al. (1995), based on speech by 45 adult males.

process by which the listener is hypothesized to compensate for these variations due to vocal tract size is known as vocal tract **normalization**. The basic idea is that the listener uses certain attributes of the acoustic signal to estimate the length of a speaker's vocal tract in order to determine the frequency parameters of that speaker's vowel space. Normalization is a procedure for factoring out systematic covariation in acoustic properties so that the apparent overlap among vowel categories can be reduced or eliminated.

13.1.1   *Extrinsic versus intrinsic normalization*

While there are many models of vocal tract normalization, two main approaches stand out: **extrinsic normalization** and **intrinsic normalization**. According to a purely *extrinsic* model of normalization, a frame of reference is established from information distributed across the vowels of a single speaker. In other words, surrounding context is thought to allow the listener to calibrate a vowel space for a given speaker such that subsequent vowel productions can be perceived with reference to that space. Evidence for this notion was first presented in a classic study by Ladefoged and Broadbent (1957). These researchers created six synthetic versions of the sentence *Please say what this word is*, each with a different range of F1 and F2. They also created four versions of a target word "bVt" (i.e. a /b/ followed by a vowel and a /t/, e.g. *bit, bet, bat*, etc.). When presented with these test words in isolation, listeners' percepts shifted from *bit* to *bet* to *bat* to *but* as F1 increased in the vowel. However, when these same words were appended to the precursor sentence, perception of a given target word changed as a function of the formant frequency range in the precursor sentence. For example, the target *bit*, perceived as *bit* in isolation, would be perceived as *bet* when preceded by the precursor in which F1 was relatively low. There was thus a contrast effect, whereby a low F1 in the precursor would make listeners perceive a given F1 in the target as relatively higher (i.e. a lower vowel), thus changing the percept from /ɪ/ to /ɛ/.

While these results provide compelling evidence for some form of extrinsic normalization, they raise questions about the kind and extent of precursor information that is most effective in the calibration of a speaker's vowel space. Perhaps the strongest evidence against the notion of extrinsic normalization is the fact that vowels are perceived with very high accuracy even when different speakers' voices are randomly mixed. In fact, vowel perception under these mixed speaker conditions is as accurate as when each target vowel is preceded by instances of the three **point vowels** /i, u, ɑ/ produced by the same speaker (Verbrugge et al. 1976). The point vowels have been claimed to provide particularly useful information for the process of calibration of the vowel space for a number of reasons: they represent extreme positions in articulatory space, they represent extreme frequencies in acoustic space, their formant frequencies are not substantially affected by moderate changes in articulatory position, and they are the only vowels for which a formant pattern can be related to a unique vocal tract area function. However, Verbrugge et al. (1976) showed that presentation of these vowels does not seem to improve vowel perception. That is, listeners' identification of vowels is highly accurate, regardless of whether or not they were preceded by instances of the point vowels.

Any theory of extrinsic normalization also begs the question of how successful perception can begin if the perception of a vowel is dependent on that of a previous vowel. One possible answer is that it would take only one vowel to be correctly perceived. The vowel /i/ is the most likely candidate, since Nearey (1978) pointed out that the [i] of any speaker can always be identified as an instance of the vowel /i/ because of its unique formant pattern. In other words, a single token of the vowel /i/ by a given speaker would immediately allow for the estimation of that speaker's vocal tract length. This is an example of an approach known as **point normalization** since it requires only one known point in a speaker's vowel space. A variant is **range normalization**, which requires at least two known vowels.

An alternative to extrinsic normalization is *intrinsic* normalization. According to this view, all the information necessary to identify a vowel is contained within the vowel itself. Overlap among vowel categories is thought not to exist, or at least to be significantly reduced, when the acoustic properties of vowels are appropriately evaluated. This approach typically seeks to derive vowel representations that are similar to those that the human auditory system derives. As discussed earlier, the auditory system imposes a number of non-linear transformations on the speech signal, especially in the frequency and amplitude domains (see Section 12.4.3). Traditionally, vowels have been represented in an acoustic space with a linear frequency scale. More recently, researchers have begun to use more auditorily based scales for frequency (e.g. Bark or ERB scales) as well as loudness (e.g. phon or sone scales). The use of these kinds of scales does seem to substantially reduce the overlap that is traditionally observed among vowel categories (e.g. Syrdal and Gopal 1986). But it should be kept in mind that simply transforming a linear scale to, for example, a logarithmic scale does not change the order of points along a scale: what is "lower" on a linear scale is also "lower" on a logarithmic scale; only the distances between points change. And when the average distance between points (which might represent vowel frequencies) becomes larger after transforming to another scale, it does not necessarily mean that the vowels can be better separated, since only the way the distances are measured has been changed and not the position of the vowels relative to each other.

In addition to the use of more auditorily based scales, researchers have also explored different ways of combining information that is provided by the location of individual formant frequencies. For example, Miller (1989) added F_0 and F3 to the traditional parameters of F1 and F2 to represent vowels in a three-dimensional space whose axes were defined as follows: $x = \log (F1/F_0)$, $y = \log (F2/F1)$, and

$z = \log$ (F3/F2). This approach grew out of formant ratio theory according to which vowel quality depends on the ratios between formant frequencies rather than their absolute values. The idea is that a change in vocal tract length changes all formant frequencies for a given vowel by the same proportion. Thus, computing ratios can factor out differences in vocal tract length. This approach also serves to separate vowel categories quite well.

We started this section by describing normalization as a process that removes idiosyncratic information from the speech signal to obtain abstract prototypical, non-overlapping, categories. Recent research, however, suggests that categories that retain such information may offer certain advantages. In **exemplar-based theories,** a perceptual category (e.g. a consonant or vowel) is thought to consist of all experienced instances of the category. An exemplar consists of an association between a set of acoustic or auditory properties and a set of category labels. Since all relevant acoustic (e.g. detailed spectra) and linguistic and indexical information (e.g. linguistic category, speaker gender) is retained in the exemplar, new items can be categorized by reference to any of these dimensions. The assumption is that "clouds" of exemplars that comprise individual speech categories tend to occupy more or less unique regions of the higher-dimensional space that is generated by all of this information. Johnson's (1997) results from simulations with an exemplar-based model of vowel identification show highly accurate vowel recognition without any explicit form of speaker normalization. The extent to which exemplar-based models can accommodate other sources of variability in the speech signal is still under debate (see Johnson 2003).

Finally, it is important to note that the approaches to vowel representation mentioned thus far are all based on formant frequencies measured in the middle of the vowel. This midpoint measurement is as far away as possible from flanking segments and is considered to be least affected by contextual effects such as coarticulation. In other words, the formant frequencies measured at vowel midpoint may provide the "purest" representation of a vowel. However, when focusing on the steady-state portion of the vowel, other potentially important information is lost. Specifically, dynamic properties such as the duration of the vowel and the formant transitions into or out of the vowel may provide important cues to vowel quality. Indeed, some experiments (e.g. Strange et al. 1976; but see Macchi 1980) have shown that vowels in a CVC context were more accurately perceived than isolated vowels, suggesting that listeners do not exclusively base their vowel perception on steady-state information but use dynamic information as well. Further support for the importance of dynamic information comes from a perception experiment by Hillenbrand and Nearey (1999). Listeners were presented with synthetic "hVd" (e.g. *heed, hid, head*) stimuli for identification. Two synthetic versions were created: one was a close copy of natural productions; the other contained no formant transitions since the formant values were set to those measured at the "steadiest state" of the vowel. Results showed that vowel identification was significantly worse for the stimuli without transitions (74 percent) than for the stimuli in which spectral change was preserved (89 percent).

13.2 Consonants

Perception of consonants is often considered more complex than vowel perception since the acoustic characteristics of consonants are thought to be more variable. Among the sources of variability that may influence the acoustic characteristics of consonants are vocal tract size, phonetic context, speaking rate, and stress. We will begin with approximants since they are most similar to vowels.

13.2.1 *Approximants*

Approximants are produced with a small constriction. The tongue approximates the passive articulator but does not come very close. As a result, the acoustic properties of approximants resemble those of vowels in many respects. Perceptually, the formant transitions into and out of the approximant are an important cue to place of articulation (see Section 10.2.1). The onset frequency of the F2 transition has been shown to be a primary cue to the distinction between /w/ and /j/. Since /w/ has a bilabial constriction (in addition to its velar constriction), all formant frequencies are a bit lower (see Section 10.2.1) and a low F1 and F2 are its main perceptual cues. Since /j/ has a palatal constriction, the front cavity is shorter and a high F2 is its primary cue. The distinction between /ɹ/ and /l/ seems to be carried by a number of cues. The most obvious difference between these two sounds is the location of F3: /ɹ/ has a very low F3, well below that for /l/. However, the onset frequency of F2 (low for /ɹ/, higher for /l/) and the transition duration of F1 (long for /ɹ/, shorter for /l/) have also been shown to contribute to the perception of the /ɹ/–/l/ distinction.

Research on the cues to approximant manner of articulation has focused on the distinction between the plosive /b/ and the approximant /w/. One important cue to this distinction is the duration of the formant transitions, particularly F2. /b/ has short transitions while /w/ has relatively long transitions. Using synthetic speech, a reasonable-sounding /b/ can be changed into an acceptable /w/ by lengthening the F2 transition duration while keeping all other parameters constant. Any time a distinction is carried primarily or exclusively by a temporal parameter, variations in speaking rate are likely to affect the perception of this distinction, as indicated in a change of the **category boundary**, that is, that value of one or more acoustic parameters (in this case, F2 transition duration) that listeners identify 50 percent of the time as a member of one category (e.g. /b/), and 50 percent of the time as a member of the other (e.g. /w/). (See Section 13.3.1 for a more detailed discussion of category boundaries.) Indeed the category boundary between /b/ and /w/ has been shown to shift as a function of speaking rate: an increase in speaking rate, experimentally induced by shortening the vowel following the initial consonant, results in an increase in the number of /w/ responses (Miller and Liberman 1979). This is thought to occur because a shorter vowel makes a given transition duration seem relatively longer. This is an example of the context-dependent nature of acoustic cues.

However, manipulating F2 transition duration as the sole cue to the /b/–/w/ distinction may be a simplification. As discussed in Section 10.4.1, the difference between stops and glides in terms of rapid versus gradual release affects amplitude as well as transition duration. For example, /b/ has a sudden increase in amplitude at the moment of release while /w/ shows a very gradual change. In natural speech, both transition duration and amplitude, as well as a variety of more subtle cues, all contribute to the /b/–/w/ distinction. And when this distinction is signaled by all these cues simultaneously, the effect of speaking rate has been shown to substantially diminish or disappear altogether (Shinn et al. 1985), although the rate effects tend to come back in the presence of background noise (Miller and Wayland 1993).

13.2.2   *Fricatives*

Fricatives are relatively long and are quite steady throughout their duration. Two defining features of fricatives are the fricative noise itself and the transitions from the fricative into the following vowel. Acoustically, spectral peak location and relative amplitude (see Section 10.2.2) serve to distinguish fricatives in terms of place of articulation.

Perceptually, the role of spectral peak location has been investigated in several studies. Most notably, Heinz and Stevens (1961) synthesized fricatives by systematically varying the location of the spectral peak from 2 to 8 kHz. Listeners' responses showed that fricatives with a peak below 3 kHz were identified as /ʃ/; fricatives with a peak between 4.5 and 6.5 kHz were identified as /s/, and those with a peak above 6.5 kHz were perceived as /f/ or /θ/. However, listeners were unable to distinguish /f/ from /θ/. Research investigating the role of vocalic context on the perception of /s/ and /ʃ/ has also shown that an /s–ʃ/ continuum can be successfully created by varying spectral peak location (e.g. Mann and Repp 1980; Whalen 1981). In sum, these studies indicate that spectral peak location is a reliable perceptual cue to the distinction between sibilant /s, ʃ/ and non-sibilant /f, θ/ fricatives, and peak location also serves to perceptually distinguish /s/ from /ʃ/.

Recent research suggests that relative amplitude is also a perceptual cue to place of articulation in fricatives. In particular, Hedrick and Ohde (1993) showed that the amplitude of friction relative to the amplitude of vowel onset affects listeners' perception of /θ/, /s/, and /ʃ/. It is as yet unknown whether relative amplitude is a cue in the perception of distinctions *within* the class of non-sibilant fricatives.

Evidence in support of the perceptual significance of other properties of the friction noise is mixed at best. Behrens and Blumstein (1988) showed that noise amplitude alone is not a reliable cue to fricative perception. In addition, noise duration does not seem to be an important perceptual cue to fricative place of articulation.

Finally, support for the role of transition information is provided by Harris (1958) and, more recently, Nittrouer (2002). Harris recorded fricative-vowel syllables consisting of all English fricatives and four vowels. She then created stimuli for a perception experiment by **cross-splicing**[1] the friction noise from one syllable onto the vocalic portion of another syllable. Results showed that the sibilants were identified on the basis of the friction noise: combining the noise portion of /s, z, ʃ, ʒ/ with any of the vocalic portions resulted in perception of /s, z, ʃ, ʒ/ respectively. However, perception of /f, θ/ was largely determined by the vocalic portion. For example, stimuli with /f/ or /θ/ noise were perceived as /f/ when followed by vocalic portions excised from /f/, and perceived as /θ/ when followed by any other vocalic portion. Based on these results, Harris (1958) assumed that listeners first decide, on the basis of the friction noise, whether they heard /s, ʃ/ or /f, θ/, and that they then use the vocalic portion to decide whether they heard /f/ or /θ/.

This notion is further supported by the finding that listeners' perception of /f, θ/ was significantly above chance when presented with only the fricative-to-vowel transitions, while perception of /s, ʃ/ was not. In addition, perception of /s, ʃ/ did not suffer from removal of the transitions. In sum, there is evidence that formant transitions play a role in the perception of the non-sibilant fricatives.

The voicing distinction is primarily cued by the presence versus absence of vocal fold vibration during the fricative, seen acoustically as the presence versus absence, respectively, of low-frequency energy. While voiceless fricatives are generally longer than voiced fricatives, duration per se does not seem to be a sufficient cue to fricative voicing. Finally, fricatives are distinguished from other obstruents in terms of their onset characteristics: fricatives have a long rise-time, plosives have a short rise time, and affricates fall in between. As long as the onset characteristics are preserved, even fricatives that have been severely shortened are still perceived as fricatives (Jongman 1989).

13.2.3 Nasals

Nasal stop consonants have a number of defining characteristics, including the pattern of formants and anti-formants during the nasal murmur, and the formant transitions into and out of the nasal. The cues to the nasal *manner* of articulation are relatively straightforward while those to place of articulation are more complex. The nasal murmur portion contains several cues to the nasal manner of articulation, including weak formants with large bandwidths, a low-frequency resonance (at approximately 300 Hz) known as the nasal formant, and anti-formants (see Section 10.2.4). The presence of this murmur is a sufficient cue for the perception of the nasal manner of articulation. When an oral vowel is followed by a nasal, the velum is typically lowered during the latter portion of the vowel. The weakening of the higher formants in the vowel spectrum as the result of the opening of the velar port also provides a perceptual cue to the upcoming nasal.

The perceptual cues to *place* of articulation reside both in the nasal murmur and the formant transitions. While early research (e.g. Liberman et al. 1954; Malecot 1956) concluded that the transitions, but not the murmur, carried cues to place, more recent studies indicate that listeners use both sources of information. Specifically, while identification of place of articulation seems comparable on the basis of either the nasal murmur or formant transitions, identification is superior when listeners are presented with a few pulses of both murmur *and* transitions (Kurowski and Blumstein 1984; Repp and Svastikula 1988).

13.2.4 Plosives

Acoustically, plosives are characterized by a number of events: consonant closure, release burst, and formant transitions (both from a preceding segment into the plosive and from the plosive into a following segment). Each of these properties can be analyzed in terms of its frequency, amplitude, and duration. Voice onset time (VOT) is an additional temporal parameter that serves to distinguish plosives. In terms of manner of articulation, plosives are unique because of their closure portion, release burst, and rapid formant transitions. Research has shown that listeners correctly identify them as plosives when presented with only the first 10–20 ms of CV syllables. Plosive voicing can be cued by a number of parameters. Relative to voiced plosives, voiceless plosives typically have a longer closure portion, typically with no or only brief glottal pulsing, a more intense release burst, a positive VOT, and higher F_0 and F1 onset frequencies in the following segment.

Most research on the perception of plosives has focused on cues to place of articulation. Two acoustic characteristics containing information about place are the frequency of the release burst and the formant transition pattern. Over the past 50 years, a great many researchers have attempted to determine if and to what extent these properties, either alone or in conjunction, enable listeners to identify a plosive's place of articulation. Early research indicated that burst frequency per se is not a very reliable cue to place of articulation. Using synthetic speech, so that the artificially generated speech allowed researchers to vary one acoustic property while keeping all others constant, Liberman et al. (1952) created a series of release bursts, ranging in frequency from 360 Hz to 4,320 Hz. These bursts were followed by a series of two-formant (F1 and F2) patterns representing seven different English vowels. Listeners were presented with these synthetic stimuli and asked to indicate whether they thought the initial consonant was /p/, /t/, or /k/. The results are shown in Figure 13.2. While the bursts consistently elicited plosive responses, place of articulation identification of the bursts was heavily influenced by the vowel context. In general, high-frequency bursts were always identified as /t/, and very low-frequency bursts were predominantly perceived as /p/. This finding matches our discussion of acoustic cues to place of articulation in Section 10.2.3. However, a mid-frequency burst, around 1,400–2,000 Hz, was perceived as /k/ when followed by /ɛ, a, ɔ/ but as /p/ when

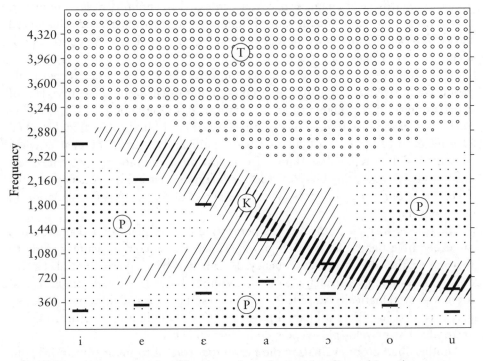

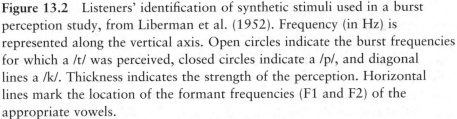

Figure 13.2 Listeners' identification of synthetic stimuli used in a burst perception study, from Liberman et al. (1952). Frequency (in Hz) is represented along the vertical axis. Open circles indicate the burst frequencies for which a /t/ was perceived, closed circles indicate a /p/, and diagonal lines a /k/. Thickness indicates the strength of the perception. Horizontal lines mark the location of the formant frequencies (F1 and F2) of the appropriate vowels.

followed by /i, e, o, u/. Burst frequency did not seem to be a reliable cue to place of articulation, particularly for velars.

Subsequent experiments used cross-spliced natural speech stimuli to examine the perception of place of articulation. For example, Cole and Scott (1974) recorded the English voiced and voiceless plosives before the vowels /i, a, u/. They then removed the consonant from one vowel context and cross-spliced it onto a different vowel context. For example, the burst and aspiration of /ti/ "t(i)" was spliced onto the vocalic portion taken from /tu/ "(t)u", and vice versa. Cole and Scott (1974) showed that identification of bilabials and alveolars was highly accurate regardless of changes in vowel context. Perception of velars, however, was much poorer. Applying the same technique to labial, alveolar, and velar voiced plosives spoken before nine different vowels, Dorman et al. (1977) reported poor identification of place of articulation.

Some studies presented for identification only the release bursts of naturally produced plosive-vowel syllables and reported that listeners could identify place of articulation with reasonable to good accuracy (e.g. Winitz et al. 1971; Kewley-Port et al. 1983). Indeed, Tekieli and Cullinan (1979) showed that listeners' identification of place of articulation was significantly better than chance when presented with only the first 10 ms of voiceless plosives followed by eight different vowels. Overall, this body of research suggests that burst frequency may be a necessary but not a sufficient cue to the perception of place of articulation in stop consonants.

The role of formant transitions as perceptual cues to place of articulation has also been investigated in a variety of experiments. In a complementary study to the one on the role of burst frequency described above, Liberman et al. (1952) created synthetic two-formant patterns (without bursts) in which the F2 transition was systematically varied. Perceptual results indicated that most listeners perceived a rising F2 as a bilabial plosive but that a falling F2 was heard either as an alveolar or velar plosive, depending on the vowel.

Another method of evaluating the perceptual role of formant transitions is to remove the burst from naturally produced plosive-vowel syllables, leaving only the formant transitions. Results from such studies indicate that identification rates of place range from moderate to good for voiced plosives but are substantially worse for voiceless plosives. (e.g. LaRiviere et al. 1975; Dorman et al. 1977).

The most careful and comprehensive study to date examining the contribution of bursts and formant transitions to plosive identification was conducted by Smits et al. (1996) for the Dutch plosives /p, t, k, b, d/ followed by the vowels /i, y, a, u/. Using digital cross-splicing and filtering techniques, burst-only, burstless, and cross-spliced stimuli were created. Average recognition rates for the burst-only and burstless stimuli are shown in Table 13.1.

Cross-spliced stimuli were created by combining the burst of a plosive at a given place of articulation (e.g. the burst from /pa/ "(p)a") with everything but the burst of a plosive at a different place of articulation (e.g. from "(t)a" or "(k)a"). The resulting stimuli are known as **conflicting-cue** signals because they combine cues to conflicting percepts. In this case, the burst signaled one place of articulation while the formant transitions signaled a different place of articulation. Responses to the voiceless cross-spliced stimuli corresponded to the burst identity in 49 percent of the cases and to the transitions in 43 percent of the cases. In addition, the /k/-burst was a stronger cue to place than the /p/- and /t/-bursts and /p/, /t/, and /k/ transitions were equally strong cues to place of articulation. For the voiced cross-spliced stimuli, responses corresponded to the burst identity in only 26 percent of the cases and to the transitions in 74 percent of the cases. The /d/-burst was a stronger cue than the /b/-burst.

Table 13.1 Correct identification (in percentages) of place of articulation, averaged across vowel contexts, for burst-only and burstless stimuli (after Smits et al., 1996)

	Percentage correct identification of . . .						
Stimulus	[p]	[t]	[k]	Mean	[b]	[d]	Mean
Burst-only	80	50	91	74	65	57	61
Burstless	95	64	47	69	96	87	92

In sum, this study confirms and extends our understanding of the relative importance of bursts and transitions as cues to place of articulation in plosives. While cue strength varies with place of articulation, vowel context, as well as speaker, a number of generalizations emerge. In general, the burst is the strongest cue to place perception in front vowel contexts while the transitions are most important in back vowel contexts. Moreover, the bursts of voiceless plosives provide a stronger cue than those of voiced plosives while the transitions of voiced plosives provide more information than those of voiceless plosives.

As mentioned in Section 10.4.1, the fact that individual acoustic properties such as burst frequency and formant transition frequency often show a high degree of context-dependency has led some researchers to consider the role of global, rather than local, properties as perceptual cues to place of articulation. For example, we mentioned in Section 10.4.1 that Lahiri et al. (1984) found that the change in distribution of high-frequency energy as compared to low-frequency energy between consonant onset and the onset of the following vowel provides a stable cue. Perception experiments in the same study confirmed that listeners integrate these two cues, burst onset spectrum and vowel onset spectrum, to make a phonetic decision.

13.3 Contributions of the Motor Theory of Speech Perception

As discussed in Section 10.4, Liberman and colleagues conducted a great many careful experiments in their search for correlates of phonemic distinctions. However, they failed to find acoustic correlates that were stable in the face of contextual variability. The lack of acoustic invariance raised the question of which other sources of information listeners use to perceive speech. Liberman and colleagues concluded that it must be articulatory information and formulated the **motor theory of speech perception**. According to *motor theory*, as it is commonly abbreviated, speech perception is more closely related to articulation than to acoustics. Motor theory claims that speech is perceived by reference to articulation: the articulatory movements and their sensory effects mediate between the acoustic stimulus and its perception. Motor theory essentially hypothesizes that listeners interpret the received auditory patterns in terms of articulatory patterns that would produce those auditory patterns. Thus, the invariant cues to speech sounds are the articulations that produce them. One of the attractive features of this theory was its direct link between the perception and production of speech. The assumption that the processes by which speech is produced and perceived have much in common may be intuitively more appealing than a view under which the two are unrelated. Early articulatory studies provided support for the theory that articulatory positions and movements classify a speech sound despite its acoustical variation (Liberman 1957). Unfortunately, it was also observed that the same speech sound can be realized by quite different articulatory movements (MacNeilage 1970), hence the sequence of articulatory movements was as variable as the speech signal itself. The motor theory was therefore modified, such that the motor commands to the articulators, rather than the movements themselves, classify speech sounds (Liberman 1970). Consequently, the listener's knowledge about the effect of the motor commands on the vocal tract serves as units of the perception process (Liberman 1982). The theory was further extended to the **revised motor theory**, namely that the **intended gestures** are perceived and thus, without even being realized, enable the perception of speech (Liberman and Mattingly 1985). Listening, in this view, is the perception of the intended gestures that lead to the coarticulated and highly variable speech signal.

Another gestural account of speech perception is **direct realism** (Fowler 1986, 2003). Direct realism is a theory of perception in general, not just auditory perception. In terms of speech perception, motor theory and direct realism both posit that the immediate objects of perception are articulatory gestures. However, while for motor theory the objects of perception are intended gestures, or the commands that would give rise to these gestures, direct realism assumes that these objects are actual vocal tract movements. Analogous to the way in which our eyes perceive objects rather than the physical reflections of light, our ears perceive articulatory gestures instead of the physical changes in frequency, amplitude, and duration of the speech signal. Such a view requires that vocal tract movements are uniquely recoverable from the acoustic signal, which does not seem to be the case since there are multiple articulatory ways to produce a given acoustic signal.

The major criticism of the original motor theory was the missing explanation of how the articulatory positions and movements can be perceived from the speech signal and how a child learns this conversion. Even in the revised motor theory, no actual mechanism is proposed. Recent neurological research may support the possibility of motor recruitment in speech perception posited by motor theory. Rizzolatti and colleagues discovered a group of neurons – **mirror neurons** – in monkeys that are active in the matching of observed events to similar internally generated actions. Specifically, these mirror neurons discharge both when monkeys perform an action such as tearing a piece of paper and when they only hear the sound of paper tearing (e.g. Rizzolatti and Arbib 1998; Kohler et al. 2002). This is an exciting finding that will stimulate further research on the link between the production and perception of speech. It is currently too early to tell whether the notion of mirror neurons vindicates motor theory. For example, neurons responding to the sound of paper being torn could be shaped by associative learning as part of a system that evolved for rapid responses to environmental situations. For now, it is clear that motor theory has inspired an impressive body of research, by both its proponents and critics, that has led to important insights into the nature of speech perception.

13.3.1 *Categorical perception*

Perhaps the best-known finding by Liberman and colleagues is that of **categorical perception**. Categorical perception refers to the fact that stimuli, equally spaced along some physical continuum, are perceived as belonging to one or another perceptual category instead of as varying as a function of their physical values. In the case of speech, the phenomenon of categorical perception refers to the way in which certain distinctions are perceived. Categorical perception requires tests of listeners' abilities to identify and to discriminate speech sounds. In general, people are much better at **discriminating** sounds (i.e. hearing the difference between a pair of sounds) than at **identifying** (labeling; i.e. saying "this is a *C sharp* note" and "that is a *B*") them. For example, listeners can discriminate hundreds of different pitches yet identify fewer than 10.

An example will make this clear. Consider the voicing distinction in English syllable-initial plosives. Voiced plosives typically have a short positive VOT while voiceless plosives have a long positive VOT (see Section 10.2.3). Using either synthetic or manipulated natural speech, it is possible to create a series of stimuli that systematically differ in terms of their VOT. The first member could have a VOT of 0 ms, the next member a VOT of 10 ms, and so on until the last member with a VOT of 80 ms. This would result in a voicing continuum, say from /dɑ/ to /tɑ/, with nine members. Several repetitions (for example 10) of each member are then created and the order of these 90 tokens is **randomized**. Randomization simply arranges the stimuli in arbitrary order. The randomized stimuli are then presented to listeners who have to identify them as either /dɑ/ or /tɑ/. In other words, a listener may be presented with the 40 ms VOT stimulus on the first trial, the 0 ms VOT stimulus on the second trial, the 60 ms VOT stimulus on the third, and so on. We would expect the 0 ms and 80 ms VOT stimuli to be identified as /dɑ/ and /tɑ/, respectively. How would the other members be identified? A reasonable guess would be that as VOT increases, the number of /dɑ/ responses decreases in a linear fashion, as illustrated in Figure 13.3. However, typical results of such an identification experiment look more like Figure 13.4.

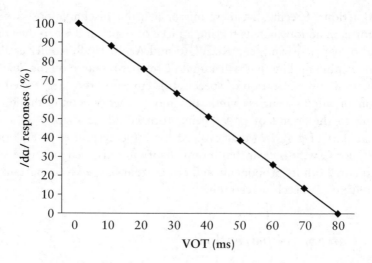

Figure 13.3 Expected result of identification experiment in which VOT is systematically varied.

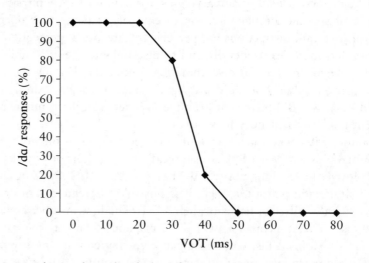

Figure 13.4 Obtained result of identification experiment in which VOT is systematically varied in 10-ms steps from /dɑ/ to /tɑ/.

The change from /dɑ/ to /tɑ/ is not gradual but abrupt or categorical. The listener divides the stimuli into two sharply defined categories, "da" and "ta." The category (or phoneme) boundary between these two categories, computed as the VOT value at which /dɑ/ (and /tɑ/) identification is at 50 percent, corresponds to a VOT of approximately 35 ms. Notice that there is very little difference in the identification of stimuli that are assigned to the same category. For example, both the 0 ms and 10 ms VOT are consistently identified as /da/. However, the identification of two stimuli on opposite sides of the boundary is very different, even though they are separated by the same physical distance. That is, the 30 ms VOT stimulus is perceived as /da/ 80 percent of the time while the 40 ms VOT receives only 20 percent /da/ identifications.

In addition to a sharp identification function, categorical perception also involves a characteristic discrimination function. Since a prerequisite of categorical perception is that discrimination is no better than identification, a discrimination experiment will have to be conducted as well (otherwise this pattern of results cannot be called categorical perception). There are several ways of conducting a discrimination experiment and we will focus on the most commonly used method, the **ABX** or **odd-ball task**. In this particular version of a discrimination experiment, three stimuli, A, B, and X, are presented on each trial. A and B are always different stimuli while X always matches either A or B. The listener's task is to indicate whether X matches A or B. For example, with A and B chosen such that they are always separated by one continuum member (known as "two-step discrimination" because two steps are necessary to go from A to B), there would be seven possible combinations of A and B for the 0–80 ms VOT continuum discussed earlier (0 and 20 ms VOT, 10 and 30, 20 and 40, 30 and 50, 40 and 60, 50 and 70, and 60 and 80). Thus, a trial could consist of the triad 0–20–20 and the listener has to indicate whether the final 20 ms VOT stimulus sounds more like the first 0 or the second 20 ms VOT. Again, 10 or so repetitions of each triad are created and randomly presented to listeners for discrimination. If the two stimuli are easy to distinguish, the listeners' accuracy should be at or near 100 percent. If the two stimuli are difficult to distinguish, listeners will identify a given stimulus X half the time as A and half the time as B, resulting in an accuracy of 50 percent. Results from the discrimination experiment are shown in Figure 13.5.

The discrimination function is flat at both ends and has a peak in the middle. There is indeed one stimulus pair that is apparently very easy for listeners to distinguish, as indicated by the peak in the discrimination function, and it consists of the 20 and 40 ms VOT stimulus pair. In other words, listeners are very good at telling these stimuli apart. Recall that in the identification experiment, these stimuli were identified as members of two different categories, "da" and "ta," respectively. The figure also shows that discrimination accuracy hovered around 50 percent for virtually all other stimulus pairs. This indicates that listeners were able to distinguish the two members of a pair only half of the time. In other words, half of the time they thought the members were the same and half of the time they thought they were different. In essence, then, listeners were simply guessing. For these stimuli, performance is said to be at chance level. That is, with only two response categories ("same" or "different"), guessing would result in an accuracy level of 50 percent. Notice that all stimulus pairs for which discrimination was at chance level consisted of stimuli that in the identification experiment had been identified as members of the *same* category.

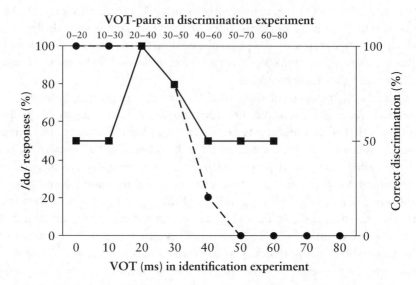

Figure 13.5 Results (solid line) from a two-step discrimination experiment using the same VOT continuum members as in identification. The dashed line again shows the identification results.

In sum, these results show that discrimination is indeed no better than identification, which is rather different from what we said about pitch perception at the beginning of this section. There is no difference in identification of stimuli that are perceived as belonging to the same category. In addition, the ability to discriminate between members of the same category is at chance level (50 percent) while discrimination is very good for the stimulus pair that straddles the phoneme boundary. This pattern of identification and discrimination is the hallmark of categorical perception. In addition to the perception of voicing, perception of place of articulation (e.g. using a /ba–da–ga/ continuum in which the F2 transition is systematically modified) has also been shown to be categorical. Categorical perception of plosives is a very robust finding. It has been extensively replicated across different languages and listeners (for an extensive overview, see Repp 1984).

In contrast, vowel perception seems to be continuous. When a vowel continuum is created, for example from /ɪ/ to /ɛ/ by raising F1 in a number of equal steps, perception of this continuum is not categorical. Instead, it looks more like that in Figure 13.3, displaying a gradual, continuous change. The fact that plosives, but not vowels, are categorically perceived was initially taken as support for motor theory. Perception was seen as mimicking production. Since the plosives /b, d, g/ are produced by categorically different gestures, they are perceived in a categorical way. Vowels, on the other hand, are produced much more continuously, and they are perceived in a continuous way.

Subsequent research, however, has suggested that this difference in perception between plosives and vowels may not be related to articulatory differences. These two types of sounds also differ in duration: vowels are relatively long and plosives are relatively short and, maybe more importantly, dynamic. When vowels are shortened to the extent that they are of comparable duration to plosives, their perception becomes categorical as well.

The initial interpretation of categorical perception that listeners can only distinguish stimuli from different categories is probably too strong. The original claim that listeners are not able to distinguish among different stimuli from the same category may have been due to limitations of the experimental task. The use of two additional response measures, **reaction time** and **goodness ratings**, indicates that listeners do perceive differences among members of the same category. *Reaction time* is often used as a measure of amount of processing, particularly in psycholinguistic research. Typically, the more ambiguous a stimulus, the more time it takes for a subject (i.e. a listener in an experiment) to process it, and the time to perform a certain reaction (e.g. pressing a button) will be longer. *Goodness ratings* indicate how good an instance a given token is, as judged by a subject. For example, a subject has to decide whether he hears a /ta/ and has to give a rating from "this is a good /ta/" to "this is a bad /ta/." Alternatively, there could be a line with /ta/ on one end and /da/ on the other and the subject has to make a cross on the line to indicate how close the presented item was to a /ta/ or a /da/; that is, how well a stimulus (the presented item) matched the target (/ta/ or /da/). The initial identification results show that all stimuli within a category are identified as if they are all identical (e.g. 100 percent /da/). However, using reaction time and category goodness ratings, categories have been shown to have internal structure in that stimuli closer to the phoneme boundary are identified more slowly and receive lower goodness ratings. Recent studies using measures such as eye movements and EEG provide additional support for the notion that within-category detail is important in speech perception (e.g. McMurray et al. 2002; Sharma and Dorman 1999). Thus, these kinds of studies have caused us to rethink the original notion of categorical perception. While it is probably efficient to ignore subtle acoustic differences between sounds if they do not signal a difference in phoneme category, that does not mean that listeners are not aware of those differences. In this sense, the phenomenon of categorical perception in which discrimination is not better than identification is a form of equivalence classification (see Section 13.1).

13.3.2   Is speech "special"?

The finding that human adults perceive plosives in a categorical fashion naturally triggered interest in the origin of categorical perception. Specifically, the debate focused on whether categorical perception was an innate attribute, due to the structure of the auditory system, or arose as the result of exposure to language. Researchers recognized that a logical way of addressing this question would be to explore the nature of plosive perception in newborn human infants, since they lacked significant exposure to language. However, it was not until the late 1960s that a technique was developed that allowed the testing of infants. This technique, known as the **high amplitude sucking (HAS)** paradigm, was first introduced in a classic study by Eimas et al. (1971). Briefly, this paradigm exploits the fact that an infant's sucking rate increases when presented with a novel stimulus. The infant sucks on a pacifier that is wired to a transducer so that the sucking rate can be monitored. A given stimulus is repeatedly presented over loudspeakers. As the novelty of the stimulus wears off, the infant's sucking rate decreases, a process known as habituation. The critical question is what happens when the infant is subsequently presented with a different stimulus: if the infant treats the stimulus as different from the previous one, we would expect the sucking rate to increase; if not, we would expect the rate to remain stable or decrease even further. The infant is therefore engaged in a discrimination task.

Eimas and colleagues tested 4-month-old English-speaking infants to investigate perception of the voicing distinction in English syllable-initial plosive consonants. A synthetic /ba–pa/ continuum was created in which VOT increased from 0 to 80 ms in 20 ms steps. As shown in Figure 13.6, these infants performed very similarly to adults. The leftmost panel indicates that infants were able to discriminate between two stimuli that for adults belong to two distinct categories. Infants clearly differentiate between a 20 ms VOT as one category and a 40 ms VOT as another category. The middle panel shows that infants did not distinguish stimuli that for adults were members of the same category. Thus, infants did not discriminate a stimulus with a 0 ms VOT from one with a 20 ms VOT. Likewise, infants did not discriminate a stimulus with a 60 ms VOT from one with an 80 ms VOT, both of which are categorized by adults as voiceless. Finally, the control condition on the rightmost panel confirms that sucking rate continues to decrease when the presented stimulus does not change.

While these results are sometimes interpreted as showing that infants perceive plosive voicing in a categorical manner, a true demonstration of categorical perception requires the results of both a discrimination and an identification test to converge. While it may prove impossible to obtain identification data from infants, one has to be cautious in the interpretation of the discrimination results. Nevertheless, the infant perception results suggest that the categorical perception observed in adults is not due to linguistic experience. Instead, this behavior seems to be present at birth. Adult-like perception has been shown by infants for a variety of linguistic distinctions in addition to voicing.

The finding that the perception of certain linguistic distinctions did not seem to require linguistic exposure led to the debate about whether or not human speech perception makes use of mechanisms that evolved especially for the processing of speech. This debate, sometimes referred to as the **speech is special** debate, centers around two competing hypotheses, referred to by Kuhl (1989) as the **special mechanism account (SMA)** and the **general mechanism account (GMA)**. According to SMA, speech is perceived directly as the result of specialized, speech-specific mechanisms that exist only in humans. According to GMA, speech perception is based on general auditory and cognitive mechanisms and does not require

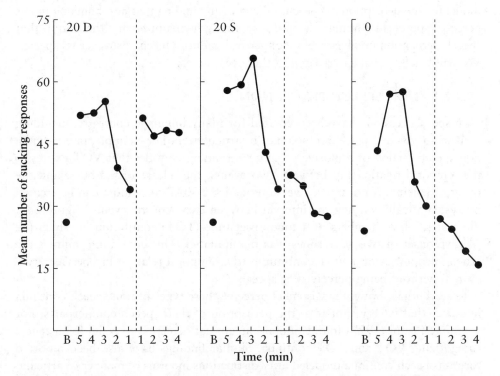

Figure 13.6 Results from Eimas et al. (1971). Mean number of sucking responses for 4-month-old infants as a function of time and experimental condition. The dashed line indicates the occurrence of the stimulus shift, or, in the case of the control group (right panel), the time at which the shift would have occurred. The left panel shows responses to a change from a 20 ms to a 40 ms VOT. The middle panel shows responses to a change from a 0 ms to a 20 ms VOT. The right panel shows responses to no change in VOT. B indicates baseline sucking rate. Time is measured with reference to the moment of stimulus shift and indicates the 5 minutes prior to and the 4 minutes after shift.

Reproduced by permission of the American Association for the Advancement of Science.

innate speech-specific processes. Critical evidence in this debate typically consists of comparisons between the perception of speech and non-speech by humans as well as the perception of speech by humans and non-human animals.

Non-speech signals mimic the speech signal in certain crucial respects. For example, while non-speech is not perceived as speech, it can be created to resemble speech in terms of rapid changes in frequency and amplitude. Experiments on non-speech test the claim that speech-specific mechanisms are required for the perception of speech. Clearly, this claim is weakened by any finding that non-speech is perceived in a way similar to speech, supporting a general auditory mechanism model for the perception of speech. Likewise, any finding that non-human animals perceive speech like humans would also strengthen support for the notion that speech perception involves the use of general auditory mechanisms across species. We will briefly consider research in these two areas.

13.3.2.1   NON-SPEECH PERCEPTION

Non-speech versions have been created for many linguistic contrasts, including consonant voicing, place, and manner of articulation. For example, in creating a non-speech analog of a plosive voicing continuum, consider that VOT expresses the temporal relationship between two events, the release of the burst and the onset of voicing. A non-speech version of such a VOT continuum can be created by systematically varying the interval between two acoustic events. Figure 13.7 illustrates a few members of a tone onset time (TOT) continuum in which the relative onset of two pure tones was manipulated. This continuum mimics the crucial properties of a VOT continuum (the temporal relationship between two events) without being perceived as speech.

Research has shown that listeners perceive these types of non-speech continua in a way that is very similar to the perception of their speech counterparts. For example, Pisoni (1977) found similar categorical perception results for listeners categorizing VOT and TOT continua. Similar findings have also been reported for non-speech continua modeled after distinctions in terms of manner of articulation (e.g. /b–w/ and /ɹ–l/) and place of articulation (e.g. /d-g/), suggesting a general mechanisms account of speech processing.

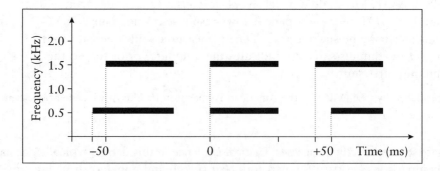

Figure 13.7   Stimuli from Pisoni (1977). Schematic representation of three of the stimuli used in a tone onset time analog of a VOT continuum. Each stimulus consists of a 500 Hz and a 1500 Hz tone. The relative onset of the two tones is systematically varied. The left panel shows the lower tone leading the higher tone by 50 ms, simulating a −50 ms VOT. In the middle panel, both tones start simultaneously, simulating a 0 ms VOT. In the right panel, the lower tone lags the higher tone by 50 ms, simulating a +50 ms VOT.

13.3.2.2 ANIMAL PERCEPTION

Early studies on categorical perception in non-human animals were conducted by Kuhl and Miller (1975). These researchers compared the perception of VOT continua by humans and chinchillas. The chinchillas (furry mammals from Latin America whose auditory system is quite similar to that of humans) were first trained to identify the endpoints of the continuum using shock avoidance. That is, in response to one of the endpoint stimuli, the chinchillas were taught to avoid mild electric shock by moving from one half of their cage to the other half. For the other endpoint, the chinchillas were trained to stay put and inhibit this crossing response. Correct inhibition was rewarded with drinking water. Once they had been taught to distinguish these stimuli, the remaining members of the continuum were included for identification. Results showed that the chinchillas' voicing boundary was very similar to the humans'. Kuhl and Miller compared perception of the voicing distinction at three places of articulation: bilabial, alveolar, and velar. They found a very close correspondence in that as the human VOT boundary shifted to increasingly longer VOTs at each place of articulation, so did the animal boundary.

Studies on animal perception have included additional linguistic contrasts (e.g. place and manner of articulation) as well as a variety of species (e.g. rhesus monkeys, macaques, and Japanese quail). In general, results from these studies indicate that there is a close correspondence between the ways in which humans and animals perceive linguistic distinctions.

What do results from experiments on the perception of non-speech and the perception of speech by animals tell us? Caution is required when interpreting these results. The demonstration that non-speech is perceived in a way similar to speech seems to indicate that an account of basic speech perception processes does not need to invoke the notion of speech-specific mechanisms. General auditory processes can account for the perception of both speech and other auditory signals. Likewise, the finding that animals perceive speech like humans indicates that basic speech perception phenomena can be understood in terms of the use of general auditory mechanisms. For example, it has been hypothesized that a voicing boundary at a VOT of 20 ms or more directly reflects the temporal resolution of the auditory system. Hircsh (1959) showed that listeners can only judge the temporal order of two auditory events when they are separated by at least 20 ms. If the onsets of the two events occur within 20 ms of each other, listeners are unable to determine which event occurred first. Translated to VOT (or TOT), one event is the release of the burst; the other is the onset of voicing. The implication of Hirsh's finding is that if release and onset of voicing occur within 20 ms of each other, the listener will treat them as occurring simultaneously, which results in the perception of a voiced plosive for a language like English. If, however, the onset of voicing occurs 20 ms or more after the release, the listener can distinguish two separate events and tell that voicing lagged release, which results in a voiceless percept. Thus, the voicing boundary could stem from general properties and limitations of the auditory system. Indeed, recent research with non-speech indicates that basic auditory sensitivities affect the extent to which categories can be learned: participants more quickly learned to distinguish two distributions when the boundary between them fell at a TOT of 20 ms as compared to two distributions whose boundary occurred at a TOT of 40 ms. The latter distinction presumably was more difficult to learn because a 40 ms TOT does not correspond to any known peak in discrimination and because one of the distributions was centered around a 20 ms TOT, which is a known area of increased sensitivity (Holt et al. 2004). This finding suggests that learnability may shape language sound inventories.

Finally, we do not claim that animals will be able to perform just about every speech or non-speech perception task that humans do. One possible area where the close correspondence between human and animal performance may break down is that of higher-level equivalence classification. For example, while infants have been shown to detect a correspondence between the vowel sounds /a/ or /i/ and the sight of a person producing them, a similar pattern in animals has not been reported.

13.4   The Role of Linguistic Experience in Speech Perception

So far, we have assumed that speaker and hearer speak the same native language. However, in many cultures, bilingualism or trilingualism is the norm; speakers may be equally proficient in both or all three languages, or have one dominant language. In addition, many people leave their native countries for ecological, political, educational, economic, or even touristic reasons. As a result, conversations in which some or all participants share a second language are always common in many areas of the world. Research on non-native production and perception of speech constitutes a relatively new area, known as the **phonetics of second language acquisition**. The study of non-native speech perception proper is often referred to as the study of **cross-language speech perception**. We will briefly review some of the issues in this area.

When an adult learns a second language (L2), the native language (L1) has already been firmly established over a number of years. A basic issue therefore concerns the extent to which this L1 system influences the perception of the L2. Early work on cross-language perception was dominated by the categorical perception paradigm. Research explored whether listeners with different native languages show any language-dependent differences in their placement of the voicing boundary along a VOT continuum. Specifically, a wide-ranging /ba/–/pa/ VOT continuum from −150 ms to +150 ms was presented to native speakers of English, Spanish, and Thai. As discussed in Section 6.3, word-initially, English contrasts plosives with a negative or short positive VOT to plosives with a long positive VOT, Spanish contrasts plosives with a negative VOT to plosives with a short positive VOT, and Thai makes a three-way distinction between plosives with a negative VOT, a short positive VOT, and a long positive VOT. Identification results showed that, when presented with the identical continuum, English listeners placed the bilabial voicing boundary at +20 ms, Spanish listeners at −5 ms, and Thai listeners showed two boundaries, one at −20 ms, the other at +40 ms. Results from additional discrimination experiments also showed that listeners only distinguished well between stimuli from different categories. English and Spanish listeners each showed two distinct categories and Thai listeners showed three distinct categories. In sum, the way in which listeners divide a continuum is determined by language-specific experience (Abramson and Lisker 1970; Williams 1977). Subsequent studies corroborated these findings for a variety of languages and consonantal distinctions.

The results raise the question of whether these perceptual patterns change as listeners gain more experience in the L2.

The ability to override or adapt L1 settings when processing L2 is thought to reflect the brain's **plasticity**, that is, its potential to reorganize its structure and function in response to experience. The notion of plasticity is closely tied to the **critical period hypothesis**, according to which there exists a particular window of opportunity during which native proficiency in a language can be obtained (Lenneberg 1967). There is as yet no consensus about the existence or duration of this critical period, but it is clear that there is a high degree of plasticity in the perceptual system, not only in infants and children, but in adults as well. Under optimal circumstances for L2 learning – that is, when L2 exposure begins at a very early age – near-native or native proficiency can be obtained. Research along these lines forms part of the study of **bilingualism**. However, research has shown that even L2 learners who have managed to distinguish difficult non-native contrasts may not use the same acoustic cues as natives (Underbakke et al. 1988).

For older children, modification of L1 patterns is possible with sufficient exposure. Research has shown that the more time Spanish-speaking children (ages 8–10 and 14–16) spent in the US, the more English-like their voicing boundary became. However, even after three years in the US, the Spanish children's voicing boundary still occurred at a substantially shorter VOT than that of monolingual American children (Williams 1979). For adults as well, perception can be substantially improved by means of a brief training regimen that focuses on a specific difficult L2 phoneme contrast. Ten to twenty hours of training in which participants are exposed to target speech sounds produced by a variety of speakers and in different phonetic contexts yield substantial improvement in participants' ability to perceive and even to produce difficult contrasts (Logan et al. 1991; Wang et al. 1999).

While children and adults show some malleability in their phonetic categories, infants as young as 2–4 months are sensitive to a great variety of subtle acoustic differences, regardless of whether these differences serve to differentiate phonemes in their ambient language. That is, infants categorically discriminate among the phonemes of their native language as well as many other non-native phonemes. This sensitivity, however, seems to weaken at the end of the first year of life. Thus, the native language acts as a filter in the first 12 months that emphasizes native sound contrasts while de-emphasizing non-native ones. For example, infants from both a Hindi- and an English-speaking environment discriminate a dental /t/ from a retroflex /ʈ/, two sounds that contrast phonemically in Hindi but not in English. However, while adult speakers of Hindi continue to distinguish these two sounds, adult speakers of English do not. It turns out that at age 10–12 months, English-speaking infants no longer discriminate the two sounds (Werker and Tees 1984; see Cheour et al. 1998 for a similar conclusion based on EEG).

Results from the perception of vowels show an influence of the native language at an even earlier age. In her research on the "perceptual magnet effect", Kuhl (Grieser and Kuhl 1989; Kuhl 1991) showed that both adults and infants find it more difficult to distinguish a prototypical instance of the vowel /i/ from variants that surround it in acoustic space as compared to distinguishing a non-prototypical instance of the vowel /i/ from its variants, even though the auditory distance between (non)prototype and variants is the same for both conditions. In Kuhl's terms, the prototype acts as a magnet, attracting other members of the category and thereby shrinking the space. Subsequently, this magnet effect was shown to be determined by the ambient language: American 6-month-olds showed a magnet effect for prototypical English /i/ but not for prototypical Swedish /y/. In contrast, Swedish 6-month-olds showed a magnet effect for prototypical Swedish /y/ but not for English /i/ (Kuhl et al. 1992). Thus, for vowel perception, the effect of language experience can be detected as early as 6 months.

Returning to adults, it is not the case that monolingual adults cannot distinguish among any non-native phonemes. While some non-native contrasts are discriminated poorly, others are discriminated at near native-like levels. It has been shown that the relation between the sound inventories of the L1 and L2 is a major predictor of the way in which an L2 phoneme will be perceived. There are currently two major models of L2 phonetic category acquisition, the perceptual assimilation model (PAM; Best 1994) and the speech learning model (SLM; Flege 1995). As emphasized by Best and Tyler (2007), PAM is a model of non-native speech perception by naïve listeners unfamiliar with the target language. Non-native contrasts are perceived in terms of their gestural similarity to the phonological categories in the native language. Consideration of the way in which the members of a contrastive pair of phones are perceptually assimilated allows PAM to make specific predictions about discrimination performance. Very good discrimination should obtain when the two non-native phones are perceived as exemplars of two different native phonemes ("two category" assimilation). Poor discrimination occurs when the two non-native phones are perceived as equally good (or poor) instances of the same native phoneme ("single category" assimilation). Intermediate discrimination is predicted when two non-native phones are perceived as instances of the same native phoneme but with different category goodness ratings ("category goodness" difference). In addition to these different degrees of assimilation, it is possible that one or both members of the pair are not perceived as instances of any native phoneme (are "uncategorized"). PAM predicts very good discrimination for categorized–uncategorized contrasts while discrimination of two uncategorized phones depends on the extent to which each phone maps on to a distinct native phoneme.

A classic example is the acquisition of the distinction between /ɹ/ and /l/ by Japanese learners of English. While Japanese has a sound resembling /ɹ/ (which is often realized as a retroflex tap /ɽ/) it does not have /l/ and Japanese learners have difficulty distinguishing the two (Strange 1992). According to PAM, this difficulty arises from the fact that both /ɹ/ and /l/ are treated as poor instances of the native Japanese /ɽ/ category, an instance of single-category assimilation. In contrast, native English speakers accurately distinguish the Zulu distinction between the voiceless lateral fricative /ɬ/ and its voiced counterpart /ɮ/. While neither fricative occurs in English, this is an example of two-category assimilation whereby English speakers map Zulu /ɬ/ onto English /s/ and Zulu /ɮ/ onto English /l/ (Best et al. 2001).

SLM is specifically concerned with ultimate attainment of L2 pronunciation and posits that errors in L2 production mostly have a perceptual basis. Like PAM, the relation between sounds in the native language and L2 plays an important role in the perception of non-native sounds. Unlike PAM, SLM does not specify whether this similarity is acoustic or articulatory in nature. SLM makes a distinction between "new" and "similar" phones. New L2 phones have no counterpart in the native language and therefore differ from all L1 phones. For example, the high front rounded French vowel [y] is a new phone for English learners of French. Similar L2 phones resemble but are not identical to L1 counterparts. Consider French /t/: although French /t/ is not identical to English /t/ since it is dental and unaspirated, it is clearly similar to English /t/. SLM predicts that the process of equivalence classification prevents L2 learners from creating a new category for similar, but not new, sounds. Thus, L2 learners are predicted not to achieve native-like pronunciation for similar phones. However, given sufficient exposure, L2 learners should be able to produce new phones authentically.

Research by Flege and colleagues has shown that there is indeed a difference in the acquisition of new and similar phones (e.g. Flege 1987). Advanced English learners of French mastered French /y/, a new phone, but not French /u/, a similar phone. Interestingly, not only do L1 categories affect L2 sounds: acquisition of L2 categories affects the production of L1 sounds as well. For example, native French speakers who had been living in the US for more than 10 years produced both English and French /t/ with VOT values in between the native norms for those two languages (Flege 1987).

For both PAM and SLM, the notion of phonetic similarity is crucial in predicting how listeners will treat L2 sounds. However, a clear empirical test for the assessment of phonetic similarity that is independent of L2 perceptual difficulties remains to be developed (see Strange 2007).

In sum, monolingual adult listeners have difficulty perceiving many non-native contrasts. However, perception is not uniformly poor. The perceptual difficulty that the adult listener encounters cannot be predicted solely on the basis of a comparison between the L1 and L2 phoneme inventories. Instead, research indicates that several other factors need to be taken into account, including the specific acoustic cues to mark a phonemic distinction, the allophonic distribution of phonetic segments in L1 and L2, the age of the speaker, as well as the amount of exposure to the L2, the quality of the L2 input, and the extent of usage of both the L1 and L2. Nevertheless, the perceptual system exhibits considerable plasticity such that phonetic categories can be modified even in adults.

13.5 Summary

The process by which listeners extract information from the speech signal, allowing them to comprehend the speaker's message, is complex and as yet not fully understood. While there is a reasonably good understanding of the acoustic cues to individual segments, there is debate as to whether these cues are variable or stable. Also, consensus on the basic units of speech perception is still lacking. An additional issue concerns the question of whether speech perception is based on general auditory mechanisms or on mechanisms that evolved especially for the processing of speech. Finally, while the perceptual system displays considerable plasticity, our native language affects the way in which we perceive speech.

Exercises

1   What are the arguments for and against extrinsic normalization? How does extrinsic normalization differ from point and range normalization?
2   What are the perceptual cues to place of articulation for fricatives? Where in a syllable are these cues located?
3   What are the perceptual cues to place and manner of articulation for plosives? Which cues are context-dependent? Give examples.
4   What is the motor theory of speech perception? In your description, include evidence supporting and opposing the theory.
5   What two types of experiments must be conducted in order to test categorical perception? Illustrate the use of these experiments with a "ba" to "pa" continuum. How does categorical perception differ from continuous perception?
6   What evidence is there that categorical perception is an innate feature of human language? How was that evidence collected? What evidence is there to the contrary?

7   What are the perceptual assimilation model and the speech learning model? How are they different? Would either or both of these models predict that American learners of Korean would have difficulty with the contrast between the rounded back vowel [u] and the unrounded back vowel [ɯ]? Explain your answer.

Note

1   Two corresponding pieces of reel-to-reel audio tape with the relevant signal portions were swapped with each other and joined together. Nowadays, splicing is done digitally, using a "cut and paste" action on the computer.

Appendix A

A.1 Mass, Force, and Pressure

The **mass** is determined by the substance matter of the object, or to be precise, by the molecules that form the object, which includes liquids and gases. The mass of an object remains the same, independent of its location, whether it is on earth, on another planet, or in zero gravity in space. Mass is measured in **grams (g)**.

The **weight** of an object is the force it exerts on a supporting surface. The weight depends on the *mass* of the object and on the *gravitational force* of the planet where the object is located. The gravitational force causes an object to accelerate toward the center of a planet. This acceleration even exists when the object is supported by a surface. In that case, the object does not move, since it is "restrained" by the supporting surface; as a result, it exerts a force upon the surface. This force is nothing else than its weight. The weight of an object is greater on earth than on the moon, because the gravitational force of the earth is stronger than the gravitational force of the moon. Force, and therefore weight as well, is measured in **newtons (N)**. One newton (1 N) is the force exercised by about 102 grams ($\approx$ 3.6 ounces) of matter upon its supporting surface, independent of the size of that surface. On earth, 1 kg of matter therefore weighs about 10 N.

On earth, the mass (in kg) of an object has to be multiplied by the gravitational force of the earth (9.81 m/s^2) in order to obtain the force (in newton) that the object exerts on a supporting surface. The value of 9.81 m/s^2 expresses the gravitational force of the earth: an object, when dropped from an airplane, increases its speed *every second* by 9.81 m/s (ignoring the air resistance). In other words, the object accelerates by 9.81 meters per second *per second*:

$$\frac{9.81 \, \text{m/s}}{\text{s}} = 9.81 \times \frac{\text{m}}{\text{s} \times \text{s}} = 9.81 \, \frac{\text{m}}{\text{s}^2}.$$

In everyday speech, we are mostly unaware of the distinction between *mass* (the "presence of matter") and *weight* (the force with which the matter is accelerated), since people do not usually move from one planet to another. A bathroom scale, for example, erroneously indicates weight in kg (that is, with the unit of measure of mass), although what it measures is in fact the force exerted by the person on the scale. (Displaying the weight in lbs actually hides the nature of the physical dimension because pounds are used for both mass and weight, confusing the matter even more.) This can be shown by using a scale, which usually has the unit "kg" for *mass* written on it, although it measures *force*. Placing a scale in an elevator and standing on it, it indicates a higher force when the elevator is accelerated upwards than when it starts to go down. In other words, the weight (measured in newton), exerted by a person as a function of her mass, changes according to whether the elevator goes up or down. But the mass of the person on the scale does not change with the direction of the elevator. The unit of measure "kg" printed on bathroom scales is therefore wrong, for in fact they measure a force in newton (N), not a mass in kilogram (kg). But since bathroom scales are seldom used in elevators or on other planets, this error usually goes unnoticed.

Pressure is force applied to a given surface. If a large force is applied to a small surface, the pressure is high; if the same force is applied to a large surface, the pressure is lower. This effect can be illustrated by means of a cone (Figure A.1). If the cone rests on its broad (flat) side, its weight is distributed over a large surface; the pressure applied to that surface is therefore low (Figure A.1a). But if the cone is turned upside down and put on its tip, its entire weight rests on a small surface; the pressure applied to that surface therefore is high (Figure A.1b). In both positions, the cone is exactly the same, with the same mass and the same weight, exerting the same force on its support. Only the size of the surface makes the difference between a high and a low pressure. Pressure is measured in **pascal (Pa)**.

One pascal is the pressure exerted by a force of one newton (N) on a surface of one square meter (1 Pa = 1 N/m^2 ≈ 0.0209 lbs/sqft ≈ 0.000145 psi). Thus, the term "air pressure" does not refer to the weight of the air (that is, to the force of the entire air mass pushing against the surface of the earth), but to the force exerted per unit of surface. In other words, each individual air molecule has a given mass; the gravitational force between the masses of the molecules and the

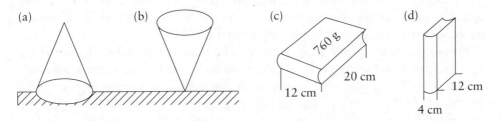

Figure A.1 Pressure changes for the same weight depending on the surface area.

earth gives it a certain weight. This weight causes the molecule to exert a force onto a small part of the surface of the earth, and this force, applied to a restricted surface, exerts a pressure on that surface.

An example should help to clarify the relation between pressure, force, and mass. Imagine a book with a mass of 760 grams, measuring 12 cm by 20 cm by 4 cm (Figure A.1c), lying flat on a table (its supporting surface being, therefore, 12 cm × 20 cm). What pressure does it apply to the table?

$$\text{pressure [Pa]} = \frac{\text{force [N]}}{\text{area [m}^2\text{]}} = \frac{\text{mass [kg]} \times \text{earth's acceleration [m/s}^2\text{]}}{\text{width [m]} \times \text{height [m]}}$$

$$= \frac{0.760 \text{ kg} \times 9.81 \text{ m/s}^2}{0.12 \text{ m} \times 0.2 \text{ m}} \approx \frac{7.5 \text{ N}}{0.024 \text{ m}^2} \approx 310.6 \text{ Pa}.$$

If the book is placed on its side (Figure A.1d), its supporting surface is reduced to 12 cm × 4 cm. The pressure of the book on the table is:

$$\text{pressure [Pa]} = \frac{\text{force [N]}}{\text{area [m}^2\text{]}} = \frac{0.760 \text{ kg} \times 9.81 \text{ m/s}^2}{0.12 \text{ m} \times 0.04 \text{ m}} \approx \frac{7.5 \text{ N}}{0.0048 \text{ m}^2} \approx 1,553 \text{ Pa}.$$

As can be seen, if the same force (here: the same weight of 7.5 N) applies to a smaller surface (the book standing on its side), the pressure exerted on that surface is higher. If the same force is distributed over a larger surface (the book lying flat on the table), the pressure is lower. This principle is important for understanding how the middle ear functions (Section 12.2.1).

To summarize: the pressure (in pascal) depends on the force (in newton) and the surface area (in square meters); the force, in turn, is determined by the mass (in kilogram) and the gravitational pull of the planet.

A.2   Energy, Power, and Intensity

The concepts of energy, intensity, and power are closely related. As a result, they are often confused. In addition, the everyday use of these terms is not always in agreement with their definition in physical terms.

Energy is a fundamental property. It can be transformed into different forms, for example, heat energy, electrical energy, kinetic energy (= energy of movement), potential energy (= energy of position), or transferred by a wave, but it cannot be "lost" or "generated." For example, a loudspeaker transforms electrical energy, which arrives through the loudspeaker cable from the amplifier, into heat energy (= warmth) and sound energy (= sound waves). The conversion into heat during this transformation is an undesirable effect. Of all the energy fed into a loudspeaker, only about 1 percent is transformed into sound energy and the rest into heat. Since so much heat is produced, loudspeakers can "blow out" when there is too much electrical energy. Nevertheless, electrical energy is transferred into acoustic energy. A sound wave therefore carries energy. Although the kinetic energy of the oscillating air molecules does play a role in the energy transmission, the sound wave does not transport any matter through the room, as is shown in Section 7.1.2.

Energy is a property of matter or waves.[1] It is measured in joules (J), a unit that can be derived from the units kilogram (kg), meter (m), and second (s), as follows:[2]

$$\text{energy [J]} = \text{mass [kg]} \times \text{velocity}^2 \text{ [m}^2\text{/s}^2\text{]}$$

$$= \text{mass [kg]} \times \text{acceleration [m/s}^2\text{]} \times \text{distance [m]}$$

$$= \text{force [N]} \times \text{distance [m]}.$$

This unit for energy and its relation to force and distance is not very intuitive. Consider the following example. An object lying on the floor has less potential energy than the same object lying on a table. The weight of the object (in newton, N) is almost the same in both cases; that is, its mass (in kg) multiplied by the gravitational force on earth. In fact, the weight is a bit less on the table, since the object is further away from the center of the earth. The major difference between the object on the floor and the one on the table is precisely the height, expressed in meters. The potential energy can be easily calculated by multiplying the weight of the object (in newton = kg × m/s^2) by the height (in meters). This is exactly what is expressed in the formula above: energy = force × distance (or, energy = mass × velocity^2).

Just like mass, energy is a dimension existing independently of time. An amount of matter, for example, one liter of paraffin, has a certain amount of energy. This energy can be delivered slowly, for instance if the paraffin is used for hours in a paraffin lamp, but it can be delivered very quickly, for instance in less than a second if the paraffin explodes. The energy embodied in one liter of paraffin is exactly the same in both cases – the only difference lies in the amount of energy delivered per unit of time. This dimension of "energy per time unit" is called **power**. If a large quantity of energy is transformed in a short period, this corresponds to high power. If the same amount of energy is distributed over a longer period, the power is lower.

The following image may help to understand this concept. Imagine someone carrying 1,000 kg from the ground floor up to the third floor of a house. A certain amount of energy is needed to do so, since the 1,000 kg possess more potential energy when they are on the third floor than when they are on the ground floor. This amount of energy depends only on the height, the gravitational force of the earth, and the mass. If someone carries the 1,000 kg up in a week, this does not require a lot of power since the energy is spread over a long time.

But carrying the same mass up to the third floor within an hour requires a large power. Power is measured in **Watt (W)**, and is nothing but energy per unit of time:

$$\text{power [W]} = \frac{\text{energy [J]}}{\text{time [s]}} = \frac{\text{force [N]} \times \text{distance [m]}}{\text{time [s]}}.$$

It should be noted that the unit Watt is used for other forms of energy. Electrical power, for example, is measured in Watt, as in the case of light bulbs. A 100 Watt light bulb transforms twice as much energy into light and heat as a 50 Watt bulb. (Note that the everyday expression "a light bulb consumes 100 Watt" is not correct from a physical point of view, since energy cannot be consumed; the 100 Watt are transformed into light (and heat) energy.) In order to obtain the total amount of energy transformed within a given period, the power (in Watt) is multiplied by the duration of this period (in seconds or hours). This leads to the unit "kilowatt-hour" (kWh), which is a measure of energy, since the power (which is energy per time unit) is multiplied by time:

$$\text{power [W]} \times \text{time [s]} = \frac{\text{energy [J]} \times \text{time [s]}}{\text{time [s]}} = \text{energy [J]}.$$

Writing "1 kWh" is just a different way of writing "3.6 million joule": 1 kWh = 1,000 Wh = 1,000 × 3,600 Ws = 3,600,000 J = 3.6 MJ.

Imagine a sound source located at a single point in a room. In the ideal case, the power of a sound, as emitted by this "zero-dimensional" loudspeaker, spreads equally fast in all directions. The spreading sound wave can be compared, in a sense, to a spherical surface moving away from the loudspeaker (its center). The further the sphere moves away from the loudspeaker, the larger its surface becomes. The **intensity** of the sound wave becomes lower the further it is removed from the center of the sound source. This is represented in Figure A.2. At a distance r from the loudspeaker, a sound reaches a surface, represented by a square with sides a. The surface of this square is $a \times a = a^2$. If the distance is then doubled to $2 \times r$, the sides of the square are doubled to $2 \times a$, which means that the surface is multiplied by 4: $(2 \times a) \times (2 \times a) = 4 \times a^2$. In other words, doubling the distance corresponds to multiplying the surface by four; that is, the surface increases by the square of the distance. For a surface of a fixed size, this

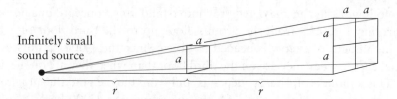

Figure A.2   Surface area increasing with the square of the distance.

implies that the intensity of the sound (the energy reaching the surface within a given time) decreases by the square of the distance between the surface and the sound source. At a distance $2 \times r$, the power affecting the surface $a \times a = a^2$ is only a quarter of the intensity affecting the same surface a^2 at a distance r. The dimension of intensity has no unit of its own; it is simply expressed in power (in Watts) per surface (in square meters):

$$\text{intensity} = \frac{\text{power [W]}}{\text{area [m}^2\text{]}} = \frac{\text{force [N]}}{\text{distance [m]} \times \text{time [s]}} = \frac{\text{mass [kg]}}{\text{time}^3 \text{ [s}^3\text{]}}.$$

In theory, a sound wave can spread infinitely far, although its intensity becomes infinitely low. But the sound energy of a sound wave is in fact continuously trans-formed into heat, so that after a certain time, the sound wave disappears since it has been entirely transformed into heat. The same principle is used in sound insulation: sound energy is not "destroyed"; it is instead transformed into heat. Since the amount of energy in a sound wave is very small, the sound-absorbing material does not become hot.

To summarize: energy is embodied in the presence of matter or a wave. It can be transformed into different forms, but it cannot disappear. Power is the amount of energy occurring during a given period of time. Intensity is power affecting a surface.

It should be noted that the energy of a sound wave is very small. In order to obtain a loudness sufficient for a living room, the amplifier of a stereo set pro-duces about 1 Watt of electrical power. Since only about 1 percent of the energy is transformed into sound energy by the loudspeaker, in a living room, the sound power is about 10 milliwatt. Even in a noisy disco, the sound power is just sufficient to illuminate a small lamp.

A.3   The Decibel (dB)

A measure (or, more precisely: a calculation rule) that is very important for sound is the decibel (dB). Decibels often appear in this book, and when you buy HiFi equipment or a dishwasher, or if you follow a discussion on noise pollution, the term "dB" pops up to express the loudness of an acoustic signal or the quality of a device that handles acoustic signals. A term that is often introduced in the latter case is the *signal-to-noise ratio* (S/N), which is given in decibels. This term expresses rather well what decibels are: a relation between two values; more specifically, the relation between a signal and noise. Nevertheless, the deriva-tion of this measure and the understanding of its "behavior" are not easy. We elaborate on this measure rather extensively because we know that the concept can be difficult to grasp.

We discuss the concept in many small steps that are supported by numerical examples. As a warning, while many numbers and formulas appear in the subsequent text, they should not distract but should serve to shed light on the subject area.

A.3.1   *RMS amplitude*

Amplitude is a rough measure to describe the loudness of a signal. The signal shown in Figure A.3a reaches its maximum amplitude only once, being quite small the rest of the time (see Section 7.3.2 for the definition of amplitude). Although the signal in Figure A.3b has the same amplitude as the one in Figure A.3a, it is near its maximum amplitude for a long time. On average, the signal of Figure A.3a is not as loud as the signal of Figure A.3b. Instead of measuring maximum amplitude, a different method to describe the loudness of a signal is needed.

One way to determine the loudness of a given signal is by adding up all the displacements as they can be seen in an oscillogram. However, this procedure does not work. On average, the movements "up" and "down" within a signal are similar in size, because each air density maximum is followed by a corresponding minimum. Simply adding up all positive and negative displacements leads to a sum that is always close to zero.

A second point to consider is the fact that it is very easy to move an air molecule just a little bit from its resting position, but that it requires more energy to move it further away. This fact must be reflected in the way of calculating loudness. A simple way of solving both problems, (1) adding up positive and negative values without the sum being zero, and (2) attaching a higher value to larger deviations, consists of squaring the deviations. This simply consists of multiplying each air pressure value by itself.[3]

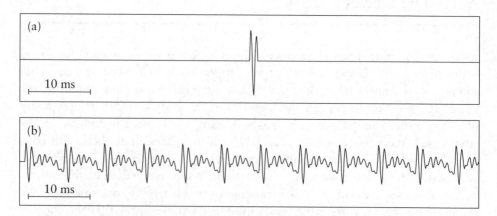

Figure A.3   Two signals with the same amplitude.

Two examples illustrate the squaring process. If at some point in a sound wave the air pressure (relative to the atmospheric air pressure) is −10 Pa, that is, the displacement measures −10 Pa, then the squared value is (−10 Pa) × (−10 Pa) = 100 Pa^2. If the air pressure is 0.01 Pa = 10 mPa, the squared value is 0.01 Pa × 0.01 Pa = 0.0001 Pa^2 = 0.1 mPa^2 = 100 μPa^2.

Adding up all squared displacements yields a measure that is related to the energy of the signal. This sum of course becomes larger when more displacements are taken into account. Therefore, this sum must be divided by the number of displacements that went into the sum – in other words, the "average sum" or "arithmetic mean" is calculated. And since the individual displacements have initially been squared, this has to be corrected by extracting the square root of the average sum. Finally, the "root of the mean of the squared values" or the root mean square (RMS) is obtained:

$$\text{RMS amplitude} = \sqrt{\frac{\text{sum of all squared displacements}}{\text{number of displacements}}} = \sqrt{\frac{\sum_{i=1}^{n} x_i^2}{n}}$$

(x_i being the value of the individual displacements, n the number of displacements; the notations Σ [the sum symbol] and x_i [to indicate variables] are discussed in Appendix B.2).

An example (see Figure A.4 and its corresponding calculation) should help to clarify this formula. It concerns a very simple and brief signal, which can be described by ten displacement values ($x_1 \ldots x_{10}$).

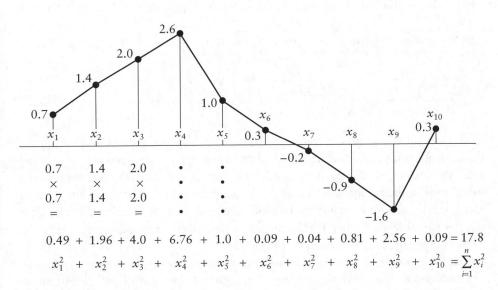

$$0.49 + 1.96 + 4.0 + 6.76 + 1.0 + 0.09 + 0.04 + 0.81 + 2.56 + 0.09 = 17.8$$

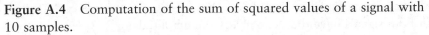

Figure A.4   Computation of the sum of squared values of a signal with 10 samples.

Inserting these values into the formula (17.8 being the sum of the squared values, 10 being the number of values) gives:

$$\sqrt{\frac{\sum_{i=1}^{10} x_i^2}{10}} = \sqrt{\frac{17.8 \text{ Pa}^2}{10}} = \sqrt{1.78 \text{ Pa}^2} \approx 1.3 \text{ Pa}.$$

For this example, the resulting RMS amplitude ("mean amplitude") is about 1.3 pascal.

Since the displacements are squared, large displacements become more prominent in comparison to the smaller ones. If two signals with equal amplitude are compared, the signal with the larger number of large displacements therefore has the higher RMS amplitude. Note that a signal which contains *many* large displacements contains high frequencies, because a high frequency means that something happens *often*. This may be clarified by the following example. A stretch of signal with an amplitude of 10 and the eight displacements 0, 5, 10, 5, 0, −5, −10, and −5, has the following RMS amplitude (see Figure A.5a):

$$\sqrt{\frac{0^2 + 5^2 + 10^2 + 5^2 + 0^2 + (-5)^2 + (-10)^2 + (-5)^2}{8}}$$

$$= \sqrt{\frac{0 + 25 + 100 + 25 + 0 + 25 + 100 + 25}{8}} = \sqrt{\frac{300}{8}} \approx 6.1.$$

Another signal with the same amplitude (10) and the displacements 0, 10, 0, −10, 0, 10, 0, and −10, has the following RMS amplitude (see Figure A.5b):

$$\sqrt{\frac{0^2 + 10^2 + 0^2 + (-10)^2 + 0^2 + 10^2 + 0^2 + (-10)^2}{8}}$$

$$= \sqrt{\frac{0 + 100 + 0 + 100 + 0 + 100 + 0 + 100}{8}} = \sqrt{\frac{400}{8}} \approx 7.1.$$

Therefore, signals with high frequency components have a higher RMS amplitude than signals with the same amplitude, but low frequency components. This may seem strange at first, but the reason is straightforward: if large displacements occur often (that is, their frequency is high) in a particular signal, then it obviously takes more energy to move the air molecules from their rest position and back. That is, that signal has a higher RMS amplitude than a comparable signal where the same displacement is reached less frequently.

The RMS amplitude provides us with a measure to compare the average amplitude of signals. For example, the signal in Figure A.3a has an RMS amplitude of 0.25 Pa, whereas the signal in Figure A.3b has an RMS amplitude of 1.10 Pa – although both signals have the same maximum amplitude of 2.70 Pa.

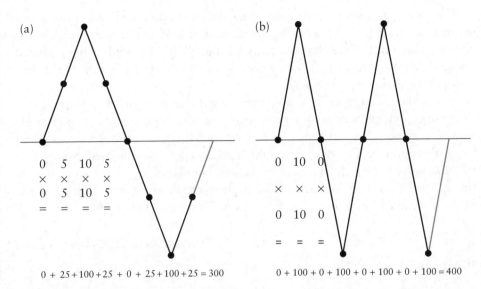

Figure A.5 Computation of the sum of squared values of (a) a low-frequency and (b) a high-frequency signal.

A.3.2 *RMS amplitude and loudness*

The RMS amplitude is a rough measure for loudness.[4] However, Weber and Fechner already established in the nineteenth century that people most often perceive change relatively, not absolutely. This phenomenon is familiar from sensory perception. For example, a weight of 2 kg seems considerably heavier than a weight of 1 kg, but the same difference of 1 kg is not perceived at all (or perceived only slightly) when lifting 51 kg as compared to 50 kg.

The same is true of loudness: in a silent environment, even small air pressure changes can be perceived, but in a noisy room, a large change is needed in order to evoke the same perception of difference. For example, the air pressure changes belonging to a sound wave with an RMS amplitude of 0.4 mPa are perceived to be twice as loud as those of a sound wave with an RMS amplitude of 0.2 mPa. However, a distinction between 20.4 mPa and 20.2 mPa cannot be perceived. In other words, we do not perceive *absolute* differences, but only *relative* distinctions.

A relative measure is usually represented as a ratio: 2 kg relative to 1 kg equals 2 kg/1 kg = 2; therefore 2 kg are two times as heavy as 1 kg. A weight of 51 kg, on the other hand, in comparison to a weight of 50 kg, gives 51 kg/50 kg = 1.02, and is therefore barely heavier. Along the same lines, an RMS amplitude of 0.4 mPa relative to 0.2 mPa is 0.4 mPa/0.2 mPa = 2. But an RMS amplitude of 20.4 mPa relative to 20.2 mPa is 20.4 mPa/20.2 mPa ≈ 1.01; it is therefore hardly louder. Although in absolute terms, the difference is the same in both cases (0.2 mPa), the ratio expresses the perceived difference in loudness between the sounds.

When using proportions, the units of measurement do not appear, irrespective of which units are used (e.g. pounds, pascal, micropascal, centimeters, inches, volts, or any other unit). Note that the units kg and Pa disappeared in the relations above. The ratio is just a number without any unit of measure specified. This fact proves very useful at a later stage.

Large values require larger changes than small values in order to be perceived to the same extent. Now consider a weight that is multiplied by ten (for example from 0.1 kg to 1 kg), and then multiplied by ten again (from 1 kg to 10 kg). Doing this multiplication twice has multiplied the weight by a hundred (from 0.1 kg to 10 kg) and *not* by twenty. If the weight is multiplied by ten yet another time (from 10 kg to 100 kg), then this triple multiplication has multiplied the original weight by one thousand, and so on. To summarize:

	Weight	Factor	Number of multiplications by ten
100 grams =	0.1 kg	1	0
	1 kg	10	1
	10 kg	100	2
	100 kg	1,000	3
	1,000 kg	10,000	4

Although the weight in this table has only been multiplied four times, it has increased from 0.1 kg to 1,000 kg; that is, it has been amplified by a factor of ten thousand. At the same time, we have the impression that the weight has only become four times heavier (if we were able to lift 1,000 kg).

Exactly the same is true for loudness. The following table contains the air pressure variations necessary to make a listener perceive an increase in loudness by a factor of ten. The first entry in the table is the lowest loudness value that can be perceived by a human being under ideally silent conditions (20 µPa); the last entry is the highest loudness that can be tolerated by a human. This gives the following:

Air pressure		Factor	Number of multiplications by ten
20 µPa =	0.00002 Pa	1	0
200 µPa =	0.0002 Pa	10	1
2 mPa =	0.002 Pa	100	2
20 mPa =	0.02 Pa	1,000	3
200 mPa =	0.2 Pa	10,000	4
	2 Pa	100,000	5
	20 Pa	1,000,000	6

Thus, if a listener has only six times the impression that a sound has become ten times as loud, the air pressure amplitude is in fact a million times greater.

As stated before, the impact of a particular percept does not depend on its absolute value, but on its level relative to an initial value. Instead of just measuring absolute air pressure amplitudes in pascal, it is therefore more useful to calculate their relation to an initial value, or alternatively, the number of times an initial value has been multiplied by ten. The latter principle of "counting the number of multiplications" is exactly the effect of the logarithmic function. For example, entering the number 1,000 on a calculator and then pressing the "log" button gives the number 3, indicating that the number 10 needs to be multiplied by 10 three times to yield the number 1,000.[5]

We have now introduced almost all the factors needed to calculate the loudness of a signal. To do so, we need to take the ratio of the signal amplitude and the minimal perceivable amplitude, and calculate the logarithm of the value thus obtained:

$$\log\left(\frac{\text{RMS amplitude}}{\text{minimal perceivable RMS amplitude}}\right).$$

The unit of this calculation is called the Bel. This unit essentially expresses the number of times the denominator (under the division line) has to be multiplied by ten in order to obtain the value of the numerator (above the division line). Since this results in very low values (6 Bel being the proportion between the maximum loudness which can be tolerated and the minimum loudness which is just perceivable), the obtained value is always multiplied by 10. The resulting unit is then "one tenth of a Bel," and is therefore called the decibel (dB) (that is, 6 Bel are 60 decibel).

It is important at this stage to take into account an effect which has already been mentioned in the description of the RMS amplitude: large deviations from the atmospheric air pressure are much more prominent than small deviations. For this reason, the amplitude values are squared whenever a loudness is being calculated, and this applies to the calculation of dB values. In addition, a value in decibels may be calculated with reference values other than the "minimum perceivable RMS amplitude" of 20 μPa. In principle, any amplitude may serve as reference value; this of course causes the dB value to change, but it does not affect the nature of the formula. In phonetics, the most common formula to calculate loudness is:[6]

$$10 \times \log\left(\frac{\text{RMS amplitude}}{\text{RMS reference amplitude}}\right)^2 = 20 \times \log\left(\frac{\text{RMS amplitude}}{\text{RMS reference amplitude}}\right).$$

Note that this formula only contains a generic reference to an "RMS reference amplitude." This expresses the fact that it is not important whether the calculation is based on sound pressures (in pascal), microphone output (in volts), distances within an oscillogram (in centimeters or inches), or any other dimension expressed in any unit of measure, since the unit of measure itself is canceled out in the calculation of the decibel values. If the calculation is performed on sound pressure values, and if the reference amplitude is set to be the lowest perceivable RMS amplitude (20 μPa), then the formula is said to express the sound pressure level (SPL), indicated as dB_{SPL}.

When using dB values, the kind of decibels used must be indicated, since the term decibel only says that the logarithm of a proportion, multiplied by ten, has been taken. For example, dB_{SPL} (*decibel, sound pressure level*) should be specified for the sound pressure level, or dB_{RMS} (*decibel, root-mean-squared amplitude*) for the RMS amplitude, or dB_A for an intensity which corresponds approximately to the subjective impression of loudness, taking the differential sensitivity of the human hearing system to lower and higher amplitudes into account.

The existence of different dB scales may seem confusing, but it has an important advantage. Since dB values express a proportion between two values whose units of measurement disappear during the calculation of the ratio (see above), it is easy to compare dB values obtained from different physical domains. The sound pressure level, for example, is a proportion between air pressure differences, but in a microphone the air pressure is transformed into electrical voltage (volt) or current (ampere). Calculating the dB values enables us to compare the microphone data with the air pressure data, although they represent entirely different physical dimensions. In a graphical representation, the values are measured in centimeters or inches; with the dB scale, these values can also be directly compared to the air pressure differences.

An important advantage of the dB scale is the fact that it makes use of proportions rather than absolute values. Someone who makes a recording on a recorder first selects an appropriate recording level by turning a knob. Then, during playback, the person turns the volume control in order to obtain a comfortable listening level. This process of setting recording and playback levels alters of course the absolute loudness values, but it does not change the relation between loud and soft passages. Thus, the dB scale makes it possible to calculate the relative amplitude characteristics of a signal, without any reference to the setting of the recording and playback levels.

Finally, it is important to note that "dB" is not a unit of measurement like "meter," which is a unit of measurement for the dimension "length," but dB is a calculation convention. But just as "length" can be expressed in different units, such as meter, inch, or mile, proportions can be expressed in different kinds of dB values, such as dB_{RMS} or dB_{SPL}.

A.3.3 *Calculations with dB values*

The derivation of the dB scale is a bit complicated, since it expresses a proportion to a reference value and uses a logarithm in its formula. Performing calculations with dB values has some peculiarities that do not occur with units of measure like "meter" or "inch." This section presents two important points to keep in mind when working with dB values.

First, as the calculations are based on proportions, there is no absolute zero point. This means that a statement like "the sound pressure level is 0 dB$_{SPL}$" does not mean that there is no sound pressure (which is relative in any case to the atmospheric air pressure of 1,013 hPa). This statement only means that the sound pressure equals the minimum perceivable sound pressure, 20 µPa, but it is *not* 0 µPa.[7] This is comparable to measuring temperature in degrees Celsius or Fahrenheit. The statement "the temperature is 0 °C" does not mean that there is no temperature, but only that the temperature is equal to a given reference temperature.

Just like temperature values, dB values can be negative. That is, if the sound pressure is lower than the reference value, the ratio of sound pressure and reference pressure is smaller than 1, and the corresponding logarithm is negative. For example:

$$20 \times \log\left(\frac{10\ \mu Pa}{20\ \mu Pa}\right) = 20 \times \log(0.5)\ dB_{SPL} \approx 20 \times (-0.3010)\ dB_{SPL} \approx -6\ dB_{SPL}.$$

Second, if the sound pressure becomes twice as high, this does *not* mean that the corresponding dB value is multiplied by two. In fact, doubling the sound pressure corresponds to an increase of the sound pressure level by approximately 6 dB:[8]

$$20 \times \log\left(\frac{\text{double sound pressure}}{\text{given sound pressure}}\right) = 20 \times \log\left(\frac{2 \times \text{given sound pressure}}{\text{given sound pressure}}\right)$$

$$= 20 \times \log(2)\ dB \approx 20 \times 0.3010\ dB \approx 6\ dB.$$

Thus, doubling the sound pressure corresponds to an increase of the sound pressure level by approximately 6 dB. If the sound pressure becomes four times as high, the sound pressure level increases by about 12 dB; if it becomes eight times as high, the sound pressure level increases by 18 dB, etc. Each time the sound pressure is doubled, the sound pressure level increases by about 6 dB. The same holds true for a reduction in sound pressure level.

$$20 \times \log\left(\frac{\text{halved sound pressure}}{\text{given sound pressure}}\right) = 20 \times \log\left(\frac{0.5 \times \text{given sound pressure}}{\text{given sound pressure}}\right)$$

$$= 20 \times \log(0.5)\ dB \approx 20 \times (-0.3010)\ dB \approx -6\ dB.$$

Thus, halving the sound pressure corresponds to a reduction of the sound pressure level by approximately 6 dB; reducing it to one fourth of the original level corresponds to a reduction of about 12 dB, etc.

Another behavior that runs counter to "normal" intuition about numbers is the way dB values behave when two signals are added. When adding signals, phase plays a crucial role. If both signals are in phase and have a sound pressure level of, for example, 0 dB (that is, the signals are as large as their reference value), then the sound pressure of the sum of the signals is 6 dB. On the other hand, two signals with opposite phase cancel each other out completely. Even if they each have a sound pressure of, for example, 70 dB, their sum has a value of "infinite" since the sound pressure value of the added signal (which is canceled out) is "0" and the logarithm of "0" is actually not defined.

In general, when computing with dB values, it helps to think of "signals" that are added and not numbers that are added. As a last example, consider two signals in phase, one with a sound pressure of 70 dB and the other with a sound pressure of 58 dB. Adding them leads to a signal with a sound pressure of less than 72 dB, as the following formulas show:

70 dB = 20 × log(3,162); 58 dB = 20 × log(794);

20 × log(3,162 + 794) = 20 × log(3,956) ≈ 72 dB.

As mentioned before, the derivation and calculation of the dB scale is not easy and may not be immediately understood by everyone. If that is the case, there is no need to worry: an understanding of the dB scale is not essential to understanding this book, even though this particular scale is used a lot in phonetics. Just remember that the dB scale is a universal scale which facilitates the representation of amplitude differences. On the dB scale that is used throughout this book, an increase of 6 dB always means that the sound pressure becomes twice as high.

Notes

1   It is the wave itself which carries the energy, not the molecules involved in the transmission. This is obvious in the case of electromagnetic waves, such as light, which carry energy even when they pass through a complete vacuum, where no matter is present at all.
2   Often the unit "calorie" is used to measure energy, where 1 cal ≈ 4.19 J.
3   A more profound reason for squaring the displacements is the fact that the speed of the oscillating molecules is influenced by the amplitude and the frequency of a wave, as already mentioned in Section 7.3.2.
4   Loudness, like any other percept, is a subjective impression which cannot be deduced directly from a physical measure (see Section 12.6). However, the subjective impression can be estimated from a physical value, as is done in this chapter.
5   In case the value "6.9077..." appears on the display of the calculator, it uses the so-called "natural" logarithm, not the logarithm to the base 10 which is used here. In order to transform a value from the natural logarithm into the logarithm to the base 10, it has to be multiplied by 0.4343: 6.9077 × 0.4343 ≈ 3.
6   Without going into the mathematical rules for calculating powers and logarithms, it is sufficient to accept that $(a^2/b^2) = (a/b)^2$, and $\log(a^2) = 2 \times \log(a)$.
7   $20 \times \log(20\ \mu Pa/20\ \mu Pa) = 20 \times \log(1)\ dB_{SPL} = 20 \times 0\ dB_{SPL} = 0\ dB_{SPL}$.
8   In an intensity dB scale, doubling the intensity means an increase in 3 dB.

Appendix B

B.1 Physical Terminology

In physics, a distinction is made between a *dimension* that is being measured, and the *unit of measurement* used to express that particular dimension.

Dimensions, such as speed, distance, or time, are indicated by abbreviations of Latin terms. For example, c for celeritas (speed), v for *velocitas* (velocity, speed with a direction), l for *longitudo* (distance), s for *spatium* (displacement, distance with a direction), and t for *tempus* (time) are used.

These abbreviations should be distinguished from the **units** in which the dimensions are measured. These are often surrounded by square brackets: m for *meter*, s for *secundus*, Hz for *Hertz*, and so forth. A distance l is therefore measured in meters [m], a time t in seconds [s]. Table B.1 gives an overview of several important dimensions and their units of measure.

To avoid writing too many zeros, scaling factors are commonly used. These are Greek or Italian words which are put before the unit. For example, "1,000" is indicated by the letter **k** (for "kilo"). Instead of writing "1,000 g" one can write "1 kg." The most common scaling factors are listed in Table B.2. Note that *billion* means something different in British and American English.

It should be noted that in computer terms, indications like kilo, mega, giga, or tera are not based on thousands (1,000), but on units of 1,024, which is a "natural" multiple for computers.[1] Since these units are almost equal to thousands, the same Greek words and letters are used – but they are written in uppercase: K for kilo in computer terms ($= 1,024 = 2^{10} \approx 10^3$), M for mega ($= 1,024 \times 1,024 = 2^{20} \approx 10^6$), G for giga ($= 2^{30} \approx 10^9$), and **T** for tera ($= 2^{40} \approx 10^{12}$). The factor "m" may lead to some confusion: a lower case m indicates "milli-" (one thousandth), whereas an uppercase M means either "mega-" (one million = 1,000,000), or the computer-based multiple "Mega-" ($2^{20} = 1,048,576$).

Some examples:

- A distance l can be measured in thousandths of a meter (millimeter [mm]).
- Pressure is indicated by p; 1 µPa is one millionth of a pascal.
- A frequency f of one thousand oscillations per second corresponds to **1 kHz**.

Table B.1   Physical units: their names, derivations, dimensions, and symbols along with their units

Dimension		Symbol	Unit	Formula
Distance		l	Meter	[m]
Mass		m	Kilogram	[kg]
Time		t	Second	[s]
Area		$A = l^2$	Square meter	[m²]
Frequency	Cycles per second	$f = \dfrac{1}{t}$	Hertz	$[Hz] = \dfrac{1}{[s]}$
Speed	Distance per time	$c = \dfrac{l}{t}$	Meter per second	$\dfrac{[m]}{[s]}$
Acceleration	Change of speed per time	$a = \dfrac{\Delta c}{t}$	Meter per second squared	$\dfrac{[m]}{[s^2]}$
Force		$F = m \times a^2$	Newton	$[N] = \dfrac{[kg \times m]}{[s^2]}$
Pressure	Force per area	$p = \dfrac{F}{A}$	Pascal	$[Pa] = \dfrac{[kg]}{[m \times s^2]}$
Energy (work)	Force by distance	$E = m \times c^2$ $= P \times t$ $= F \times l$	Joule Wattseconds Newtonmeters	$[J] = [Ws] = [Nm] = \dfrac{[kg \times m^2]}{[s^2]}$
Power	Work per time	$P = \dfrac{E}{t}$	Watt	$[W] = \left[\dfrac{J}{s}\right] = \dfrac{[kg \times m^2]}{[s^3]}$
Intensity	Power per area	$I = \dfrac{P}{A}$	Watt per square meter	$\left[\dfrac{W}{m^2}\right] = \dfrac{[kg]}{[s^3]}$
(Level)			Decibel (formula, not a unit)	[dB]

In addition to these physical dimensions, some dimensions indicate subjective impressions, for example loudness, pitch, and timbre. In principle, these dimensions can only be measured by means of experiments in which judgments are obtained from listeners. However, once these experiments have been conducted, formulas may be found that approximate the physical dimensions and units (for example, frequency in Hertz) on the basis of the corresponding subjective dimensions and units (for example perceived pitch in Bark). Table B.3 gives an overview of the most common subjective units. Section 12.6 introduces some formulas that are used to approximate the corresponding physical dimensions.

Table B.2 Scaling factors: their abbreviations, Greek or Italian origin, British and American names, the number and the representation as a power of 10

Abbreviation	Greek/ Italian	British	American	Number	Power
t	Tera	Billion	Trillion	1,000,000,000,000	10^{12}
g	Giga	Milliard	Billion	1,000,000,000	10^{9}
M	Mega	Million	Million	1,000,000	10^{6}
k	Kilo	Thousand	Thousand	1,000	10^{3}
h	Hecto	Hundred	Hundred	100	10^{2}
da	Deca	Ten	Ten	10	10^{1}
d	Deci	Tenth	Tenth	0.1	10^{-1}
c	Centi	Hundredth	Hundredth	0.01	10^{-2}
m	Milli	Thousandth	Thousandth	0.001	10^{-3}
μ	Micro	Millionth	Millionth	0.000001	10^{-6}
n	Nano	Milliardth	Billionth	0.000000001	10^{-9}
p	Pico	Billionth	Trillionth	0.000000000001	10^{-12}

Table B.3 Physical dimensions and levels with their units and their subjective equivalents

Physical		Perceptual	
Dimension/level	Unit	Dimension	Unit
Length in time	Seconds [s]	Duration	–
Fundamental frequency	Hertz [Hz]	Pitch	mel $bark_{CB}$ $bark_{ERB}$
Sound pressure level	dB_{SPL} dB_{RMS}	Loudness	dB_A phon sone

B.2 Mathematical Notations

In mathematics, a simplified notation is used to represent systematic sums calculated by adding up all the numbers of a series (in mathematical terms, this is called a *sequence*). For example, if all the pressure values as measured by a barometer are added up, one possibility is to write the measures in a table (Table B.4).

Table B.4 Example of a table of air pressure measurements, when they were taken, and the number of measurements

Number of measurement	Time and date	Value (hPa)
1	6:00 am, May 2, 2004	1,015
2	6:00 am, May 3, 2004	1,023
3	6:00 am, May 4, 2004	1,031
4	6:00 am, May 5, 2004	927
5	6:00 am, May 6, 2004	986

Table B.5 Addition of five air pressure measurements

First measurement	Second measurement	Third measurement	Fourth measurement	Fifth measurement	Sum
1,015 +	1,023 +	1,031 +	927 +	986 =	4,982

In order to calculate the average pressure of this series, one then adds up all measures (Table B.5).

Finally, the sum must be divided by the number of measurements:

$$\frac{4,982}{5} = 996.4.$$

In more general terms, this procedure can be represented as follows:

$$\text{average air pressure} = \frac{\text{1st + 2nd + 3rd + 4th + 5th measurement}}{5}$$

It is useful to make this procedure more general, so that it can be used for any number of measures, not just five. In everyday language this gives something like:

"Add up all measures, and divide this sum by the number of measurements."

In a simple case such as this, this sentence is perfectly understandable. But if more complex calculations are involved, a formulation in everyday terms can become very unclear. This is precisely the reason why symbols are used in mathematics, for example, "+" for "plus" and "×" for "times". The operation "add up all numbers" has its own mathematical symbol, the Greek symbol for "S" as an abbreviation for "sum": Σ. When using this symbol it is necessary, of course, to specify exactly which numbers are to be added up, and what "all" means. Since measures (or any other series of values) can be indicated by a serial number (1st measure, 2nd measure, etc.), it is sufficient to specify the index of the value (that is, which place it occupies in the series), and the total number of measures. The index is usually indicated by the letter *i* (for *index*), whereas the total number of values is indicated by *n* (for *numerus*).

In mathematical notation, the phrase "add up all measurements" (or, more precisely, "add up all measured values from measurement '1' up to measurement 'n'") is expressed as follows:

$$\sum_{i=1}^{n} x_i.$$

Dividing this sum by the number of measures (*n*) is simply expressed as follows:

$$\frac{\sum_{i=1}^{n} x_i}{n}.$$

For the example given above, this abstract notation is then put to use by filling in the five real, measured values:

$$\frac{\sum_{i=1}^{5} x_i}{5} = \frac{1{,}015 + 1{,}023 + 1{,}031 + 927 + 986}{5} = 996.4.$$

This notation has the important advantage of avoiding any possible confusion as to how values are calculated, whereas a formulation in everyday language usually allows for several interpretations, which may lead to errors.

Note

---

1 Digital computers operate on the basis of the number "2." One obtains 1,024 by multiplying the number "2" by itself ten times: $1{,}024 = 2^{10} = 2 \times 2 \times 2 \times 2 \times 2 \times 2 \times 2 \times 2 \times 2 \times 2 \times 2$.

Appendix C

C.1 Formant Frequency Values

Table C.1 Formant frequency values for 10 vowels of American English, as produced by children, female adults, male adults, and the means of these three groups, according to research by Peterson and Barney (1952; P&B), and by Hillenbrand et al. (1995; HGCW). Peterson and Barney measured wide-band spectrograms, while Hillenbrand et al. determined the formant frequency values by calculating LPC spectra. Although the results of both investigations differ in some respects, they show similar tendencies for individual vowels

	Gender	Investi-gation	Vowel									
			i	ɪ	ɛ	æ	ɑ	ʌ	ɔ	ʊ	u	ɚ
F1	Child	P&B	360	534	700	1,017	1,030	855	694	560	432	569
		HGCW	452	513	740	718	992	738	836	571	493	586
	Female	P&B	310	441	608	863	864	758	587	469	378	503
		HGCW	437	484	727	676	921	760	804	519	460	524
	Male	P&B	267	392	526	664	718	631	568	437	307	489
		HGCW	343	429	588	591	756	621	656	469	380	475
	x̄		362	464	648	749	886	729	679	504	405	522
F2	Child	P&B	3,178	2,744	2,616	2,334	1,383	1,592	1,064	1,402	1,193	1,806
		HGCW	3,073	2,556	2,279	2,497	1,689	1,538	1,303	1,506	1,404	1,721
	Female	P&B	2,783	2,474	2,334	2,049	1,229	1,409	915	1,162	961	1,641
		HGCW	2,761	2,369	2,063	2,335	1,526	1,416	1,188	1,229	1,106	1,588
	Male	P&B	2,323	2,034	1,803	1,930	1,309	1,181	1,023	1,123	992	1,379
		HGCW	2,294	1,993	1,854	1,727	1,091	1,192	836	1,023	876	1,360
	x̄		2,744	2,367	2,154	2,142	1,370	1,395	1,024	1,231	1,066	1,556
F3	Child	P&B	3,763	3,604	3,564	3,366	3,188	3,328	3,263	3,332	3,250	2,194
		HGCW	3,702	3,409	3,297	3,289	2,937	3,126	2,951	3,076	2,992	2,154
	Female	P&B	3,312	3,063	2,999	2,832	2,783	2,768	2,736	2,685	2,666	1,977
		HGCW	2,273	3,057	2,953	2,973	2,832	2,901	2,834	2,829	2,735	1,930
	Male	P&B	2,937	2,569	2,481	2,420	2,442	2,377	2,403	2,245	2,239	1,709
		HGCW	3,001	2,687	2,604	2,595	2,535	2,548	2,521	2,435	2,355	1,711
	x̄		3,346	3,065	2,991	2,902	2,790	2,863	2,774	2,764	2,703	1,930

C.2 Fundamental Frequency Values

Table C.2 Fundamental frequency values for 10 vowels of American English, as produced by children, female adults, and male adults, according to research by Peterson and Barney (1952; P&B), and by Hillenbrand et al. (1995; HGCW). Column x̄ contains the averaged values of the three groups. It clearly shows that children have the highest fundamental frequency, while male speakers have the lowest F_0. In addition, the "high" vowels [i, ɪ, u, ʊ] can be seen to have higher mean values for fundamental frequency than the lower vowels [ɛ, æ, ɑ, ʌ, ɔ]

	Gender	Investigation	Vowel										
			i	ɪ	ɛ	æ	ɑ	ʌ	ɔ	ʊ	u	ɚ	x̄
F_0	Child	P&B	272	269	260	251	256	261	263	276	274	261	249
		HGCW	246	241	230	228	229	236	225	243	249	236	
	Female	P&B	235	232	223	210	212	221	216	232	231	218	221
		HGCW	227	224	214	215	215	218	210	230	235	217	
	Male	P&B	136	135	130	127	124	130	129	137	141	133	131
		HGCW	138	135	127	123	123	133	121	133	143	130	
		x̄	209	206	197	192	193	200	194	208	212	199	

References

Abramson, A.S., and Lisker, L. (1970). Discriminability along the voicing continuum: Cross-language tests. In *Proceedings of the Sixth International Congress of Phonetic Sciences*. Prague: Academia, pp. 569–573.

Behrens, S., and Blumstein, S.E. (1988). Acoustic characteristics of English voiceless fricatives: A descriptive analysis. *Journal of Phonetics* 16, 295–298.

Békésy, G. von (1928). Zur Theorie des Hörens: Die Schwingungsform der Basilarmembran. *Physikalische Zeitschrift* 22, 793–810.

Best, C.T. (1994). The emergence of native-language phonological influences in infants: A perceptual assimilation model. In J.C. Goodman and H.C. Nusbaum (eds.), *The development of speech perception: The transition from speech sounds to spoken words*. Cambridge, MA: MIT Press, pp. 167–224.

Best, C.T., and Tyler, M.D. (2007). Nonnative and second-language speech perception: Commonalities and complementarities. In O.S. Bohn and M.J. Munro (eds.), *Language experience in second language speech learning: In honor of James Emil Flege*. Amsterdam: John Benjamins, pp. 13–34.

Best, C.T., McRoberts, G.W., and Goodell, E. (2001). Discrimination of non-native consonant contrasts varying in perceptual assimilation to the listener's native phonological system. *Journal of the Acoustical Society of America* 109, 775–794.

Bjuggren, G., and Fant, G. (1965). The nasal cavity structures. *Quarterly Progress and Status Report*, Royal Institute of Technology, Stockholm, pp. 5–7.

Blumstein, S.E., and Stevens, K.N. (1979). Acoustic invariance in speech production: Evidence from measurements of the spectral characteristics of stop consonants. *Journal of the Acoustical Society of America* 66, 1001–1017.

Broad, D.J. (1973). Phonation. In F.D. Minifie, T.J. Hixon, and F. Williams (eds.), *Normal aspects of speech, hearing and language*. Englewood Cliffs, NJ: Prentice-Hall, pp. 127–167.

Broad, D.J. (1979). The new theories of vocal fold vibration. In N. Lass (ed.), *Speech and language: Advances in basic research and practice*, vol. 2. New York: Academic Press, pp. 203–256.

Carr, P. (1999). *English phonetics and phonology: An introduction*. Oxford: Blackwell.

Cheour, M., Ceponiene, R., Lehtokoski, A., Luuk, A., Allik, J., Alho, K., and Näätänen, R. (1998). Development of language-specific phoneme representations in the infant brain. *Nature Neuroscience* 1, 351–353.

Chiba, T., and Kajiyama, M. (1941). *The vowel: Its nature and structure*. Tokyo: Tokyo-Kaiseikan.

Cho, T., Jun, S., and Ladefoged, P. (2002). Acoustic and aerodynamic correlates of Korean stops and fricatives. *Journal of Phonetics* 30, 193–228.

Cole, R.A., and Scott, B. (1974). Toward a theory of speech perception. *Psychological Review* 81, 348–374.

Cooper, W.E., and Sorensen, J.M. (1977). Fundamental frequency contours at syntactic boundaries. *Journal of the Acoustical Society of America* 62, 683–692.

Dang, J., Honda, K., and Suzuki, H. (1994). Morphological and acoustical analysis of the nasal and the paranasal cavities. *Journal of the Acoustical Society of America* 96, 2088–2100.

Delattre, P.C., Liberman, A.M., and Cooper, F.S. (1955). Acoustic loci and transitional cues for consonants. *Journal of the Acoustical Society of America* 27, 769–773.

Dorman, M.F., Studdert-Kennedy, M., and Raphael, L.J. (1977). Stop-consonant recognition: Release bursts and formant transitions as functionally equivalent, context-dependent cues. *Perception & Psychophysics* 22, 109–122.

Eimas, P.D., Siqueland, E.R., Jusczyk, P.W., and Vigorito, J. (1971). Speech perception in infants. *Science* 171, 303–306.

Ferrein, M.A. (1741). *De la formation de la voix de l'homme*. Recueil de l'Académie Royale des Sciences de Paris, 402–432.

Flanagan, J.L., and Landgraf, L. (1968). Self-oscillating source for vocal tract synthesizers. *IEEE Transactions Audio and Electroacoustics* AU-16, 57–64.

Flege, J.E. (1987). The production of "new" and "similar" phones in a foreign language: Evidence for the effect of equivalence classification. *Journal of Phonetics* 15, 47–65.

Flege, J.E. (1995). Second language speech learning: Theory, findings, and problems. In W. Strange (ed.), *Speech perception and linguistic experience: Issues in cross-language research*. Baltimore, MD: York Press, pp. 233–278.

Fletcher, H. (1940). Auditory patterns. *Reviews of Modern Physics* 12, 47–65.

Forrest, K., Weismer, G., Milenkovic, P., and Dougall, R.N. (1988). Statistical analysis of word-initial voiceless obstruents: Preliminary data. *Journal of the Acoustical Society of America* 84, 115–123.

Fowler, C.A. (1986). An event approach to the study of speech perception from a direct-realist perspective. *Journal of Phonetics* 14, 3–28.

Fowler, C.A. (2003). Speech production and perception. In A. Healy and R. Proctor (eds.), *Handbook of psychology*, vol. 4: *Experimental psychology*. New York: John Wiley & Sons, pp. 237–266.

Grieser, D., and Kuhl, P.K. (1989). Categorization of speech by infants: Support for speech-sound prototypes. *Developmental Psychology* 25, 577–588.

Handbook of the International Phonetic Association: A guide to the use of the International Phonetic Alphabet (1999). Cambridge: Cambridge University Press.

Harris, F.J. (1978). On the use of windows for harmonic analysis with the discrete fourier transform. *Proceedings of the IEEE* 66, 51–83.

Harris, K.S. (1958). Cues for the discrimination of American English fricatives in spoken syllables. *Language and Speech* 1, 1–7.

Hayes, B. (1995). *Metrical stress theory: Principles and case studies*. Chicago, IL: University of Chicago Press.

Hayes, B., and Lahiri, A. (1991). Bengali intonational phonology. *Natural Language and Linguistic Theory* 9, 47–96.

Hedrick, M.S., and Ohde, R.N. (1993). Effect of relative amplitude of frication on perception of place of articulation. *Journal of the Acoustical Society of America* 94, 2005–2026.

Heinz, J.M., and Stevens, K.N. (1961). On the properties of voiceless fricative consonants. *Journal of the Acoustical Society of America* 33, 589–596.

Helmholtz, H. von (1863). *Die Lehre von den Tonempfindungen als physiologische Grundlage für die Theorie der Musik*. Braunschweig: Vieweg.

Hillenbrand, J.M., and Nearey, T.M. (1999). Identification of resynthesized /hVd/ utterances: Effects of formant contour. *Journal of the Acoustical Society of America* 105, 3509–3523.

Hillenbrand, J.M., Getty, L.A., Clark, M.J., and Wheeler, K. (1995). Acoustic characteristics of American English vowels. *Journal of the Acoustical Society of America* 97, 3099–3111.

Hirano, M. (1974). Morphological structure of the vocal cord as a vibrator and its variations. *Folia Phoniatrica* 26, 89–94.

Hirsch, I.J. (1959). Auditory perception of temporal order. *Journal of the Acoustical Society of America* 31, 759–767.

Holt, L.L., Lotto, A.J., and Diehl, R.L. (2004). Auditory discontinuities interact with categorization: Implications for speech perception. *Journal of the Acoustical Society of America* 116, 1763–1773.

Hombert, J.M. (1978). Consonant types, vowel quality and tone. In V. Fromkin (ed.), *Tone: A linguistic survey*. New York: Academic Press, pp. 77–111.

Hughes, A., and Trudgill, P. (1996). *English accents and dialects: An introduction to social and regional varieties of British English*. London: Edward Arnold.

Husson, R. (1950). Étude des phénomènes physiologiques et acoustiques fondamentaux de la voix chantée. *Éditions de La revue scientifique*, Paris, 1–91.

Hyman, L.M. (2006). Word-prosodic typology. *Phonology* 23, 225–257.

Ishizaka, K., and Flanagan, J.L. (1972). Synthesis of voiced sounds from a two-mass model of the vocal cords. *The Bell System Technical Journal* 51, 1233–1268.

Ishizaka, K., and Matsudaira, M. (1968). What makes the vocal cords vibrate? *Proceedings of Sixth International Congress of Acoustics*, Tokyo, pp. B1–3.

Johnson, K. (1997). Speech perception without speaker normalization. In K. Johnson and J.W. Mullennix (eds.), *Talker variability in speech processing*. San Diego, CA: Academic Press, pp. 145–166.

Johnson, K. (2003). Speaker normalization in speech perception. In D.B. Pisoni and R.E. Remez (eds.), *The handbook of speech perception*. Oxford: Blackwell, pp. 363–389.

Jongman, A. (1989). Duration of frication noise required for identification of English fricatives. *Journal of the Acoustical Society of America* 85, 1718–1725.

Kemp, D.T. (1978). Stimulated acoustic emissions from within the human auditory system. *Journal of the Acoustical Society of America* 64, 1386–1391.

Kewley-Port, D. (1983). Time-varying features as correlates of place of articulation in stop consonants. *Journal of the Acoustical Society of America* 73, 322–335.

Kewley-Port, D., Pisoni, D.B., Studdert-Kennedy, M. (1983). Perception of static and dynamic acoustic cues to place of articulation in initial stop consonants. *Journal of the Acoustical Society of America* 73, 1779–1793.

Kingston, J., and Diehl, R. (1994). Phonetic knowledge. *Language* 70, 419–454.

Kirk, P.L., Ladefoged, J., and Ladefoged, P. (1993). Quantifying acoustic properties of modal, breathy and creaky vowels in Jalapa Mazatec. In A. Mattina and T. Montler (eds.), *American Indian linguistics and ethnography in honor of Laurence C. Thompson*. University of Montana Occasional Papers in Linguistics, no. 10. Missoula, MT: University of Montana, pp. 435–450.

Klatt, D.H. (1973). Discrimination of fundamental frequency contours in synthetic speech: Implications for models of pitch perception. *Journal of the Acoustical Society of America* 53, 8–16.

Kohler, E., Keysers, C., Umiltà, M.A., Fogassi, L., Gallese, V., and Rizzolatti, G. (2002). Hearing sounds, understanding actions: Action representation in mirror neurons. *Science* 297, 846–848.

Kuhl, P.K. (1989). On babies, birds, modules, and mechanisms: A comparative approach to the acquisition of vocal communication. In R.J. Dooling and S.H. Hulse (eds.), *The comparative psychology of audition: Perceiving complex sounds*. Hillsdale, NJ: Lawrence Erlbaum, pp. 379–419.

Kuhl, P.K. (1991). Human adults and infants show a "perceptual magnet effect" for the prototypes of speech categories, monkeys do not. *Perception & Psychophysics* 50, 93–107.

Kuhl, P.K., and Miller, J.D. (1975). Speech perception by the chinchilla: Identification functions for synthetic VOT stimuli. *Journal of the Acoustical Society of America* 63, 905–917.

Kuhl, P.K., Williams, K.A., Lacerda, F., Stevens, K.N., and Lindblom, B. (1992). Linguistic experience alters phonetic perception in infants by 6 months of age. *Science* 255, 606–608.

Kurowski, K., and Blumstein, S.E. (1984). Perceptual integration of the murmur and formant transitions for place of articulation in nasal consonants. *Journal of the Acoustical Society of America* 76, 383–390.

Kurowski, K., and Blumstein, S.E. (1987). Acoustic properties for place of articulation in nasal consonants. *Journal of the Acoustical Society of America* 81, 1917–1927.

Ladd, D.R., and Silverman, K. (1984). Vowel intrinsic pitch in connected speech. *Phonetica* 41, 31–40.

Ladefoged, P. (1967). *Three areas of experimental phonetics*. Oxford: Oxford University Press.

Ladefoged, P. (1996). *Elements of acoustic phonetics*, 2nd edn. Chicago, IL: University of Chicago Press.

Ladefoged, P. (2006). *A course in phonetics*. Boston, MA: Thomson Wadsworth.

Ladefoged, P., and Broadbent, D.E. (1957). Information conveyed by vowels. *Journal of the Acoustical Society of America* 29, 98–104.

Ladefoged, P., and Maddieson, I. (1996). *The sounds of the world's languages*. Oxford: Blackwell.

Lahiri, A., Gewirth, L., and Blumstein, S.E. (1984). A reconsideration of acoustic invariance for place of articulation in diffuse stop consonants: Evidence from a cross-language study. *Journal of the Acoustical Society of America* 76, 391–404.

LaRiviere, C., Winitz, H., and Herriman, E. (1975). Vocalic transitions in the perception of voiceless initial stops. *Journal of the Acoustical Society of America* 57, 470–475.

Laver, J. (1980). *The phonetic description of voice quality*. Cambridge: Cambridge University Press.

Laver, J. (1994). *Principles of phonetics*. Cambridge: Cambridge University Press.

Lehiste, I. (1970). *Suprasegmentals*. Cambridge, MA: MIT Press.

Lenneberg, E.H. (1967). *Biological foundations of language*. New York: John Wiley & Sons.

Liberman, A.M. (1957). Some results of research on speech perception. *Journal of the Acoustical Society of America* 29, 117–123.

Liberman, A.M. (1970). The grammars of speech and language. *Cognitive Psychology* 1, 301–323.

Liberman, A.M. (1982). On finding that speech is special. *American Psychologist* 37, 148–167.

Liberman, A.M., and Mattingly, I.G. (1985). The motor theory of speech perception revised. *Cognition* 21, 1–36.

Liberman, A.M., Delattre, P.C., and Cooper, F.S. (1952). The role of selected stimulus-variables in the perception of the unvoiced stop consonants. *American Journal of Psychology* 65, 497–516.

Liberman, A.M., Delattre, P.C., Cooper, F.S., and Gerstman, L.J. (1954). The role of consonant–vowel transitions in the perception of the stop and nasal consonants. *Psychological Monographs: General and Applied* 68, 1–13.

Lindblom, B. (1963). On vowel reduction. *Report no. 29, Speech Transmission Laboratory*, The Royal Institute of Technology, Sweden.

Lisker, L., and Abramson, A.S. (1964). A cross-language study of voicing in initial stops. *Word* 20, 384–422.

Logan, J.S., Lively, S.E., and Pisoni, D.B. (1991). Training Japanese listeners to identify English /r/ and /l/: A first report. *Journal of the Acoustical Society of America* 89, 874–886.

Macchi, M.J. (1980). Identification of vowels spoken in isolation versus vowels spoken in consonantal context. *Journal of the Acoustical Society of America* 68, 1636–1642.

Mack, M., and Blumstein, S.E. (1983). Further evidence of acoustic invariance in speech production: the stop–glide contrast. *Journal of the Acoustical Society of America* 73, 1739–1750.

MacNeilage, P.F. (1970). Motor control of serial ordering of speech. *Psychological Review* 77, 182–196.

Maddieson, I. (1984). *Patterns of sounds*. Cambridge: Cambridge University Press.

Maeda, S. (1993). Acoustics of vowel nasalization and articulatory shifts in French nasal vowels. In M. Huffman and R. Krakow (eds.), *Phonetics and phonology: Nasals, nasalization, and the velum*, vol. 5. New York: Academic Press, pp. 147–167.

Malecot, A. (1956). Acoustic cues for nasal consonants: An experimental study involving a tape-splicing technique. *Language* 32, 274–284.

Mann, V.A., and Repp, B.H. (1980). Influence of vocalic context on perception of the [ʃ]–[s] distinction. *Perception & Psychophysics* 28, 213–228.

Markel, J.D., and Gray, A.H. (1976). *Linear prediction of speech*. Berlin: Springer-Verlag.

McClean, M.D. (2000). Patterns of orofacial movement velocity across variations in speech rate. *Journal of Speech, Language, and Hearing Research* 43, 205–216.

McLaughlin, F. (2005). Voiceless implosives in Seereer-Siin. *Journal of the International Phonetic Association* 35, 201–214.

McMurray, B., Tanenhaus, M.K., and Aslin, R.A. (2002). Gradient effects of within-category variation on lexical access. *Cognition* 86, 33–42.

Mikuteit, S., and Reetz, H. (2007). Caught in the ACT: The timing of aspiration and voicing in East Bengali. *Language and Speech* 50, 247–279.

Miller, J.D. (1989). Auditory-perceptual interpretation of the vowel. *Journal of the Acoustical Society of America* 85, 2114–2134.

Miller, J.L., and Liberman, A.M. (1979). Some effects of later-occurring information on the perception of stop consonant and semivowel. *Perception & Psychophysics* 25, 457–465.

Miller, J.L., and Wayland, S.C. (1993). Limits on the limitations of context-conditioned effects in the perception of [b] and [w]. *Perception & Psychophysics* 54, 205–210.

Moore, K.L., and Dalley, A.F. (1999). *Clinically oriented anatomy*. Philadelphia, PA: Lippincott, Williams & Wilkins.

Nearey, T.M. (1978). *Phonetic feature systems for vowels*. Bloomington, IN: Indiana University Linguistics Club.

Nittrouer, S. (2002). Learning to perceive speech: How fricative perception changes, and how it stays the same. *Journal of the Acoustical Society of America* 112, 711–719.

Patterson, R.D. (1976). Auditory filter shapes derived with noise stimuli. *Journal of the Acoustical Society of America* 59, 640–654.

Payan, Y., and Perrier, P. (1997). Why should speech control studies based on kinematics be considered with caution? Insights from a 2D biomechanical model of the tongue. *Proceedings of Eurospeech 97, Rhodes, Greece*, pp. 2019–2022.

Peterson, G.E., and Barney, H.E. (1952). Control methods used in a study of the vowels. *Journal of the Acoustical Society of America* 24, 175–184.

Pisoni, D.B. (1977). Identification and discrimination of the relative onset time of two component tones: Implications for voicing perception in stops. *Journal of the Acoustical Society of America* 61, 1352–1361.

Repp, B.H. (1984). Categorical perception: Issues, methods, findings. In N.J. Lass (ed.), *Speech and language: Advances in basic research and practice*, vol. 10. New York: Academic Press, pp. 243–335.

Repp, B.H., and Svastikula, K. (1988). Perception of the [m]–[n] distinction in VC syllables. *Journal of the Acoustical Society of America* 83, 237–247.

Rizzolatti, G., and Arbib, M.A. (1998). Language within our grasp. *Trends in Neurosciences* 21, 188–194.

Selkirk, E.O. (1984). On the major class features and syllable theory. In M. Aronoff and R.T. Oehrle (eds.), *Language sound structure: Studies in phonology presented to Morris Halle by his teacher and students*. Cambridge, MA: MIT Press, pp. 107–113.

Sharma, A., and Dorman, M.F. (1999). Cortical auditory evoked potential correlates of categorical perception of voice-onset time. *Journal of the Acoustical Society of America* 106, 1078–1083.

Shinn, P.C., Blumstein, S.E., and Jongman, A. (1985). Limitations of context-conditioned effects in the perception of [b] and [w]. *Perception & Psychophysics* 38, 397–407.

Sluijter, A.M.C. (1995). Phonetic correlates of stress and accent. Doctoral dissertation, Leiden University, The Netherlands.

Sluijter, A.M.C., Van Heuven, V.J., and Pacilly, J.J.A. (1997). Spectral balance as a cue to linguistic stress. *Journal of the Acoustical Society of America* 101, 503–513.

Smits, R., Ten Bosch, L., and Collier, R. (1996). Evaluation of various sets of acoustic cues for the perception of prevocalic stop consonants. I. Perception experiment. *Journal of the Acoustical Society of America* 100, 3852–3864.

Stevens, K.N., and Blumstein, S.E. (1981). The search for invariant acoustic correlates of phonetic features. In P.D. Eimas and J.L. Miller (eds.), *Perspectives on the study of speech*. Hillsdale, NJ: Lawrence Erlbaum, pp. 1038–1055.

Stevens, S.S., and Volkman, J. (1940). The relation of pitch to frequency: A revised scale. *American Journal of Psychology* 53, 329–353.

Strange, W. (1992). Learning non-native phoneme contrasts: Interactions among subject, stimulus, and task variables. In Y. Tohkura, E. Vatikiotis-Bateson, and U. Sigasaka (eds.), *Speech perception, production, and linguistic structure*. Tokyo: Ohmasha, pp. 197–219.

Strange, W. (2007). Cross-language similarity of vowels: Theoretical and methodological issues. In O.S. Bohn and M.J. Munro (eds.), *Language experience in second language speech learning: In honor of James Emil Flege*. Amsterdam: John Benjamins, pp. 35–56.

Strange, W., Verbrugge, R.R., Shankweiler, D.P., and Edman, T.R. (1976). Consonant environment specifies vowel identity. *Journal of the Acoustical Society of America* 60, 213–224.

Sussman, H.M., McCaffrey, H.A., and Matthews, S.A. (1991). An investigation of locus equations as a source of relational invariance for stop place categorization. *Journal of the Acoustical Society of America* 90, 1309–1325.

Sussman, H.M., Hoemeke, K.A., and Ahmed, F.S. (1993). A cross-linguistic investigation of locus equations as a phonetic descriptor for place of articulation. *Journal of the Acoustical Society of America* 94, 1256–1268.

Syrdal, A.K., and Gopal, H.S. (1986). A perceptual model of vowel recognition based on the auditory representation of American English vowels. *Journal of the Acoustical Society of America* 79, 1086–1100.

Tekieli, M.E., and Cullinan, W.L. (1979). The perception of temporally segmented vowels and consonant–vowel syllables. *Journal of Speech and Hearing Research* 22, 103–121.

Traunmüller, H. (1982). Der Vokalismus im Ostmittelbairischen. *Zeitschrift für Dialektologie und Linguistik* 49, 289–333.

Underbakke, M., Polka, L., Gottfried, T.L., and Strange, W. (1988). Trading relations in the perception of /r/–/l/ by Japanese learners of English. *Journal of the Acoustical Society of America* 84, 90–100.

Van den Berg, J., Zantema, J.T., and Doornenbal, P., Jr. (1957). On the air resistance and the Bernoulli effect of the human larynx. *Journal of the Acoustical Society of America* 29, 626–631.

Verbrugge, R.R., Strange, W., Shankweiler, D.P, and Edman, T.R. (1976). What information enables a listener to map a talker's vowel space? *Journal of the Acoustical Society of America* 60, 198–212.

Wang, Y., Spence, M., Jongman, A., and Sereno, J. (1999). Training American listeners to perceive Mandarin tones. *Journal of the Acoustical Society of America* 106, 3649–3659.

Warner, N., and Arai, T. (2001). The role of the mora in the timing of spontaneous Japanese speech. *Journal of the Acoustical Society of America* 109, 1144–1156.

Weibel, E.R. (1984). *The pathway for oxygen. Structure and function in the mammalian respiratory system*. Cambridge, MA: Harvard University Press.

Werker, J.F., and Tees, R.C. (1984). Cross-language speech perception: Evidence for perceptual reorganization during the first year of life. *Infant Behavior and Development* 7, 49–63.

Whalen, D.H. (1981). Effects of vocalic formant transitions and vowel quality on the English [s]–[ʃ] distinction. *Journal of the Acoustical Society of America* 69, 275–282.

Williams, B. (1983). Stress in modern Welsh. Doctoral dissertation, University of Cambridge.

Williams, L. (1977). The perception of stop consonant voicing by Spanish-English bilinguals. *Perception & Psychophysics* 21, 289–297.

Williams, L. (1979). The modification of speech perception and production in second-language learning. *Perception & Psychophysics* 26, 95–104.

Winitz, H., Scheib, M.E., and Reeds, J.A. (1971). Identification of stops and vowels for the burst portion of /p, t, k/ isolated from conversational speech. *Journal of the Acoustical Society of America* 51, 1309–1317.

Wolfram, W., and Schilling-Estes, N. (1998). *American English*. Oxford: Blackwell.

Zemlin, W.R. (1998). *Speech and hearing science: Anatomy and physiology*. Boston, MA: Allyn and Bacon.

Index

THE INTERNATIONAL PHONETIC ALPHABET (revised to 2005)

CONSONANTS (PULMONIC)

	Bilabial	Labiodental	Dental	Alveolar	Postalveolar	Retroflex	Palatal	Velar	Uvular	Pharyngeal	Glottal
Plosive	p b			t d		ʈ ɖ	c ɟ	k ɡ	q ɢ		ʔ
Nasal	m	ɱ		n		ɳ	ɲ	ŋ	N		
Trill	B			r					R		
Tap or Flap		?ⱱ		ɾ		ɽ					
Fricative	ɸ β	f v	θ ð	s z	ʃ ʒ	ʂ ʐ	ç ʝ	x ɣ	χ ʁ	ħ ʕ	h ɦ
Lateral fricative				ɬ ɮ							
Approximant		ʋ		ɹ		ɻ	j	ɰ			
Lateral approximant				l		ɭ	ʎ	L			

Where symbols appear in pairs, the one to the right represents a voiced consonant. Shaded areas denote articulations judged impossible.

CONSONANTS (NON-PULMONIC)

Clicks	Voiced implosives	Ejectives	
ʘ Bilabial	ɓ Bilabial	ʼ	Examples:
ǀ Dental	ɗ Dental/alveolar	pʼ	Bilabial
ǃ (Post)alveolar	ʄ Palatal	tʼ	Dental/alveolar
ǂ Palatoalveolar	ɠ Velar	kʼ	Velar
ǁ Alveolar lateral	ʛ Uvular	sʼ	Alveolar fricative

OTHER SYMBOLS

ʍ Voiceless labial-velar fricative	ɕ ʑ Alveolo-palatal fricatives
w Voiced labial-velar approximant	ɺ Voiced alveolar lateral flap
ɥ Voiced labial-palatal approximant	ɧ Simultaneous ʃ and x
ʜ Voiceless epiglottal fricative	
ʢ Voiced epiglottal fricative	Affricates and double articulations can be represented by two symbols joined by a tie bar if necessary.
ʡ Epiglottal plosive	k͡p t͡s

VOWELS

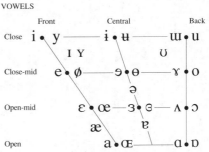

Front — Central — Back

Close: i y — ɨ ʉ — ɯ u
ɪ ʏ — ʊ
Close-mid: e ø — ɘ ɵ — ɤ o
ə
Open-mid: ɛ œ — ɜ ɞ — ʌ ɔ
æ ɐ
Open: a ɶ — ɑ ɒ

Where symbols appear in pairs, the one to the right represents a rounded vowel.

SUPRASEGMENTALS

ˈ	Primary stress
ˌ	Secondary stress ˌfoʊnəˈtɪʃən
ː	Long eː
ˑ	Half-long eˑ
˘	Extra-short ĕ
ǀ	Minor (foot) group
ǁ	Major (intonation) group
.	Syllable break ɹi.ækt
‿	Linking (absence of a break)

DIACRITICS

Diacritics may be placed above a symbol with a descender, e.g. ŋ̊

̥ Voiceless	n̥ d̥	̤ Breathy voiced	b̤ a̤	̪ Dental	t̪ d̪
̬ Voiced	s̬ t̬	̰ Creaky voiced	b̰ a̰	̺ Apical	t̺ d̺
ʰ Aspirated	tʰ dʰ	̼ Linguolabial	t̼ d̼	̻ Laminal	t̻ d̻
̹ More rounded	ɔ̹	ʷ Labialized	tʷ dʷ	̃ Nasalized	ẽ
̜ Less rounded	ɔ̜	ʲ Palatalized	tʲ dʲ	ⁿ Nasal release	dⁿ
̟ Advanced	u̟	ˠ Velarized	tˠ dˠ	ˡ Lateral release	dˡ
̠ Retracted	e̠	ˤ Pharyngealized	tˤ dˤ	̚ No audible release	d̚
̈ Centralized	ë	̴ Velarized or pharyngealized	ɫ		
̽ Mid-centralized	e̽	̝ Raised	e̝	(ɹ̝ = voiced alveolar fricative)	
̩ Syllabic	n̩	̞ Lowered	e̞	(β̞ = voiced bilabial approximant)	
̯ Non-syllabic	e̯	̘ Advanced Tongue Root	e̘		
˞ Rhoticity	ɚ a˞	̙ Retracted Tongue Root	e̙		

TONES AND WORD ACCENTS

LEVEL			CONTOUR		
e̋ or	˥	Extra high	ě or	˩˥	Rising
é	˦	High	ê	˥˩	Falling
ē	˧	Mid	e᷄	˦˥	High rising
è	˨	Low	e᷅	˩˨	Low rising
ȅ	˩	Extra low	e᷈	˧˦˧	Rising-falling
↓		Downstep	↗		Global rise
↑		Upstep	↘		Global fall